LOST Thought

Edited by Pearson Moore

By Pearson Moore:

LOST Humanity
The Mythology and Themes of LOST

LOST Identity
The Characters of LOST

Cartier's Ring

Game of Thrones Season One Essays

Direwolves and Dragons Volume 1.01
Thesis and Symbolism

Direwolves and Dragons Volume 1.02
Bran and Jon

Coming in late 2012:
Intolerable Loyalty:
The Invasion of Canada, 1775

LOST Thought:

Leading Thinkers Discuss LOST

Edited by Pearson Moore

<u>Contributors:</u>

Amy Bauer, Ph.D.
Cynthia Burkhead, Ph.D.
Erin Carlyle
Sarah Clarke Stuart
Jeffrey Frame
Delano Freeberg, Ph.D. (Hon.)
Jennifer Galicinski
Jo Garfein
Julia Guernsey-Pitchford, Ph.D.
Gozde Kilic
Michelle Lang, Ph.D.
Kevin McGinnis
Sam McPherson
Cory Milles
Pearson Moore, Ph.D.
Erika Olson
Ryan Ozawa
Andy Page
Antonio Savorelli, Ph.D.
Jamie Smith
Nikki Stafford
Paul Wright, Ph.D.

LOST Thought:

Leading Thinkers Discuss LOST

Published by Inukshuk Press

ISBN: 978-0-61-560378-0

To the production crew
of the ABC television series *Lost*,
illi qui nos omnes delectant:

Vos creatis; nos humiliamur.

Table of Contents

The Structure of LOST

The Characters of LOST

Afterword

Featured Artists

Citations

Glossary of Terms

Notes

Introduction

Pearson Moore

Introduction:
In the Shadow of Greatness

By Pearson Moore

We are Lost.

To those who remain entranced by the Island's power, this statement conveys a sobering note of authenticity that rings through our daily reality. While a television program may have struck the original chord, the majestic score of our lives—this sequence of fighting and corruption, destiny and redemption, life, death and rebirth—continues, but in ways we never could have imagined before a fuselage with attached wing fell ten thousand meters from the sky on September 22, 2004.

The truth of the statement, however, does not originate with the television series that crashed into our living rooms on an early autumn evening several years ago. The statement was as true before Flight 815 as after; the power of LOST is found not in detached adventure or in vicarious epic, but in unreserved engagement. We are LOST, because without us the Island has no meaning. We are Lost, because the jungle trails and the shoreline beaches are the paths of our lives. We are lost, because the journey toward discovery of Self, Other, and Society never ends.

LOST has enduring relevance because we believe our lives to contain not only meaning and structure, but a uniqueness of our own making. When, inevitably, circumstance forces us to surrender, we do not go gentle into that good destiny.

With Sawyer, we rage, rage against Jacob: "What made you think you could mess with my life? I was doin' just fine 'til you dragged my ass to this damn rock."

We recognize Sawyer's protests as feeble counterpoint to Jacob's grand symphony. We know, too, that our own existence is no happier than Sawyer's, or Kate's, or Jack's. Jacob did not address Sawyer, but every one of us, uncomfortable on the edge of our sofas and easy chairs: "You are all flawed. I chose you because you are like me. You are all alone. You are all looking for something you couldn't find out there. I chose you because you need this place as much as it needs you."

We feel the emotion of Sawyer's words, but our heart is not the only aspect of our being touched by his resolve to burn and rage at close of day. Our gut tells us much more than simple feelings are at issue. In fact, if we bring the full weight of thought to bear on the proceedings at this final meeting of Candidates, we realize that something even more profound than the instinct to survive is under discussion.

Sawyer's curses and fierce tears are appropriate, eloquent, and central to this great symphony in six movements. We cannot shrink from our Island-imposed duty to enumerate the most fundamental questions of human existence:

1. Do our flaws render us prisoners to fate, or do our imperfections catalyze growth and change?
2. To what extent does an individual human being control her own destiny?
3. Does life have meaning and value only to the extent that we endow significance, or does existence carry moment and solemnity independent of deeds and beliefs?
4. What is the nature of our identity as human beings?
5. What does it mean to "live together, die alone"?
6. How do histories and mothers and fathers affect our lives?
7. And the biggest question of all: What does LOST mean?

Common wisdom tells us that to rage, rage against the dying of the light is noble, but futile. What does LOST say on the matter? Is Sawyer's refusal to acquiesce to destiny merely a caricature of dignified but pointless human pride, or do his words hint at a deeper meaning attached to the dancing flames of Jacob's fire? Did Jack's death exemplify final human destiny, or do life, death, and rebirth in LOST carry significance at odds with common wisdom?

LOST is many things to many people, but it will never be designated as common. We may consider it an adventure story, but if so, it is grand adventure, and unlike any epic ever portrayed on the small screen. We may consider it above all a story about interesting characters, but nothing as mundane as a character study has within itself capacities to drive tens of millions to sustained sorrow, unrestrained joy, and warm tears. We may believe LOST is first of all an intricate tale of powers and forces physical and supernatural, but the Cork Stone controls more than electromagnetic waves and travel forward and back through place and time.

It is precisely because we are Lost—because we are susceptible to Jacob's Progress—that LOST endures. Most of the contributors to this anthology refer to LOST as an open, living text. The book of LOST cannot be closed because a definitive judgment of its meaning will never be achieved.

In preparing this collection for publication I edited each of the essays. In one of the more profound contributions I identified what I took to be an error: The author began the essay in past tense, moved briefly to present tense, then reverted to past tense for the concluding paragraphs. I marched through the essay with my red pen and turned every instance of a present tense verb into past tense, believing I had corrected a simple problem. The author was gentle in his response. "*Lost* is a living, breathing text," he wrote. LOST, he said, will continue to speak to us in ways we have not previously understood, and therefore, we do well to express LOST as a present-tense reality. The author was correct on every point. His essay—rendered in its original mixed-tense format—occupies an honored place in our anthology.

It goes without saying that LOST is open to interpretation. But in this nonlinear story we are obliged to go much further in granting analytical license. Not only does LOST live as mutable, organic text, but its design and format change with the redactor. That is, form, substance, and even the text itself must be considered fluid, and entirely subject to the chronologies and priorities applied by each interpreter. Most contributors to this anthology consider that the meaning of LOST cannot be separated from the interpretation applied by viewers. This is because LOST is an exemplar of nonlinear storytelling; the structural hierarchy of the story's events, character interactions, and even its cause and effect relationships (etiologies) must be ***provided*** by the viewers. Whether LOST is considered a postmodern text or cinematic metadrama, those taking in the drama are not passive observers of unassailable fact, but rather active players in the construction of the presentation. We are not viewers, but participants, not observers, but fellow actors in the play. Strictly speaking, there are no "observers" or "viewers" of LOST, because no mechanism exists for the logical placement of events. If we do not accept our responsibility to engage fully in every scene, if we do not work ceaselessly to divine a narrative structure consonant with every faculty of our minds, we will never uncover the meaning of LOST.

The Excellence of Mittelos

LOST awakens us to our hungers.

All too often we are aware of human existence as drudgery, as numbing compromise preventing the full realization of our potential as beings who ponder, create, and dream. There are realities so grand as to defy complete understanding, truths we can only glimpse in fleeting moments of clarity, destinies that seem to demand our full engagement, and yet elude us in their complexity—or is it their simplicity that challenges us? Perhaps we are comfortable in our mediocrity, happy in our adherences to the well-worn paths of trite stereotype, easy judgment, and social conformity.

Abraham Heschel wrote on our tendency toward inner compromise in *Moral Grandeur and Spiritual Audacity* (1,2):

> We dwell on the edge of mystery and ignore it… Accepting surmises as dogmas and prejudices as solutions, we ridicule the evidence of life for what is more than life. Our mind has ceased to be sensitive to wonder… we lose sight of what fate is, of what living is… How could we have lived in the shadow of greatness and defied it?

What lies in the shadow of the statue? *Ille qui nos omnes servabit*. LOST saves us from conformity and stereotype, thrills us in its uncompromising expectation of engagement at every level of spirit, mind, and heart. All of us, we realize, are standing in the shadow of the statue, but we stand in awe, not defying or denying, but seeking, searching, finding value and wonder and delight in Jacob's Progress, in the discovery of new ways to celebrate our true identity as beings of the Light. Walking the beaches and jungles of our Island, we're invigorated, alive to our senses, aware of ourselves and our world as if for the first time. We hunger for the fullness of reality, and we find in LOST the richest, most diverse banquet ever prepared.

The volume you hold in your hands is a contribution to the celebration of our happy place in the shadow of the statue. Twenty-two of the best-known bloggers and academic experts on LOST have shared in these pages something of their fascination with Mittelos, and their commitment to discovering those glimpses of Light most visible from a place in the shadow of greatness.

Possibly the most enduring quality of LOST is its rare ability to affect us personally, in ways unique to each of us. The first section of this anthology, therefore, "The Culture of LOST," treats some of the very personal reactions to this most intimate of television creations. Nikki Stafford (*Finding Lost*) captures the essence of our individual and social connections to LOST and provides the perfect introduction to a volume deeply affected by the emotional, spiritual, and conceptual bonds that permeate our discourse on this breathtaking television epic. Erika Olson (Long Live Locke) and Jo Garfein (Jopinionated) discuss LOST in its capacity as "culture disguised as television," while Ryan Ozawa and Andy Page explain the nuts and bolts behind two of the greatest LOST-inspired communication efforts of the early 21st century: *The Transmission* podcast series and the Dark UFO website.

In the second section, devoted to the mythology of LOST, Dr. Cynthia Burkhead presents one of the most fascinating analyses I have ever read on the place of dreams in LOST. This paper is followed by Jo Garfein's playful discussion of the Alice in Wonderland allusions that suffuse LOST and point to the major themes of the series. Sam McPherson, Administrator of Lostpedia.com, provides an insightful discussion of some of the ancient Egyptian symbols and artifacts of the Island, and comes to some striking conclusions. Also in this section, I explain my take on the thesis of LOST, this time concentrating on the Cork Stone as intellectual totem, but weaving together concepts in disorientation, chaos theory, and literary analysis to support my argument.

Jennifer Galicinski and Dr. Paul Wright are the only contributors to the theology section of this anthology, but do not be misled: Theirs is one of the longest sections in the book, and they analyze some of the most intriguing ideas relating to the philosophical and theological underpinnings of LOST. Galicinski's paper speaks to me at several levels, and I find myself particularly intrigued by the notion that LOST stands in opposition to both modernist and postmodernist ideologies. Dr. Wright's paper is so dense in its thought, yet so simple in its core message, I gain new insights into the connections he makes every time I read the essay.

LOST peers into the lives not only of the survivors, but of their fathers as well, bringing multi-tiered definition to the generational bonds that were strained, riddled with imperfections, and fundamental to the Island drama. If anything, mothers were more important than fathers, with Rousseau, Claire, and Jacob's "mother" serving as complex reflection of the nurturing yet wounded Island that could as easily kill as heal. Gozde Kilic addresses "Daddy Issues" in her engaging essay, while Erin Carlyle focuses on the mother image in visual creations that bring new perspective to the Island and its inhabitants.

The dilemma of free will versus destiny was a recurring theme and a constant presence during the six years of LOST. Dr. Amy Bauer and Kevin McGinnis shed new light on the topic and deliver some thoughtful and challenging conclusions in the Free Will section.

Adequate comprehension of the multi-faceted nature of LOST requires that we travel numerous connected, intersecting, and parallel paths. The multi-dimensionality of LOST is captured in essays by four contributors. Jeffrey Frame provides an engrossing account of four-dimensionalism in LOST, invoking St. Augustine, William Faulkner, and Jeff Jensen to support his point. Sarah Clarke Stuart and I go head to head in a far-flung discussion of our (somewhat!) conflicting theses, and come to a conclusion that may surprise you. Dr. Amy Bauer applies literary and psychoanalytic tools to better understand fate and causality and their effect on Desmond, Charlie Pace, Daniel Faraday, John Locke and Benjamin Linus. Finally, Cory Milles looks at LOST as story, describing the manner in which LOST rises to new heights by bringing nuanced emphasis to characters and nonlinear plot. He demonstrates that our connection to the characters and their plight is the result of a very carefully mapped storytelling style that demands viewer participation.

One of the most controversial and fascinating areas of inquiry is the proposition of LOST's literary structure. Dr. Michelle Lang examines the question of whether LOST can be considered poststructural or postmodern, while Dr. Delano Freeberg provides a spirited defense of his interpretation of LOST as a postmodern creation, applying the principles of quantum mechanics to make his point, with several well-studied examples from the show. Dr. Antonio Savorelli presents an engaging personal reflection on The End in which he indicates sympathetic admiration for a conclusion he found surprising though also in some ways disappointing. Finally, Dr. Michelle Lang offers her position that LOST can be understood as employing the techniques of the Neo-Baroque, particularly as this set of artistic methods and principles was articulated by Dr. Angela Ndalianis.

Several characters serve as vehicles for Lindelof and Cuse's commentary on current social convention and expectation. One of the most challenging characters in this regard was Sayid Jarrah, and the final section of the anthology begins with Jamie Smith's piercing analysis of the character and his significance to viewer-participants in the West. Smith focuses on the Western appreciation of Islam, and the ways in which LOST forces a reevaluation of our prejudices. Dr. Julia Guernsey-Pitchford juxtaposes LOST with *Paradise Lost*, demonstrating that the Island plays a pivotal role in directing the development and transformation of major characters. Finally, any LOST anthology in which I am a participant must include an essay on the enigmatic Dr. Christian Shephard. My third and most surprising take on the good doctor serves as the final essay in this volume.

In The Shadow of Greatness

For all our thousands of hours of study, we are but visitors to the Island (Episode 2.11).

> MR. FRIENDLY: Let me ask you something. How long you been here on the island?
> JACK: Fifty days.
> MR. FRIENDLY: Oooo, 50 days. That's what—almost two whole months, huh? Tell me, you go over to a man's house for the first time, do you take off your shoes? Do you put your feet up on his coffee table? Do you walk in the kitchen, eat food that doesn't belong to you? Open the door to rooms you got no business opening? … This is not your island. This is our island. And the only reason you're living on it is because we let you live on it.

Mr. Friendly was wrong. It is not his island. Even Jacob, Jack, and Hurley, important as they are, are but temporary caretakers. People come and go. We fight and we make peace, we destroy and we rebuild. We corrupt and we create because we are Jacob, and we are the Man in Black. We are say-it-like-it-is Hurley and parse-your-words-carefully Ben Linus. But even the broadest collection of polar opposites cannot express the fullness of our beings. We are neither Other nor survivor, neither father nor son, neither slave nor free.

"Taweret" © Pearson Moore 2011

Mr. Friendly got one thing right: This is not our island. With Jacob, Jack, and Hurley, we are visitors. It only ends once, but we never witness the end with our own eyes, we never know the extent to which we contribute to creation and corruption. We can never call the Island our own. Jacob is "not a man you go and see. This is a man who summons you." (Episode 3.20) If in our ignorance and nonchalance we are unworthy to just "go and see" Jacob, we are far less worthy of an audience with the Protector's taskmaster, the Island.

Yet the Island is the destiny of everyone onboard Flight 815. That is to say, the Island is our destiny. If we are not worthy to darken the shadow of the statue this is nevertheless where we stand, where destiny bids us abide. We stand in the shadow of greatness. No one can ever own the Island. It is the Island that calls us, directs us, **owns** us. The Island is our destiny because we do not accept "surmises as dogmas and prejudices as solutions." The Island compels us to reject the spiritual death of complacency, conformity, and mediocrity. There is nothing compromising or halfway in the Island's call to exploit every faculty of the mind so that we might ponder, create, and dream.

Here then, in these pages, meditations and missives—dispatches and messages—from the object of our fascination: the Island.

4:51 PM
January 23, 2012

The Culture of LOST

Nikki Stafford
Jo Garfein
Erika Olson
Ryan Ozawa
Andy Page

Haikus for the Journey: The Life-Changing Reality of *Lost*

By Nikki Stafford

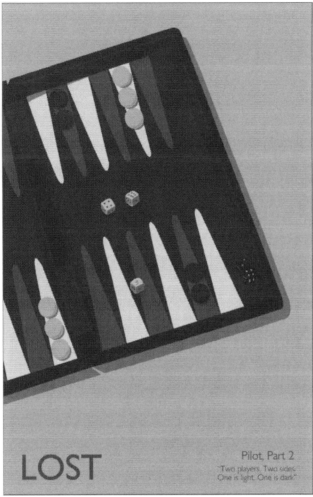

"Pilot, Part 2" by Gideon Slife
Used with permission

Where do I begin? "At the beginning" just seems so… predictable. And linear. And *Lost* was neither of those things. What *Lost* was, in its very title, was prescient. "Lost" was a word that not only described the physical state the characters were in — being literally lost in the world — but their emotional states. Through flashbacks the viewers were given glimpses into these very personal worlds and how these characters were lost long before they ever set foot on that plane. Many of them didn't even know it.

Like the characters, fans didn't know we were missing anything, that we were lost. On September 22, 2004, when *Lost* premiered, television was in a golden age. *The Wire, The Sopranos, Six Feet Under,* and *Deadwood* were not just shows that proved HBO was king, but were stretching the boundaries of what television could be. On the horizon were more cable networks about to step up and show the world what they could do — Showtime was about to unveil *Dexter* and *Weeds*; AMC was just a few years away from becoming HBO's chief rival with shows like *Mad Men* and *Breaking Bad*. F/X was already airing *The Shield* (the show that has ruined all other cop shows for me) and *Rescue Me*. On network television, genre fans had just finished Joss Whedon's *Angel* (and had enjoyed *Buffy the Vampire Slayer* for seven years previous to that), while J.J. Abrams fans were currently enjoying *Alias*. Television had truly shown us what it was capable of.

And then *Lost* showed us just how much further it could go.

Until *Lost*, no other show had taken such huge risks, had built up such an intensely serialized drama that it risked losing viewers just to maintain its top-notch storytelling. No other show had expected its audience to not only keep track of every tiny detail over 120 episodes, but to be well versed in obscure literature, psychology, popular physics, philosophy, history, world religions, and even biology. We had no idea that we'd been lost until this show came along.

Lost changed everything — what we expect from television; how television shows are marketed; how the internet can be used to pull in fans; how television can become an interactive experience. We not only watched the show, we participated in it. We tried to get ahead of the characters by following the clues and solving the puzzles before they could. Fan reactions to certain characters (particularly Henry Gale) changed the trajectory of certain storylines and kept actors on who were only supposed to have guest roles. At the time of this writing, almost two years have passed since *Lost*'s final episode aired, and its impact on television is everywhere. *Lost* references pop up everywhere in television and film as other writers and producers pay homage to one of their favorite shows. (How many times have we seen Hurley's numbers appear prominently?) Flashbacks have become the norm. Flashforwards have formed the basis of an entire series. Time travel and sci-fi elements are finding their way into straight-ahead, non-genre shows. And Liz Lemon and Tracy Jordan are constantly cracking *Lost* jokes on *30 Rock*.

Lost was that unique show that we all watched together, and yet also watched alone. We brought our own personal beliefs and experiences to it week after week. *Lost* fans talked about the show so incessantly they became the butt of many jokes. You can always spot a *Lost* fan: we're the ones who see the number 23 and have an inexplicable urge to jump to the nearest social networking site to tell everyone about it.

Over the course of *Lost*'s run, I published a series of five companion guides called *Finding Lost*, and blogged incessantly on it. I've talked about it on radio and television and in print, wrote articles about it, and became one of *those* people (you know, the one who everyone is trying to avoid because they know I'll start talking about *Lost*). I've published over a million words on the show, but now that I'm being given the opportunity to write anything I want on it, I've decided to become less analytical, and more personal. *Lost* was an intensely personal show for me, and as such, I have intensely personal feelings about it.

I started my blog, Nik at Nite, during *Lost*'s third season, to an audience of two. By the end of *Lost*, I was getting over 20,000 hits a day, like many other *Lost* blogs and sites, and yet somehow that community on my blog seemed close-knit and small. We truly became a family. Day after day, week after week, we filled our time chatting about every aspect of the show, while coming up with a ton of inside jokes. We wrote weekly haikus about that week's *Lost* episodes. We went back and rewatched earlier seasons. We discussed aspects of the show vehemently, but it was always respectful and fun, even when it was passionate. One time a disagreement broke out over the arrangement of the houses in Dharmaville in Season Five, so one member of our group constructed an elaborate map based on screen shots and directions people walked from one house to the next, and posted it for all of us so we could all continue to debate it while adding to it and moving houses around. There was something so hilarious about that person's reaction: instead of throwing his hands up and yelling at the group that they knew nothing, or that he wasn't going to waste his time arguing with us (the sort of fan argument you'd see on a lot of fan forums for this and other shows) he took the challenge and sat down to construct his argument in pdf format. And we loved him for it.

Oddly enough, more than the show itself, it's the conversations the show sparked that I miss the most.

May 23, 2010. The day of the finale. All day I had a feeling of excitement, but also overwhelming dread. A rock had taken up temporary residence in my stomach. Yes, there was a fear that the finale wouldn't deliver, that it would have been built up so much in all our hearts and minds that it couldn't possibly be as good as we needed it to be. But more than that, there was a sense that it would be over. All the questions would be answered. No more speculation, no more discussions, no more disputes, no more insane theories. All the things I loved about *Lost* were about to come to an end.

But I needn't have worried. The finale was polarizing, yes, but luckily, I loved it (101). I loved almost every single thing about it. And the answers weren't offered on a plate. The speculation, discussions, disputes, and insane theories could continue!

Except . . . they didn't. Because even our very close-knit community was torn asunder when half the fans didn't like it, and couldn't bring themselves to argue with the other half who loved it. Suddenly, that camaraderie I'd loved so much was the very thing that stopped discussions in their tracks. Worried that things would get nasty, half the group disappeared and didn't talk about it, while the other half chattered away happily about how great the finale was.

There are people out there who hated the finale when they saw it, and still feel that way. There are others who hated it at first but now have reconsidered their initial reaction, and have grown to either like it, or even love it. There are those who loved it from the beginning, and have either tempered that (maybe they've realized they really did want more answers) or, like me, continue to be passionate about it. I studied every moment of this series very closely, and by the end, realized we knew the answers all along. We didn't need the showrunners to show us. I went back and checked the questions I had at the end of each season, and realized just how many of them had been answered.

I miss the camaraderie that *Lost* fans had week after week. I miss the weekly discussions that began moments after an episode happened and continued through to moments before the next one began. I never thought I'd say this, but I even miss that panicky mad scramble to get my lengthy post up the night of the episode.

I miss *Lost*.

I miss our haiku.

I miss making fun of Jack.

I miss Jack. Terribly.

I miss coming up with superlatives to describe my affection for Desmond. (I'm still waiting to see you in the next life, bruthah.)

I miss the mad Google searches after every episode seeing if I caught a hidden anagram or reference to a piece of literature.

I miss the delight of finding a new book that I'd never heard of, and reading it because Sawyer or Ben Linus was reading it.

I miss the delight of seeing Sawyer or Ben Linus discover a book I already knew and loved.

I miss the anticipation of what new curveball would be thrown this week, and whether I'd come out of the episode seeing someone in a new way.

I miss the puzzle. I know many fans think we spent six years trying to piece together a puzzle only to get to the end and all the important pieces were missing, but I'm enjoying still staring at that almost-complete puzzle and trying to imagine what those missing pieces are.

I miss the wonder. I haven't found that in any show since.

I remember.

I remember meeting the characters for the first time in Season One, and the twists and turns discovered through their backstories. I remember the shock of thinking I knew a character only to realize there was a dark secret in their past that utterly changed who they were for me. I remember wishing Terry O'Quinn could be in every show I watch.

I remember the tension of Season Two, whether it was with the new Tailies being introduced, or the fact that ABC had wonked up the schedule so much it was difficult to keep track of everything, and I remember how the writers took what we knew in Season One and turned it on its head.

I remember the utter grief of watching Charlie die at the end of Season Three, followed by the thrill of realizing that the flashback we'd just seen was actually a flashforward.

I remember the excitement of Season Four, the beauty of *The Constant* (*that phone call!*) and the rivalry between Widmore and Ben. I remember wishing Michael Emerson could be in every show I watch.

I remember the complexity of Season Five, and how much fun we all had trying to piece it together. And how it was the season where I realized I could no longer really explain to non-viewers what *Lost* was about.

I remember the crazy anticipation we all had leading up to Season Six, the fan videos that were appearing, the way we were piecing together bits of the story we'd seen so far to figure out where the story would go next, linking John Locke and the Man in Black and learning of Jacob being in there. I remember how Season Six built up quickly with every episode, and the panic that began to slowly creep in when half the season was gone and we hadn't gotten many answers, and thinking the writers would run out of time.

I remember crying like I've never cried before when the show ended. From the thrill of seeing my favorite characters discover their constants in the sideways world and "moving on," to Jack lying down on the ground with Vincent by his head, there was so much beauty in this episode it brought me to joyous tears over and over again.

Lost was a show that ended with a simple message: that it's not about where you end up, but the journey you took to get there. It's about the connections you make in your life, which is why every character on the island seemed to have been interconnected even before they got on the plane. It's about who you touch emotionally, and how those experiences and memories are the only things you can take with you to the next life. It's about constancy. It's about love and hope.

The sideways world turned out to be a place where everyone went after they died, with no memory of having been on the island at all, but instead working through their issues – the very issues that made each person so emotionally lost when they crashed on that island in the first place — without the island helping or hindering them along the way. When they came to a revelation about who they were or what their purpose was — a revelation that could only come through a connection — they could suddenly see everything, past present and future, clearly. And once they could see clearly, they knew that it was important to help other people come to that clarity, and only then could they move on to the afterlife. Jack was the last one to come on board, because he simply couldn't step back from the minutiae of his life and see the big picture. He suddenly realized that, like Dorothy, he had had the answers all along.

Some fans have complained that the ending is too spiritual. Yes, the church setting could certainly make one say that, but the church itself is simply a visual cue in this case. It's not meant to evoke a religion, but to suggest that the scene we are seeing in front of us is spiritual. We don't need to look to higher powers to find spirituality; it's within us, and in the connections that we make. The friendships that everyone had on the island with each other, the connections and relationships they forged with one another, they were spiritual. They might not have seemed it, but in the end, they are what mattered. The church setting simply said, "What you are watching right now? It's spiritual. Not in a God sense, but in an uplifting of the soul sense."

Lost was an intensely personal show. In a way, it was like a religion. You can read the bible, or go to church and listen to a church official interpret the bible for you, but in the end, you will still make your own decisions and have your own take on things. You will feel your own personal relationship to God. Religion doesn't hand you the answers; it gives you the tools with which to find those answers. Life doesn't give you answers, but if you follow the right path and connect with the right people, you will determine what answers work for you.

Lost didn't offer up answers, but it gave us the story of people who were similarly seeking them, and showed us how they went about finding them. We, too, need to look within and outside ourselves to find those answers. Our very discussions on my blog were a way of us looking for those answers within the context of the show. We connected to each other, and were able to find some of the answers we sought just by talking it out with each other.

"The End" was extraordinary. But for me, the real beauty of *Lost* was the fun in getting there, both in watching the show and discussing it.

The key lesson that Jack learns at the end of the series is to "Let go." Fans have joked that if you're still talking about *Lost* years later, you haven't learned Jack's important lesson. But I disagree; Jack learned you have to let go of the things that weigh you down and embrace the meaningful things in our lives. *Lost* really was so much more than a television show, because it made us think about these things. It made us look around us and appreciate the people in our lives, the connections we've made, the time we spend together. We need to let go of disagreements and hostilities and find happiness and peace within communities like Jack did. On the island, Jack realized it was his fellow survivors who changed his life and made him who he was. Off the island, fans formed new friendships and camaraderie among like-minded people, friendships that go far beyond the show. Our eyes were opened to new ways of thinking, and if we could just let go of the things in the finale that we didn't like, we'd realize there were so many things in the dozens of episodes that preceded it that we loved.

In May 2010, it was time to say goodbye to the experience of seeing new episodes of *Lost*, but that didn't mean we had to say goodbye to everything the show taught us. *Lost* is firmly entrenched in my heart as not just a television show, but as an experience I will never forget.

Nikki Stafford is the author of the critically acclaimed _Finding Lost_ series, a five-volume collection of guides to the television show _Lost_ (the Season Six volume contains a 50-page discussion of the finale). _Newsday_ has referred to Nikki as "one of the show's leading scholars," and _Entertainment Weekly_'s Jeff Jensen wrote, "_Lost_ is over, but I know I'll be thinking about it for years to come. And in those mental trips to The Island, I'll be taking three things: my Bible, my comic book collection, and all of Nikki's insightful and comprehensive _Finding Lost_ books." Nikki has appeared on TV and radio as a respected commentator on pop culture and television, and has been quoted by several media outlets, including the _New York Times_, _USA Today_, _Philadelphia Inquirer_, the _Globe and Mail_, the _Washington Post_, Associated Press, and many others. She was a keynote speaker at the first _Lost_ academic conference in October 2011 (New Orleans, Louisiana) and blogs about television at Nik at Nite, and lives in Toronto.

Culture Disguised as Television

LOST in Conversation:
LOST Bloggers Jo Garfein and Erika Olson Revisit the Series and Finale

By Erika Olson and Jo Garfein

"Television" icon by Everaldo Coelho and YellowIcon 2006
GNU Lesser General Public License vers. 3.0

Jo: One of my favorite aspects of LOST was that it was a history and literature lesson disguised as a television series.

Erika: How dare they attempt to make us smarter!

Jo: I can't think of another series that has been as influential regarding the promotion of literature, mythology, and history. In that sense, I think that LOST will be studied in classrooms for years to come.

Erika: I have to wonder how many casual viewers missed much of that simply because they weren't paying close enough attention or heading to message boards/blogs after each episode. I'm sad for them—it added so much to the show to have that deeper connection. So many layers beyond the character dialogue and on-screen action, you know?

Jo: Agreed. Although I've spoken with many people who considered themselves casual fans, who never did more than watch it once a week, and moved on with their lives. And I can't fault them for that.

Erika: Yes, I can't hate on the "normal people!" I'm just happy they watched it at all and didn't give up.

Jo: I've always been interested in the specific use of character names on LOST, like Faraday, Locke, Hume, etc.; whether or not they chose those names in advance, knowing they would implement the philosophies and sciences of the real figures in history.

Erika: It's funny because I remember when the first show started—with a character like John Locke being SUCH an obvious reference to the real-life philosopher—all of us got so excited.

Jo: Yes!

Erika: I think in the beginning, with the main cast, the names were definitely purposeful. As the seasons went on, however, I started wondering, "Are they just throwing in these references and allusions to mess with us?!?"

Jo: It certainly appealed to those of us who are inclined to research the significance and similarities

Erika: But I ALWAYS appreciated it, because I like learning about new concepts that I might not have had exposure to before. There's certainly never been another TV series (that wasn't the nightly news) that made me want to dig into something further.

Jo: I am very fond of the fact that they named Locke's dad Cooper, as the real Anthony Cooper was an associate of the real John Locke, who actually saved Cooper's life when he had a liver infection (which is why Locke giving Cooper his kidney on LOST was a fantastic touch).

Erika: I didn't even realize that until recently (after the series ended)! That's VERY cool.

Jo: I believe that Darlton and the writers started to realize the scope of their influence, and embedded even more literary and historical Easter eggs for those of us who paused our DVRs for every instance on screen and ran to our computers to research them. But don't get me started on people who gave up on LOST. That is a concept I find baffling.

Erika: Absolutely agree. It was the writers' big chance to have a greater impact than they might have initially realized they could, and I am extremely thankful they took that road.

Jo: The fact that they added an official LOST Book Club was genius.

Erika: Yes—and I'm sure there were a ton of other offshoots of fandom that even you and I don't know about! That's what's so cool.

Jo: I strongly believe that LOST completely altered the television landscape, from showrunner communication with fans to negotiating the number of seasons.

Erika: Of course. There's no doubt about that in my mind, either.

Jo: To this day, I am still discovering pockets of LOST-related fans and websites. The interest has not waned at all. I love it. Have you had the opportunity to re-watch any of LOST?

Erika: I've only re-watched *The End* and Season One.

Jo: I did a re-watch before Season Six; it was extensive and exhausting, but also rewarding. So I will re-watch the entire series in a year or two. I cried in the exact same spots during each viewing of the series finale. It starts with Jin and Sun's flash-sideways awakening in the hospital with Juliet, and ends with Jack and Christian.

Erika: I kind of like to totally forget details before re-watching... I put six years between my initial viewing of Season One (in 2004) and my re-watch in 2010. I LOVED catching so many things that would come into play later that I had forgotten about. It made me realize how much care they took in setting things up, despite how not every single little question was "answered" in an obvious way.

Jo: The only flash-sideways scene that has never made me cry: Sayid and Shannon. Wait, six years?! Well to be fair, you did publish a book and have quite a busy schedule!

Erika: I also hated the Sayid/Shannon reunion scene—BOGUS.

Jo: THAT can be an entire chapter and separate conversation. Sigh. But let's address it.

Erika: I feel like it was just a ploy to get Maggie Grace back. But it made zero sense in the whole scheme of Sayid's story.

Jo: I have always been very openly on Team Nadia on my blog. Organically, it made sense for her to be Sayid's soul mate/Constant/Church companion. There are those who believed that it was an issue of actress availability (i.e. Can we get Maggie back? Okay great!). There are those who believe that Sayid didn't DESERVE Nadia. If Sayid didn't deserve to move on in the afterlife with his Constant, why did he deserve Shannon? It seemed convenient and odd and stood out as THE only flash-sideways resolution with little emotion. Locke was in that church alone in the end without Helen, so in my opinion Sayid should have also been there alone (if he didn't deserve to be with Nadia).

Erika: I have to believe that for "finale hype" reasons they might have been inclined to gun for Maggie to return. Whenever there's something about the show that's frustrated me, I can usually find a way to justify it by remembering that the showrunners were ultimately still responsible to The Man (aka ABC/Disney/the suits). I tried to keep in mind the reality that the show was—like it or not—a revenue stream and a business for the network. So Maggie Grace coming back helped to hype the finale... even though it made no sense for the storyline. It was disappointing, but I guess it could've been worse—at least Nadia was in Sayid's flash-sideways up until that point!

Jo: Very diplomatic and well said.

Erika: And great point about Locke without Helen.

Jo: Boone was alone, too. Shannon couldn't have been *both* Sayid and Boone's Constants! I've also been told that Nadia wasn't in the church because she wasn't on the island. Well, neither was Penny.

Erika: Yes, that was always my argument against Shannon/Sayid—the fact that Penny was there with Desmond. The whole "who was with whom" in the church at the end definitely makes for a strange debate—not sure how well thought out it was.

Jo: I agree that it might have been influenced by actor availability and corporate influence, but I'd be curious to find out what Darlton REALLY had planned in their ideal world for that church.

Erika: And wasn't little Aaron back to being a baby? He is forever Turniphead.

Jo: The only explanation I have for Aaron's presence in the church as a baby is that —for Claire—it represented her happiest time. The flash-sideways they created was under ideal circumstances. Before she went nuts and lost her hairbrush, Claire had time on the island with baby Aaron. Do you think maybe they had alternate choices for who was paired up?

Erika: Maybe for the ten-year anniversary DVD we'll get that information. I would love to know where their heads were at on this one, too.

Jo: I seriously doubt we'll ever get alternate endings or additional answers, actually. Regardless of future gigantic box-set specials for anniversaries. Which leads to our next topic at hand: unresolved mysteries. Should everything have been answered or addressed? Are there lingering questions still stuck in your head? Some fans felt robbed without obvious answers, yet they missed subtle ones along the way (i.e. polar bears: they explained their existence on the island when Charlotte discovered the Dharma collar in Tunisia—the bears were used to test the frozen donkey wheel and exit point in Tunisia, and helped to explain why it was kept at such cold temperatures down at the wheel).

Erika: I know a lot of people don't agree with my take on this one, but to me I was just never all that concerned with getting "an answer" to everything. Sure, I'd spend 14 hours a week nerding out over theories and possible explanations about what was going on with all of the different mysteries, but finding out a *definitive* answer for each and every question I had was NOT my motivation.

Jo: Me either! The show was designed for us to interpret in our own way. Some people really don't like a choose-your-own-adventure style of storytelling, but obviously you and I did.

Erika: I liked hearing way-out-there theories that I would've NEVER thought of on my own but that actually made sense to me when someone else explained them—regardless if they ended up being realized on the show or not.

Jo: And as you mentioned earlier, when you go back and watch the entire series again, they actually provide far more answers than you thought. Some are quite subtle and implied, while others hit us over the head. How many times have you had to answer questions from fellow fans about lingering mysteries that were actually already addressed? I used the polar bear as an example because I still get questions about why they were on the island.

Erika: I think if more people were comfortable with not being spoon-fed answers or given completely black-and-white responses to questions, then not only this country, but also this world would be a much better place. I get very frustrated when people can't tease out something on their own or just use their imagination for two seconds. But I digress.

And to your question, yes, SO MANY PEOPLE missed major things.

Jo: So. Many.

Erika: The biggest one being that EVERYTHING ON THE ISLAND HAPPENED and so therefore THEY WERE NOT DEAD THE ENTIRE TIME.

Jo: I've made it a goal in life to change the minds of those who did not like the finale because of the last ten minutes. I am constantly referring them to Christian's speech.

Erika: People just freaked out at the end of the series and never re-watched Christian's speech, which pretty much spelled out the fact that the entire series *wasn't* a fake-out.

Jo: I literally listed out, character by character, who died and when. Including those we NEVER SAW DIE. Like the ones who flew out on 316. Ben and Hurley. Rose and Bernard. Desmond.

Erika: I have a right to be angry with those people because I, too, assumed the wrong thing when I first watched it, and it was my husband who said, "I think you misinterpreted what just happened."

Jo: Absolutely.

Erika: And so if I can be humble enough to realize I might've misconstrued the end of "The End" after considering myself a "LOST master" for so many years, everyone else can, too!

Jo: There were those who were already frustrated with the lack of answers, ready to pounce on how the series wrapped up, because of their anger.

Erika: Yes. They wanted to be pissed and don't want to be told otherwise.

Jo: Frankly, I will never comprehend how a person can dedicate six years of their lives to an amazing show, only to say it ruined their lives or marred the series because they didn't love or understand the finale.

Erika: I don't get it, either. It makes me sad for those people. Talk about your extreme reactions!

Jo: Yes! I've been accused (and I'm sure you have, too) of being a LOST apologist; that I am incapable of criticizing the show. To which I always respond: read the last four years of my LOST blog. The proof is online, people.

Erika: Had my husband not immediately helped me out, I KNOW I would've re-watched the ending within a day—just to *ensure* I had understood everything. To have simply given up on the show and never look back is unthinkable to me.

Jo: We were both spoiler-free and constructive in our criticism. That was not everyone's cup of tea.

Erika: What's funny is that whenever I DID rip on something or some character, people wouldn't like that, either!

Jo: Catch 22!

Erika: I remember being called a "woman hater" when I was joking about how Juliet's psychologist Harper looked like she had too much Botox. Now all of a sudden I hate women. Sweet.

Jo: I was openly critical of Kate for years and really only applauded her character and actions in the series finale. You can imagine how well that went over with Skaters and Jaters. But let's change gears for a minute and talk about what we thought might happen in the finale, versus what actually happened. Did you ever imagine how the flash-sideways would be resolved or explained? Over a year later, are you satisfied? Closure achieved?

Erika: I'm pretty sure that about 85% of my initial confusion over the end of the series was due to the fact that I kept waiting for the "two timelines" to merge somehow.

Jo: Oh really? I didn't think they would at all. I was asked to predict how it would end, but I really and truly had NO idea. My guesses, much like 99% of my theories over the years, were entirely off base.

Erika: I was SO CONFIDENT that was how it would end: with one reality influencing or affecting the other, or one of them (the island or the flash-sideways) ultimately "winning out." And then the characters would only have faint memories of the other timeline/reality. It would be like a little special secret they all shared if they ever ran into each other, even though they wouldn't necessarily KNOW each other (assuming the flash-sideways won out). But I always felt that the action on the island was real.

Jo: Yes. We had to know that whatever happened, happened. But starting off the final season on 815 and not crashing...that blew my mind. We'd seen flashbacks and flash-forwards, so what the hell were we witnessing?

Erika: I definitely would've felt cheated if it had all been a dream, or nothing on the island ever happened, etc., which is why I think I was freaking out the first time I watched *The End*. Perhaps I was SO fearful that my worst nightmare was coming true that it was almost like I was willing myself to hear it.

Jo: I had a feeling that they wouldn't have made it purgatory or a dream. But to have studied each episode down to every detail and with great frequency over the years, and then to still not have any idea how it would end—I found that thrilling and fantastic.

Erika: People felt like they'd been fooled, and instead of saying, "Wow, that was clever," they instead got angry. I am always impressed when a show or a book or a movie is able to surprise me. I mean, give credit where credit is due, people!

Jo: Clever is precisely the word I would use to describe the flash-sideways.

Erika: I would LOVE to see any of the critics write even one TV episode that comes anywhere close to the worst episode of LOST.

Jo: In retrospect, I appreciated the details, like Jack's neck bleeding and then his wound on the island.

Erika: Even though I haven't re-watched anything other than Season One, I would say there were actually "letting go" references (and other things that ended up pertaining to Season Six/*The End*) throughout the entire series.

Jo: I do want to ask you about Desmond. People argue that he was the only one who knew (on the island) what was happening in the flash-sideways.

Erika: Hmm, I'm not totally sure even *he* knew what was going on.

Jo: Did you get the sense that when Desmond was being lowered down to the Source and told Jack that "none of this matters" that he had had a vision? After all, Faraday told him (and us) that he was "uniquely and miraculously special." My interpretation is that we finally saw that statement come to life. I believe that after Widmore subjected Des to the electromagnetic torture box, and he flashed...he KNEW.

Erika: I would agree he had a vision, but I believe he thought what he experienced and saw in the flash-sideways was a TRUE reality back in the real, physical world. I definitely do not think he realized it was some sort of afterlife. He seemed too weirded out when he regained consciousness on the island... kind of like, "Why am I back here?"

Jo: But then he was at peace, and looked more peaceful and comfortable than we'd ever seen him.

Erika: I just chalked up his peace to him knowing that in some other instance of his existence he was back with Penny and off of the freaking island.

Jo: One might argue that Widmore's goal with the torture box was to awaken Desmond…

Erika: I think when he was dragged back to the island by Widmore, he truly thought he would die there and never see Penny or his son again. And speaking of Widmore, he's definitely a character that I think got the shaft, death-wise. Too anticlimactic.

Jo: The real David Hume, a philosopher, was known as a giant skeptic. Of everything. Desmond certainly didn't believe (or want to believe) in the island. And to me, he finally understood his purpose and destiny after being zapped. Again, that is just my interpretation. I agreed about Widmore. They built up this entire war between Ben and Widmore, but in the end that was overshadowed by Jacob and the Man in Black.

Erika: I just feel like after he was zapped, Des saw that there was this other "existence" where he was back with Penny. And I think perhaps he thought that in order to make that vision a reality, he (and everyone else) HAD to fulfill his/their destiny on the island first... and then once they did, they'd all be flipped over to this other reality. I think if he had known it was THE AFTERLIFE, he might have freaked because then that would still mean he'd never actually see Penny again in the life he was currently in. He would think he was about to die on the island, for good.

Jo: Interesting! This is why I love and will always appreciate talking about LOST. There are myriad interpretations of scenes.

Erika: I was also confident that someone was going to kidnap little Charlie [Desmond and Penny's son] in Season Six. And that clearly didn't happen.

Jo: You notice that little Charlie was nowhere to be found in the church. Nor Ji Yeon.

Erika: It was weird that those kids weren't there—another reason why I fear that scene might have been thrown together a little haphazardly.

Jo: By the way, I love the conspiracy theories that Charlie Hume was actually Charlie Pace. I myself may have created an insane paragraph about that theory at one point.

Erika: I remember those theories. They made my brain hurt.

Jo: I think it was very purposeful that Ji Yeon wasn't there. That child did not represent the best time in their lives. Jin and Sun clearly created an ideal circumstance where they were together, which is all they cared about. Look at their parenting decisions: Sun with a gun, leaving the baby with Kate (of all people), Jin deciding to die with her on the island rather than live and get home to take care of the baby. Look, Sun chose to go back to the island rather than raise their baby. End of story.

Erika: If you want to talk about things I am definitely critical about with the series, Sun and Jin at the end is near the top of my list! I was not a fan of Jin deciding to stay with Sun and drown. Hello, selfish!

Jo: I am more fascinated by the concept that in an ideal world, Desmond and Penny chose not to include their son. Because up until they reunited and then had Charlie, their world was sad and apart and upside down.

Erika: I can't find a way to make the absence of Little Charlie [in the church at the end] make sense, so that's why I have to justify it with "must have been an oversight; the writers/producers/directors are only human." Which I think is a fine justification, actually. I wouldn't ever want to be under the pressure they were under by the time the finale rolled around. Many things were bound to slip through the cracks—I'm just glad they nailed (in my opinion) almost all of the major stuff.

Jo: Let's talk about David Shephard. Another concept I explain often to the baffled masses.

Erika: Ah yes, David. The Boy Who Never Actually Existed.

Jo: To me, David existed in Jack and Juliet's ideal world for two specific reasons: for Jack to prove that he could be a better father than his own, and for Juliet to successfully deliver a baby that survived (since she couldn't on the island and because she never was able to meet her nephew).

Erika: I am with you on this one.

Jo: Excellent! So many people were up in arms that he didn't ever exist. I try not to get frustrated and seem what I call Blog Snobby. Which is to say, I get it. I got almost all of it and still do. But I understand why others have trouble grasping certain concepts from the final season and finale.

Erika: I think Jack's need to be a good dad was obvious, Juliet's reasons were less so, but still—the woman had MANY regrets in life. Talk about Blog Snobby—if someone's never watched LOST, I'm actually okay with that because I realize they might not have had time or didn't have any friends into it so they didn't hear how good it was, etc. But if someone HAD watched the show and then gave up on it, I have very strong opinions about their level of intelligence. I don't have much patience for those who didn't have patience!

Jo: I just question their true reasons for giving up. Was it the content? The direction? The mythology?

Erika: Blog Snobby and proud!

Jo: You must admit that "our" show was jam-packed with deep mythology and extensive storytelling, and that is not for everyone. But I certainly implore all to go back and try it again, especially now that all seasons are available in so many ways. I love when friends watch for the first time and text me with questions or exclamations like, "Ben is the leader of the Others?!"

Erika: I guess... but I feel like LOST stood on its own as an action/adventure series as well; it was really easy to overlook all of the mythology if you weren't into that. There was still a lot going on. I LOVE convincing people to watch it now who never had before, too. I guess it must be like when parents kind of rediscover the joys of little things through their kids.

Jo: Compared to most shows that aired before and are on the air now, LOST was dense in terms of the number of characters and storylines to follow. But I LOVED that. No other show kept me up at night, thinking about the possibilities.

Erika: I always say, "Just watch the first four hours. If you're not into it by then, fine." Because if Locke's first flashback in *Walkabout* doesn't get them, nothing will!

Jo: And I say the first five. Because Locke got *you* and almost everyone else in that episode, but for me it has always been episode 1.05, *White Rabbit*.

Erika: Yes, "White Rabbit" was definitely another chill-inducing one.

Jo: That is the episode that hooked me in forever.

Erika: I honestly don't think there will ever be another show like LOST. But I am very much okay with that.

Jo: Me too. I think it will be five to ten more years before another series even comes close in terms of fandom, community, and inspiration.

Erika: I don't actually want there to be "another LOST." I want there to be something ELSE that is totally unique and original and creative on its own terms. A game changer. And I agree with you that it will probably be nearly a decade before that happens. Right now everyone in the biz is trying to cash in on knock-offs, not only of LOST, but also of any other series that was ever even the slightest bit successful and revenue generating. The same thing happens in the film industry— and in several other industries. It's just human nature, I think.

Jo: LOST changed my life—altered it in positive ways that continue to open doors and inspire me to pursue less-traveled paths. If another show or film never achieves that effect again, so be it.

Erika: Same here—LOST literally changed my life and my career... and I have a feeling its influence over me will last for quite a while.

Erika Olson spent a ridiculous amount of time theorizing about LOST on her blog LongLiveLocke.com during the series' six-season run. The site's popularity motivated her to leave the financial services industry in 2007 and pursue a freelance writing career; she became a film critic and movie blogger for Redbox in 2008, and in 2010 her first book, Zero-Sum Game: The Rise of the World's Largest Derivatives Exchange, was published by Wiley. LOST's influence on Erika's life continues—her son, Desmond, was born in early 2012.

Jo Garfein is a pop culture sponge who covered LOST extensively for years, with an emphasis on in-depth analysis and elaborate speculation. She is now a freelance entertainment writer, focusing primarily on primetime television.

The Journey Has Just Begun: Building *The Transmission*

By Ryan Ozawa

Radio Tower by ROmas 2008
WMC PD

When I first considered starting a podcast, it was still called audioblogging, and my wife didn't want to have anything to do with it. But it turned out to be the thing that grew our marriage into a wonderful, creative partnership.

Our LOST podcast was originally a spinoff from an earlier show, but that little side project ended up taking over our lives. And while "The Transmission" saw early success, that success overwhelmed us. We found ourselves being more famous for quitting than for starting.

LOST combined everything I loved, from deep and daring storytelling, to powering a passionate fandom and transmedia storytelling, to showcasing the scenic diversity of my island home. But it was a franchise that, it's fair to say, didn't love me back.

You could say it's complicated.

Getting Into Podcasting

Today, with NBC and BBC and NPR churning out podcasts, and with even independent shows finding audiences that are larger than a typical television or radio show, it may be difficult to imagine a time when only the geekiest of the geeky were putting shows online.

I first heard about podcasting in 2004 at a monthly local geek lunch that was organized by Burt Lum, today my public radio co-host and partner in crime. At these meetups, which are still going strong today, tech enthusiasts and early adopters eagerly shared their latest discoveries. Many of us had been blogging since well before it was called blogging, and podcasting was a natural extension of online expression.

Audio was the next dimension, using the same basic mechanisms to publish sounds as we'd used to publish written words. In those early days, geeks were obsessed with the architecture, the underlying plumbing. How do we attach an audio file to a blog post? How can we automatically collect and play back these attachments on computers and iPods? There was handwringing over RSS specs and polling and payloads.

The most popular podcasters were the geeks that were trying to build and promote the technology at the same time. Blogging pioneer Dave Winer and former MTV veejay Adam Curry were superstars... at least to a very small but passionate community of media makers. All the "navel gazing" and "monkeys with typewriters" jokes made at bloggers' expense were easily applied to this bunch, with the biggest podcasts consisting of people talking about podcasting.

And putting out a podcast was only half the challenge.

Once you'd recorded, encoded, and uploaded your audio file, and hacked your blog to serve them up, you had to find an audience. Though people could just download the MP3 right off your website, the "magic" required a program that would check your website regularly and automatically download files whenever a new one appeared. And then you had to get that file onto an iPod or into your music library. There were programs that did this, but you had to be pretty geeky to know about them, and be interested enough into listening to other geeks talking to themselves.

In February 2005, a bunch of local geeks created the "Hawaii Association of Podcasters," a fancy name for a simple group of tech heads trying to sort it all out. I plugged a $7 Radio Shack microphone into my old PC, recorded a file in the free Audacity sound editor, and posted it to a blog I'd set up at HawaiiUP.com, one of many random domain names that I'd registered before I knew what I'd do with it.

I'm pretty sure the only people who listened to that first show were the five other members of the "association."

Still, I kept at it, and slowly but surely built up a small, devoted audience. My show basically recapped local news, and featured local music (with permission, one of the stickiest parts of podcasting to this day). Former Hawaii residents who'd moved away were hungry for island updates and tunes, and helped each other find my show and the software needed to subscribe to it.

I experimented with recording audio while out and about in Honolulu, reviewing restaurants with friends, recording while driving home from work, and capturing the sounds of waves crashing on the beach. I also nagged my wife, Jen, to contribute. But to say she was reluctant would be an understatement. When she finally started to warm to the idea, the first name of her segment was "Annoy the Wife," as I was basically dragging her into my geeky little world.

But listeners really liked hearing another regular voice on the show, and getting a conversation rather than a monologue. Jen was surprised and energized that people liked hearing what she had to say, and began to enjoy thinking up topics to cover during her segment. We talked about our kids. We talked about movies and music and television shows. (More on that in a bit.) We were having fun.

Looking back now, this was a small but magical shift for us. Podcasting could have just been the next shiny new thing to take me away from her. Another obsession to keep me huddled in the den while she did her own thing in the next room. But it became something we did together.

Tipping Point

By the summer of 2005, there were thousands of podcasts covering hundreds of topics. People with a real talent for audio, and access to serious equipment, were putting together shows that sounded as good as professional, commercial radio. Video content was also increasingly common as well (I uploaded my first shaky, grainy video posts in April).

Podcasters were a fast-growing, passionate community of people who felt they were at the leading edge of a revolution. Just as the web and blogs threatened to turn the publishing world inside out, we imagined a world where everyday people would have access to the tools to create audio and video content for a global audience that could challenge the mainstream media.

But there were still major barriers between us and the rest of the world. Apart from a handful of overstuffed web directories, it was still hard to find podcasts. And keeping up with them, downloading them, and listening to them still required special software or awkward hacks that seemed downright scary to the average person.

That all changed in June, when Apple released iTunes 4.9.

iTunes was already one of the most popular music management programs out there, on both Windows and Mac systems. It was the way people listened to music on their computers, and put that music on their iPods. And with the release of iTunes 4.9, Apple built in support for podcasts.

And not only did millions of people suddenly have an easy way to subscribe to and listen to podcasts, but they had a way to find them. Apple seeded the system a directory of over 3,000 shows, including HawaiiUP.

On July 1, I reported on "The iTunes Effect," which exploded our audience from hundreds to thousands and briefly knocked my website offline. Our little podcast about life in Hawaii climbed to #65 in the iTunes Top 100 podcasts list, and we heard from new listeners across the country and around the world. Our first comment from Belgium made us giddy.

Even then I griped about how Adam Curry and his friends dominated the charts, but we enjoyed the minor novelty of living in Hawaii. People from Hawaii, planning to visit Hawaii, or merely curious about Hawaii were subscribing, listening, and sending in comments and questions. We talked about life in the islands. And we talked about one of our favorite television shows, that just happened to be filmed in Honolulu.

Right Place, Right Time

I like to say we were fans of LOST before it ever hit the airwaves.

The town was abuzz early in 2004 when J.J. Abrams and ABC decided to film their $10 million pilot on Oahu. (And there were also two other network shows being shot on the island at the same time.) Folks laughed at stories of people coming across the jet wreckage on the beach and calling 911 to report a crash. The trailers and lights and crowds of crew brought to mind memories of "Magnum P.I." shooting around town in the '80s.

I worked at a bank in Chinatown at the time, and our building was near the epicenter of early LOST flashbacks. On the corner of the same block, the "Walkabout" travel agency. Across the street, the police station where Sawyer almost met Boone. I loved the behind-the-scenes stuff as much as I loved the fantastic show that it turned into a few months later.

So Jen and I talked about LOST on our Hawaii podcast. And we started to talk about it more than the other varied topics that we would cover. And some of our listeners thought we were going a little overboard with the television show about a mysterious island. And others thought our LOST chats were the best part of our show.

On September 9, we reviewed the first season of LOST on DVD. The following week, we gushed about catching the Season Two premiere on the beach in Waikiki. We were giddy in our joint fandom, but not everyone else was. So we made "an announcement that should please both fans and non-fans alike" with the start of "The Transmission."

Finally we were free to fully indulge our obsession with LOST, dedicated entire shows to individual episodes, picking apart little details, indulging in theories about what was happening on the show. And a whole new community of listeners joined us, posting map coordinates of where the island might be located, and guessing at who Alex might be.

Our little spinoff did even better than our Hawaii show. It hit #56 after our first episode, popping up amidst reliably popular "Harry Potter" shows. Over the next few days, "The Transmission" climbed to #40, then #30.

Then, on October 12, Steve Jobs took to the stage and announced iTunes 6. All the world's geeks were watching, waiting for his trademark "one more thing," the closing extra that was often the most important announcement.

"We're doing for video what we've done for music," he said, and revealed that you could now use iTunes to buy television shows. Or, at least, television shows from Disney and its subsidiary ABC. And there on stage, larger than life, was the LOST logo. Photos of Jobs on stage with that logo hit front pages around the world, and mentions of the show were everywhere. LOST fans were ecstatic.

But it was an even bigger moment for us. Because on that day, both our little podcast, and one of the most popular shows on television, were being served up on the same plate. Curious media-hungry iTunes users, of which there were millions, would search for LOST, and in addition to the ABC series, would find "The Transmission."

Two days later, "The Transmission" hit the iTunes homepage at #12. Our show climbed as high as #7, my wife and I listed alongside national radio networks and major media companies like NPR and ESPN.

I had to move our show to another server. Our inbox exploded. It was surreal.

The More the Merrier

As a rising tide lifts all boats, our podcast wasn't the only one to find an exponentially wider audience. It was an early bonding experience for the few LOST podcasters that were around at that time, as we all dealt with site outages and bandwidth limits. People like father and stepson duo Jay & Jack Glatfelter, who are still going strong, Jason and Anna of the Delta Park Project, and John Keehler and friends over at "LOSTCasts."

I had already been trading notes with Jay Glatfelter, geeking out over compression settings and feed glitches, and we were blown away by what was going on. We were also being contacted by podcasts unrelated to LOST asking for advice, and hearing from other LOST fans wanting to start their own shows. (One of the most interesting new podcasts to pop up during that time was "In the Hatch," featuring episode reviews by a 13-year-old boy named Rusty.)

We joked about competing with each other—the "LOSTCasts" crew declared war on "The Transmission," and we played along with the rivalry, even though some fans took it seriously. But we worked well together, offering very different styles and perspectives. We celebrated new voices in the mix. So early on, I set up the "LOST Podcasting Network," a serious sounding organization that was basically a mailing list and a shared blog.

The network, which is still around today, basically provided a single podcast subscription that included episodes from several different shows. In its heyday, it included shows from over 30 different podcasts dedicated to LOST. For every 47 minutes of content broadcast on ABC, there was more than a full day of recorded discussion to go along with it.

Perhaps the greatest validation of what we were doing, and the potential of alternative media distribution and commentary, came less than a month later.

To be sure, ABC and the creators of LOST were very aware of the thriving online fan community that surrounded its show, and members of the cast and crew were already following and even participating in fan message boards and blogs. Indeed, I think LOST arrived at the perfect time to take advantage of the rapid evolution and growth in social networks and web tools that made it easy for anyone to have a voice online. Fan reaction was not just instantaneous, but coming from countless diverse sources. And most notably, the people behind the show weren't just listening. They were participating in the conversation.

So as podcasts inched closer to the mainstream, it was inevitable that the LOST team would join the fray. On Nov. 8, amidst half a dozen fan shows, "The Official LOST Podcast" launched. Kristopher White, a multimedia master, simply recorded chats between showrunners Damon Lindelof and Carlton Cuse. It was beautifully sparse, casual, sometimes a little awkward. But it was earnest, it felt real, and a big step forward for mainstream media.

Sure, behind-the-scenes featurettes and making-of DVD extras were nothing new. But "The Official LOST Podcast" couldn't benefit from 20-20 hindsight. We were getting a peek behind the curtain while action was still unfolding on the stage. Like fan podcasts, Lindelof and Cuse would unpack the latest episode to air and tease what was coming up next. But we also got a sense of what it was like to work on such a massive production, how the writers' room worked, and who the people behind LOST really were.

Sometimes they revealed answers that fans never suspected. And sometimes they revealed that they didn't think half as hard about a plot point as fans did. But they mostly revealed that they were human, both fun and fallible, and that added a huge dimension to the enjoyment of the show.

Today, every popular television show has a number of fan podcasts dedicated to it, and if the showrunners are smart, they've got an "official" podcast as well. But back in 2005, when the New Oxford American Dictionary named "podcast" the word of the year, it was LOST that set the standard.

Yet as much as I loved "The Official LOST Podcast," I also loved the fact that fan podcasts were still more popular.

Unfortunately, our podcast got a little too popular.

Quitting While We're Ahead

"The Transmission" was doing fantastically well. Thousands of new listeners meant thousands of new contributors of feedback and theories, and the start of dozens of new friendships that we still treasure today.

Our podcast benefited greatly from the fact that we lived on the island where the show was filmed, and could share little observations and tidbits about location shoots and cast sightings. Other podcasts would cite our show for LOST spoilers (more on that in a bit), as did fan blogs and forums, boosting our listenership even higher.

The Hawaii International Film Festival hosted a special LOST panel, which we attended, recorded, and posted to our feed. We came up with special episodes focused on LOST websites and favorite characters to help fans survive the agonizing re-run gaps between new episodes. LOST star and fan favorite Jorge

Garcia even called into our show, and a few other podcasts, to offer his own take on the latest episode. Jen and I were blown away.

We were getting dozens of blog comments, emails, and phone calls each week, which I dutifully summarized and organized in the notes we prepared for each podcast—notes that were starting to run six or seven pages long, including our trademark episode recaps, reactions, theories, and show spoilers. (If we'd included every voicemail message we received each week, our show would be twice as long.) Since we stubbornly stuck to our format and I meticulously edited our audio, a one-hour podcast took several hours of prep work.

It was overwhelming. We were both exhilarated and exhausted. And we were having trouble keeping up.

It would be one thing if we were full-time podcasters. But I had a full-time job, and Jen was a full-time mom. I had just gotten a big promotion at the bank, and was starting to stress out over additional responsibilities and training requirements. Our youngest son Alex was 16 months old and a handful and a half, in addition to our then three-year-old son Zac and seven-year-old daughter Katie.

So one week our podcast was late. Another week, we missed posting a show completely. We just chalked it up to the hiatus and the holidays, and braced ourselves for the return of new LOST episodes in January.

But two episodes in, we crashed and burned. Just three months after breaking into the ranks of the most popular podcasts, we announced our retirement.

We loved what we were doing, but we couldn't keep doing it, at least not without making compromises we didn't want to make in the show, or in our lives. And as we were always amazed and humbled by the number of people who inexplicably enjoyed listening to us, it truly felt like we had instigated a heart-wrenching breakup, a broken promise, a betrayal.

A lot of people were upset, although fortunately most of them understood. People knew podcasting was a labor of love, a free gift to fellow fans, so shutting down was hardly a crime. But as a wholly different wave of comments, emails, and calls came in, we were doubly traumatized. I'm not ashamed to say there were a lot of tears. A lot of nights spent awake, stricken with what we'd done, second guessing and dreaming of ways to start over.

And despite our brief success, it was our departure that became our first claim to fame. A week after we signed off, urging our listeners to try other shows like Jay & Jack and to sample the Lost Podcasting Network, we were written up in Wired magazine.

"Podfading takes its toll," the headline read, and Steve Friess wrote, "In a plot twist worthy of the hit television show itself, the Hawaii-based couple suddenly marooned their audience and shut down."

From Quitters to Show Spoilers

Though we decided we couldn't keep our podcast going, we didn't stop being fans of LOST, or fans of LOST fandom. And we definitely didn't want to lose our connection with the many, many great people who'd been part of our wild LOST journey. So even though we didn't record audio files, we still took notes, we still hypothesized and debated, and we still shared our take on each episode as good old-fashioned blog posts.

And we were gratified to find that people still enjoyed reading our opinions about the show, with our reviews sometimes garnering hundreds of comments.

Indeed, it was after we'd stopped our podcast that some of the most interesting things happened.

First of all, I managed to snag an opportunity to work as a background extra on the show, and got to spend a day on the set as the episode "Lockdown" was filmed. I wore a suit and walked back and forth outside a bank while Terry O'Quinn drove up in his truck and ran inside, over and over and over again. The two minute sequence took six hours to shoot, clogging up traffic in downtown Honolulu. And then it was cut entirely from the show, not even making the DVD extras.

Secondly, Jen and I had one of our most cherished opportunities as LOST fans. We got to take both Jorge Garcia and Daniel Dae Kim to lunch at The Willows, a neat restaurant in Mo'ili'ili. It turned out Kim was a listener as well, and he showed us our podcast on his iPod as proof. We ate, talked story, and then both actors were gracious enough to sit down for a joint interview that I later posted as a very special podcast.

(That interview made Kim late for his next appointment, an imposition that I still regret to this day.)

Jen and I remained active in the wider community as well, following other podcasts, blogs, and message boards, sending audio segments to Jay & Jack, and participating in Q&As with other fan sites. I also still kept an eye out around town for LOST filming, and reported on interesting things I saw, sometimes posting photos and video clips. And these reports often ricocheted across the web through an increasingly voracious network of spoiler sites.

It didn't take long before we went from being "the fans that quit podcasting" to "the fans with the spoilers." But it was a much more controversial place to be.

People take spoilers seriously. Fan sites have elaborate rules on what counts as a spoiler (i.e. previews versus interviews versus original source material), and what types of details can be discussed when (i.e. be vague for the first few days after airing, but all bets are off after a week). And while I'm the type of person who loves to know what's going to happen, who doesn't mind knowing about the big twist in advance, I completely understood the extreme caution. I totally got why some people hate spoilers.

Whether for our podcast or our blog, my spoilers were always wrapped in warnings and disclaimers. "Spoil responsibly," I would say, never wanting to spoil someone who didn't want to be spoiled. But I always knew it was possible for someone to have their experience ruined by an over-eager website or a careless friend.

48

So the information I gathered was at once both in great demand, and a little dangerous.

Sometimes, I'd stumble on big reveals without even trying. One day in October 2006, Jen and I were meeting our friend Gail at a restaurant in Chinatown. It was only after we were seated at a window table that we noticed something strange about the police cars parked out on the street. They were LAPD cruisers, not HPD, and there was definitely something different about the female police officer directing traffic.

It was Michelle Rodriguez, who played Ana Lucia on the show, hamming it up in her police uniform between takes. And if you caught my YouTube video, or blog post, you knew that Ana Lucia was a cop in her previous life months before the rest of America.

But sometimes, I would go a little too far in following the production around the island.

Late in Season Two, I heard about an elaborate village of huts being built out near Makapuu Point. LOST had taken over the rocky shoreline below the hiking trail to set up a fake camp that would eventually be revealed to be a fake "Others" camp. I drove out there to check it out over the weekend, but was dismayed to find a security guard stationed in his truck, parked on the access road.

I got the bright idea to try and sneak down into the camp from above. So I hiked halfway up Makapuu Lighthouse trail, then boldly struck off down the side of the mountain.

Mountains tend to be a lot taller and steeper than they look from a distance. It was a precarious climb, and a couple of times along the way, I thought about turning back, only to realize it would be even harder to get back up. It took over an hour to crawl down to the set, earning me skinned knees, scratched elbows, and a badly bruised ego.

But I did reach the village, and I got to walk around and photograph the huts and props. I was just beginning to wonder how I'd leave, possibly having to talk my way the wrong way past the security guard, when I saw a local family walk down the access road, right past the guard, and into the village to swim.

Confused, I asked them how they got past the guard.

"Public beach," the guy said. "They no can stop anyone."

That location turned out to be one of my favorite LOST sets (and sets of LOST set photos), but it was also an important lesson in common sense. Something that, I admit, I still sometimes lack.

Another time, I learned that LOST was filming way up in the mountains above Pearl City. I drove out there early in the morning, up a winding road, to Waimano Trail. But in the dark, in the rain, I didn't realize that I'd driven right into the heart of the production until it was too late. I parked my van between two large construction company pickup trucks, then slouched in the back seat as more trucks and cars poured in and everyone got to work.

I got to see Nestor Carbonell in a suit, and a couple of women in nurses' uniforms, but other than that, I got to see a lot of the back side of a storage trailer. I was trapped in the belly of the beast for most of the day for just a tiny tidbit of news. They had been filming the inauspicious birth of John Locke.

As the seasons progressed, the mysteries on LOST got more and more convoluted. As the show gained a reputation for secrets and big reveals, the spoiler industry got more heated. Set security got more and more aggressive. During Season One, I was able to walk into Boone and Sawyer's police station and sit at a cop's desk to chat with the carpenter. By the last two seasons of the show, local fans were sometimes being kept blocks away.

I certainly wasn't the only one tracking LOST location shoots on the island. It's hard to hide giant trailers, cranes, and crew tents when their presence often shut down streets and neighborhoods. And new tools like Twitter, which didn't even exist in 2004, made it possible for sightings to spread like wildfire. Just as I learned to recognize other fans pacing along the trailers and barricades, the LOST production crew definitely became familiar with my ugly mug.

I'd like to think I was pretty good at stalking the show. I might even attribute some of it to my journalism training, which otherwise didn't get put to much use. I nurtured relationships with anonymous sources on the crew. I kept up with the hotline that extras would use to get locations and call times. But mostly I just honed my skills at finding and following public information, from city permits to offhanded posts on social networks. All of my friends and family knew I was a huge LOST fan, and they would call me when the show turned up in their neck of the woods.

Eventually, I had cultivated a network of LOST spotters, from fellow residents and businesspeople (many of whom had been enlisted to provide services to the show) to hardcore fans visiting on vacation.

All this, of course, was of great concern to ABC and the show's creative team, and with good reason. Some of the show's biggest twists (like the end of Season Three) had been ruined for many fans by leaks from within the production. As careful as I tried to be with the information I put out there, having fans following their crews around obviously didn't help things, either.

This led to a few tense moments, for sure. A few angry shouts, some creative blocking maneuvers, and one retracted invitation for an official event. But I'm happy to say that most of the time, there was a shaky but respectful truce in place. I knew my public spaces and rights of way, they knew their private property lines. I knew where I could stand and where I couldn't, and when I should take pictures and when I shouldn't.

Having hung around for so long, I was on downright friendly terms with some of the crew (including location gurus Jim and Dustin) and security guards (like Lou, Danny, and Lance). We could sit and talk as long as no one from the network was around. And in at least one case, when a fellow local fan was starting to get a little too pushy, they called me to ask her to lay off.

Still, I didn't want to cause trouble, and sometimes it was clear that my mere presence made things more complicated for the crew. Eventually I started to send fans visiting from out of state to watch them work instead. They'd contact me after landing in Honolulu, and I'd steer them to the right places, in exchange for the first opportunity to report on what they saw. It was a great setup, as hardcore fans got the LOST vacation of a lifetime, I got the scoops, and the production crew didn't have to keep tabs on me all day.

When Locke Met Rose

I had stopped going out to find LOST. But during the final season, LOST came to find me.

By then I was working at a real estate data company in the Dole Cannery complex. Our office building had previously hosted flashback scenes for Jack and Ana Lucia. For Season Six, the show was revisiting some of the backstories we saw at the start of the show, including John Locke's employment at a box company. The original location, however, was no longer available, so the LOST locations staff were on the hunt for another bland, soulless bank of cubicles to recreate that office.

They came in through the front door, saw potential in our IT department, and headed over to meet with my boss. To say they were surprised to see me at a desk would be an understatement.

Ultimately, they decided that Hawaii Information Service would work better as a temp agency than a box company, but either way they'd be using our office to shoot a scene. We cleared our staff out and emptied their cubicles. Then the LOST set crew swooped in, hung an "OC Staffing" sign on the wall, rearranged some furniture, then carefully transformed our empty desks back into lived-in desks with coffee cups, family photos, and post-it notes. It was an impressive level of detail... especially considering the fact that almost none of it made it on screen.

The local crew was able to keep my personal connection to the set quiet right up until the last minute, though there were reportedly some tense phone calls. On filming day, Dustin came over to my desk to ask me to please try and stay out of sight. So that day, while I could hear the director call "action" from the next room, the closest I got was catching a glimpse of Terry O'Quinn on our lobby couch on my way to lunch.

It's a good thing I went out to lunch, too, since a second unit was filming a few hundred yards away. Jorge Garcia was there with his bright yellow Hummer, visiting the box company.

The tension between the show and its spoiler-hungry fans obviously reached a crescendo as the series finale entered production. And when LOST set up at Sacred Hearts Academy in Kaimuki to film the penultimate church scene, a woman was even enlisted to loiter around the set in a wedding dress to throw fans off the scent. And I admit, I fell for it.

It was only good business for LOST to protect one of its main assets, that being the answers to its infamously challenging questions. Though I suspect there was some genuine personal animosity aimed at me and fellow spoiler hounds, I hope there was also the understanding that people like us were probably some of the show's biggest fans.

Even if we got some answers early, even if we didn't like those answers, we loved how the story was told. And in the end, it seemed even the show's creators decided the main message was to value the journey, rather than the destination.

Back On The Air

Obviously, our love of LOST runs deep. And Jen and I couldn't stay silent forever.

The end of Season Three left us breathless. In September 2007, we got to attend "The Lost Symphony," the first public performance of Michael Giacchino's symphonic score, at the Waikiki Shell. We got to meet Giacchino in person, and I even got to hang out backstage, called into service as one of the torch-carrying Others. After we saw the Season Four premiere in January 2008, we knew a blog post wouldn't be enough.

With no warning, and not much of a plan, we restarted "The Transmission" podcast. And we received a wonderful welcome back from the podcasting and fan community. Most of our long-time listeners were still there, and once again we started to make new friends and hear new voices. It was almost as if we had never left, but the fan community was even bigger and even better than it was three years earlier.

Several of our listeners started their own podcasts and blogs. And some of our regular callers became stars within "The Transmission." Jon from North Carolina regularly registered his astonishment at each new reveal with a "holy freaking crap." Soon the phrase took on a life of its own, with "HFC" becoming a unit of measurement used by others. A Texas man calling himself "Knives Monroe" always had succinct, sharp commentary, some of it critical. We were so accustomed to his tough, no-nonsense style, we were floored by one of his last voicemails in which he choked back tears.

After Season Four, we went back and recorded podcasts for every episode we had missed.

After Season Five, we decided to attend our first Comic-Con in San Diego. It was an incredible, unforgettable, life-changing experience that could warrant a whole separate essay. But in short, while we were excited to experience the last official LOST panel, we were most touched and transformed by meeting hundreds of fellow fans and familiar online faces in person.

For the Waikiki Beach advance screening of the Season Six premiere, we helped bring over 100 fans from outside Hawaii (and even from outside the U.S.) to the island for a special LOST weekend. Working with friends in event management and the travel industry, we hosted a luau and then led our first ever (and last ever) tour of LOST locations. Taking two motorcoaches full of visiting fans around the island was nervewracking, and heartwarming.

And as the final season of LOST unfolded on television, the fan community grew incredibly close, and deeply nostalgic. We were giddy and sad at the same time. Our podcast was garnering hundreds of comments each week, more than we'd ever seen before. The mainstream media took notice of the intensity of

LOST fandom, and Jen and I found ourselves interviewed by mainland television stations, mentioned on Nightline, and even written up in the New York Times.

Anticipation for the series finale on May 23, 2010 was intense. Jen and I grew so restless, we finally took a tour of Kualoa Ranch that week. It was a long-overdue and gorgeous pilgrimage that put us in the right mindset to handle "The End." And thanks to a fan and listener named David on the East Coast, we were able to tap into his Slingbox and watch that last episode five hours before we normally would, allowing us to put our series finale podcast out early.

That podcast received over 1,100 comments.

Even though LOST was no longer on the air, the community it created was stronger than ever. Jen and I went back to Comic-Con that year, and in 2010, and are hoping to go again. But we aren't motivated by "LOST," so much as by the friendships we found around the show.

The LOST Podcasting Network is still up and running, with a handful of shows still working their way through complete rewatches of the entire series.

We put out one final episode of "The Transmission" in May 2010, a one-year-later retrospective. That same week we launched "Popspotting," our new podcast where Jen and I talk about everything, from television and movies to music and books. In a way, we're back where we started with HawaiiUP in 2005. But of course, everything else has changed.

The journey is what matters most. And it's nowhere near over.

A self-professed life-long geek, Ryan Ozawa has immersed himself in new technologies and online communities since the days before the web. From running a dial-up BBS in high school to exploring today's dynamic world of 'Web 2.0' and social media, he has long embraced and evangelized the ways in which technology can bring people together. An obsessive media maker, he and his wife are now co-hosting Popspotting, a daily pop-culture podcast.

4. Andy Page: Chased By Polar Bears

How an English Bloke Got to Run the Largest *Lost* Fan Site

by Andy Page

I remember hearing the phrase "everyone has a book in them." I'm not sure about that; in my case I think I have a chapter in me: a story about how a normal bloke from a normal town in rural England ended up somehow running the largest individual fan site for the TV show *Lost*. It's not as exciting or thrilling as being chased by polar bears, but it's the truth and it's my story.

Like most of you reading this book, my story did not start on September 22, 2004 with the plane crash of Flight 815. My story started nearly a year later, around the first week of August 2005. I can't recall how I found it or where I'd heard of it but somehow I clicked on a promo for this show called *Lost*. The clip gave me goose bumps and I thought I have to check out this show. Channel 4 was going to air the first three episodes (Pilot Part 1, Pilot Part 2 and Tabula Rasa) back to back, and I thought if the pilot does not grab me no big loss.

So I settled in with the wife and the three hours flew by in what seemed like ten minutes. When it was over my mind was racing, and I was dying to see the next episode. In the UK I would have to wait a whole week, something I don't think I would have survived. So I thought, okay, time to see if this Torrent technology would help me download the episodes I knew had aired in the USA.

I found a great torrent site and downloaded the whole of Season One. It took eons and ages on my old slow cable modem. As each episode downloaded I ripped the video onto DVD as quick as I could and after a few days I had the whole of Season One on DVD. With my happy bundle my wife and I watched three or four episodes every night until we had finished the season.

I was numb when it was over. Like a drug, I needed more... So I sought out the Internet to see what I could find. I search, clicked, googled, and finally ended up at the IMDB forums. These forums were chock full of discussions/debate/trolls/crazy folk/theories—it was everything a *Lost* fan could ask for.

Around this time I also started visiting the excellent *Lost* Cubit and The Tailsection sites. It was now September 2005 and the boards were buzzing about the likely contents of the hatch. There were all sorts of crazy theories: it was a railroad, a submarine, the pit of hell, etcetera. No one had any idea.

About the 14th or 15th of September, I was googling for more *Lost* info and I came upon this report about what was in the Hatch. I read it furiously but it was so strange! The report talked about some Scottish guy called Desmond, a Counter, a Computer and strange symbols. I thought this was too crazy to be made up so I started doing more searches and I came across this report from Hawaii from some guys who had seen the première early.

Excited by this find and confirmation, I went over to my favorite site at the time, IMDB, and posted a full blow-by-blow of the episode with a spoiler warning. (Little did I know what this would lead to eight years later, now running one of the largest spoiler sites on the internet).

The replies looking back were hilarious. They ranged from people calling me names for making this up, people saying it was fake and I'd been had, to people threatening me (!) I wish I had saved the thread but alas IMDB doesn't keep threads very long. A week later I watched the episode a few hours after it had aired with a smug grin on my face as the episode played out exactly as posted.

From this point on I was seen as somewhat of a "Spoiler Hound" and after each episode I would post links to other sites that had the promos up, interesting screenshots and any spoilers that I found while googling. After a while this become a bit tedious as the IMDB forum software was very basic and would not allow photos, videos to be added as well as the forums starting to get overrun by various trolls etc.

I think it was about halfway through Season Two that DocArzt from The Tailsection asked if I would help out doing a round-up of spoilers for his site. This was my first introduction to the Blogger software (Eight years later, I continue to use it to power my sites).

After a few weeks I thought this was great, and I decided to start my own site. So DarkUFO was born (The name comes from an old handle I had from a Band I was in as well as my name on my first site about UFOs).

The first site, Lost Mysteries (http://lostmysteries.blogspot.com/), was my attempt to catalog all the outstanding questions and mysteries from the show. These would then be updated when they were answered on the show. I was amazed that someone found this site and submitted it to the then-popular news site Digg.

The next 24 hours were unreal. We had something like 80,000 hits on the site, hundreds of comments and my inbox filled up very quickly. It was at that point that I realized just what a phenomenon *Lost* was in the Online world. It was seriously crazy. So I started to tidy up the site and added more sections: Theories, Polls, News, Spoilers, Rumors, and so on. The site just grew and grew.

Below is how the site looked at the beginning when we had all the various sections added.

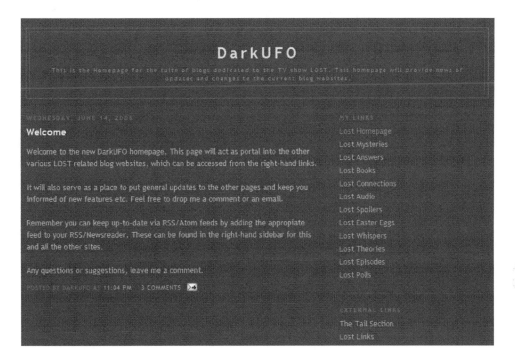

Here are the stats from the first five months that I started recording them. We went from nothing to 1.7 million in just five months.

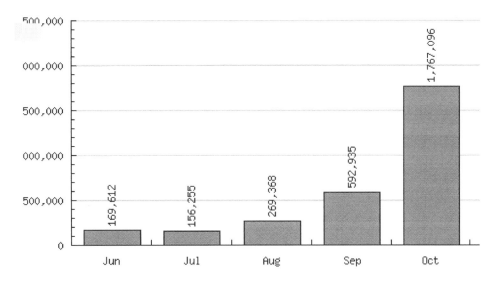

So Season Three was the first season for which I had the site fully operational and I quickly realized it was starting to take over my life. I was spending more and more time on the site, adding news, polls, theories, spoilers; it was becoming almost a full-time job.

It was around this time that I met The ODI and he started to help out with posting content on the site and to look after things when I was asleep or was away on vacation. It was a tremendous relief to have someone I trusted looking after the site.

He and I are still good friends all these years later—in fact, he helps me run SpoilerTV.

Also around 2007 we started to bring on board assistants to help keep up with the vast amount of information on the site: people like PandaVamp, b3rt4, CJ, Sandi, Dharmageddon and many others too numerous to name. Like the ODI, they remain friends today and work on my other sites.

Another contributor we added was Vozzek69 (aka Danny) who wrote the very popular "Things I Noticed" episode recaps/reviews after each episode. Danny ended up writing his own book as a result of these.

Everything was going so well. Stats for the site were growing and growing and the Season Three finale was approaching fast. Then LOSTFAN108 happened.

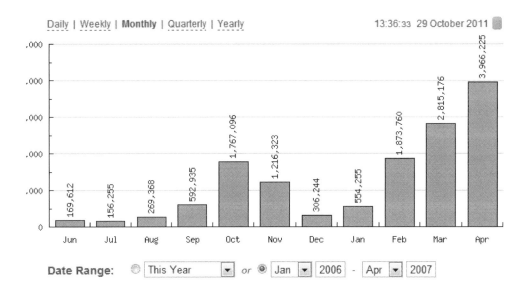

I'm not going to dwell too much on this but it's one of the facets of the site's history that's probably the most controversial. I'll post a snippet of an Interview I did with Lostpedia. LOSTFAN108 was the person who leaked the Flash-forward Twist of the S3 Finale.

Lostpedia: What was your reaction to these spoilers?
At first I called BS. [sic] Then I read them again and checked his story with some sources and it slowly become apparant that this was the real deal...

Lostpedia: Do you know how LostFan108 got them? What do you think his motives are?

I've no idea how he came across them. I can only speculate that he works in Post Production and gets to see the final version. As for motives, you will have to ask him. I'd have preferred him not to release them the way he did and can't understand why he would post them on a public board such as AICN without warning. It was pretty irresponsible of him.

Lostpedia: How difficult was the decision to post the spoilers?
Very. I pondered the first LostFan108 spoilers for a day or so and ran a poll on the site to see what our readers wanted. From my memory we had over 80,000 votes and the "yes, Post it" crowd won. The other factor that persuaded me to post them was that I felt I could release them in a slightly more responsible manner. I decided to split the posts up over a period of 3-4 days with a segment being released each day and in a graphic format that made it a little harder for people to copy and paste the text. It also gave people warning that the spoilers were coming and to avoid unmoderated boards which would help people avoid getting "shotgun spoiled."

Lostpedia: Considering fan and producer backlash, do you regret your decision about it?
Personally I had very little backlash, 95% of all feedback I got was very positive, and thankful for posting. I still don't know to this day if I did the right thing or not but I think I would have felt worse if Lostfan108 had gone to another site and released them into the wild without any warning, causing even more people to be spoiled who did not want to be. The funny thing was, that at no time did anyone from ABC ask me to remove them. If they had done so I would have removed them. As part of running our sister site, SpoilerTV, we get take down notices from CBS, FOX, NBC, etc but never once from ABC.

Lostpedia: Do you think that you have been unfairly portrayed in this situation?
I really don't know to be honest. I tried to make the best of a bad situation and did it in a way I thought best and as I said most of our users were really supportive of me and we've certainly seen no drop off in users on the site. I can certainly understand people who were unfairly spoiled being upset and like most things in life they look for someone to blame, hell I've done it myself enough times. The fact is that these were going to be released regardless of if I posted them and I think a LOT more people would have been spoiled had I not released them the way I did. As I previously mentioned, I would have rather Lostfan108 had not released the info and/or

ABC had kept a tighter reign [sic] on things but such is the nature of the industry that spoilers get out.

The Season Three finale broke all sorts of records as you can see from the chart below. The month of May brought in a staggering 8.8 million page visits.

After Season 3 the site really started to grow. More and more people seemed to see DarkUFO as the site to go to for Spoilers and *Lost* news and more and more people started sending us information and news. The whole thing started to exponentially spiral upwards.

The other new innovation, due to technology advances, was real-time Internet presentation of *Lost* episodes. We had hundreds upon hundreds of people in chat room discussing the episode as it aired. It was great fun to read all the thoughts and comments as the episode progressed. However it made for a long night as by the time the episode finished and I had made all the usual posts on the site it was normally around 6 a.m. UK time.

We also started getting more and more "inside" contacts who sent us lots of snippets and details of filming, scripts and upcoming plot-lines. One of these insiders was "insiderscoop" who got to see episodes a few days in advance and would write detailed episode synopsis for each episode for those people who wanted to read them. These large spoilers were always placed behind large "Are You Sure" buttons to ensure that people who didn't want the large spoilers would not be spoilt.

Again everything was going great until the writers' strike which put both *Lost* and our site on a sort of unofficial hiatus. It unfortunately led to a shortened 14-episode season. We took this time off to give the site a new look and feel.

As we got closer to the Season Four (three-part) finale we were once again contacted by LOSTFAN108 who again sent us some detailed spoilers for the finale where we saw the rescue ship explode and the Island "disappear."

The Season Four finale broke all site records in terms of visits, comments and reactions. It was always a double-edged sword after a finale. It meant I got some semblance of my life back but it also meant that there would be no new episode of *Lost* for nearly eight months.

We decided during this time off time to put some focus on our side project, SpoilerTV, which was just picking up and it gave me a chance to try out some new features for the site, including improved commenting system, Fantasy League game and a fun Prediction League.

Season Five was also a shorter season with only 17 hours of *Lost*, but again Season Five surpassed Season Four in terms of site hits, comments, new spoilers, as well as our Live Episode chats, which were becoming more and more popular.

Season Five flew by and before we knew it the finale was upon us, again breaking all records. When Season Five ended it was with mixed emotion as this would be the last hiatus Season Six would be *Lost*'s final season.

During the hiatus my good friend Matt gave us a new fresh look and feel. The hiatus seemed to last forever and we continued to await the resumption of filming in Hawaii. Once it did we started to get reports/photos and video from the set and the site seemed to explode into life once again.

As in previous seasons, we received reports from several sources who had access to scripts and early dailies (raw footage filmed before going into production). By the time the Season Six première aired we already had some details on the first 13 episodes of the season.

As the *Lost* staff had done a few times previously, most notably for Season Two, they had a special Sunset on the Beach event. This was for the first one-hour episode of the Season Six première, called mysteriously LA X.

Within hours of the Sunset airing, a full but blurry copy of the whole hour was online for people to see. The stats on the site took a serious spike. Although most die-hard *Lost* fans would have seen the first hour, the Live Streams and chat once again broke all previous records, with thousands of people flocking to see the second part of the première. Comments and poll votes on the site once again went through the roof and *Lost* fans flocked to the site to comment, discuss, and theorize about what was happening.

To be honest, the rest of the season pretty much flew by. We were so busy with the site posting spoilers, news, screencaps, promos, sneak peeks, theories, polls etc. that before we knew it we were getting ready for the finale. I don't think it had quite sunk in for me at this point that this would be the last ever episode of *Lost* and that my life would once again change.

As we got nearer to the finale I could sense that people on the site were getting nervous, excited and sad and probably a multitude of other emotions. The last few days seemed to go into slow-motion as we got closer to The End.

For the first time *Lost* would air on a Sunday, and the Finale would be two and a half hours. So that night I drank a load of coffee and joined our chat rooms and loaded up the live stream. I watched it in a sort of blur due to the late hour (5 a.m.-ish) and the coffee.

The episode was about 10 minutes from the end when my cable connection stopped. I couldn't believe it! The timing could not have been any worse. I rebooted, shook, shouted and cursed my modem and then in the end after 30 minutes had to go to sleep. So after six years and never having missed an episode, I missed the last ten minutes! I guess the Spoiler Gods were against me.

I got up about three or four hours later and after getting back online I took a quick look at the site stats. They were unreal. We already had over one million people view the site and the comments were just streaming in. I cursed myself for having missed everything.

I quickly found a torrent and downloaded it. I made sure not to actually read any of the comments and watched the last 20 minutes so that I could get into the mood for the last 10 minutes.

When it was over I found that I had tears rolling down my face. I had no idea I had been crying and anyone who knows me, knows I'm not a blubberer! I think the combination of the emotional final scene, the realization that my favorite show was over, the knowledge that the site would never be the same and the fact that over two days' time I'd had about three hours sleep all meant I was a tad emotional.

I slowly got to work to post the various screenshots, recaps, polls, etc on the site but it was with a heavy heart. I checked the stats at the end of the day: we had had over 1.7 million visits in a 24 hour period.

Over the next few days, things started to slow down and we closed down various parts of the site (e.g., SpoilerTV/Rumours, etc.). It was a pretty sad time.

At the time of writing this chapter here are the final site statistics:

We had over 173 Million page visits. Below is the breakdown of articles and comments made in each section of the site. Even today, over a year and half since the last episode, we still get over 75,000 page hits per month on the site.

Section	Article Count	Comments
Homepage	2940	106661
Fan Fiction	3154	7469
Media Mentions	2506	14707
Mysteries	628	16183
Polls	6338	92256
Rumours	237	8248
Screencaps	920	19251
Spoilers	3192	158801
Theories	6416	64338
Misc	1944	7431
Total	28275	495345

Looking back now on the whole experience I realize just how lucky I was to be at the center of such a fantastic show and more importantly a fantastic fandom. I don't think I understood at the time just what an impact the site and show had, not only on me, but on others as well. Reading all the emails/comments to me about the site was very cool and pretty emotional I have to say.

Would I have done things differently? Any regrets? Of course! I'm not one of those people who, when asked if they had any regrets, says, "No, Nothing." That's rubbish. Just off the top of my head, I would have set the site up differently, got more helpers from an earlier stage, added a forum at the start, improved the way we handled videos, made better use of Twitter and social media more, just to cite a few specifics.

People ask me what I thought of the finale and what was the aspect of running the site I most enjoyed. I pretty much answer the same every time: I loved the finale, the ending was perfect. As for running the site, that's easy: The most satisfying part was the privilege of meeting so many good people online. I can't and won't name them all here; they know who they are and they are still all good friends and most of them help me with my other online projects.

What I will miss the most is the massive community that we built and the sheer excitement waiting for a new episode to air and then watching it live with thousands of other fans in the chat room.

Well there you have it, the story of DarkUFO. No polar bear chases through the jungle, but an adventure nevertheless.

This is how the site looks today, and I think the tag-line in the banner is quite appropriate.

Cheers
Andy (aka DarkUFO)

Andy (aka DarkUFO) is the creator and owner of both the DarkUFO and SpoilerTV web sites. He's a professional poker player and a keen cricketer, golfer as well as being a loyal supporter of the Arsenal Football team. He's come from a Programming and Project Management background. He is based in England and married to Annie.

Disorientation, Chaos Theory, Literary Analysis, and the Thesis of LOST

by Pearson Moore

"If we can't live together, we're gonna die alone."

I understand Jack's first major speech at the end of *White Rabbit* (Episode 1.05) as a statement of intent, and a challenge. Jack's purpose on the Island, and the central objective of our quest, is the discernment of a new way of living together. LOST is not Shakespearean tragedy; the final cause is not the painful death of the hero, even though Jack does indeed give up his life in the very last frame of the opus. Neither is LOST an avant-garde tale of the futility and painful absurdity of human existence. LOST is the very antithesis of existential angst, for as Jack told Desmond at the Source, "There are no shortcuts, no do-overs. What happened, happened. Trust me, I know. All of this matters." (Episode 6.17) The forward march of destiny was a constant refrain, and a virtual call to arms, through the entire six seasons of the show. LOST does not proclaim the primacy of death, the emptiness of life, the shallowness of human or creative expression, or the touchy-feely, caprice-driven assignment of nebulous, ambiguous, or postmodern significance to its core message. Therefore, LOST must provide new account of the human ability to live together, even in the face of the fighting, destruction, and corruption that constitute the most visible signs of Jacob's Progress.

Even without proceeding past the fifth episode, we know that LOST is a dance around the central idea of humankind's ability to live together. Of course, LOST's thesis statement is not intended to apply merely to the survivors who appeared in our living rooms on September 22, 2004. The Boeing 777-200 we saw at the ocean shore did not carry 324 passengers. No, Oceanic Flight 815 from Sydney carried every one of us to that barren, wreckage-strewn beach, where we were forced to confront confusion and incivility, as well as compassion and gentle propriety. LOST does not intend the construction of temporary beach shanties, rather, it implores, beseeches, **commands** the establishment of human civilization itself. LOST proclaims a challenging, uncompromising reorientation of the essential elements of our deepest humanity.

The central idea of LOST is that people need each other to find themselves. LOST expresses this simple concept in complex ways, and prerequisite supporting concepts are neither obvious nor intuitively derived. In fact, LOST promulgates a philosophical position that may be contrary to accepted cultural thought, and therefore poses a new, stimulating set of ideas worthy of consideration and debate. In particular, the idea that love, struggle, growth, and reconciliation with the world require distinct, one-on-one personal connections is challenging—even threatening—to notions of personal autonomy. The bold statement of this premise is unique to LOST and provides the touchstone for this essay. The discussion will focus on disorientation, chaos theory, and literary analysis as revelatory of the core principle of LOST, metaphorically understood as the Cork Stone, or more appropriately, as the Boss Stone holding together the conceptual framework for the thesis.

Proto-Thesis

Jack was the leader, and he bore the responsibility of explaining our purpose on Mittelos. The particulars of his foundational speech are instructive, for they relay the core of the thesis, as well as several of the supporting themes that will recur as dominant motifs over the next six years. This is what Jack said amidst the bright flames of a dozen signal fires on the warm evening of September 27, 2004:

> It's been six days and we're all still waiting. Waiting for someone to come. But what if they don't? We have to stop waiting. We need to start figuring things out. A woman died this morning just going for a swim and he tried to save her, and now you're about to crucify him? We can't do this. Every man for himself is not going to work. It's time to start organizing. We need to figure out how we're going to survive here. Now, I found water. Fresh water, up in the valley. I'll take a group in at first light. If you don't want to come then find another way to contribute. Last week most of us were strangers, but we're all here now. And god knows how long we're going to be here. But if we can't live together, we're gonna die alone.

The proto-thesis is simple: If we can't live together, we're gonna die alone. The supporting elements are no more complicated:

1. Stop waiting. That is, no one is going to do this for us. We need to act immediately; we need to work together.
2. Prevent unnecessary death and suffering (a woman died; vigilantes tried to punish the man who attempted to save her). That is, civilization must place a

premium on human life and health. We will eventually understand this emphasis as subordinate to the recurring motif of life, death, and rebirth. This central motif is itself tied to the thesis in several ways, as I will demonstrate in this essay.

3. Every man for himself is not going to work. That is, human civilization is collaborative and respects individual contributions to the common good. This point is intimately tied to the first supporting theme.

4. Survival is essential, water is essential. After just five episodes we could not have known that water in LOST would become much more than a means of satisfying physical, biological thirst. Jack's final statement that "All of this matters" (Episode 6.17) applies with full force to this initial proclamation of LOST's thesis: Every word in Jack's declaration must be understood as bearing deep and abiding relevance to the entire text of the show.

Any valid statement of thesis will include these four elements as structural parameters, supporting axioms, or immediate corollaries.

The motif of life, death, and rebirth emerges as a forceful statement in Episode 1.20, *Do No Harm*. The sudden appearance of the beam of light from the bowels of the Swan Station was a spectacular event, presaging the opening of the hatch at the end of the first season. The importance of the event was highlighted by Boone's death and the simultaneous occurrence of Aaron's birth: Life, death, and rebirth (in the Light). But we need to gain full appreciation of the broader context of the three great events of that evening in order to understand the breathtaking majesty of this second grand proclamation of the thesis.

This first appearance of the life, death, rebirth motif occurs at a conspicuous moment. LOST incorporates religious imagery and makes frequent appeal to themes of reconciliation, communion, life, and death as drawn from Christian tradition. One such Christian theme is the notion of the saint. A saint is a person whose existence transcends life, death, and rebirth, who has moved on into the eternal light of heaven. There is on the Christian calendar a feast day that celebrates the fullness of the millions or billions of human beings whose lives are lived in the fullness of the light. In the secular world we do not mark this feast, but we do celebrate with great revelry the evening before the feast. We know this evening-before holiday as Halloween. Halloween is a contraction of the phrase All Hallow's Eve, which is a reference to the Christian holiday occurring the next day, on November first: All Saints Day.

Locke made his final attempts to open the hatch during the evening of Day 40. That same night, Claire began to go into labor. With the switching on of the Swan Station flood light, midnight arrived, and Day 41 began. It was in the early hours of Day 41 that the three momentous events occurred, essentially simultaneously: The light switched on and pierced the heavens, Boone died, and Aaron was born. Day 40 occurred on October 31, 2004—on Halloween. And in the early morning hours of the next day—All Saints Day—we experienced the full force of life, death, and rebirth.

Boone's death was the "sacrifice the Island demanded" (Locke's dream, Episode 3.03; see also Episode 1.24, Locke's speech to Jack). He risked his life to send the mayday radio message from the Nigerian plane. That the first day of November was chosen as the date of Boone's sacrifice cannot be seen as coincidental; we are justified in understanding Boone as a martyr to the cause of the greater and salutary needs of the Island. We might also propose, with some degree of support, that Aaron is a child of the Island, in the sense that the Island has an unusual mystical connection as parent to Claire's baby.

I believe the Cork Stone, the Green Pill, and the All Saints' Day shaft of light ascending the heavens are all symbols of the Heart of the Island: the three-fold foundation of Life, Death, and Rebirth that we witnessed throughout the six-year run of the series. On that terrible, wonderful All Saints Day in the first season of LOST we experienced all three of the essential elements at the Heart of the Island: Life, Death, and Rebirth. We saw that night the birth of Aaron (life), the final agonized breath of Boone Carlyle (death), and the rekindling of hope in John Locke when the bright light came on inside the hatch (rebirth). Similar events conspicuously braiding Life, Death, and Rebirth occurred throughout the series. I believe an analysis of any one of these symbols—Green Pill, Cork Stone, or shaft of light—will reveal an unrelenting assertion of the primacy of Life, Death, and Rebirth, and more importantly, a sustained assault on the prevailing cultural ideas of personhood, relation, and the acceptable range of social order. In fact, I believe the thesis of LOST constitutes a fresh view on the very nature of our humanity.

Disorientation

LOST is bewildering. I know I am not the only person within the confraternity of fandom to have spent many a long night searching the Internet and my home library for clues, ideas, connections—any information that would allow me to make sense of events or character motivations. I believe one totem, the Cork Stone, is well suited to serve as an objective point of reference around which we might build a framework for the better understanding of the series.

If we hope to understand the Cork Stone, we need to make sense of the rationale for the disorienting conditions on the Island. There is a method to the time-bending madness of LOST, and it starts with the heavy use of disorientation as a tool of understanding.

How do polar bears end up on a tropical island? What kind of statue depicts a sandal-covered foot bearing just four toes? How can an island—presumably anchored to the ocean floor—move freely about the Pacific Ocean, apparently unencumbered by any attachment to tectonic plate, scientific reason, or common sense?

It's television, and on top of that, it's science fiction. We know—two times over, in fact—that we will have to suspend our disbelief in order to accept the story on its own unusual, disorienting terms. The polar bears were brought to the Island by the Dharma Initiative. They were prime subjects for zoological studies because of their unusual intelligence and great physical strength. As we saw in the Season

Four finale, the Frozen Donkey Wheel does not turn without the application of a good deal of force, and we know at least one polar bear was successful in turning the wheel far enough that she was sent to the drop point in the Tunisian desert. The four-toed statue originally depicted Tawaret, an ancient Egyptian hippopotamus god often sculpted or painted with a four-toed but otherwise human foot. The moving Island is a bit more difficult to explain, but if we appeal to the strong magnetic charge at the Island's depths, and factor in strange behaviors operating at high magnetic strength, such as the Moses Effect, we can intuit with some degree of satisfaction a handful of scientifically valid hypotheses. If a metal cube can levitate at one Tesla, couldn't we levitate an entire island at 100 Tesla? From the well-established mythological lore of LOST, we know that magnetic forces at the Island's core exceed hundreds of thousands of Tesla; levitating an island under those conditions seems entirely plausible.

We have been taught from earliest childhood to seek logical explanation whenever confronted with inscrutable mystery. In accord with our upbringing and the Western tradition of science-based knowledge, we sense that the goal of LOST is to make sense of the strange, disconnected, random threads of the story. But this initial assessment is incorrect. LOST is soaked in mythology and relies on phenomena at the periphery of human understanding, but it does not appeal to or demand scientific rationale for etiological placement of the mythological elements of the story. The disorientations imposed by the series are not intended to result in a final reconciliation with science. The objective was not the one-on-one provision of an answer for each question posed. The real goal was to effect a realignment in conceptualization of the basic problem of the series. Disorientation was aimed at forcing us to surrender well-founded preconceptions regarding the nature not of science, but of human nature itself. Since the objective was profound, the methods used to bring us to a completely reworked cognitive framework had to be extreme, experimental, and even risky.

That the showrunners intended disorientation to resolve into unambiguous, objective understanding can be discerned from the very first frames of the series. Jack opens his eye as if startled into consciousness. The camera pulls away and we see him, dazed, his movements uncoordinated, seemingly random and without purpose. The first few seconds of LOST set the tone for the entire series: LOST was going to serve up an over-abundant, jumbled series of instances of confusion, exasperation, and disorientation.

But take a closer look at the opening seconds of the series. It might help to imagine yourself in a private home belonging to young parents. Take the freshly-carpeted stairs to the newly-painted and generously furnished children's room—the nursery. In the middle of the room you see a crib. You bend down into the crib, hovering just above the sleeping infant. Suddenly, the baby's left eye pops open. Her eye darts about, eagerly seeking something, but focusing on nothing. As you pull away from the baby you see the child's random, uncoordinated arm movements. Moving out, you take in the forest of long vertical poles that are the slats of the crib surrounding the baby. The infant looks up at you with a complexity of emotions: fear, confusion, pain. Now replace the image of the infant with that of a middle aged man in a bloody, torn, disheveled dark suit. The eye movements and the arm motions are precisely the same as those of the infant. The green bamboo forest serves as the crib in which this newborn infant has been so carefully placed. Jack, Man of Science, is on this Island reborn. "It doesn't matter, Kate, who we were - what we did before this, before the crash," Jack said in *Tabula Rasa* (Episode 1.03). "Three days ago we all died. We should all be able to start over." On that first terrifying, overwhelming afternoon on the Island, at the moment the fuselage hit the hot sand, they died. But in that same moment, Jack—and every one of us who crashed with him on the Island—experienced the awful bewilderment, the stultifying madness of rebirth into a foreign, hostile, and disorienting world.

Pitchforks and Torches

"Buonaparte 48 Hours After Landing" by James Gillray 1803 WMC PD

I could spend the next two hours cataloging every one of the mystical, metaphysical, and material questions posed by LOST—the so-called "unanswered questions"—and provide a satisfying answer to each one of them. That this has been done, over and over again, by many commentators, has not assuaged the deep resentment felt by many fans and former fans. Indeed, Nikki Stafford's keynote address at the LOST conference in New Orleans last year was titled "Dear Damon, I hope you rot in hell." On the other hand, the vast number of LOST fans who believed character stories constituted the core of the work felt richly rewarded by the series finale.

The aim of this essay is to demonstrate that the underlying assumptions of both camps are incorrect. If the devotees of the character-driven LOST truly understood the template they have applied, they would be out there with the mythology-driven LOST crowd, wielding pitchforks and torches, ready to burn Damon and Carlton at the stake. What neither camp realizes is that LOST is not character-driven and it is not mythology-driven. A deeper reservoir of significance lies at the heart of LOST.

Basis for Character-Driven Theses

If we are to comprehend the nature of both camps' misunderstanding, we should consider first any differences evident between the series as understood by the partisans of the mythology-driven story and as comprehended by the advocates of a character-driven structure.

One of the most obvious distinguishing factors between the two camps is the extent of cohesion in the two aspects of the story. The four hundred and fifty mythology-based questions require four hundred and fifty distinct answers. The statue was toppled by the force of a giant tsunami, the 30-hour discrepancy in the observed flight time of the helicopter from Island to freighter was due to an electromagnetically-induced spacetime discontinuity engulfing the Island, and so on. The character motivations and destinies, on the other hand, were all wrapped into a single hierarchy that culminated in one person: the Protector of the Island.

The Protector (Jacob) gave instruction to the Consigliere (Richard), the Candidates, or other agents, who in turn conveyed orders to their lieutenants. I imagine even the most ardent devotee of the mythology-based models of LOST would agree that the above structure is useful to our understanding not only of character hierarchies, but also to many of the important aspects of Island mythology. As for the character-driven explanations of LOST, I am not aware of any theory that does not assert the Protector as occupying the top position in the cascade of characters. Probably no one who has seen all six seasons of the show would contend that Benjamin Linus or Richard Alpert stood at the apex of the Island's command structure, or that the Protector was anything less than the person who had the greatest influence on events both on and off the Island.

Since the Protector was the most important human being on the Island, it stands to reason that if we understand his function, motivation, and objectives, we will understand the entire corpus of LOST.

The Jacob Function is "Protector of the Island." The title doesn't seem to comport with our experience, though. If the Protector's role was to ensure the Island made its passage through spacetime undamaged in any way, why did Jacob allow drilling into the Island's sensitive core, or permit the United States Army to bring a thermonuclear weapon onto the Island?

We learned the answer in "Across the Sea" (Episode 6.15), when the Guardian ("Mother") brought Jacob back to the stream just outside the cave of light:

> GUARDIAN: Do you remember what I showed you here [in the cave]?
> JACOB: The light.
> GUARDIAN: You're going to protect it now.
> JACOB: What's down there?
> GUARDIAN: Life, death, rebirth. It's the source, the heart of the island.

Even though we knew him as "Protector of the Island," according to the information provided by the Guardian, we really should have understood his role as Protector of the Source, the Heart of the Island. Jacob's single-minded focus on the Source explains his nonchalance regarding even the most severe transgressions on other parts of the Island: They simply had no bearing on the safety of the Heart of the Island. We found out during the series finale that the very core of the Source—the device holding the Source together, and therefore the most important object on the Island—was the Cork Stone. If we understand the Cork Stone, then, we understand the Protector, and through him, all of LOST.

The Cork Stone

Nowhere does canon state that the stone in the light pool at the Heart of the Island is to be called a cork. We do have it on good authority that the Island acts as a cork, holding evil inside (Jacob's words to Richard, Episode 6.09). But we need to remember there are no reliable narrators in LOST. Despite his long tenure on the Island, Jacob's perception was warped by emotionally-charged experience. Therefore we cannot accept his explanations as complete or even accurate. Rather than referring to the stone as "Cork Stone", we might more accurately think of it as a heart.

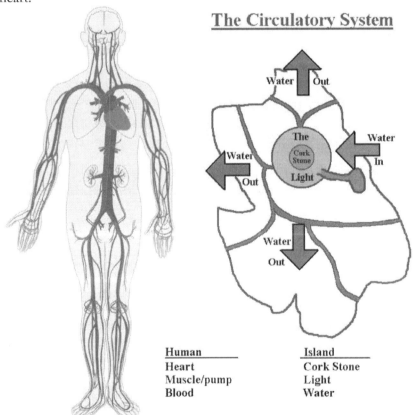

The Circulatory System

Human	Island
Heart	Cork Stone
Muscle/pump	Light
Blood	Water

However, there are many other, equally valid ways of understanding the stone at the center of the Island. I like to think of the stone as the high point of the vault in a Gothic cathedral, the balanced and perfectly-fitted mass that evenly distributes the weight of the arches to hold the cathedral together.

The Boss Stone at the apex of the central ribbed vault is the only thing preventing the tens of thousands of tons of stone comprising the roof from falling down on everyone in the cathedral. Without the perfectly balanced downward application of force ensured by the correct placement of the Boss Stone, the entire structure would become destabilized, and eventually collapse under its own weight. We saw precisely this event begin to occur when Desmond removed the Stone during the finale. Earthquakes rocked the Island, and large chunks of solid real estate began falling into the ocean.

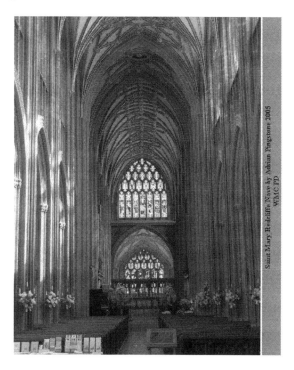

Saint Mary Redcliffe Nave by Adrian Pingstone 2005
WMC PD

Since the Smoke Monster lost his invulnerability to physical force during the Stone's hiatus, we might even make the claim that the Boss Stone analogy is more useful than Jacob's Cork Stone explanation. If the evil contained by the corked Island was rendered nearly impotent by the removal of the cork, the importance of the cork to the outside world becomes significantly diminished. On the other hand, if we think of the Island as a grand repository of human value—a cathedral built to exemplify, honor, and sustain the greatest aspects of our humanity—the Boss Stone analogy fits perfectly into the mythological scheme of the Island. For purposes of clarity, however, I will continue to refer to the stone at the Heart of the Island as the Cork Stone.

Regardless of the way in which we prefer to conceptualize the object, the Stone as seen in the series finale included certain physical attributes important to our understanding of its function. The characteristics that most draw our attention, of course, are the etchings around the perimeter of the stone inscribed in four bands.

The
Cork Stone

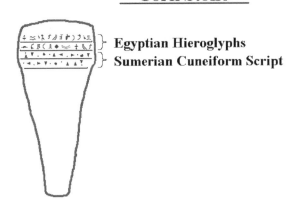

} Egyptian Hieroglyphs
} Sumerian Cuneiform Script

The upper bands contain Egyptian hieroglyphs and the lower bands contain Sumerian cuneiform script. As it happens, we have (from *Lostpedia* and the *Lost Encyclopedia*) English translations of the etchings. The Egyptian hieroglyphs are taken from the Egyptian Book of the Dead, and the Sumerian script is from the Enûma Eliš, the Sumerian story of creation.

The Cork Stone, Annotated

The
(Annotated)
Cork Stone

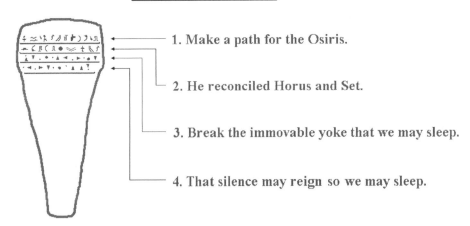

1. Make a path for the Osiris.

2. He reconciled Horus and Set.

3. Break the immovable yoke that we may sleep.

4. That silence may reign so we may sleep.

Let's take a closer look at the texts, beginning with the lowest one, "that silence may reign."

The fourth band uses the subjunctive mood ("That X may reign") to express a desire for a condition (silence) conducive to sleep. As the text occurs in a position subordinate to the other statements, the state of silence desired by the author would appear to be conditional on events or states of existence mentioned in the earlier texts. The third statement, "Break the immovable yoke," is written in the imperative, and the author has become a petitioner. She is no longer merely broadcasting a desire to any who might be interested, but she is directing her wish to some specific, higher authority, requesting that the entity take action on her behalf. It seems likely that whoever this authority might be, she is also the person who "reconciled Horus and Set." We have already established that Jacob (or anyone else occupying the office of Protector) is the final authority on the Island. We also know the Protector is entrusted with the Heart of the Island, and so it makes perfect sense that Jacob would occupy the highest position in this hierarchy of ancient texts. Osiris, according to our character-centric model, is Jacob (later Jack and then Hurley).

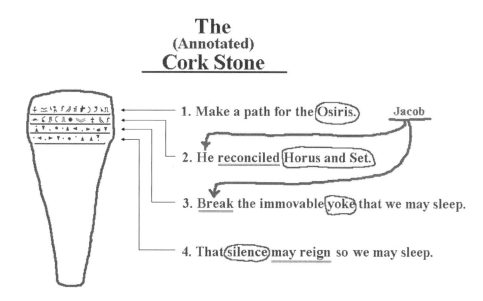

The
(Annotated)
Cork Stone

1. Make a path for the Osiris.   Jacob

2. He reconciled Horus and Set.

3. Break the immovable yoke that we may sleep.

4. That silence may reign so we may sleep.

Significance of the Cork Stone Laws

Again beginning with the lowest statement first, we can assign the symbolic meaning of each text.

Silence is the lack of noise, which we may characterize as sonic dissonance. Dissonance is disturbing or troubling to the ears and to the psyche. In simple terms, noise is that which disturbs the peace. Silence, and especially the type of silence that allows restful sleep, is tantamount to the establishment of peace. Thus, Statement #4 is an appeal for the establishment of peace.

The "immovable yoke" referenced in Statement #3 is not a physical yoke, but the psychic encumbrance caused by the unrelenting raucous din of inconsiderate people. In the opening tablets of the Enûma Eliš, from which this text is drawn, the older and less thoughtful gods are creating such a ruckus every night that the younger, less powerful gods are unable to sleep. Deprived of nocturnal rest, they go through their days exhausted and never find any happiness in their existence. They appeal to the proto-god, Tia-mat, begging her to force the other gods to end the older gods' night-time orgies of noise and discord. Thus, Statement #3 can be understood as one of the first recorded instances of a call to justice.

The
(Annotated)
Cork Stone

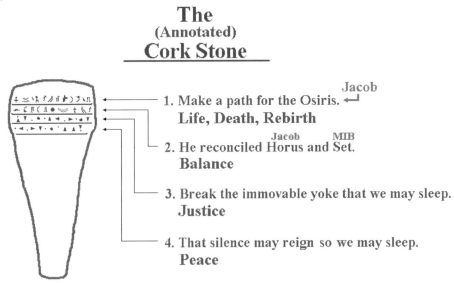

1. Make a path for the Osiris.   Jacob
   Life, Death, Rebirth

2. He reconciled Horus and Set.   Jacob   MIB
   Balance

3. Break the immovable yoke that we may sleep.
   Justice

4. That silence may reign so we may sleep.
   Peace

The second text refers to the god of daylight, Horus, and the god of night-time darkness, Set. In the context of the Island, we properly understand this second statement as a direct reference to Jacob and the Man in Black (for a complete discussion of this, please see *LOST Humanity*, Chapter 14, "The Source"). The two brothers are opposites, and the authority's action to reconcile the Man in White and his brother established balance on the Island.

The first law is all about Osiris, so it may be useful if we acquire some background information on this Egyptian god.

Osiris was Pharaoh, the most powerful human being to walk the earth. When his brother, Set, killed him, he descended to the underworld and became the god of the dead. But in a reality that included reincarnation, the job description did not end with a disinterested statement regarding custodial work in the land of the dead. He is the continually reincarnated pharaoh. Osiris alone among the gods determines life and death and rebirth. In fact, we would not be incorrect in saying Osiris *is* life, death, and rebirth.

Jacob's Sin

Placing Jacob as Osiris over Jacob as Horus in the Cork Stone hierarchy is problematic, but not irreconcilably so, at least from a logical point of view. For instance, we could envision Jacob as occupying two offices simultaneously, one office subordinate to the other. But to say that he is Osiris, that he embodies life, death, and rebirth, is simply not possible. The Guardian instructed Jacob to preserve at all costs the physical Source, since it is the Heart of the Island that controls life, death, and rebirth. She never conveyed the idea that Jacob controlled life, death, and rebirth. She did not instruct Jacob to preserve himself at all costs. Jacob—or the Protector function—is not Osiris. Osiris is the Source. Osiris is the Island.

The
(Annotated)
Cork Stone

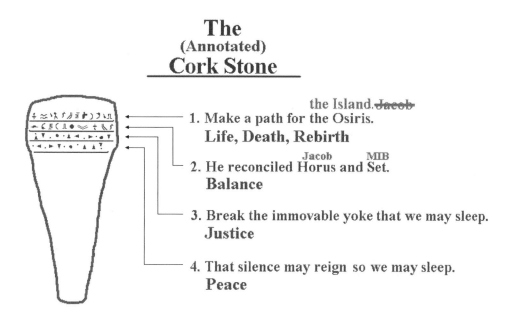

the Island. ~~Jacob~~
1. Make a path for the Osiris.
   Life, Death, Rebirth

   Jacob   MIB
2. He reconciled Horus and Set.
   Balance

3. Break the immovable yoke that we may sleep.
   Justice

4. That silence may reign so we may sleep.
   Peace

Jacob never sought to become Osiris. It was not pride that led him to throw his brother into the Source. Actually, I would say that that single act of violence against his brother in itself did not constitute a sin as the final judge, Osiris, would understand it. Osiris allowed all manner of violence on the Island, and rarely did anything to stop it. In any case, Jacob's sin ran deeper than animosity against his brother. In fact, if I understand the Island correctly, Osiris would have **_encouraged_** the feud between the Man in White and the Man in Black.

I can say this because of what I know of the life lessons absorbed by the two brothers and the nature of human relationship as I believe the Island sought to define it. The Man in Black's life lesson was "It always ends the same: They come, they fight, they destroy, they corrupt." What was Jacob's fundamental belief? "It only ends once. Anything that happens before that is just progress."

Notice that Jacob is contradicting his brother, and yet his words reinforce the minor premise. Jacob contradicts, but he does not disagree with the particulars of the Man in Black's argument. Fighting, destroying, corruption in Jacob's mind are understood not only as constructive, since they foster progress, but they are actually necessary, since all this fighting and corruption must lead to a single ending. It is the assertion of necessity and the rapt engagement of human beings in the business of progressing in their understanding that is lacking in the Man in Black's statement of human nature. And here is the true nexus of Jacob's sin: It was Jacob's early attempt to remove from his life the burr in his saddle—to destroy the negative force that pushed him toward his own progress—that was Jacob's greatest sin. Jacob sinned in disengaging from his nemesis, his Strange Attractor twin, the Man in Black.

On the Island, the opposite of fighting and corruption is not peace and preservation, but the unrestrained commitment to human progress. We get there through love and devotion to Constant, to be sure, but the more important tool in accelerating Jacob's Progress is strife.

The Hot Pocket Incident

Everyone remembers the Hot Pocket incident from Episode 5.02, *The Lie*. Benjamin Linus appeared in Hurley's kitchen, scaring him so much he threw the Hot Pocket he had just heated in the microwave. Ben implored Hurley to return with him to the Island. Now, recall early in the episode Hurley didn't want to participate in Jack's lie about the Oceanic Six. In fact, he'd rarely been able to lie. So, confronted by Ben in the kitchen, Hurley never even considered the man's request. "No way, dude... you're playing one of your mind games." That is, Hurley refused to go because he knew Ben was lying. Ironically, though, Hurley's final response to Ben's request was to tell the biggest lie in the six years of LOST: He ran out of the house to the police waiting to arrest him, shouting "I'm a murderer. I killed four people... three people. However many are dead, I killed them. I killed them."

The Hot Pocket incident revealed the logic of LOST. Superficially, Hurley lied because of his commitment to the truth, which appears to defy ordinary logic. However, Hurley was not the heroic protagonist, the virtuous crusader marching into battle to defend truth against deception, ready to defend virtue against any unsavory character. Hurley was not motivated by firm allegiance to any abstract idea, not even to truth. In fact, Hurley was motivated to do battle not with an idea, but with a character—in fact, he placed himself in opposition to *one* particular character. Virtue and the natural order are not elements of LOST. Not a single major character in LOST was motivated by abstract concepts. Every character instead was motivated by unique connections to a *single* individual. Hurley was the biased antagonist, doing everything he could to thwart the schemes of just one man: Benjamin Linus.

This was no accidental, isolated incident. LOST is all about the deep, personal connections between two individuals. Not just the Constant connection between Desmond and Penny or Charlie and Claire, but the antagonistic, "strange attractor" connection between Ben and Hurley, Jack and Locke, Sawyer and Anthony Cooper, Kate and Claire, and every other major character in the series.

Recall the two scenes in the series finale in which two men lowered a third man into the Source. First Jack and Locke—the primary strange attractor pair of the series—lowered Desmond. Later, Hurley and Ben lowered Jack into the Source. Jack had already expressed his desire not only to thwart Locke, but to kill him, yet they worked together toward a common goal. Those two scenes in the series finale constitute visual demonstration of the thesis of LOST:

We find ourselves not through abstract ideas, but in our deep connections with each other. Women and men must live and work together, both in harmony and in conflict, to preserve the personal and social connections that are the basis of human civilization.

The relationship between Hurley and Ben or Jack and Locke is chaotic, not in the popular understanding of that word, but in the scientific sense. Their relationship is not random and devoid of meaning, but governed by hard and fast equations, highly dependent on their initial relation to each other, and the very source of meaning for each other.

The Lorenz Equations, or strange attractor equations, define the rules between three variables:

The Lorenz Equations

$$\frac{dX}{dt} = \sigma(y - x)$$

$$\frac{dy}{dt} = x(\rho - z) - y$$

$$\frac{dZ}{dt} = yx - \beta z$$

The Lorenz attractor comprises three equations with three variables x, y, and z. The other terms (σ, ρ, β) are constant. The equations are dependent on each other. The x equation depends on y, the y equation depends on x and z, and the z equation depends on x and y.

Pearson Moore 2011

If we look at the result of propagating the equations in any particular dimension, we end up with a pattern that appears completely random:

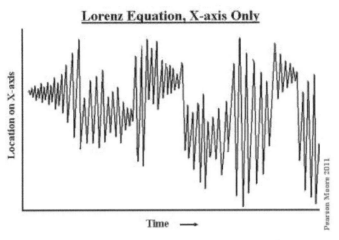

However, if we plot the equations in two or more dimensions, we end up with a grand symmetry:

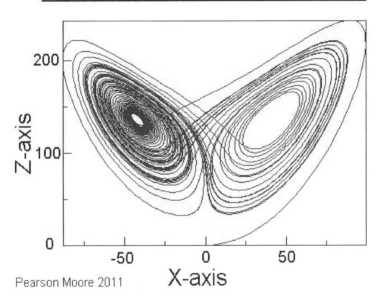

The Lorenz Equations define the butterfly effect: A butterfly flaps its wings in Brazil, causing a hurricane in New York. The two events, plotted on a single axis, appear unrelated. However, if we consider the events in higher dimensions, the symmetrical relationship becomes apparent. In the same way, Jack's skill with the scalpel would appear to be unrelated to Locke's skill with the hunting knife. At the superficial level, no connection between Jack and Locke is apparent, but at higher levels we discern a necessary connection between Jack and Locke and their struggle—their *progress*—in understanding the single, true concept that we express as the superficially opposing ideas of Faith and Science.

Survival Without Rhyme or Reason

We understood quite early in Season One that coincidence was not a structural element of the LOST universe. In *White Rabbit*, (Episode 1.05) Locke asked Jack, "What if everything that happened here, happened for a reason?" Only two episodes later (Episode 1.07), Kate held a position we already sensed had been discredited by nearly every event we witnessed on the Island:

KATE: People survive plane crashes all the time.
SAYID: Not like this one. The tail section broke off while we were still in the air. Our section cart wheeled through the jungle and yet we escaped with nothing but a few scrapes. How do you explain that?
KATE: Blind, dumb luck?
SAYID: No one's that lucky. We shouldn't have survived.
KATE: Sorry, Sayid, some things just happen, no rhyme, no reason.

Sayid was not the only one among the survivors to read into their survival an eerie presence that precluded any appeal to the vagaries of accident, luck, or coincidence. Locke, in being granted the miracle of fully functional legs, was the first one to become aware of a force guiding them toward a goal. Near the end of Season One, he understood this goal to be the opening of the Hatch. As he told Boone (Episode 1.19), "You and I are here for a reason. There's something that we were meant to find, something that's going to help us get into the hatch." By the final episode of the first season, the Island's greatest living prophet put into words the truth we already knew (Episode 1.24):

Do you really think all this is an accident—that we, a group of strangers survived, many of us with just superficial injuries? Do you think we crashed on this place by coincidence—especially this place? We were brought here for a purpose, for a reason, all of us. Each one of us was brought here for a reason.

And then the coup de grâce that forever relegated "coincidence" to the list of invalid LOST theories:

JACK: And who brought us here, John?
LOCKE: The Island. The Island brought us here. This is no ordinary place, you've seen that, I know you have. But the Island chose you, too, Jack. It's destiny.

Hurley held onto the notion of "luck," but always in the context of the Curse of the Numbers. For instance, in Episode 1.18 (*Numbers*), Hurley told his mother, "You know, ever since I won the lottery it's like we've had nothing but bad luck. Like, I don't know, like the money's cursed or something." By the end of the episode, Hurley hugged Rousseau when she confirmed, "So, yes, I suppose you're right: [The Numbers] are cursed."

Tricia Tanaka Killed Postmodernism

Hurley's argument, that his life was governed by the Curse of the Numbers, did not assert coincidence. Rather, Hurley's argument was the obverse of Locke's position. While Locke was showered with unanticipated bounties (restoration of his legs, insights into the Island), Hurley was pummeled by unhappy events (his grandfather's death, the burning down of his house, the crash of Flight 815). Hurley's "Curse" was the same as Locke's destiny, expressed in different terms but always with the awareness of an unseen force guiding the course of events.

By now we feel comfortable in the assertion that Hurley's perception of the Curse, and therefore his involvement with the Numbers, ended in the tenth episode of Season Three, *Tricia Tanaka Is Dead*. Certainly Hurley's van ride down the side of the mountain was the definitive refutation of any rational arguments deducing a curse. "You've got to make your own luck," David Reyes told his young son. Decades later, just after Hurley won the lottery, his father again said, "We make our own luck, Hugo." With these philosophical dispositions weighing heavily in opposition to his perception of number-induced plagues, Hurley's mantra, as he hurtled down the steep incline of the mountain, was simple: "There is no curse! You make your own luck!" When the rusted-out, 20-year-old engine turned over and Hurley and Charlie survived what would otherwise have been a fatal crash, the last traces of the Curse were wiped out in a symphony of joyous shouts and acclamations. But this turning point in Hurley's life did not sever his connection to the Numbers. In fact, the ride down the side of the mountain only served to confirm the unopposable force of destiny.

If the Curse was shown to have been without logical support, we ought to be obliged to dismiss from consideration the idea of destiny, since curse and fate served as two sides of the same philosophical coin. Going further, the clear supremacy of Hurley's axiom, that "We make our own luck," is the obvious precursor to Ben's final words after Hurley's installation as Protector:

HURLEY: It's my job now... What the hell am I supposed to do?
BEN: I think you do what you do best. Take care of people. You can start by helping Desmond get home.
HURLEY: But how? People can't leave the Island.
BEN: That's how Jacob ran things... Maybe there's another way. A better way.

According to Ben, not only do we make our own luck, but we make our own rules. Rules—those fabrications that contain within themselves the truth of life as we understand it—are constructs entirely dependent upon the society that creates them. Hurley, the new leader of the Island society, will change the rules to his liking, as is his prerogative.

Truth is not a universal. Truth is fickle, the expression of a social construct that guides all thought, action, and interaction among humans. That is to say, truth, and therefore any truth that LOST wishes to convey, is completely dependent on postmodern sensibility. In fact, LOST, many literary scholars and philosophers would say, is the supreme broadcast television example of postmodernism.

I tend not to put myself in the postmodernist camp, at least in my understanding of LOST. In fact, I believe the course of events subsequent to Hurley's van ride will demonstrate that Tricia Tanaka killed any valid postmodernist interpretation of LOST. This argument serves as essential corollary to my understanding of the thesis of LOST, and therefore to my interpretation of the Cork Stone as central to the philosophical position Darlton intended.

O Death, where is thy sting?

There are no disconnected threads in LOST. Hurley's van ride was not a linear precursor to the Ben/Hurley "Number One" and "Number Two" alliance that resulted in the final triumph of relativism. Intimately connected to Hurley's fate was the destiny of the man who rode shotgun during the joyride down the mountainside.

HURLEY: Snap out of it! Stop feeling sorry for yourself because someone said you're going to die. I've got an idea that's going to help us both. Now, it is dangerous. And there's a very good chance that you will die.
CHARLIE: That's supposed to convince me to come with you?
HURLEY: It is. Because if you don't die, then we win.
CHARLIE: Win?
HURLEY: Look, I don't know about you, but things have really sucked for me lately and I could use a victory. So let's get one, dude. Let's get this car started. Let's look death in the face and say, "whatever, man." Let's make our own luck. What do you say?

Hurley did not explicitly say Charlie's death sentence would be lifted if they succeeded in starting the car, but this idea was the very clear implicit message. "Let's look death in the face and say, 'whatever, man.'" But the most memorable event of the end of Season Three was Charlie's death, precisely in the manner Desmond predicted.

One could continue to legitimately argue that Charlie's fate was tied to the action of some outside force, but that no such force was at work in Hurley's life. *Tricia Tanaka is Dead* proved fate exercised no power over Hurley. If we were to grant a connection between personal volition as victor over fate and prerequisite to any relativistic postmodern interpretation of LOST, we could quite convincingly maintain that LOST is a process. Jacob's Progress means the early part of the story may have been subject to realist or modernist interpretation, but by the time we reached the final scenes, the only viable interpretation was postmodernist.

I have at my side a bucket of some very cold water. In fact, it's ice water, and it's not going to feel good at all, because the shock of being hit with this ice-cold liquid is going to cause many of you to readjust your perspective on one of the most beloved episodes in the LOST canon. Some of you, after you read the next several lines, will believe that I have destroyed the beauty and removed the fun-loving nature of *Tricia Tanaka Is Dead*. If you do not wish to risk damage to your enjoyment of this fan favorite, read no further in this essay.

Hurley's ride down the mountainside has virtually unparalleled significance in the LOST story. The basis of the episode's meaning is the reality that Hurley invited great personal risk—in fact, life or death risk—to face down the Curse. "Let's get this car started. Let's look death in the face and say, 'whatever, man.' Let's make our own luck." If he died, it would mean he could not choose his own destiny. If he lived, on the other hand, having chosen a test that virtually ensured his death, he would demonstrate for all time that fate had no control over him. There was no curse, there was no destiny. Extrapolating to the final episode of LOST, we could assert that Hurley's exercise of human volition as newly-installed Protector of the Island was the frosting on the cake, the greatest confection in LOST's postmodernist bakery.

We could consider Hurley's ride as the brave action of a man convicted in the truth of his position. But an independent observer, looking at the rocks at the bottom of the steep hill, the age of the van, and giving due consideration to the indisputable fact that the battery had been dead for over twenty years, would reasonably conclude Hurley was not brave. Rather, the evidence indicated the man was either certifiably insane, or he had a death wish. In short, reasonable observers would believe Hurley was attempting suicide. As Sawyer said just before he pushed the van toward the hill, "Well, it's your funeral."

Hurley's ride means something to us because he risked everything, even his life. If he had chosen an act without risk—a game of Connect Four, for instance—as his proof of individual autonomy, the significance would have been degraded to the point of meaninglessness—not to mention the fact that the episode would have been devoid of any shred of drama.

Okay, here it comes.

Hurley's ride, from any reasonable independent observer's point of view, was a suicide attempt. Let's imagine he had ramped up the stakes by skewing the odds even more against his odds of survival. He went down to the bottom of the hill and dug in a line of spears at driver level so he would be impaled if the engine didn't start. He had Charlie tie him up so he couldn't steer. He had Charlie light a stick of dynamite, so that even if the engine turned over and the car cleared the rocks (even without steering), he would be blown to bits in the explosion.

Dynamite would surely work, wouldn't it? Dynamite killed Dr. Leslie Arzt, didn't it? It killed Ilana Verdansky, right? It killed Richard Alpert, when he went into the Black Rock to commit suicide, and—

Well, not quite. Richard Alpert did not die. He couldn't commit suicide any more than he could die of old age. He lived, even though he asked Jack Shephard to light the fuse. What Jack knew, and what Hurley could not possibly have known when he took his joyride, is that Candidates cannot commit suicide. In fact, killing a Candidate is virtually impossible. Hurley, if you recall, was a Candidate.

Hurley could not have died during the van ride. He risked nothing.

Hurley, as one of Jacob's Candidates, was immune to death by suicide. Hurley could not die in this way, because the Island would not allow it. The fact that the engine turned over—a real impossibility, since the battery chemicals were long before neutralized to the point of uselessness—was not a proof of Hurley's victory over fate. Instead, it was yet another proof that Hurley was in the care of the Island. That is, *the van ride was a proof of destiny's complete control over every minute of Hurley's life.* Perhaps Hurley enjoyed some measure of autonomy. Perhaps he exercised volition in many areas of his life. But in those parts of his being having greatest bearing on his future and his relation with others, Hurley's life was completely subordinate to a grand plan that fully determined his fate.

The Mirage of Cultural Relativism

Proponents of postmodernist interpretations of LOST will point to the cultural potpourri highlighted in virtually every episode. Egyptian hieroglyphics, Dharma station names gleaned from ancient Greek mythology, Christian imagery, Hindu numbers, Buddhist symbols, and a mish-mash of cultural artifacts ancient, modern, and popular formed the multi-cultural, multi-textual underpinnings of LOST. The characters were thrust into an environment lacking cultural cohesion. In postmodern theory the only reality we can understand, appreciate, and appropriate to our own personal growth—to our own identity as human beings—is a socially constructed reality. Since human beings require socially-derived structure in order to find themselves, and since the survivors of Flight 815 were deprived of social order and cultural meaning of any kind—indeed, because they were forced to inhabit a topsy-turvy island rich in mix-and-match cultural confusion, they were Lost. The lesson of LOST, postmodernists would say, is that we impose meaning on our existence through the filter of social cognition. Without the cultural overlay, life is random, devoid of meaning, and denizens of this chaotic existentialist realm are— all of them—Lost.

As I argued in *LOST Humanity*, I believe Darlton made clear their positions on several artistic statements that arose during the course of the series. One of these explicit positions, I believe, regarded the value of the counter-cultural Dharma Initiative.

The Dharma Initiative was presented as the ultimate collective of hypocrites. Their motto was "For the betterment of mankind and the advancement of world peace." But as I wrote in Chapter Five of *LOST Humanity*:

> ... the organization was funded by a munitions and arms merchant [Alvar Hanso] who became wealthier with every Vietnamese village incinerated to dust by napalm bombs... the DI was run by a mathematician whose primary aim was to build "security systems." And when Horace Goodspeed's bully tactics weren't aggressive enough, Stuart Radzinsky stepped in with handguns, rifles, and machine guns.

The Dharma Initiative, I wrote, "is the story of happy image and harsh reality, idealists and schemers, the culmination of everything the Woodstock Generation believed in."

The Woodstock Generation is my generation. We're the generation that protested an unjust and illegal war in Southeast Asia. Perhaps our children and grandchildren see in our protests something worthy and noble. But what do they think of our illegal war in Nicaragua? Our quest for "weapons of mass destruction" as justification for the invasion of Iraq? Why would pot-smoking flower children who opposed an immoral war in Vietnam find an even less defensible war in Iraq entirely acceptable?

Postmodernism was a creation of the mid-20th century, and it was the post-World War II Baby Boom generation that fully embraced its cultural significance. "I'm OK, you're OK" meant "doing your own thing." Most of all, it required looking out for Number One, and that meant disentangling ourselves from any kind of social commitment. "Turn on, tune in, drop out" was our battle cry. We fulfilled the call to "turn on" by filling our lives with sex, drugs, and rock-'n'-roll. "We agitated and marched and chanted for peace in Vietnam not because we understood the war to be unjust, but because we saw no reason to die in a far-off jungle when the orgasmic pleasures of responsibility-free life beckoned. 'I'm Okay, you're Okay' and 'If It Feels Good, Do It' were closer to the governing mantra of my generation than any pacifist or humanist or religious ideals. We temporarily adopted those ideals because they suited our true objectives, which in the end proved to share not a single point of reference with any of the nobility of our parents' hearts." (LOST Humanity, Ch. 5)

Perhaps my analysis is incorrect. If so, I would expect Damon Lindelof and Carlton Cuse to have portrayed their fathers' generation in a mostly positive light. The fathers of the Flight 815 survivors, then, would have demonstrated an unusual degree of virtue, and their children's only source of angst would have been the bad choices they made after the crash. If only they had emulated the sterling example of their Baby Boomer parents, all would have been well on Mittelos.

But as we know very well, Darlton made the sins of the fathers into a major theme in LOST. In many cases, Sawyer being the most prominent example, the Baby Boomer parents were depicted as virtually destroying their children's lives.

Darlton encapsulated their disdain for their parents' hypocrisy in the Island hippie movement they called the Dharma Initiative. Quoting again from *LOST Humanity*, Chapter Five:

> LOST is emphatic about few things, but this is one of them: The Baby Boomer generation's response to life is wrong-headed, inhuman, and uncivilized... If we are to survive... if we are to realize Jacob's Progress, we must engage. We are compelled, by nature, by our truest selves, by everything holy and wise and good, to engage with this world and with each other in every dimension of life, spirit, and will. We all need

each other, for the only way into the Church of the Holy Lamp Post is with a Constant at one's side, and the only way to move on into the warmth and light beyond is as a group, the congregation of all those who have interacted in harmony with each other to improve the human condition. Goodness is not singular, but collaborative. It is not a choice. It is our truest and only sustainable destiny.

For Darlton, there is no value in a socially-dependent relativism. Society must be grounded in principles that transcend culture and social conditioning. Society, in the end, is based on carved-in-stone principles, such as those chiseled into the face of the Cork Stone.

We know the principles Darlton advocated were not intended for open interpretation of the "I'm okay, you're okay" postmodernist persuasion. The famous all-religions stained glass window in the sacristy of Our Lady of the Foucault Pendulum is not some wishy-washy statement to the effect that all religions are equally valid. No, the church window expresses the same truths as those etched into the Cork Stone: There are universal human values, **_objectively valid_** human virtues, that transcend time and place, religion and philosophy, culture and society. As Dr. Paul Wright said in Chapter Nine ("Theological Syncretism in LOST") of this volume, "… syncretism [in LOST] is not copout or capitulation; it is both common sense and a moral imperative."

The Cork Stone, inscribed with fundamental truths from two societies of disparate origin and practice, is the final proof of non-relativistic intent. LOST, at its core, asserts that the axioms of culture and society transcend place and time. The laws of the Cork Stone were as valid in Mesopotamia as in Egypt, as valid for Jacob as they are for Hurley, valid yesterday, today, and tomorrow, for as long as human beings remain bathed in the light that is life, death, and rebirth.

Finding Ourselves

Our identity as stand-alone, independent individuals, according to LOST, is a dangerous deception. The reality is that we find ourselves—we best express our humanity, and adhere to the tenets of Jacob's Progress—in engaging with distinct persons in one-on-one interactions so as to force an evolution in thought, attitude, and social relation.

I said the members of strange attractor pairs are not personally concerned with abstract ideas. However, it is certainly true that abstract ideas unite them in their binary progress toward finding themselves.

Recall the first law: Make a path for the Osiris.

The
(Annotated)
Cork Stone

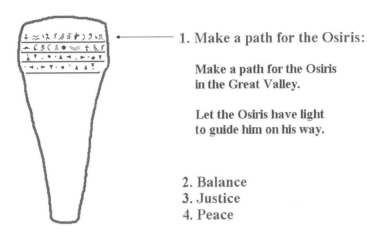

1. **Make a path for the Osiris:**

   **Make a path for the Osiris
   in the Great Valley.**

   **Let the Osiris have light
   to guide him on his way.**

2. **Balance**
3. **Justice**
4. **Peace**

Make a path for the Osiris. Give him light for his way. It is not an imperative directed at Hurley and Ben, Protector and Consigliere. Hurley and Ben are subordinate to the Osiris—to the Island, in other words. It is our collective duty to make a path for the Island in our own lives. We are obliged to assert the primacy of life, the dignity of death, the inevitable symmetry of rebirth. In doing this, we allow Osiris to make his way from the darkness of the Great Valley into the bright sunshine of life. We allow the Island into our lives and our world, to bring balance, justice, and peace. That is, we find our LOST Humanity.

We will always be Lost, because life is all about Jacob's Progress, and our work in fulfilling our destiny is never completed in our lifetime. But in engaging heart, mind, and body with beloved Constant and treacherous Strange Attractor, we find ourselves in a place without time, sitting beside our Constant in a grand antechamber, bathed in the Light, embraced by the Island, once struggling, but now found, forever balanced in justice and peace, never again Lost.

Pearson Moore is the author of *LOST Humanity*, *LOST Identity*, and over 100 essays on LOST. His first novel, *Cartier's Ring*, an action-adventure historical novel, is available at bookstores worldwide. Pearson also writes on the HBO series Game of Thrones; his first GoT collection, *Game of Thrones Season One Essays*, is available in both ebook and paperback versions.

'Tied to a Tree in the Jungle of Mystery':
Using Dreams in *Lost* to Keep Viewers Bewildered ... and Watching

By Cynthia Burkhead, Ph.D.

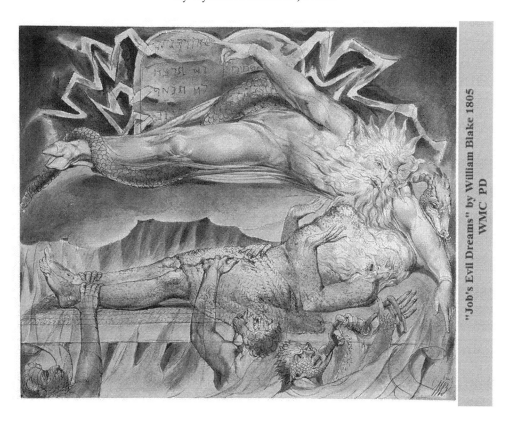

"Job's Evil Dreams" by William Blake 1805
WMC PD

Lost spent six seasons and offered multiple, often original narrative devices in the pursuit of delayed audience comprehension. In contrast to shows like *St. Elsewhere* which convinced viewers of their understanding before introducing the final autistic-boy-and-his-snow-globe ending that destabilized that sense of insight, *Lost* never allowed a moment of comprehension that wasn't undermined by another moment of confusion, until the somewhat neatly tied together final episode. In their pursuit of viewer mystification, *Lost*'s creators gave their audience multi-directional flashes and science that sent us all to Wikipedia for quick lessons in subjects like electromagnetism. It created mythology (or was it science?) that presented temporal displacement that goes awry without a constant. That last one at least helped us understand the movie *Inception*. And if we were looking for any coherence in the show's multiple allusions, we had to navigate between, for instance, the philosophy of Kierkegaard vs. the young adult literature of Judy Bloom, and the sci-fi world of *Star Wars* vs. the Bible. Its use of many and varied devices in the service of storytelling places *Lost* in the category of TV programs Jason Mittell defines by its narrative complexity. According to Mittell, "This programming form demands an active and attentive process of comprehension to decode both the complex stories and modes of storytelling offered by contemporary television." (601) Along with science and mythology and a multitude of illusions, *Lost* also uses the dream to compound narrative complexity and audience uncertainty.

Typical uses of dreams in narrative texts include exposition, foreshadowing, character development, and closure. Sometimes, as is the case in select episodes of the *Twilight Zone* and *The Alfred Hitchcock Hour*, the dream state merges with a character's reality, resulting in the horror we experienced from these programs. The important thing to remember in horror's use of the dream is that viewers anticipate an unexpected or horrific outcome when the dream is utilized. In the case of *Lost*, dreams have multiple functions, and this prevents the audience from experiencing any certainty about their meaning. Additionally and perhaps more baffling, on the island a character's subconscious is never the unquestionable source of his or her own dream. With all these myriad uses of the dream, Lindelof and Cuse add to their arsenal of devices for keeping the viewer unawares.

Before considering how *Lost*'s creators used dreams to withhold understanding of the story, it is important to look at a confusion created by dreams for which the producers had no responsibility: that is the theory among some viewers that the finale would reveal the whole show was just a dream. Although Damon Lindelof confirmed in an interview that *Lost* would have a clear resolution, not "a snow globe, waking up in bed, it's all been a dream, cut to black" (602) kind of ending, some viewers refused to budge from their finale theories. The dominant among these was that the whole thing was Jack's dream, experienced as he lay dying after the crash. Jack got to own the dream because, as the theory goes, he was the only one who had been in contact with all the passengers who were survivors in his dream. Even the sitcoms got in on the dream theory action. Three months before *Lost*'s final season began, *30 Rock's* Jenna reported that J. J. Abrams told her the Island was just Hurley's dream. The important point is not that the theories were wrong, which of course they were, but that the idea of a dream ending for *Lost* was perpetuated even after Lindelof's denial. Perhaps it was the only explanation for an ultra-complex narrative for which some viewers had a context; after all, they had seen the "snow globe, waking up in bed, it's all been a dream, cut to black" kind of endings before. Some viewers who couldn't wrap their minds around the resolution *Lost* actually presented refused to give up on their "dream" ending, justifying their own interpretations by arguing in one forum that the finale was really the "equivalent of a dream." (603) After the finale aired, *New York Times* blogger Tony Pierce even invited readers to comment on whether the entire show had been a dream or not. The confusion related to dreams in these cases occurred not through anything *Lost*'s producers did, but perhaps by what they didn't do: provide narrative comprehension early enough to prevent less inventive viewers from borrowing from other texts to write the story and its ending for themselves. As an ode to or perhaps ridicule of these viewers, *The Simpsons* episode that aired immediately after the *Lost* finale ends with Bart writing on the chalk board: "End of *Lost*: it was all the dog's dream. Watch us."(604)

While the *Lost* team did everything possible to dispel the fans' "it was all a dream" theories, the show's creators are responsible for using the oft-maligned narrative device throughout the series, which perhaps teased viewers into the dream trap.   More important to this analysis, utilizing dreams inconsistently throughout *Lost* intensified viewer uncertainty. A few choice examples illustrate this point.

Claire Littleton's first dream occurs in the Season 1 episode, *Raised by Another*. Claire is not pregnant in her dream, and when she hears a crying baby and tries to find it, she finds Locke instead. He is sitting at a table with tarot cards and a lamp – the same table and lamp later seen at the psychic reading in Claire's flashback. Locke tells Claire that she gave the baby away, and "everyone pays the price now." The cards are black and white, and when Locke looks up at Claire, he has one black eye and one white. This dream does foreshadow elements of the show, but not those viewers expect. In her dream, after running away from Locke, the white crib she finds in the jungle is the same crib at the staff station where Claire is taken after being abducted by Ethan. The mobile on the dream crib is the same mobile as on the station crib, which featured airplanes with Oceanic logos on them.

"Dreams" by Vittorio Matteo Corcos 1896
WMC PD

Of course, when Claire has the dream, we don't know what it means, nor would we expect to know because narratives typically unveil these meanings bit by bit. The episode's flashback does give some insight into Locke's comment about giving the baby away. The flashback shows that Claire did see a psychic after the baby's father left her, and the psychic warned Claire that she must raise the baby alone or it will be in danger. Between the flashback and the dream, then, it can be inferred that in the future, Claire will give the baby away, an action for which everyone will suffer. When Claire is abducted, viewers don't learn what happened to her until a flashback in the Season Two episode, *Maternity Leave*. The flashback reveals that Claire is drugged during her stay at the staff station and doesn't even realize she is on the island. At the station, she is almost ready to give the baby away until she is saved by the young woman we later learn is Alex Rousseau. When she returns to the 815ers, she has no memories of anything after the crash, including her dream or the abduction. Locke's warning, then, has no meaning for Claire herself, only for viewers. After Aaron's birth, Claire is so intent on protecting him that we dismiss Locke's warning and any action it may have foretold. At this point it is tempting to disregard the psychic's warning to Claire about raising the baby alone. Claire does not leave Aaron until Season Four, when she follows not-Christian to the cabin. By leaving Aaron, Claire has given him away, and he will eventually end up in Kate's care. Viewers now experience our own flashback to Claire's Season One dream and remember the other part of dream-Locke's warning, that "everyone pays the price" if Claire relinquishes responsibility for Aaron. The dream can now be classified as a foreshadowing device, and we must only wait to see how the rest of the Locke's warning is manifested in the narrative. But as with anything on *Lost*, nothing is that easily understood or resolved.

Going back to the dream reminds us of Locke's appearance, the black and white eyes. As part two of the series pilot has already implied symbolic significance for the two colors when Locke is explaining the game of backgammon to Walt, saying, "Two players. Two sides. One is light, one is dark," and as we have seen the black and white stones retrieved from Adam and Eve's resting place in the cave, Locke's dream eyes begin to accrue meaning. This accumulation can only happen for viewers, however; Claire did not witness the discussion about backgammon or the scene in the cave – indeed, Claire was not even in the episode *House of the Rising Sun* in which the stones were discovered. When in Episode 1.14 we learn through Charlie reading Claire's diary that she is having recurring dreams about a black rock she can't escape, the mystery compounds.   As a narrative device, then, Locke's dream eyes still function to suggest meaning that is not fully realized until Seasons Five and Six. Within the narrative, however, they suggest something else. Was it Locke speaking to Claire in the dream, or was it one or both of the Island's battling brothers, Jacob and the Man in Black? In other words, was the dreams' source mystical?

The question is important because it would suggest *Lost* is using dreams that are both Freudian in nature – Claire's subconscious repeating warnings first given her by the psychic in Australia – and supernatural. In the case of the supernatural, the dream becomes one more piece of a puzzle that, even in the tenth episode of the first season, is becoming one of the most complex in television storytelling history. The viewing experience becomes like a dream as bits and pieces of past episodes are remembered and suggest meaning, but the story is still too fragmented to allow full interpretation.

This effect is particularly important in the dreams that foreshadow the character's actions in a past they haven't even experienced yet. In the Season One episode *Deus Ex Machina* (Episode 1.19) Locke's first dream is central to some major plot elements, including the heroin-filled Madonna statues, the question mark, Yemi's corpse, and Boone's death. But the dream also foreshadows Locke witnessing the plane's crash in the past, after Ben turns the wheel causing the survivors to jump around in time. Likewise, Hurley's second season dream in *Everybody Hates Hugo* foreshadows Jin and Hurley's involvement with the Dharma Initiative in 1977, where they eventually find themselves in the time jumping experience. Until the time skipping begins, there is absolutely no way that viewers can find meaning in certain elements of these dreams as they have no relation to anything the characters have yet experienced in the narrative. Rather than providing any intellectual ability to grasp the story, they compound audience confusion.

Many of the dreams best classified as mystical serve to provide instruction for the characters. Charlie's first dream in *Fire and Water* tells him that he will save the survivors, but only if he plays. His second dream in the episode tells him he must accept responsibility for Claire and Aaron. Eko's dream in "?" not only encourages him to push the button, but also to make Locke take him to the question mark. The mystical power controlling the dream takes the form of Yemi, Eko's brother, who is the source of Eko's guilt. Likewise, Charlie's mother voices the instructions in his dream, and she is one for whom Charlie feels great guilt as a result of his addiction. In the aptly titled episode, *Further Instructions*, Boone appears in Locke's dream as a spirit guide. Boone is, of course, the person for whom Locke feels the greatest guilt, at least among the 815ers. Boone encourages Locke to save Eko and suggests he can use Eko's stick to find New Otherton. Locke's *Cabin Fever* dream tells Locke, through Horace Goodspeed, how to locate the cabin. In *There's No Place Like Home*, Claire appears in Kate's dream to warn her against bringing Aaron back to the island. While it seems these "instruction dreams" are more clear than other dreams the islanders experience, confusion still results because it is uncertain who is behind the instructions, which is further complicated when the choices are narrowed to Jacob or the Man in Black. Once that happens, viewers are left with the same options the islanders must face – to follow the light or follow the dark. And the option is as thorny for us as it is for *Lost*'s characters.

Pearson Moore argued in his keynote address at the *Lost* Mini-conference [New Orleans, October 6-8, 2011] that the confusing elements of *Lost* are the tools of our greatest understanding. I would add to that claim the word "eventually." In no other television narrative do the writers delay understanding for as long and to the degree as those telling the *Lost* story. This analysis only begins to uncover the role dreams serve in that delayed comprehension, and it has more than once created the type of confusion viewers experience when trying to use *Lost*'s narrative clues to unlock its meaning. Like John Locke's, the investigation will continue; it's what all of those who study this text do, which in the end may be the most brilliant quality of *Lost*. It won't allow its audience to "let go."

Cynthia Burkhead is an English Instructor at the University of North Alabama. She is the author of *Student Companion to John Steinbeck*, and co-editor of *Joss Whedon: Conversations* and *Grace Under Pressure: Grey's Anatomy Uncovered*. Her full-length book on dreams in television is forthcoming from Continuum in 2013.

Funny Red Pictures: Egypt and LOST

By Sam McPherson

There are some questions not even Lostpedia can answer.

How important is ancient Egypt to the mythology of LOST?

Lostpedia is undoubtedly the most useful resource for any inquisitive fan, new or old (though I may be a little biased), but the answer to the question above simply cannot be answered by the consensus-based fact-gathering of the site. Instead, the answer inhabits the realm of interpretation and conjecture. The Lostpedia user base is itself polarized by that very question; some dismiss the Egyptian mythology as a red herring while others claim it has thematic significance. For the purposes of the storyline itself, the ancient structures that littered the Island simply served as epic, exotic set pieces, with no significance beyond simply providing mysterious locations for the characters to interact in. If this were any other show, that would be all the answer necessary.

But this is LOST, and beneath the surface layer of significance, there is a rich tapestry of meaning tied to the show's Egyptian references. These meanings aren't explicitly a part of the show, but with a little interpretation, they give new context to Jacob, the Man in Black, and to the very nature of the Island itself. Egypt isn't just significant to the mythology of LOST, it redefines it.

To Summon Protection

Hieroglyphics were the first glimpse at ancient Egypt we received on LOST, first appearing in Season Two on the countdown clock in the Swan hatch when the survivors failed to press the button in time.

"The timer went all the way down to zero, and then some funny red pictures flipped up in its place," Benjamin Linus recounted in the episode *Dave*. "They looked like hieroglyphics, but I'm no expert."

Of course, Ben was lying; he knew more about those funny red pictures than he let on at the time. Hieroglyphics could be found across the entire Island, etched on ancient ruins and underground passageways -- even in a secret room in the back of Ben's closet. Naturally, these hieroglyphics have multiple, sometimes directly contradictory meanings within the series.

For instance, the Egyptian character sa (meaning 'protection') appears several times throughout the series, associated with both Jacob and the Man in Black. The Season Six episode *Lighthouse* sees Jacob lead Hurley to an engraving of sa in the Temple wall, which marks the entrance to a secret passageway out of the Temple. By leaving the Temple through this passageway, Hurley and Jack are saved from the Man in Black's assault on the Temple, which happens hours later. During that assault, which occurs during *Sundown*, Jacob's disciple Ilana uses that same sa-marked escape route to usher the rest of Jacob's followers to safety, escaping death at the hands of the Man in Black by mere seconds. In this way, it appears that the Egyptians used sa to refer to Jacob. It does seem appropriate; after all, Jacob's role was that of Protector of the Island.

As with everything on LOST, though, there is a strange duality to sa: it also refers to the Man in Black. In the season four episode *The Shape of Things to Come*, Ben enters a secret room where he summons the Man in Black (as the smoke monster) to avenge his daughter's death at the hands of Martin Keamy and his team of mercenaries. The doorway of this chamber features several hieroglyphics, including sa. When read together, they translate to loosely read, "to summon protection."

So, if sa is to be believed, the Egyptians viewed both Jacob and the Man in Black as protectors, despite the fact that Jacob was the only one with the job title. The Egyptians seemed to have a reverence for both brothers as the protectors of the Island. They believed this, interestingly, despite being aware of the constant battle that was being waged between the two.

The Two Fighters, The Guardians of Life

Somehow, the Egyptians learned about the Heart of the Island and where it was located, and were responsible for placing the cork into the Source. This task was so important to them that several of them died accomplishing it (likely from the high electromagnetism), their bodies remaining to be found by Jack and Desmond years later. It stands to reason, then, that the inscriptions on that cork—the cork that's protecting the world from Hell—are pretty significant.

The second of those four lines of text has been officially confirmed to translate to: "He hath reconciled the Two Fighters (Horus and Set), the guardians of life." Looking at the mythological Egyptian figures of Horus and Set, it seems fairly likely that they were intended to parallel Jacob and the Man in Black.

As with any mythological tale, there is no definitive version of the story of Horus and Set; many exist. Most versions describe Set as the brother of Horus's mother Isis, but in his book Who's Who in Egyptian Mythology, Anthony S. Mercatante (701) briefly mentions one version of the myth in which the two gods "came forth from the belly" at the same time; they were twins, just like Jacob and his nameless brother.

Mercatante also describes Set as "the personification of darkness," and the "natural opponent to all that was good and life-giving in the universe." (701) Set instigated the fight between himself and Horus by murdering Horus's (and, depending on the version of the myth, his own) father, the god Osiris, creating great animosity between the two. A terrible battle between the two brothers was subsequently waged, and in the end, Horus was declared the winner, and Set was cast into the darkness, though not killed.

It's interesting to note that many versions of the battle between Set and Horus feature a moment when Set gouges out Horus's left eye. While Horus's eye was later restored, the Eye of Horus became a major symbol in ancient Egyptian culture, representing safe passage to eternal life and protection from evil (not unlike sa). Given LOST's fascination with eyes, it's no surprise that the Eye of Horus made a brief appearance on the show, becoming the defining feature of Jacob's tapestry.

The events of the Horus and Set myth sound strikingly familiar to those of the Season Six episode *Across the Sea*, in which the Man in Black—LOST's own personification of darkness—kills his and Jacob's mother and initiates a battle between the two. Jacob, in his anger, causes his brother's transformation into the Monster, a "fate worse than death."

But what is this reconciliation that the cork stone speaks of? The feud between the two brothers doesn't end well; the Man in Black manipulates Ben into stabbing Locke, while Jacob's successor, Jack (along with Kate) kills the Man in Black by kicking him off the Island's lava cliffs.

The first line of text reveals that the 'he' who reconciles the Two Fighters is Osiris, the Egyptian god of the afterlife. Does this mean that the feud between Jacob and the Man in Black could only be ended by their deaths? That's entirely possible. But there's another aspect of Egyptian mythology that might indicate something further. It's called "The Secret of the Two Partners."

As you might have guessed, the two partners are Horus and Set. But what is this secret? Mercatante refers to it as "the hidden understanding between the two combatant gods." This understanding is pretty spiritual stuff. Despite their feuding, both fighters know that, "in the sphere of the eternal where there is no duality, Set and Horus are one; that is death and life... are one force. There is reconciliation in the end."

A "sphere of the eternal" where reconciliation is possible? That sounds strikingly similar to the flash-sideways afterlife we saw the survivors in throughout Season Six. Of course, Jacob and the Man in Black weren't present in this afterlife, but that's because it was made by the survivors for the survivors. The Man in Black and Jacob would have their own sphere of the eternal (where, as Christian Shephard put it, "there is no now"). And, as our survivors were given the chance to atone for their past mistakes, perhaps the brothers would finally reach the reconciliation that the Egyptians wrote about. They would be able to 'move on' into the glowing yellow light that had surrounded our survivors in the final moments of the series finale, where life and death were one force.

"What's down there?" Jacob once asked his mother, talking about the glowing light emanating from a hole in the ground.

Her response was simple: "Life, death, rebirth."

The reconciliation between Jacob and the Man in Black happens at the Source.

For Every Man There Is a Scale

Despite their possibly correct analysis of the dynamic between Jacob and the Man in Black, the Egyptians still could only express that relationship in the terms of their own deities. Jacob and the Man in Black were Horus and Set, naturally, but they also brought in other gods who had no parallels to figures on the Island. Anubis, the Egyptian god of the dead, for example, is depicted alongside the Monster in a mural seen in the Season Five episode *Dead Is Dead*.

It's easy to see how the Egyptians might have associated the Man in Black with Anubis. It all comes down to the Weighing of the Heart.

In the episode *Sundown*, Dogen explained to Sayid exactly why he had tried to kill him. "For every man there is a scale," he explained. "On one side of the scale there is good. On the other side, evil. This machine tells us how the scale is balanced. And yours tipped the wrong way."

One of Anubis's jobs as guardian of the dead was to oversee a post-death judgment ceremony known as the Weighing of the Heart. The ceremony, described in the Egyptian Book of the Dead, begins as "the deceased is led by Anubis into the judgment hall," where 42 judges are present. The deceased "then recites the Negative Confession, in which he says he has not committed any faults" from a list of forty-two sins. His heart is then weighed against Ma'at, the goddess of truth and justice. The deceased was allowed to enter the afterlife if the scales balanced, but if they did not, the deceased would be "immediately destroyed by a monster who waits at the foot of the scale."

Where have we seen something similar?

At the end of the Season Three episode *The Cost of Living*, Mr. Eko is confronted by the Man in Black, who appears to him as his dead brother Yemi.

Yemi, dressed in his priestly garb, prepares to hear Eko's confession. Eko offers this instead:

"I ask for no forgiveness, Father, for I have not sinned," Eko tells the Man in Black. "I have only done what I needed to do to survive." The Man in Black, visibly disgusted by Eko's negative confession, retreats into the jungle and, as the Monster, pummels Eko to death. This occurred, of course, after the Monster's apparent judgment of Eko in Season Two's *The 23rd Psalm*.

Likewise, in *Dead Is Dead*, the Monster confronts Ben in a similar manner, eventually appearing to him in the form of his dead daughter, Alex. Unlike Eko, though, Ben is quick to apologize for his sins, and the Monster allows him to live.

Of course, as we learned in Season Six, the Man in Black's judgments are anything but objective. He killed Eko for the same reason he spared Ben: he was looking for someone he could manipulate. The negative confession served its purpose in proving Eko's incorruptibility, though unfortunately for him, that's not what the monster at the base of the scale was looking for.

Regardless of the Man in Black's motivations, the Egyptians regarded his judgments with such reverence that they built a chamber just for that purpose, depicting him alongside their great judge, the deity Anubis. They just didn't realize that his scale was tipped the wrong way.

The Shadow of the Statue

Finally, it is time to address the largest physical aspect of Egyptian influence on the Island: the statue of Taweret. From an unknown date until the Black Rock decimated it in 1867, the massive statue stood in its entirety, a remnant of the Egyptian culture that once thrived on the Island. For the storyline of LOST, the statue's ruins became a symbol for the mystery of the Island. Sayid was disquieted at its four toes when he first spotted it back in the Season Two finale *Live Together, Die Alone*, while the Season Five finale revealed that it was the home to Jacob, one of the Island's most enigmatic figures.

So why did the Egyptians build their largest and most striking moment to Taweret, the goddess of fertility? Unlike Horus and Set, she had no obvious parallel to any Island figure the Egyptians were familiar with. No, Taweret's significance is much broader: she parallels the Island itself.

The obvious connection is fertility. Some suggest that the statue of Taweret was built to appease the goddess, as pregnancy problems were seen to plague the Island. However, those problems occurred only after Juliet Burke detonated a hydrogen bomb deep inside the Island. All the evidence we have suggests that the Island, until the Incident, was initially conducive to conception; the fact that the sterile Jin was able to father a child while on the Island seems to be the best example of what Juliet called "good odds." In 1977, Juliet disrupted what had been thousands of years of the Island's encouragement of fertility. The statue of the Island was a reflection of the blessings that the Island had bestowed upon its inhabitants: the same blessings they believed came from their goddess.

Another of Taweret's many jobs was her role in the restraint of evil. The hell that the Egyptians created the cork stone to hold back is restrained by a much larger cork, as Jacob points out to Richard in *Ab Aeterno*: the Island itself is a cork. The Island quite passively acts as a barrier between that evil and the rest of the world, but it also manages to trap the little bit of that malevolence that managed to escape: the Man in Black. In Egyptian mythology, Taweret kept Set chained at her side as part of her role as protector of the innocent (in some depictions, to reinforce her role as a protector, her hand rests on the sa).

Suddenly, the rattling noises that the Monster makes sound much more like chains.

Taweret's most important job, though, takes place in the realm of Anubis and Osiris. In the Egyptian Book of the Dead, Taweret appears in the underworld to aid in the rebirth of deceased souls into the afterlife.

In an indirect way, the Island functioned to usher the survivors into their rebirth in the afterlife. Despite the fact that the Island is at the bottom of the ocean in the flash-sideways timeline, memories of the Island were what helped the survivors to come together and 'move on.' The light that floods the church as the survivors move on is likely the light at the center of the Island, indicating that the Island's role as a source of life, death, and rebirth may not be restricted to just the physical world, just as the Egyptians believed that Taweret's influence extended into both the real world and the afterlife.

◊ ◊ ◊ ◊ ◊

Did the Egyptians intend all of these similarities? Probably not, but the similarities are still there. The question that remains is whether or not these similarities were intentional from an outside perspective. Did the writers plan for these comparisons to be made when they threw in these subtle references and clues? Are they meant to be such significant parallels to the events and characters of the Island? Do they even matter?

That's the question that Lostpedia cannot answer. Perhaps it's a question that Lostpedia should not answer. LOST is finished; all the definitive pieces have been presented. The only importance of the Egyptian mythology to the story is what we assign to it. You can either see funny red pictures or complex allegories. They look like complex allegories to me.

But I'm no expert.

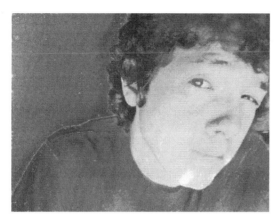

Sam McPherson is an administrator of the popular LOST fansite Lostpedia.

Since July 2009, he has served as a contributing editor for TVOvermind.com.

The Island of the Allegorical: Alice In Wonderland Gets LOST

By Jo Garfein

"Alice in Wonderland" by Arthur Rackham 1907
WMC PD

The television series LOST and Lewis Carroll's classic novel "Alice's Adventures in Wonderland" and "Through the Looking Glass" are two very distinctive yet similar tales about the experience of being transported to a mysterious land of self-discovery and destiny.

Alice had contemplated, "How nice it would be if we could only get through into the Looking-glass House."

Like Alice, the passengers of Oceanic flight 815 and island inhabitants had each stepped through a looking glass upon arrival on the island; traveling down rabbit holes of their own, facing temptations and confronting their pasts along the way. Both Wonderland and The Island represented unique opportunities for all involved to change their lives by making different choices.

"I could tell you my adventures – beginning from this morning, but it's no use going back to yesterday, because I was a different person then." – Alice

From arrival on the island through Flash Sideways revelations, I'm going to weave you a tale, in typical non-linear LOST fashion.

While there were many obvious nods to "Alice's Adventures in Wonderland" and "Through the Looking Glass" throughout all six seasons of LOST (the Looking Glass station, Ben Linus' many bunnies, his mother Emily in episode 3.20 - appearing as a ghost attired in a very blue Alice dress, Jack's 'son' reading "The Annotated Alice" in episode 6.05, etc.), and even a few subtle touches (the rabbit through Eloise Hawking's wine glass in episode 5.14)…I am going to focus on what I have interpreted to be the more allegorical aspects of the homage.

PANOPTICON AS LOOKING GLASS/DHARMA OBSERVATION STATIONS

We're all familiar with the name Jeremy Bentham, as Charles Widmore assigned it to Locke to use as his off-island pseudonym in Season Five. The real Jeremy Bentham was a British philosopher who designed a building called a Panopticon, which allowed observers to watch people…unbeknownst to them. His plan was to implement the Panopticon as a prison system where interested parties would be able to view the prisoners at all times, but the prisoners themselves would never know who was watching them.

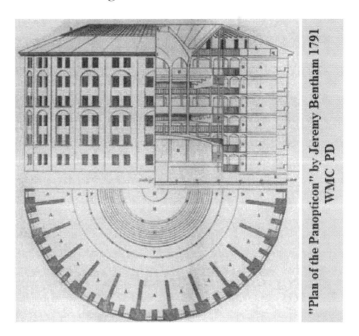

"Plan of the Panopticon" by Jeremy Bentham 1791 WMC PD

It appears as if the Dharma Initiative had a Panopticon in mind when they designed their station layout on the island; it clearly resembled Bentham's observation system, and this was their installation of an on-island Looking Glass. As illustrated on the Swan hatch blast door map, the Dharma Pearl Station (marked with a ?) was located exactly and ideally in the center of the island, much like the observation tower in Bentham's Panopticon.

The Dharma Initiative created several clandestine Panopticon-style locations with video monitoring throughout the island, including the Hydra Station, the Flame communications station and the Pearl Hatch (where the Dharma Initiative stationed employees to take notes on what they observed around the island).

The irony is, of course, that the Pearl surveillance teams themselves were part of a greater psychological experiment, and their observations were irrelevant. Their notebooks were simply discarded in a huge pile on the island.

We, as the viewing audience, observed the activities on the island from a Panopticon perspective, and watched the stories weave and unravel through the looking glass of our television monitors. The jury is still out, of course, whether or not *we* were simply part of a greater psychological experiment.

DRINK ME: THE RABBIT HOLE TEMPTATIONS AND ISLAND TRANSFORMATIONS OF JACK SHEPHARD AND JOHN LOCKE

"Alice ventured to taste it, and finding it very nice, she very soon finished it off."

Just as Alice uncorked her own adventure by partaking of the liquid in the infamous Drink Me bottle, the survivors of 815 ingested their specific, individual island temptations of their own free will; some discovered elixirs along the way, and others perished in search of their remedies.

Before arriving on the island, Jack Shephard's 'drink of choice' was an obsession with fixing people and situations. He suffered from a general lack of faith in himself, because as his father Christian once told him, "You don't want to be a hero, you don't try and save everyone, because when you fail...you just don't have what it takes." (Episode 1.05)

As an adult, Jack had dug his own rabbit hole – a giant chasm between him and his father. Christian Shephard was an alcoholic, pushed to the brink after being fired due to Jack's actions. By the time Jack was forced to travel down that hole in search of Christian, it was too late; he was unable to fix their fractured relationship before his dad passed away.

Once on the island, Jack quickly got a taste of what would become his solution and elixir: leadership. But he expressed serious doubt about his abilities. "I'm not a leader. I don't know how to help them. I'll fail. I don't have what it takes."

Jack's journey toward what would become his island rabbit hole adventure really began when he saw his own version of Alice's White Rabbit; the ghost of his deceased father Christian in episode 1.5 of LOST, aptly titled *White Rabbit*.

A few days after the crash, Jack spotted Christian standing in the ocean, dressed to the nines in a perfectly pressed suit. Just as the White Rabbit was "splendidly dressed, with a pair of white kid gloves," CS was splendidly dressed in a suit with crisp white tennis shoes. "Burning with curiosity, she ran across the field after it." Like Alice and her White Rabbit, Jack felt compelled to pursue Christian.

Alice's faith was tested on more than one occasion while traversing Wonderland; she stated with great certainty that "one can't believe impossible things." In the integral "White Rabbit" episode of LOST, Jack told Locke that it was "impossible" for his father to be walking around on the island. But toward the end of his adventures on the island, Jack finally understood what Locke had long believed. In the wise words of Alice, "SO many out-of-the-way things had happened lately...few things indeed were really impossible."

At the end of six seasons on LOST, 'Drink Me' quite literally signified transfer of island leadership from Jacob to Jack, after partaking of the water from the heart of the island. "Now you're like me." Those are the very words that Jack likely wished he'd heard from Christian.

Jack had what it took, despite what his father had always said. He just needed to go down that rabbit hole on the island in order to believe in himself and in the extraordinary circumstances that had enveloped him since arriving there. By series' end, by physically putting a cork in the island, Jack faced and fixed his past, and secured both his destiny and that of his friends who were still alive on and off the island.

Like Jack, John Locke's initial journey down a rather horrible rabbit hole began before he crashed on the island, courtesy of a *different* kind of push from *his* father, Anthony Cooper.

After that descent into physical and mental anguish, Locke's 'drink of choice' was an obsession with proving what he was capable of; he did NOT like being told what he couldn't do. Once on the island, Locke quickly got a taste of what would become his solution and elixir: freedom.

After traveling down the rabbit hole, Alice wondered, "If I've changed in the night? Let me think: was I the same when I got up this morning? I almost think I can remember feeling a little different. But if I'm not the same, the next question is, who in the world am I? That's the great puzzle."

Unlike Jack, Locke had reason to believe in the impossible when he first landed on that island. His miraculous ability to walk again restored his faith, and kicked off an incredible adventure down several different rabbit holes – and the most obvious example was the Swan Hatch.

Alice had wanted to enter the Rabbit's house, and asked the Footman: "How am I to get in?" He responded with, "Are you to get in at all? That's the first question, you know." It was, no doubt; only Alice did not like to be told so." It was her version of "Don't tell me what I can't do!"

Alice in Wonderland
Peter Newell 1890 WMC PD

Just as Alice went down her rabbit hole, "never once considering how in the world she was to get out again," Locke was determined to get inside that hatch - and that he did…among many others.

One of the most compelling, foreshadowing and relevant conversations on LOST took place between Jack and Locke in *White Rabbit* (Episode 1.05).

Locke: Why are you out here?
Jack: I'm chasing something – someone.
Locke: The white rabbit. Alice in Wonderland.
Jack: Yeah, Wonderland, because who I'm chasing – he's not there.
Locke: But you see him?
Jack: Yes, but he's not there.
Locke: Is your white rabbit a hallucination? Probably. What if this person that you're chasing is real?
Jack: That's impossible.
Locke: Even if it is, let's say it's not.
Jack: Then what happens when I catch him?
Locke: I don't know. You need to finish what you started. A leader can't lead until he knows where he's going.

Locke's immediate faith in the impossible and in the island was a constant source of disdain for Jack throughout the series, but they rescued one another from many potentially fatal and unnecessary rabbit hole journeys along the way. In Alice's world, the Unicorn assured her that "If you'll believe in me, I'll believe in you." If only Jack had believed Locke from the beginning…if only he had chosen to follow that White Rabbit rather than his father. It certainly is a fascinating alternative outcome to ponder.

LET THE GAMES BEGIN! 2 PLAYERS, 2 SIDES: ONE IS LIGHT, ONE IS DARK

Alice declared, "It's marked out just like a large chess-board! There ought to be some men moving about somewhere – and so there are! It's a great huge game of chess that's being played – all over the world – if this IS the world at all." In the pilot episode of LOST, John Locke informed us of the island rules, of the shape of things to come. "Two players. Two sides. One is light, one is dark."

There were indeed two players; two brothers. The survivors of 815, the Others and former Dharma folks were among the many pawns to have been used between Jacob and the Man in Black from the beginning of time through The End. One brother was responsible for bringing the Dharma Initiative and flight 815 to the island, to send them down necessary rabbit holes, and one brother was responsible for making sure that each island inhabitant was put through hell along the way. Jacob illuminated their paths, and the Man in Black extinguished many of their lights from start to finish. The ongoing game between the brothers consisted of many tragic levels, layers and players, and the exchanges between the two were very similar to conversations with various characters in Alice's world.

The March Hare offered to Alice, "Have some wine." She said, "I don't see any wine." March Hare: "There isn't any." Alice: "Then it wasn't very civil of you to offer it." March Hare: "It wasn't very civil of you to sit down without being invited." When Alice encountered the White Knight and Red Knight, they were discussing the "rules" of their game: "You will observe the Rules of Battle, of course?" The Red Knight responded with, "I always do." Alas, the Red Knight was yet to discover his own loophole.

One of the more memorable and game-changing conversations on LOST took place between the two brothers in the Season Five finale, *The Incident*.

MAN IN BLACK: Do you have any idea how badly I want to kill you?
JACOB: Yes.
MAN IN BLACK: One of these days, sooner or later... I'm going to find a loophole, my friend.
JACOB: Well, when you do, I'll be right here.

That loophole led to both John Locke's and the Man in Black's death, as well as Jack's ultimate emergence as a leader. Man in Black: 1, Jacob: 2. They came. They fought. They destroyed. They corrupted. It didn't end the same and it *was* progress.

The game between Jacob and the Man in Black had far darker consequences than that which Alice came upon in her adventures. The island inhabitants were unaware that they were all pawns in the ongoing game between the two brothers, and that their rabbit hole adventures and outcomes were equally influenced and dictated by Jacob and the Man in Black.

When Alice noted that, "The game's going on rather better now," the Duchess added that "The moral of that is – 'tis love that makes the world go round." On the island, unfortunately, it was the lack of brotherly love that perpetuated the games and ultimately altered the worlds of those who ever set foot there.

FLASH SIDEWAYS: BREAKING THROUGH THE LOOKING GLASS MIRRORS

As Alice herself said about items through her Looking Glass house, "things go the other way." Alice awoke from her adventures in Wonderland, questioning whether or not it was all a dream. She had stepped back through the Looking Glass with a new sense of adventure and countless tales to tell.

The Flash Sideways world was not a dream, but rather a series of scenarios that began when each survivor and island inhabitant crossed over to the other side and stepped through the looking glass (in this case, a rear view mirror on their lives after they'd passed on). The Flash Sideways were altered versions of their former lives that represented ideal circumstances, created by Jack and his friends - so that they could find one another. Because the most important part of their lives was the time that they spent with each other.

Jack's Flash Sideways scenario allowed for reconciliation and redemption; it represented the end of his rabbit hole journey. In this ideal world, Jack had created a son for himself to prove that he was capable of being a better father than his own. And Christian Shephard was the one who appeared in the end to provide the clarity and closure that Jack had long been seeking.

In Wonderland, the Queen noted that with "the effect of living backwards…there's one great advantage in it; that one's memory works both ways."

Although those in the Flash Sideways were unaware of it at the time, each experienced a "mirror moment" of pause, of subconscious reflection back to their time on the island. Following those mirror moments, once each of them experienced their island epiphany awakenings, they discovered that they had collectively stepped through the Looking Glass and instantly realized that…whatever happened, happened.

Alice had wondered, "Then it really has happened, after all! And now, who am I? I will remember, if I can! L, I know it begins with an L!" Yes, Alice, it does. You, too, were LOST for a time.

"Thus grew the tale of Wonderland:
Thus slowly, one by one,
Its quaint events were hammered out –
And now the tale is done;
And home we steer, a merry crew,
Beneath the setting sun."

Jo Garfein is a pop culture sponge who covered LOST extensively for years, with an emphasis on in-depth analysis and elaborate speculation. She is now a freelance entertainment writer, focusing primarily on primetime television.

The Theology of LOST

Paul Wright
Jennifer Galicinski

Reconcilable Differences? Philosophical and Theological Syncretism in *Lost*

By Paul R. Wright, Ph.D.

"Fire + Water" by Gideon Slife
Used with permission.

Editor's Note: Syncretism is the fusion of different belief systems, often achieved through combining the thought and practice of diverse philosophical or theological traditions. Syncretism can result in the unification and equation of originally distinct schools of thought, especially in religious theory and practice, leading to inclusive tendencies toward other faith traditions. While the concept is most frequently applied to the interface between philosophy and theological inquiry, the idea has been used to express movements in politics, culture, society, and the arts.

In this essay, Dr. Paul Wright argues that the syncretism of Lost must be considered with a mature cognizance of its multi-textual complexity, with special deference given to the long history of theological syncretism, beginning in the Italian Renaissance, that informed the studied and literate fusion of disparate thought that constituted the creative work of multitudes of writers, actors, film professionals, musicians, and viewers—the creation we know as Lost.

Introduction: Viewer Schisms in the "Church" of Lost

In the provocative and controversial series finale of *Lost* (*The End*), this singularly ambitious narrative's final moments unfold in a church that—as careful viewers will recall—is located directly above the Dharma Initiative "Lamp Post" station administered by Eloise Hawking. The Lamp Post station featured prominently in three Season-Five episodes (*The Lie*, *This Place Is Death*, and *316*). In a season dedicated to the intricacies of the island as a moving target in both space and time, these episodes complicated the genre pedigree of a series that was already defiantly genre-bending. The Lamp Post station was seemingly the only Dharma station to exist off the island and was a direct link to Los Angeles, the original destination of Oceanic Flight 815. In the key Season Five episode *316*, which refers to the Ajira Airways flight that Jack Shephard will take in order to return to the island, both the Lamp Post and the church above it are essential to the narrative and thematic turn taken by the entire series.

In the basement station, we come to see Eloise Hawking (first seen in the Season Three episode *Flashes Before Your Eyes*) in a new context, as the caretaker (and possibly usurper) of the Dharma station whose purpose was to locate the island as a function of time. Situated above an electromagnetic pocket of energy much like that on the island itself, the station has as its centerpiece a calibrated and perpetually swinging pendulum, tipped with chalk to mark a floor map of the world in an effort to predict the island's next appearance. An allusion to physicist Léon Foucault's pendulum and to the Umberto Eco novel of the same name (901), the Lamp Post pendulum in *Lost* grounds the time travel narrative of Season Five in both science and science-fiction. And yet while many viewers and interpreters of *Lost* have treated the church as merely a front for the Dharma secret beneath it, the episode foregrounds the religious space of the church in very important ways. Rather than simply being the curtain behind which one uncovers the science-fiction mysteries of *Lost*, that church—long before its pointed deployment in the series finale—was an essential narrative and moral space for the series. This is directly evidenced in scenes of Eloise's instruction that, on the Ajira return flight to the island, Jack will need to take John Locke's body as a proxy for Jack's father. When Eloise directs him to place something belonging to his father on Locke's body, she reminds the ever-skeptical Jack that a "leap of faith" is required to instantiate the "science" of the whole enterprise. As Jack wrestles with his decision in the church above the station, Benjamin Linus points out to him Caravaggio's 1601 painting *The Incredulity of Saint Thomas*, leaving him with the observation that "We're all convinced sooner or later, Jack."

What we must understand and appreciate is that, long before the series finale, the *Lost* narrative had already moved well beyond the facile opposition between faith and reason established in Seasons One and Two with the conflict between Jack and Locke (and in the conflicts between many other characters as well). In retrospect, episode *316* forced viewers to reassess completely the character dynamics, thematic tropes, and philosophical foundations of *Lost*; this was accomplished in large measure by the episode's insistence that rational decision-making and trusting faith are in fact mutually constitutive. In this essay, I contend that the meaning and conclusion of the entire series must be examined in a far more generous light than many critics or viewers brought to bear in the days and months after the airing of the finale—and that the series must be examined in the richer context of a history of philosophical and theological syncretism that is conceptually connected to the show's genre improvisation.

Among the iconic final images viewers were left with in the series finale is the scene in which Jack confronts the nature of the so-called "flash sideways" world to which roughly half of Season Six was dedicated. As Jack leans over his father's coffin in the Lamp Post church and comes to realize that he himself died long ago on the island and is now reuniting with other friends who have died—"some before you, some long after you," as his father, Christian Shephard, tells him—we see in the stained glass church window an apparent visual and economical summation of the show's many religious themes.

Our Lady of the Lamp Post Stained Glass Window
copyright Pearson Moore 2012

The stained glass window unites religious symbolism drawn from various world faiths: the star and crescent of Islam; Judaism's star of David; the Aum of Hinduism; the Christian cross; the Dharmacakra of Buddhist tradition; and the Taoist yin-yang disc. For viewers who embraced the spirituality of the show, that window embodied the ecumenical spirit and pan-theological respect that was the hallmark of the series. For others with particular faith traditions, it represented a non-denominational copout, and for some who were wedded to the science-fiction threads in the *Lost* narrative, it was a betrayal of an altogether different sort—a betrayal of genre through the over-simplification of mass-marketed religious allegory. I will endeavor to demonstrate how these various reactions to the series are not fair or subtle enough to account for what is going on in *Lost* as a hybrid narrative and as a work of popular culture driven by philosophical and religious inquiry. Note the emphasis here on *inquiry* as opposed to *certainty*; it is essential to approach the entirety of *Lost*, both in its methods and meaning, in this generous spirit. At its heart, *Lost* was an "essay" in the classical sense, and not always a tidy or coherent construction; it was, pun very much intended, a good-faith effort to document where our various traditions of religion, philosophy, science, and narrative might intersect and inform one another. It is in this sense that I identify *Lost* as a meditation on and practice of syncretism.

The Theological "Combo Meal": Responses to *Lost* Syncretism

As I make my case for *Lost* as a syncretic project, I want to begin by confronting a few viewer objections to the stained glass window and to the finale. Consider this cross-section of responses informed by the perception that *Lost* concluded in a banal religious vein. One blogger, identified only as Rusty, ranted: "Why not just have Jack ascend to heaven in a Prius with a 'coexist' bumper sticker?" (902) Yet another, Patrick George McCullough, a Ph.D. student in New Testament origins at UCLA opined that the finale was "nauseating religious soup." The exasperated McCullough posed an entertaining yet ultimately reductive question: "Why do the final moments of the LOST finale feel like an after-school special on the importance of respecting religious diversity? There we were, wondering about the mythology of LOST, which questions would be answered and how, following the epic story, and then, we were being homilized. And it's not even a good homily at that." (903) And as McCullough rightly notes, even the writers of *Lost* had a playful sense of humor about their narrative's religious references and sensibilities, as is evidenced in the finale when Kate Austin offers an aside that surely reflects what many viewers had been saying since Season One: "Christian Shephard? Seriously?"

This ironic take on the finale by its own writers was hardly new and had in fact been a hallmark of the series from its beginnings. Comic irony clearly was a strategy to manage fan expectations on the part of show-runners Damon Lindelof and Carlton Cuse (the infamous "Darlton" of fan lore and ire), whose podcasts alternately teased fans with narrative hints and teased them for their own inexhaustible desire for closure and answers. And yet while we should acknowledge the playfulness of *Lost* and its many creators, we should also note that the fury and condescension of some commentators on the finale arises from *precisely* the same uncomfortable place—namely, that postmodern anxiety about religious convictions in an age of multiculturalism, technological wonders bordering on the magical, and profound uncertainty. Whether we are laughing along with its creators or raging with its detractors, *Lost* remains a thoughtful reflection on the power and the limits of faith, science, and various other forms of knowledge that make claims on coherence and on our exclusive allegiance.

In this light, mockery and dismissiveness are equally inadequate responses to *Lost*. If the show spawns so much passion, it is because the series is as good a touchstone as any for the vital questions raised by human beings throughout history as they attempt to survive and process the world around them—and then to accommodate competing explanations of that world. Those who attempt to accommodate competing ideas have often been those who would *reconcile* things in the most profound and ambitious sense—and those who risk misunderstanding and humiliation in the process. Reconciliation is clearly a key theme of *Lost*, but not merely in terms of characters and emotional payoffs, but moreover in terms of the history of ideas. In this context, syncretism and syncretists have always been with us, and *Lost* participates in that discourse in ways that deserve fuller investigation. The fact that *Lost* sought cultural and conceptual reconciliation calls on us to explore the objectives *Lost* was implicitly trying to attain as a syncretistic project, as opposed to focusing on whether *Lost* achieved whatever each viewer wanted it to be. My operative premise in this paper is that rather than dismissing syncretistic efforts like *Lost*, we ought instead to forego the temptations of reader-response theory for the harder road of historical and philosophical inquiry.

Contextualizing *Lost* Syncretism:
The History and Epistemology of the Syncretic Act

For the purposes of both historical narrative and assessing the televisual narrative of *Lost*, syncretism need not only be understood in the context of religious accommodation or philosophical-theological recombination. What I am stressing here is the broader effort to negotiate and reconcile traditions, worldviews, knowledge systems, modes of thought and belief, cultures, discourses, and even ideologies that otherwise appear to be mutually exclusive or downright hostile toward one another. Negative responses to syncretism have historically been driven by diverse motives and concerns, and it is indeed in the realms of religion and philosophy that the contempt for syncretism has been most strongly pronounced. Among the anxieties provoked by syncretism is the sense that the act of syncretism cheapens or compromises one or more of the faith traditions or knowledge systems being reconciled. This is typified by certain reactions to the efforts to reconcile Christian theology and pre-Christian Greek and Roman philosophy; late medieval Christians such as Aquinas (and literary inheritors such as Dante) were in the vanguard of this syncretistic accommodation between the two traditions, while other Christians (Luther among them) were more troubled by the humanist effort to fuse scripture and the world of Plato and Aristotle. Yet thinkers such as Machiavelli and, much later, Nietzsche, would infamously reject this syncretism from the other side of the temporal looking glass, suggesting that Christianity had contaminated the purity of classical thought and culture.

Even where syncretism might otherwise find a sympathetic hearing, it may find itself refused if the syncretic act is viewed (perhaps fairly so) as heavy-handed, inept, immature, or condescending to the traditions being brought into contact with one another. It is not my purpose here to argue that all acts of syncretism are equally skillful, persuasive, valid, or justified—although I will build to a conclusion suggesting that all attempts to understand the world coherently do depend on syncretic and recombinant operations. This is also not an effort to promote a simplistic Hegelian model of "synthesis" of the sort that tends not even to honor the complexities of Hegel's own project, itself a key milestone in the history of syncretism. Rather, the goal here is to assess the power of syncretism as a conceptual alternative to the zero-sum competition model that too often drives the history of ideas (and, not coincidentally, the history of human civilizations and politics).

If we are to understand better the pop cultural contribution of *Lost* to this historical conversation on the mediated and inclusive nature of truth, we need to see *Lost* as an artistic intervention in a much older and more complex debate. As with everything else, *Lost* is certainly a product of its specific cultural moment; yet, also like everything else, *Lost* has its roots in all that has gone before, of which William Faulkner famously reminded us: "The past is never dead. It's not even past." (904) If there is a common denominator in all acts of syncretism, it is perhaps this—syncretism always comes into being in reaction and relation to an *orthodoxy* of some kind or another, and this is the pre-condition for the eventual cultural assessment of that syncretism, whether it is embraced or denounced, whether it thrives for centuries or dies on the epistemological vine.

The syncretistic impulse seems in every case to assert that an existing orthodoxy or orthodoxies are wanting, inadequate, misleading, or simply wrong. The aims and operations of a given syncretic act may be selective, borrowing elements of a finite number of existing discourses for particular ends. The example of the doctrine of "universal salvation" in the Christian tradition (a controversial doctrine dating back to Origen, and hardly universally embraced) demonstrates precisely this principle of selectivity. This doctrine—borne out of centuries of theological improvisation and wrestling with the principles of original sin and damnation—retains most of orthodox Christian theology as an article of faith, but nonetheless incorporates a new logic of salvation that presumes God's grace is so mysterious and omnipotent that it overcomes every sin. *Lost* itself, a drama steeped in questions of moral responsibility and potential redemption, clearly engages with these questions, however generically—particularly with characters such as Benjamin Linus, Sayid Jarrah, and the so-called "Man in Black." This doctrine, like so many others in the Christian drama of the West, required logical, theological, and even literary operations on the raw material of scripture (itself a product of the syncretic negotiation of an official biblical canon over centuries). In instances such as these, there is an effort to refine and recalibrate an existing orthodoxy where it is perceived to have erred, or perhaps just not to have gone far enough in its own implications (e.g., universal salvation takes the logic of God's inexhaustible grace and extrapolates from it the negation of all damnation). As radical as these syncretic challenges to orthodoxy may be in context and in their consequences for the human beings living out these theological questions, from the eagle's eye view of the history of ideas, this kind of syncretism amounts to a tweaking of an otherwise accepted premise.

Other syncretic acts are potentially more global and radical in nature, however. Here we must think of those efforts to integrate and thereby transmute all existing discourses into a new operative truth. This comprehensive approach to the complete reform and integration of all existing knowledge is characteristic of something like the "Theory of Everything" movement in the contemporary hard sciences. These efforts, mostly driven by the conjectures of theoretical physicists since the twentieth century, focus on mathematical and logical models that can potentially account for all physical phenomena and for the workings of the universe itself. A syncretistic move like this seeks to reconcile all hitherto competing and discrete sciences into a kind of transcendental, comprehensive scientific inquiry; this move is both a methodological statement on the pursuit of existing questions, and a manifesto demanding the raising and answering of new ones. Among the precursors of the Theory of Everything approach is the nineteenth-century scientific philosophy of physicist and chemist Michael Faraday, from whom *Lost*'s Daniel Faraday takes his name and part of his agenda—the exploration of the unities of gravitational theory and electromagnetism.

"Michael Faraday" by Mathew Brady ca. 1855
WMC PD

Yet even a cosmic-level syncretism such as the Theory of Everything runs the risk of reductionism and must at the end of the day (or the cosmos?) *take itself into account*—a virtual impossibility if Heisenberg's uncertainty principle is taken as axiomatic for theories themselves and not just for the particles explained and measured by them. The dilemma here is comparable to the problem of the immanent critique in philosophy—namely, what are the limits of our knowledge of the whole from any point inside of that whole, be it our empirical senses, a political system, ideology, or the universe itself? Put differently—and in the context of other disciplines and ways of knowing the world around us—while the realization of the Theory of Everything, if accomplished, might seem comprehensive and final, would it really even begin to account for all the other mysteries of the universe, including the meaning of human existence itself? From this perspective, the Theory of Everything is yet another syncretism refusing all orthodoxies, and yet trapped within the modern orthodoxy telling us that hard science will explain everything—or at least everything that science deems to matter.

Once we apply the realities of historical change and cultural perspective to these issues, syncretism becomes even more complex, perilous, and yet unavoidable. Knowledge and epistemologies one person or culture dismisses as facile syncretism may be another's truth—and in turn a potential new orthodoxy that will itself be later challenged, revised, or even abandoned. Like the island of *Lost*, both our ideas and we as human beings are moving targets in space and time. With these considerations in mind, *Lost* is both less and more of a syncretistic project than those to which I have already alluded. Less, in that the show is fundamentally a work of art and an entertainment that makes no unilateral claims on us as a doctrinal statement or commitment—i.e., surely no one will be burned at the stake for loving or hating the *Lost* finale. This is not to suggest that *Lost* is not intellectually serious or ambitious; it is indeed, whether we find it moving and persuasive or not (and we are certainly entitled to render our own individual judgments). But *Lost* is not in essence a fully-realized orthodoxy, and this is precisely where it strives to be more than a typical act of intellectual syncretism. The show is in this sense decidedly *unfinished* as its syncretistic moves are in the service of a narrative that is by definition interpretively open-ended (and as I suggest later on, a narrative work that was always and remains "in progress" in the minds of its creators and viewers).

If *Lost* has a salutary lesson to all would-be syncretists, perhaps it is the recommendation that understanding the world is not about *taking sides*, but about seeing that there are *multiple and ultimately linked lenses* through which we need collectively to view our problems—be they the structures of time and space, or of the human mind and heart. As perhaps is clear from this philosophical reflection on syncretism thus far, it may well be the case that we are all syncretists, that all systems of thought and all human experiences are in essence epistemological improvisations that we are continually tempted to render stable and unquestionable—thereby forgetting the important pre-history of our own untidy beliefs about the world and ourselves.

Historical Syncretism and the Orthodoxies of the *Lost* Era

As I have been stressing, every era in the history of the West has had its syncretizing impulses stimulated and shaped in reaction to entrenched orthodoxies. In the pre-modern Mediterranean world dominated by Greece and Rome, syncretism was arguably the *de facto* survival mode for individuals, cities, and growing empires. This is exemplified in the classical polytheism and Hellenistic worldview disseminated in the wake of the conquests of Alexander the Great and his successor generals. In a culturally-charged and changing situation like this, syncretism was itself the orthodoxy of the day, both conceptually and practically. By the time we reach the medieval and early modern periods, syncretism—especially in the transitional Renaissance—operated in the context of the orthodoxy and hegemony of Christianity (and the related notion of Christendom, a powerful unifying concept historically distinct from our modern notions of nationhood or of Europe proper). (905) Put simply, syncretic efforts to reconcile Christian faith with other traditions (and with the challenging realities of new peoples and cultures in Asia, Africa, and the so-called "New World") had always to maneuver in these periods under the watchful eye of the "jealous God" of the Judeo-Christian order.

With modernity, the Judeo-Christian order found itself challenged and supplanted by the new orthodoxy of Enlightenment rationality and science. As in the medieval period, syncretism in the modern era found itself confronted at every turn with new gods against which all things were to be measured—positivism and efficiency. Yet as philosophers like Theodor Adorno and Max Horkheimer argued (906), the horrors of the Second World War, the Holocaust, and the nuclear age ushered in a new era of displacement in which both God and reason were horrified—and were found wanting. That "postmodern" moment—and we truly lack for a better term—is our moment and seems almost a return to the conceptual chaos and promise of the classical era, where instead of polytheism *per se*, we have instead a kind of discursive "polygamy." Ours is the era, we are told, of inter-textuality and irony; cultural cross-pollination and globalism; multi- and inter-disciplinarity; *bricolage*; and what Lyotard famously called the death of "meta-narratives" of all sorts. (907)

It may rightly be said that today's historians are indeed the stepchildren of Nietzsche, Kuhn, and Foucault—those philosophers who traced the "genealogy of morals," scientific "paradigm shifts," and the epistemological "order of things" shifting unnoticed beneath our feet (908). Hence we must examine the untidy practice of syncretism in *Lost* in the epistemological and historical context of our own anxious moment. It may be the case that at present we have no clear orthodoxies against which to define our resistance or reconceptualization of truth, and therefore no easy or obvious targets for the operations of syncretism. I suspect, however, that despite my confidence in the broad outlines of the historical periods discussed above, *every era* experiences its moment as one of dislocation, alienation, and crisis. In this long view, every orthodoxy is more fragile than we imagine, yet no less deeply entrenched for it, precisely because the orthodoxies that matter most—what Kuhn called in the sciences "paradigms"—are hegemonic and undetectable until they have been superseded by those to come. If postmodernity can make a claim to being uniquely unsettling in this regard, perhaps it is because we are so *hyper-aware* of the situation that it borders on paralysis—such that we are caught oscillating between skepticism about any strongly articulated belief and contempt for those beliefs which are not asserted strongly enough.

This is precisely the spectrum of responses to the *Lost* finale, which caused some to see in it a pat religious solution to all the show's dilemmas, and others to find in it an act of spineless and market-safe theological appeasement. To avoid both of these reductive assessments of *Lost*, we must restore the show to its agonistic place (however minor) in the entire history of syncretism I have been outlining here. This of necessity takes us beyond the misleading question of whether *Lost* is a postmodern narrative, a claim with which Pearson Moore and others have rightly taken issue. Like Moore, I too see the narrative strategies and characterization on the show as having postmodern elements, but see the thesis of *Lost* as anything but postmodern. I would argue that this is because *Lost* comes to its claims about responsibility, existence, and the ethical nature of memory and experience through a creative process and intellectual approach that is almost classically syncretistic. Like the Christian injunction to be in this world, but be not of it (909)—an injunction whose message is hardly restricted to the Christian tradition—*Lost* can be said to live in postmodernity, but to be qualitatively not of it. I would caution that this does not make *Lost* a specifically Christian narrative (and certainly not in any respect an orthodox one); however, the other world that is the soul of *Lost* is the entire historical tradition of syncretic efforts to reconcile the irreconcilable.

Whether this was a conscious and perfectly sustained goal of the writers or not is debatable. Whether the end result of the series was satisfying, edifying, or neither is again a matter of interpretive free will upon which I am uninterested in encroaching. Certainly the conceptualization, writing, and televisual execution of the show as both a work of human art and as a commercial product are very complicating factors. Episodically, by season, and as a whole, *Lost* was the consequence of hundreds of collaborations and contributors, followed by millions of interpretive encounters between the show's "text" and viewers, between the creators and viewers, and between the viewers themselves. All of these stages of producing and consuming *Lost* are in fundamental ways *improvisational*. The meaning of the plots and characterizations, as with all films and television shows, comes into being at the nexus of production constraints, writing and directing, the actors' dramatic practices, post-production, viewer response, and subsequent critical assessment of the sort exemplified in this volume. To expect the meaning of *Lost* to be reducible to any one message is the very opposite of what I am suggesting here. What I am insisting on here is that *Lost* is a part of this rich and vexed tradition of syncretism in the West. The infelicities and frustrations of the *Lost* narrative (and especially the conclusion of that narrative) are themselves reflective of this messy tradition, as I hope some specific historical comparisons will illustrate.

An Inductive Comparison: *Lost* and Renaissance Syncretism

One of the most illustrious and controversial syncretists of the Italian Renaissance was the precocious young Count Giovanni Pico della Mirandola (1463-94). (910) In addition to his association with Florentine Neo-Platonists like Marsilio Ficino, Pico is best known for his 1486 *Oratio de hominis dignitate* (*Oration on Human Dignity*), a highly crafted exposition of a philosophical methodology almost obsessively concerned with syncretic inclusiveness. Pico strives to reconcile (among many other things) Christian theology, classical philosophy, Arabic science, and

"Giovanni Pico della Mirandola" ca. 1490 Anonymous, Italian School WMC PD

Cabalistic mysticism—all in the service of what he calls a "poetic theology." Pico's interest in the unity of all truth becomes the framework for a conception of human nature as inherently malleable and indeterminate. In his piece, Pico wrote one of the most famous defenses of fluid human nature, a rhetorical flourish that influenced the likes of Shakespeare in *Hamlet*. Pico writes:

> I have placed you at the center of the world, that you might hence more readily survey whatever is in it. Neither heavenly nor terrestrial, neither mortal nor immortal, We have made you, so that freely and honorably, as if the sculptor and moulder of yourself, you may safely fashion yourself into whatever form you wish. You may degenerate into those lower forms that are brutish; you may be regenerated into the higher, which are divine, all at the direction of your own spirit. (911)

Earlier in 1486 Pico had published his nine hundred theses on subjects "philosophical, cabalistic, and theological," intending to submit them to public debate in Rome the following year. The rich young noble even went so far as to offer to finance travel expenses for visiting scholars. Pico's *Oration* was formulated as an introduction to the debates, an opening blow in the literary and philosophical wrestling match he wished to oversee; unfortunately, Pico would never actually make it into the ring. Pope Innocent VIII suspended the debate after Pico's theses were found to be potentially heretical in some thirteen instances, particularly those theses that postulated the Hebrew Cabala as a viable subtext of Christian doctrine. Pico's troubles with the Church prompted him to flee to France and publish a defense of his ideas and syncretic approach.

Aside from demonstrating that syncretists have always drawn fire for being too willing to reconcile disparate and seemingly incompatible belief systems, the example of Pico also gives us a fuller sense of the historical richness of syncretism as a conceptual and rhetorical mode. The passage quoted above contextualizes for us a long-standing, thematic attention to the fluidity of human character and the tension between our sense of agency and our attendant fears of being fated—all themes touched on throughout the series run of *Lost*. Pico also writes of the pursuit of human and divine truth using the powerful mythological and theological figures of Jacob, Osiris, and Phoebus:

> Lest we be satisfied to consult only those of our own faith and tradition, let us also have recourse to the patriarch, Jacob whose likeness, carved on the throne of glory, shines out before us. This wisest of the Fathers who though sleeping in the lower world, still has his eyes fixed on the world above, will admonish us. He will admonish, however, in a figure, for all things appeared in figures to the men of those times: a ladder rises by many rungs from earth to the height of heaven and at its summit sits the Lord, while over its rungs the contemplative angels move, alternately ascending and descending. ... When we shall have been so prepared by the art of discourse or of reason, then, inspired by the spirit of the Cherubim, exercising philosophy through all the rungs of the ladder—that is, of nature—we shall penetrate being from its center to its surface and from its surface to its center. At one time we shall descend, dismembering with titanic force the "unity" of the "many," like the members of Osiris; at another time, we shall ascend, recollecting those same members, by the power of Phoebus, into their original unity.

I am not suggesting any facile connection between Pico and the writers of *Lost*, despite the direct allusion to Jacob here. The mythical and philosophical dimensions of *Lost*, Jacob, and the Osiris myth have been far more thoroughly addressed by Pearson Moore than I could do justice to here. What Pico offers us, however, is a wonderful methodological statement of how syncretism operates in something as ambitious as *Lost*. Like Pico, the *Lost* narrative exhorted us to be "sleeping in the lower world, ... eyes fixed on the world above," to confront and integrate competing truths, "lest we be satisfied to consult only those of our own faith and tradition." The alternate dismemberment and unity of Osiris is a powerful metaphor not only for the fragile community of castaways on the island as they fracture and reconstitute their bonds with one another. It also captures the interpretive dynamics of the series, which must always be understood (and unapologetically so) as an improvisational attempt to build structures of coherence around a philosophical narrative that was continually evolving and inescapably rough around the edges.

Other evocations of Renaissance culture, in two cases drawn from the visual arts, can also help to illuminate the conceptual ancestry of *Lost*. For one, consider the pop cultural pervasiveness of the Da Vinci *Last Supper* model in recent visual celebrations of television's best shows. At the vanguard of this visual trope was Annie Leibovitz's *Last Supper* shoot of *The Sopranos* cast for the December 1999 issue of *Vanity Fair*. Other shows have followed suit over the last thirteen years, including *Battlestar Galactica* and of course, *Lost* for *Entertainment Weekly* in January 2010, the show's final year on the air. The *Lost Last Supper* provocatively put actor Terry O'Quinn in the position of Christ, and in retrospect this foreshadowed a key thematic element of the final season—as O'Quinn portrayed both the murdered John Locke and the Man in Black who inhabited his body and, according to Jack Shephard, betrayed the memory of Locke's fundamental decency.

Consider, however, another work of Renaissance art that might be a far better analogy for *Lost*'s syncretism in practice. In what is perhaps the greatest visualization of syncretism from the Renaissance period, the master artist Raphael in the early sixteenth century attempted to bring into one metaphorical room the greatest philosophers of the Greek and Roman worlds in his incomparable *School of Athens* fresco, a partial detail of which is depicted below.

The School of Athens, detail of Plato and Aristotle Raphael ca. 1509 PD

Commissioned for the Stanza della Segnatura in the Vatican, this fresco is the most iconic of an entire chamber filled with evocations of the syncretic reconciliation of classical antiquity and the Christian world. This stunning room also boasts Raphael's *Disputation of the Holy Sacrament* (which does for Christian theologians what *Athens* does for classical philosophers), as well as depictions of *The Cardinal Virtues* and of *Parnassus*, home of the muses and source of all the arts. When we consider this entire room as a virtuoso performance and as a complex, multi-dimensional commentary on the sum total of human learning known in the era of Raphael, we come to realize that Raphael's syncretistic argument goes well beyond the most famous image in the *Athens* fresco—that central depiction of Plato and Aristotle, one with a hand raised to the heavens and the other with a hand leveled to indicate a focus on the things of this earth.

In the context of *Lost*, one might understandably be tempted to replace Plato and Aristotle in the fresco with John Locke and Jack Shephard. And yet *Lost* always strove to transcend the schematic depiction of faith and reason in conflict, with characters as mere pawns in an intellectual drama. As I suggested earlier, this stark and typological conflict was sufficient as an establishing plot device in Seasons One and Two, but by later seasons Locke and Jack were each forced to confront their own weaknesses and also the qualities the two of them had in common. In fact, one of the great lessons of the intertwined journeys of Locke and Jack was that their deepest failings were revealed when they were most tempted to view themselves as mere typologies—one styling himself the hero of intuition and defender of the island, the other styling himself the hero of material rationality and escape from the island. By the end of the series, these typologies had cost both characters a great deal in hubris and moral failure, and both had become inextricably connected, even beyond the grave—discovering genuine heroism only in the syncretic fusion of their seemingly opposing views. If we were truly to analogize the intellectual drama of *Lost* with Renaissance syncretism, we would need more than a simple *Last Supper* gimmick and more than Raphael's Plato and Aristotle alone. We would be obliged to populate the entire Stanza della Segnatura with *Lost* counterparts. Even then the entire project would still only hint visually at a meaning greater than the sum of its conceptual parts or visual tropes—for at the end of the day, *Lost* worked as a syncretic drama precisely because the show's best characters transcended their parts and were fleshed out as human beings and not merely as principles or allusions. A contemporary case study in the need to see proponents of faith and reason as more than mere typologies can be found in the provocative yet humanizing dialogue between secular neo-Marxist Jürgen Habermas and Catholic theologian Joseph Ratzinger, the future Pope Benedict XVI. (912)

These powerful analogies to Renaissance syncretism and contemporary debates on reason and religion put into better context many of the complaints of *Lost* detractors about the disappointments of its "incomplete" narrative and what McCullough calls its "nauseating religious soup." Viewer reactions to the show in general and to the finale in particular were largely shaped by two competing impulses—the desire for one's idiosyncratic reading of the show's meaning to be realized, and the desire to be *given* and *have revealed* a meaning that would somehow have to have been (quite impossibly for television) constructed *a priori* to the show's execution over the course of six seasons. Even when the end date of the narrative was finally established by negotiations between the show-runners and ABC, this hardly solved all narrative dilemmas as fans so often demanded. Even with an endgame in mind, the actual execution of the final two seasons of *Lost* was undoubtedly a process of continual improvisation on the part of producers, writers, and directors—an improvisation as difficult (if arguably not as successful) as Raphael's frescoes or Pico's intellectual brinkmanship.

Viewer frustrations inevitably manifested in contradictory and over-wrought objections—e.g., that the series failed to provide adequate answers to its own narrative and philosophical puzzles; that the answers provided were simplistic copouts; that the series was coherent, but in an intentionally arcane and pretentious manner; and that the series never had a coherent plan or *telos* at any point. To be fair, there has arguably never been a narrative—even one solely constructed by a singular author, let alone the "vast narrative" by committee that was *Lost* (913)—that has not generated similar frustrations on the part of its interpretive consumers. This is precisely because the very nature of all narrative is infelicitous and incomplete, and in the case of anything as ambitious as *Lost*, narrative itself becomes inherently syncretistic—as a function of content, genre, and the conditions of production.

The Conundrum of Genre and the Realities of Television Production

It is somewhat reasonable to ask of *Lost* whether it was merely genre-bending or genre-confused. The conclusion of Season Six and the resolution of the "flash sideways" mystery lead one to wonder whether the science-fiction and time-travel narrative was consciously abandoned at the beginning of Season Six, or only once and for all in the eleventh hour of the series. It would have been fascinating to eavesdrop on the debates among the writers of *Lost* as they struggled to come to a consensus on the show's conclusion and overall meaning, which would of course be arbitrated at last by show-runners Lindelof and Cuse. From a viewer's perspective, the time-travel explanation remained plausible until almost the final episode of the series, such that those looking for the show's science-fiction pedigree to be fully embraced were only disappointed at the bitter end.

Alternatively, one might ask whether the issue of genre is properly framed in this way at all. Instead, did the science-fiction elements of the series ultimately fuse syncretically with the philosophical, mythological, and theological elements of the show? In this light, making claims on *Lost*'s genre purity or genre failures avoids the messy reality of any narrative that cross-pollinates styles and modes—and what narrative does not at last? There is no denying that *Lost*'s hybridization of elements (from genre to theology and everything in between) was both an intellectual statement, but also an effort to please (or at least not to alienate) multiple and diverse audiences. It is indeed fair to suggest that *Lost*'s refusal to be just one thing was at once a creative and commercial choice—always and of necessity both. And the various loose threads of the narrative (everything from the outrigger of Season

129

Five to characters being prematurely written out of the show, such as Mr. Eko) also remind us that the entire mode of *Lost*'s creation and execution was always work-in-progress—interpretively, that work goes on even today, but now among "readers," among whom are those still invested in carving out their own fan narratives and explanations to fill in the perceived gaps.

Yet rather than casually dismiss *Lost* because of its genre or intellectual "impurities," we would do better to see its syncretism (both creative and conceptual) as a specific response to an age of hyper-conscious televisual auteurism and exegetical viewership facilitated by unprecedented social media. If there is an orthodoxy *Lost* struggled to define itself within and sometimes against, it is the orthodoxy of reader-response-driven event television. This is the current "focus group" culture of television production in which show-runners may draw on or ignore—yet must always confront—viewer responses and interpretations in what is literally a "real time" (and often predatory) online environment. The nature of this situation is to intensify a culture of escalated investment and inevitable disappointment in "vast narratives" like *Lost*, *The Sopranos*, *Battlestar Galactica*, and so many other series in this latest "golden age" of television drama. In this climate, for better and sometimes for worse, the creators *and* viewers of *Lost* collaborated on a narrative that was not fashionably postmodern but was instead a syncretic improvisation that both fascinated and exasperated in equal measure.

As should be clear from my entire argument, these narrative realities are not a matter for easy complaint or celebration, but for critical engagement and reflection. *Lost* could never have been what any one of us wanted it to be, not even what its creators thought they wanted it be. Something like *Lost*—by the historical, economic, and creative conditions of its production—can only be assessed as multi-dimensionally and generously as possible. To call *Lost* cynical, rudderless, or pointless not only denies its improvisational nature and meaning; it also denies the fundamental nature of all meaning-making acts, which are by definition messy, impure, and incomplete. Syncretism in its specifically religious and philosophical form has always been this way, and a method that nearly got Pico della Mirandola excommunicated kept *Lost* afloat for six compelling, albeit uneven seasons.

The writers of *Lost* were themselves continually seeking the syncretic truth of their project, and not merely communicating that truth. Damon Lindelof, in a recent interview some sixteen months after the *Lost* finale, describes the dilemma imposed on a writing project of this scope:

> There were these two things happening on the show from the minute it began. The first thing was that the audience really wanted to feel like they had an impact on the show … And the other thing was, you didn't want us to be making it up as we went along. You wanted us to have a plan, you wanted us to have a big binder with the entire show and you didn't want us to deviate from it. And the audience didn't realize that there's a huge contradiction between these two ideas. If you want to have a say, then there can't be a binder. And if there is a binder, then we're basically going to

be like, "We don't care what you guys have to say. We're just turning to page 365 and we're doing [Lapidus]." … The show had to become sort of an exercise in, "Here's what it's going to be, guys: We're going to come out and we're going to play our set, and once the set is over you guys can shout out what songs you want to hear and we'll do those for the encore." And that was the way that we modulated it, and maybe it worked and maybe it didn't. (914)

Again, whether *Lost* "worked" or not is for every reader of it to assess. And certainly the passion and intelligence of both casual and dedicated viewers—some of whom misconstrued the narrative stakes of *Lost* as mere transmission and decoding, or as merely an exercise in reader-response shaping a narrative—were nonetheless also constitutive of the syncretized meaning of the series. These shifting structures of improvisational meaning manifested in the naming and interaction of characters; the narrative interlacing of multicultural and historical allusions; the collision and cross-pollination of genres; fan response online and on podcasts; and the elaboration of subsidiary *Lost* narratives developed by both the creative team and by fans independent of that team. To ask all of these *Lost* threads to cohere symmetrically or without fissures showing in the narrative edifice is to forget that *all* narrative practice is at heart not only improvisational, but also a function of continued semantic negotiation and compromise among all participants in the act of making meaning. And we would do well to remember the virtues of negotiation and compromise—above all seeing the limits of our own most deeply-held beliefs and potentially tyrannizing orthodoxies—as these virtues in essence shaped the communal ethos of *Lost*'s creative process and the ethical universe that its characters continually struggled to navigate. In this light, syncretism is not copout or capitulation; it is both common sense and a moral imperative.

Dr. Paul R. Wright is Assistant Professor of English and Co-Director of the Honors Program at Cabrini College in Pennsylvania.

The Lord is My Jack Shephard:
From System and Spectacle to Sacred Story

by Jennifer Galicinski

"There are three rows of figures.
The upper part has in it the figure of Christ as the Good Shepherd,
surrounded by floating angels carrying scrolls inscribed with verses from the 23rd Psalm."

    All our stories come from a particular, socially constructed point of view; this notion is central to my thesis. It will emerge soon enough which perspective I myself am writing from, though I will say now that this essay was originally written for a post-modernity class at an Anglican graduate school in Toronto, Wycliffe College. For this reason, I am particularly interested in the challenge LOST offers the Church, though this critique can also be applied to the wider society as well. It is essential to note that because I belong to the Christian faith tradition, this essay is a critique of my own tradition. It is my struggle to come to terms with its sometimes oppressive history, its way of knowing and being in the world. For those who are not a part of this tradition, I hope you will not feel excluded, but that you will enjoy and learn from the conversation. I do believe that it has implications for those who belong to other traditions, as well as for those who have none or are forming their own.

The series finale of LOST outraged thousands of fans. Many were furious that the show failed to provide concrete answers for the hundreds of questions it raised during its six year run. Fans viewed creators Damon Lindelof and Carlton Cuse as storytelling gods. And now they feel their gods have betrayed them. I do not share their view. I believe LOST is the greatest, most prophetic work of fiction ever to have graced the small screen. LOST proclaims the necessity of faith and trust. But it does so much more. LOST provides those of us who embrace the story's message—who embrace faith and trust—a means of finding our way through the postmodern jungle by abandoning our modernist, systematic, and dangerous ways of knowing (epistemology) and interpreting both our human heritage and religious texts, such as the Christian Scriptures (hermeneutics). We must embrace the narrative nature of human and religious traditions and find our place within an epic drama of a socially-embodied Sacred Story.

The genius of LOST—this epic tale of redemption—is not compromised by the mysteries it left unresolved. To the contrary, the lack of answers is intentional and serves as a brilliant literary device to help the viewers feel as displaced, disillusioned, and 'LOST' as the characters in the narrative. The creators are inviting us to see the story of LOST as our story, a reflection of humanity in this disorienting postmodern age. For Jack, Kate, Sawyer, and Locke – who represent us – the greatest mysteries of life can never be fully be grasped. Those seeking ultimate, objective answers will be endlessly frustrated because they are essentially asking the wrong questions. Damon Lindelof said, "For [the writers], the real mystery of the show wasn't 'Where is the island?' but 'Who are these people?'" For at its heart, LOST is a character study; an exploration of what makes people the way they are and the results that spring forth from their behavior. Specifically, it is an exploration - and a critique - of the modernist quest to master the unknown. All the characters that attempt to conquer, control, and harness the mysteries of the Island inevitably do violence to the 'other' and are eventually led to their own demise: the DHARMA Initiative; the Man in Black; Charles Widmore. The characters that appear to have ultimate knowledge are revealed in the end to be nothing more than a social construct with a skewed and limited perspective of reality: Benjamin Linus; Eloise Hawking; Jacob.

While LOST condemns the modernist project, this 'metaphysics of violence,' it is also a reflection—and a critique—of the postmodern disorientation that results from being liberated from it.(1002) The smorgasbord of cultural references and seemingly random patchwork of mysteries creates a sense of being 'lost at sea' for characters and viewers alike.(1003) Yet in the midst of the tumultuous storm, the transformative journey of Jack Shephard offers us a prophetic allegory, a vision for living on stable ground. Initially a self-reliant, controlling Man of Science, Jack finds redemption by abandoning his modernist ways, accepting a life based on faith, and embracing his place in the larger Story of the Island. His ability to save everyone is only realized once he stops trying to fix everything and places his faith in something much bigger than himself—the

Island—to bring ultimate healing, within and through a community of beloved pilgrims.

A Failed Social Experiment

Those who demand that all the questions of LOST be answered according to their own logic-based standards do not view the mysteries as something to be wrestled with on a journey of discovery, but conquered. This is nothing more than a modernist quest to master the unknown. During the ages of the Reformation, the Enlightenment, and the Scientific Revolution, (roughly between the 17th and 20th centuries), the great mysteries of life, like those of LOST, were seen as puzzles to solve. The questions, "What is the best way to achieve freedom in society?", "What is the true nature of salvation?" and "Why does an apple fall to the ground?" were thought to have definitive, black-and-white answers that could be discovered through one infallible vehicle: human reason. It was a time to throw off the shackles of church and civil authority and embrace the freedom and progress that could be achieved through human rationality. The British philosopher John Locke (whom our beloved 'Man of Faith' on the Island is ironically named after) believed that the "reasoning power of a human being…is competent to answer his deepest questions."(1004) This included the questions of religious faith – he believed that God could be known absolutely through human logic. Likewise, Jean-Jacques Rousseau (the namesake of the insane French woman who lives in the jungle) believed that humans are rational, good, and capable of achieving great progress. The ultimate goal was a "prosperous, happy, peaceful society that would be constructed on the basis of a rational, scientific understanding of humanity."(1005)

Sounds pretty good, except for the fact that the century immediately following the height of the Enlightenment was the bloodiest century of human history. For as Middleton and Walsh say in their book *Truth is Stranger than it Used to Be*, the modernist quest is at its foundation an "impulse to mastery and ultimately to violence."(1006) The various executions of the Catholics, the Anabaptists, or the Reformers, depending on who held the throne of England, were the result of each monarch believing they had mastered 'the Truth.' The First and Second World Wars proved that even the countries most influenced by the Enlightenment could engage in tremendous amounts of needless slaughter. The Holocaust demonstrated the scientifically calculated methods that an evil regime could apply to genocide. Modern advances in technology led to the development of nuclear weapons that could eradicate millions of people at the touch of a button. Beliefs in a 'One True Culture', which had been 'enlightened', led to imperialistic oppression and colonization so the 'savages' could be 'enlightened' as well. The development of capitalism and democracy, which was promised to 'lift all boats' and provide freedom for the masses only lead to an increase of global wealth disparities, social inequalities, and an oppression of a new kind. This 'metaphysics of violence' was the result of seeking to "grasp the infinite, irreducible complexities of the world as a unified and homogeneous totality."(1007) As postmodern philosopher Jean-

Francois Lyotard put it, the modernist quest to master the unknown has given us "as much terror as we can take."(1008)

The Island Will Not Be Mastered

In LOST, the Island is the Great Unknown that many people, time and time again, have tried to master and yet have catastrophically failed to do so. From the moment Oceanic flight 815 crashed there, we knew it was no ordinary island. It healed John Locke's paralysis and Rose's cancer. It was home to a polar bear, an insane French woman who had been stranded for 16 years, and a mysterious jungle-dwelling Smoke Monster that killed whomever it chose. Jack Shepherd saw visions of his dead father. The large and lovable Hurley saw his friend from the mental institution where he lived before the crash. The beautiful and strong Kate, a fugitive for killing her abusive stepfather, saw the horse that had once helped her escape the police. The Island contains 'unique electromagnetic properties' that seem to be able to bend the space-time continuum. It is outside of time and thus not visible to the outside world. It requires special knowledge to find (unless Jacob, the enigmatic Island Protector, mysteriously draws one to it). It is not surprising then, that many people wanted to conquer, control, and manipulate the powers of Island for themselves. People like the DHARMA Initiative, the 'Man in Black,' and Charles Widmore. However, following in the footsteps of the modernist quest to master the unknown, they committed great violence upon the 'other', which inevitably led to their destruction.

Noble Hippie Scientists Turned Massacred Conquerors

The DHARMA (Department of Heuristics And Research on Material Applications) Initiative, a multi-research project founded in the 1970s, came to the Island to conduct scientific research in various disciplines that would supposedly "save the world as we know it." The word 'dharma' in a Hindu context means "one's righteous duty," which emphasizes their belief in themselves as saviours of humanity.(1009) It was revealed in the Lost Experience, an alternate reality online game designed to engage fans and expand the storyline, that a mathematical calculation called the 'Valenzetti Equation' was used to predict the exact day that humanity would destroy itself through either environmental crisis or nuclear warfare. The numbers 4, 8, 15, 16, 23, and 42—the numbers that are seen hundreds of times in various ways throughout the six seasons (on clocks, soccer jerseys, cans of soups, etc)—are explained as the numerical values to the core environmental and human factors of the Valenzetti Equation. The supposed purpose of the DHARMA Initiative was to change the numerical values of any one of the core factors in the equation in order to give humanity a chance to survive, effectively by changing doomsday.(1010) The mysterious powers of the Island would play a huge role in this research, and it was these powers the DHARMA Initiative sought to harness. They built over 10 research stations in secret locations throughout the

136

Island for the purpose of their experiments. At the Swan Station, they drilled deep into the ground for the purpose of tapping into a pocket of electromagnetic energy, which they were hoping to use to 'manipulate time', thereby giving humanity more time to survive based on their calculations.

A noble mission, one could argue – much like the original goals of the modernist project which sought to better humanity – to produce a society of order, peace, and prosperity. The DHARMA folks began as a peaceful group. They greeted each other with 'Namaste' meaning the 'Divine in you greets the Divine in me.' They lived on the Island in a sort of hippy commune and worked together to save humanity from its own destruction. They believed that their project was of utmost importance, never doubting the truth of the science behind the Valenzetti Equation. Yet as James Olthuis says, the "unity of truth is purchased only at the cost of violence, by repressing what doesn't fit and erasing the memory of those who have questioned it."(1011) Totalizing aspirations, such as those of the DHARMA Initiative, inevitably seeks to conquer, destroy, or 'dissolve into a homogeneous unity' those that who are different, those seen as 'other.'(1012) This is precisely what happened with the DHARMA Initiative. They were not the only ones on the Island. There were original inhabitants that they called 'the Hostiles' (who our plane crash survivors would eventually call 'the Others'). They had an ongoing conflict with the Hostiles and would kill or capture those that were on 'their territory.' Stuart Radzinsky, the controlling, determined Head of Research in the DHARMA Initiative, was so paranoid about the Hostiles discovering his plans to build 'the Swan' station, that he sought to kill those that he believed were 'spies.' Even though he was warned that drilling into the pocket of electromagnetism would release an enormous amount of energy – like Chernobyl – he refused to give up drilling, which caused the catastrophic 'Incident.' As a result, the energy was contained in tons of concrete, but small amounts needed to be released every 108 minutes by entering 'the Numbers' into a computer. Radzinsky, devastated by the cosmic failure of his research, did this job for a number of years before he shot himself in the head. The rest of the DHARMA Initiative was eventually killed by 'the Hostiles' in a holocaust-like genocide referred to as 'the Purge.' Their modernist quest to master the Island and 'save humanity' resulted in nothing but a bloody, horrific tragedy – much like the wars of the 20th century. Yet this was not the first time a catastrophe of this magnitude had occurred on the Island. Centuries before the DHARMA Initiative was ever founded, the Man in Black also desired to manipulate the powers of the Island.

Curious Boy Turned Evil Smoke Monster

He was not a trained scientist, nor did he desire to do complex experiments, nor did he seek to 'save humanity.' The Man in Black's aim was simple: he wanted to leave the Island. He was born there, along with his twin brother Jacob (the 'Man in White,' who later became the 'Protector of the Island'), after their mother was shipwrecked. He was raised by the woman who was the current 'Protector of the Island.' This woman had murdered the boys' mother immediately after their birth so she could raise them as her own. She told him that nothing was across the sea, that the Island was all there was. When he and Jacob were young boys, she took them to a cave that contained The Light (which the DHARMA folks later would call 'electromagnetic energy'). But for them it was simply the warmest, most brilliant light they had ever seen. She told them that it was the 'heart of the Island' and it was 'life, death, and rebirth.' These words are easily assimilated into a traditional faith context. For example, in Christian terms, we could say the Light was the "Alpha, Omega, and Author of Salvation" or the "Light of the World." In Hindu tradition the Light might become "The radiance of the 108 faces of Lord Shiva." She told them that a little bit of this Light was inside every person, but that they always want more. She said that she was protecting it from the dangerous people who tried to conquer and manipulate the Light. According to her, "they come, they fight, they corrupt, they destroy; it always ends the same." She told them that eventually her time would be up, and when she was gone, one of them would have to become the 'Protector of the Island' in order to protect the Light. For when people try to capture the Light, it would go out, and once it did, humanity would cease to exist.

"Across the Sea" © Gideon 2010
Used with permission

The day that his dead birth-mother appeared to him in a vision, the Man in Black learned that the woman who had been raising him was a liar and a murderer. His real mother told him that there were many things across the sea, and that her people who had been shipwrecked on the Island lived on its other shore. Shocked and angry, the Man in Black confronted his guardian mother and told her that he was going to live with 'the other people.' He tried to get Jacob to join him, but Jacob did not believe his story and was loyal to his guardian mother. For the next 30 years, the Man in Black lived with the other people, who were 'smart men who were curious about how things work.' They discovered that there were places on the Island where 'metal behaves strangely' (due to a force the DHARMA folks would call 'electromagnetism'). When they discovered it, they dug, and found the Light / electromagnetic energy. The Man in Black, along with his people, had developed a system where they would 'channel the Light and water.' They installed a giant wheel that would harness the power of the Light, which would mysteriously transport them to another place, off the Island, and across the sea.

When Jacob told his 'mother' about the Man in Black's plan to harness and manipulate the Light, she transformed herself into the Smoke Monster (1013) and murdered his entire village of people (an act which would be replicated with 'the Purge' of the DHARMA Initiative centuries later). Knowing that the Man in Black would seek to kill her, 'mother' took Jacob back to the cave of the Light and performed a ceremony that made him the new 'Protector of the Island.' When she arrived back at her camp, the Man in Black, who would now not be able to leave the Island, murdered her in a fit of rage. Jacob arrived just in time to see his 'mother' stabbed to death by his brother, and angrily beat him. Jacob then dragged him back to the Light and threw him into the cave. This caused the Man in Black to be forever separated from his body and his spirit transformed into the Smoke Monster. His desire to control and harness the Light, no matter what his motivations were, resulted in horrific violence and a terrifying end. As with the final end of the DHARMA Initiative, his attempt to master the mysteries of the Island led to the Man in Black's demise. Unfortunately, no record of this lesson would be passed on to future generations, and so history continued to repeat itself on the Island. A generation after 'the Purge' of the DHARMA Initiative, Charles Widmore, a powerful industrialist living in Los Angeles, sought to find the Island and capture it for himself.

Betrayed Island-Lover Turned Ruthless Tyrant

He had once lived in peace on the Island as the leader of 'the Others' but had been banished by Benjamin Linus, an aspiring leader of the group, who had discovered his 'questionable' misconduct. Ben believed that Widmore was an unworthy leader because he was disobeying Jacob's 'rules.' Once he banished Widmore from the Island, the two became mortal enemies. Widmore hired a freighter of people – a mercenary team and scientists – to find the Island and kill Ben and everyone on the Island (which at this time included our beloved plane crash survivors) so that he could resume his leadership on the Island and claim its powers for himself. Widmore's plan to conquer the Island was systematic, ruthless, and inherently violent.

As with the DHARMA Initiative and the Man in Black, things did not end well for the power-mongering conqueror. Like the Spanish Conquistadors who sought the riches, fame, and glory of the American Continent, Widmore had no concern for the people already on the Island. He ordered his mercenaries to kill everyone, including Ben's sixteen-year-old daughter, Alex. Though they were unsuccessful in killing everyone and capturing Ben, Alex was murdered right in front of Ben. Enraged, he made it his purpose to take revenge on Widmore and eventually succeeded, years later, by shooting him. Widmore's quest to master, control, and harness the powers of the Island led to much needless bloodshed, including his own.

The DHARMA Initiative, the Man in Black, and Charles Widmore, though in different time periods and with different motivations, all sought to become what Rene Descartes called "masters and possessors of nature."(1014) They all had faith in their own rationalistic methods of harnessing the unknown which led to catastrophic violence against all the 'other' who did not share their totalizing worldview. The tragic stories of these characters portray the modernist's faith in reason and science as a 'metaphysics of violence' that must be rejected. The Island, or The Light, will not be mastered. As an allegory for God, it will not allow itself to be domesticated, placed in a box, or submit itself to be known fully by human reason. As LOST analyst Pearson Moore insightfully suggested,

> The point of LOST is that there are things completely beyond our control, completely beyond our understanding, beyond our grasp. I like to say we are like dogs trying to read a newspaper. We only understand a few of the black-and-white photographs. That's it. The full reality of God is there in the newspaper, but we will never be able to read it, never completely understand it.(1015)

This echoes the sentiment in the New Testament: "For now we see in a mirror dimly, but then face to face. Now I know in part; then I shall know fully." [1 Cor 13:12] Human reason is too limited to understand the great mysteries of life. If, as LOST demands, we acquire and maintain faith, we must come to believe in a beginning and an end, and an entity beyond our rational means of knowing; we must accept on faith an Author of Creation. We can know this Author, but such knowledge requires something much more holistic than logic. This holism begins with understanding that all of our "knowledge" is a mere interpretation. Just as those on the Island were required to surrender in order to achieve redemption, we too must give up our "knowledge" to gain redemption. True knowledge through faith transcends in all respects the partial "knowledge" afforded through logic. For as we shall see in the life stories of Benjamin Linus, Eloise Hawking, and Jacob, what originally appears to be their ultimate, objective knowledge is little more than a socially-constructed and limited interpretation of reality.

Good-bye Objectivity

The French philosopher Jean-Jacques Derrida asserted, "There is nothing outside the text," or in other words, "everything is an interpretation". According to the contemporary philosopher James K. A. Smith, Derrida believes that the whole concept of people being able to reach absolute, objective "Truth" is in fact a faulty epistemology that stems from modernist philosophers such as Rousseau.(1016) Rousseau believed that language prevents us from experiencing the world "as it really is." As soon as there is language, he believed, there is a distorted interpretation of our experience. Rousseau believed that the "state of Nature" is a place of direct knowing, where mediated interpretation is not necessary; we just "know things as they are."(1017) Like cold, hard facts that are simply "floating in space" with no connection to time, culture, or space; they somehow exist independently of everything.

According to Smith, Derrida believes that 21st century thinkers are "Rousseaueans are heart." In other words, many believe they can know things objectively, "as they really are." For example, Smith points out that some authorities believe that only with difficult texts, such as certain religious texts and allegories, it is necessary to go through a process of interpretation in order to get the meaning behind the text. According to these authorities, the rest of the time we are "simply reading" and seeing things "as they really are"–and no interpretation is taking place. However, Derrida believes there is never a time when we are not interpreting.(1018) Everything that we read, and more significantly, every time we use language, we are engaging in a humanly constructed, mediating process of interpretation. Here he agrees with Rousseau – language means interpretation. However, unlike Rousseau, Derrida does not believe that language is a pesky obstruction of reality, something that we need to remove or get past in order to understand things "as they really are." Derrida believes that we can never experience things "as they really are." Rather, "everything must be interpreted [through language] in order to be experienced."(1019) Thus, language/interpretation is the arena in which our experience, and thus our truth, takes place. Therefore, our sense of the world, our truth, is constructed through the lens of history, culture, time, and place. This is LOST's most powerful critique of the modernist sensibility: no one person or group of people can hold objective knowledge because there is no such thing as objective knowledge. It is all a façade, like the Wizard of Oz, a quivering little old man behind the curtain. It was a failed social experiment in the human ability to master the unknown that resulted in the most violently imperialistic atrocities of human history. Later, I will elaborate on the idea that we need not throw out the concept of truth, for there are in fact more holistic ways of knowing truth than simple objectivity. In LOST, characters such as Benjamin Linus, Eloise Hawking, and Jacob, who initially appear to have ultimate knowledge, are eventually discovered to have only a socially constructed and finite perspective of reality.

Benjamin Linus: Omnipotent Leader or Bluffing Manipulator?

Benjamin Linus is not only the most complex and compelling character on LOST, but perhaps in all of television history. A leader of 'the Others' who helped plan 'the Purge' of the DHARMA Initiative, Ben is wickedly deceitful, conniving, and downright creepy. His menacing, cold stare is enough to give anyone the chills. When we first meet him, he is caught in a trap in the jungle and claims, quite convincingly, to be a survivor of a hot-air balloon crash. This was his first of many lies. Throughout the next five seasons Ben vehemently claims that his ways, though obviously evil (genocide, kidnapping, and torture, to name a few), are for the 'good of the Island.' He seems to have ultimate knowledge about the Island's mysteries, and the viewers are led to believe that if anyone has a 'God's-eye-view" of the Island, it is Ben. He is absolutely ruthless in his loyalty towards it, as well as towards Jacob from whom he claims to 'take orders'.

After Jack is able to make contact with Widmore's freighter (which he believes to be a rescue boat), Ben pleads with him to not let them come to the Island, as they are not 'good people' and will kill them all. Jack does not listen, and Widmore's mercenaries come and hold Ben's daughter hostage in an attempt to capture him. Instead of doing everything he can to save his daughter, Ben refuses to leave the Island, and she is killed. Ben is shocked, and whispers "He changed the rules," implying again that he has ultimately knowledge about the 'rules' of the Island. Then, in an attempt to hide the Island from Widmore, Ben 'moves' it, through time, by turning a mysterious frozen wheel (the wheel that the Man in Black was going to install centuries earlier) far below the surface of the Island. This causes it to disappear from sight, and transports him off the Island to the middle of a Tunisian desert. He spends the next three years manipulating the Oceanic Six— some of the plane crash survivors who were later rescued—to return to the Island because they "were never supposed to leave."

Again, Ben seems to have an ultimate knowledge of the Island and the survivors' 'special purposes' on it. He has a master plan for returning to this Island, which includes convincing the Oceanic Six that they all need to go back. The friends they left behind, he says, "are in danger." Ben appears to know what is happening on the Island, even though he has not been there in three years. His seemingly all-knowing ways convince us that he must have ultimate knowledge that will unlock the mysteries of the Island for us all.

We eventually learn however, that Ben was nothing more than a bluffing, emotionally scarred man who desperately wanted to be 'special.' After returning to the Island, he confessed to Locke that he had never even met Jacob and had deceived everyone in order to hold his power. He knew nothing about The Light or other mysteries of the Island, only that the Island was unique and needed to be protected. Yet Ben was not born a manipulative seeker of power. His behavior was socially constructed. His flashbacks reveal that he was brought to the Island as a child by his father, a member of the DHARMA Initiative. His father was an alcoholic who blamed him for the death of his mother, who died in childbirth. Ben was consistently beaten and insulted by his father, which caused him to feel powerless and dejected.

When he saw a vision of his dead mother, he followed her into the jungle where he met Richard Alpert, the ageless representative of Jacob who lived with 'the Others.' After telling Richard that he followed his dead mother out there, Richard told Ben that because he could see his mother, he must be 'special,' and that he could join them if he wanted. Ben, desiring to feel valuable, eventually helped the Others to kill the DHARMA Initiative, which earned him respect in the eyes of the group. Eventually he became their leader, and slowly his desire to feel special grew into a love of power, which he eventually became willing to protect at all costs.

In the end, Ben was regretful and repentant about his manipulative ways, and sought the forgiveness and well-being of all those he had hurt. His life story is a critique of the modernist belief in ultimate and objective truth. For although we were led to believe that Ben possessed infinite knowledge about the Island, in the end we learn he was nothing more than a broken, lonely man whose perspective was merely a socially constructed, limited interpretation of reality.

Eloise Hawking: Oracle of Destiny or Student of Her Murdered Son?

A similar pattern is echoed in the life of the seemingly all-knowing, time-traveling guru, Eloise Hawking.(1020) We first meet her as an elderly woman who guides Desmond (1021) towards his 'fate' of crashing on the Island in order to push the button. She talks much of people's 'destiny' and what is 'supposed to happen' and 'sacrifice' for the 'sake of the Island.' She appears to know all about the unique nature of the Island, what will happen next, and what needs to happen for the 'good of humanity.' She is a stoic woman who tells Ben that if the Oceanic Six don't return to the Island then 'God help us all.' She also tells Desmond that he must return with them as "the Island is not done with you yet." She is the one who informs us all—by telling some of the Oceanic Six in a mysterious DHARMA station in Los Angeles called 'the Lamp Post'(1022)—that the Island is outside of time and is constantly moving.

She tells them that they must get on Ajira flight 316 (a reference to the biblical verse describing God's plan of salvation—a foreshadowing allegory for the Island's plan of redemption) that will fly over a portal to the Island at a specific time that will get them back. In all she says and does, she seems to have a mystical union with the Island and ultimate knowledge about its mysteries.

"Seems" being the key word, for nothing is as it appears on LOST. For in a number of flashbacks we learn that in her late thirties Eloise was once the leader of 'the Others' who had an affair with Charles Widmore, who was her co-leader. Shortly after she became pregnant with his son, she shot a 35-year-old man who had entered their camp waving a gun. As he lay dying, he told her that he was her son. This man was Daniel Faraday, a physicist who had time-traveled back to the 1970s in order to prevent the chain of events that would lead to the crash of the survivors' plane.(1023)

After he died, Eloise looked at his notebook full of highly advanced equations concerning time travel and saw a note in her handwriting, signed, "Love Mother." She was shocked, and took the notebook for herself. In another flashback, we see Daniel as a small child, in America, and a grief-stricken Eloise, ten years after she shot her adult son on the Island, telling him that it is his 'destiny' to pursue science. She pushes him through school, and he earns a PhD in Physics and specializes in the research of space-time. He is sent on a mission to the Island by his father—Charles Widmore—with the other freighter people who were ordered to capture Ben and kill everyone else.

Eloise knew that Daniel would be on the Island when Ben turned the mysterious wheel, which would cause the Island to move through time. She knew that Daniel and the others would end up in the 1970s—when she was the leader of the Others—where he would eventually storm into her camp and she would shoot him. Even though it pained her to send Daniel to his death at her young hands, it was his journal, with all the advanced time travel equations, that allowed her to manipulate the Island's time-traveling capabilities. Without that journal she would not be able to travel through time and space, and she would not know so much about the people who eventually came to the Island. Originally, Eloise appeared to have ultimate, infinite knowledge about the Island, but as we discover, everything she knows is because of the space-time equations in her son's journal. In reality, we find that she is a plain woman who once made a horrible, ill-fated mistake, one that just happened to provide her with scientific knowledge from the future.

Jacob: Demigod or Flawed and Lonely Mama's Boy?

We didn't see him till the end of the fifth season, yet if anybody held ultimate knowledge on the Island, it was the enigmatic, god-like leader of all leaders, Jacob. During the first 102 episodes of LOST, we constantly heard Ben and the Others mention 'Jacob's lists', and whether or not Jack or Kate were 'good' enough to be written there. We also heard them talk of "Jacob's orders" and "Jacob's rules," of which we were given little information. The mere mention of his name caused those present to straighten their posture or bow their heads in reverence. In a brainwashing film that the Others forced a young "traitor" to watch, all sorts of eerie images and sounds flashed before him including a three-second flash of the phrase "God loves you as he loved Jacob" in bold bubble letters. Like the Jacob of the Bible, the island's Jacob seemed to be some sort of chosen patriarch, the truest and highest father, the one who knew all of its deepest mysteries. His children – those he was able to mysteriously 'bring' to the Island – seemed to be wandering in the 'wilderness' of the Island's jungle for many years, obeying his every command.

"Jacob" by ArtGUS
Used with permission.

When we first see him in the last episode of Season Five, he is a young man, blonde, and wearing a white tunic. He is living alone, in a chamber under a statue of the Egyptian goddess of birth and rebirth, Taweret. He is weaving a tapestry full of Egyptian hieroglyphics and Greek phrases. He catches a fish and while sitting on the beach, his adversary, the Man in Black, appears. He sits and sees an old ship coming in the distance. Their dialogue feels Shakespearean.

MIB: You brought them here. Still trying to prove me wrong?
Jacob: [Looks calmly at him] You are wrong.
MIB: Am I? They come; they fight; they destroy; they corrupt. It always ends the same.
Jacob: It only ends once. Anything that happens before that…is just progress.
MIB: [Pause] Do you have any idea how badly I want to kill you?
Jacob: Yes.

145

MIB: One of these days, sooner or later, I'm going to find a loophole, my friend.
Jacob: Well, when you do I'll be right here.

It seems they have been having this conversation for centuries. We later learn that Jacob believes mankind is good and capable of loving sacrifice for others; while the Man in Black believes 'it is in their very nature to sin' (to destroy and corrupt). We soon see a contemporary Jacob in the flashbacks of many of the Oceanic survivors, touching them at some pivotal moment in their lives – Kate when she steals a lunchbox as a child, Locke when his father pushes him out of a window, and Jack after his father humiliated him during his first spinal surgery. He touches all six of the 'Candidates' – those he has chosen as his potential replacements as Protector of the Island. He seems wise, kind, and compassionate – a father figure to all of the Candidates who, we have learned, all have dysfunctional relationships with their fathers. At the same time, it appears that Jacob may be using those he brings to the Island as pawns in a centuries-old game to prove his nemesis wrong.

His backstory though, reveals a much different picture. Jacob is not a god, nor is the Man in Black. As I mentioned earlier, they were twin brothers whose mother arrived on the Island after being shipwrecked. Jacob clung to his guardian 'Mother' and always felt a bit stung when she seemed to favor his brother (the opposite of the Biblical story in which the mother favors Jacob). After the Man in Black left to join the other camp of people, Mother brought Jacob to The Light again and told him he has to be the one to protect it, for as long as he can, and then he will have to find his replacement. Jacob, far from his stoic, calm, wise self that we had come to know, reacts like a mere whiny child.

Jacob: I don't wanna protect it.
Mother: Someone has to.
Jacob: [rebelliously] I don't care!
Mother: My time is over.
Jacob: [confused and afraid] Why? Why is your time over?
Mother: It has to be you, Jacob.
Jacob: No it doesn't! You wanted it to be him! [Angrily] But now I'm all you have.
Mother: It was always supposed to be you Jacob. I see that now. And one day you'll see it, too. But until then, you don't really have a choice.

Jacob reluctantly takes the cup of wine and assumes responsibility for the role of Protector. The next morning, his brother, the Man in Black, kills his mother. Jacob throws his brother into the Light, turning him into the Black Smoke and for the next few centuries, he would bring people to the Island, trying to find his replacement. He revealed to the remaining four Candidates, Jack, Kate, Sawyer, and

Hurley, that he chose them because they were like him—flawed and alone, and in need of the Island as much as it needed them.

Flawed and alone. Though he had confidence that people were capable of choosing good (which Jack proves in the end), Jacob chose the Candidates because they were in need of healing and redemption—which they would find by struggling together on the Island. He knew this not because he was an all-knowing, all-powerful, god-like leader as we were led to believe for almost six full seasons. He knew because he was able to travel through time and meet them at various times in their lives. In the end, we learn that, like Ben and Eloise, he too was a simple, broken, lonely person who crashed on a special Island and regrettably turned the last of his family into a cloud of evil smoke.

Benjamin Linus, Eloise Hawking, and Jacob were all characters who initially appeared to have ultimate knowledge but who ended up simply being regular people who made terrible choices that resulted in much heartache. As much as we trusted in each of them to be the ones that would unlock the mysteries of the Island, they all were as just as 'lost' as we were. In weaving these characters' stories into the heart of the narrative, the writers are pounding yet another nail into the modernist coffin. If we believe that it is possible to know things 'ultimately,' 'objectively,' and 'rationally,' we are deceiving ourselves, as these characters deceived us, into thinking that our upbringing, surroundings, and culture have no effect on us. No one is capable of having a "God's-eye perspective," or "The Absolute Answer to it All" because all of our experiences and knowledge, like those of Ben, Eloise, and Jacob, are limited interpretations of reality, which are merely socially-, historically-, and culturally-constructed. It is this concept that the Church tends to feel uncomfortable with.

But the Church need not be alarmed, for just because a perspective is an interpretation, it does not mean that all interpretations are equally valid; relativism is not the automatic alternative to objectivity. James K.A. Smith's words are both insightful and encouraging for those with whom the Christian gospel resonates:

> To assert that our interpretation is not an interpretation but objectively true often translates into the worst kinds of imperial and colonial agendas, even within a pluralistic culture. Acknowledging the interpreted status of the gospel should translate into a certain humility in our public theology. It should not, however, translate into skepticism about the truth of the Christian confession. If the interpretive status of the gospel rattles our confidence in its truth, this indicates that we remain haunted by the modern desire for objective certainty. But our confidence rests not on objectivity but rather on the convictional power of the Holy Spirit (which isn't exactly objective); the loss of objectivity, then, does not entail a loss of kerygmatic boldness about the truth of the gospel.(1016)

Recognizing our perspective as an interpretation is simply a more authentic and humble epistemology (theory of knowledge) that will prevent the arrogant violence of modernity and open up space for the voices of the suppressed and marginalized—who were silenced during modernity to be heard. But what is the difference between a 'true interpretation'—as Smith suggests—and 'Objective Truth'? This is an important question, and one that I'll explore during our discussion of Jack Shepherd's transformative journey. For now, the stories of the characters we have looked at so far serve as a warning to us about the dangers of the modernist sensibility. If the desire to conquer the unknown by seeking ultimate, rationalistic, objective answers leads only to violence against the 'other' and ignores the socially constructed nature of our perspectives, we must reject this desire. The postmodern sensibility though, is not much easier to swallow.

A Chaotic, Complex Cacophony of Cultural Confusion

Like the alliteration above, there is a method to the madness of LOST. While the narrative offers us a weighty critique of modernity, the literary devices used throughout the story offer a reflection of the postmodern response. LOST is a 'pastiche' - a random, hodge-podge of various philosophical, literary, religious, mythological, and pop culture references - that is intended to make us feel as disoriented as the plane crash survivors who discover a polar bear on a tropical island. Characters are named after philosophers, religious icons and spiritual or literary figures: John Locke, Desmond Hume, Danielle Rousseau, Jeremy Bentham, Jack and Christian Shephard, Kate Austen, James "Sawyer" Ford, Richard Alpert (the birth name of Baba Ram Das, a contemporary spiritual teacher), Charlotte Staples (C.S.) Lewis, and the Island's patriarch, Jacob. There are literally hundreds of direct and indirect references to Star Wars, as Hurley (the large, hilarious, genuine, and most-loved character) regularly compares their situation to those in the films. He refers to Jack's healing of another survivor's asthma by simply calming her down as a 'Jedi moment' and Jacob's vague instructions on how to protect the Island as 'worse than Yoda.' As the characters discover various DHARMA Stations, we regularly see the octagon DHARMA symbol which is an allusion to the Noble Eightfold Path of Buddhism. There are hundreds of Egyptian hieroglyphics discovered on secret doors in the homes of 'the Others,' in the various DHARMA stations, in caves, on the walls of underground passages, and the Temple. Jacob lives under the statue of the Egyptian goddess Taweret. In one of the last scenes of LOST, the characters all meet at a multi-faith church, and there is a significant camera focus on a stained-glass window that is literally a patch-work of six different religious/philosophical symbols – a Yin-Yang, a Star of David, a Christian cross, a Buddhist Dharma Wheel, a Hindu Omkar (Aum), and an Islamic Star and crescent (Ottoman symbol). Far from the 'One True Culture' that would have been represented by the Christian cross, or the scientific Atom symbol, a variety of perspectives is seemingly put on a level playing field.

There are also hundreds of examples of hyper-textuality (the postmodern theory about the inter-connectedness of all literary works and their interpretation) that serve to broaden the scope of the confusion. Characters are seen either reading, looking at, or displaying on their bookshelf texts such as *Alice in Wonderland* by

Lewis Carroll, *The Brothers Karamazov* by Dostoevsky, *Are You There God? It's Me, Margaret* by Judy Blume, The Bible, *Catch-22* by Josephy Heller, *Our Mutual Friend* by Charles Dickens, *The Turn of the Screw* by Henry James, *Ulysses* by James Joyce, and *Watership Down* by Richard Adams, among dozens of others. Characters also make direct references to *The Lord of the Flies* by William Golding, *Of Mice and Men* by John Steinbeck, Superman by Jerry Siegel, and *The Wonderful Wizard* of Oz by L. Frank Baum, amongst many others. Furthermore, Damon and Carlton (the creators) have mentioned that Stephen King's *The Dark Tower* trilogy (which describe a "Gunslinger" and his quest toward a powerful tower), and the post-apocalyptic horror/fantasy novel *The Stand* are both extremely influential on the story of LOST. The multitude of connections to other texts, all with their own themes, ideas, and critiques, provides a limitless realm of exploration for viewers who are seeking to understand their significance for LOST. As Cari Vaughn asserts in her article "Lost in Hypertext":

> This virtual enlargement of the already complex entity of Lost provides the willing viewer/reader, with a virtually limitless string of interconnected characters and themes, one that encourages a more personal and individual experience of the show. Allowing, even encouraging, viewers and readers to create meaning is the very definition of reader response and hypertext theory.(1024)

By linking the story of LOST to hundreds of stories outside of the narrative, the writers create a sense of interaction by leading the viewers on a journey far outside of LOST, one that leads down a labyrinth of rabbit holes with no clear exit in sight. All this combined with the myriad of mysterious happenings, questions that remain unanswered, and fragmented storylines that are revealed in a non-linear fashion through flashbacks, flash-forwards, and flash-sideways, the writers are creating a sense of vertigo that enables the viewers to feel as dizzy and confused as the characters in the narrative.

"COME IN AND GET LOST!"

This advertisement on the outside of the bargain superstore Honest Ed's in downtown Toronto captures a foundational aspect of the postmodern sensibility. The huge, sprawling, carnival of gaudiness that is Honest Ed's, with its blinking show-tune lights and signs is disorienting to say the least. Replacing the circus of modernity with its one great central performance (calling itself the 'Greatest Show on Earth' or the 'One True Culture'), the carnival that is post-modernity offers us hundreds of sideshows.(1025) At Honest Ed's there are sideshow-like displays of plastic Elvis statues, jumping dolphin clocks, and polyester socks all competing for the consumer's attention. The walls are plastered with old newspaper clippings, wacky signs, and framed pictures of random celebrities who have visited the store, further adding to the confusion. The choice of consumer products and the chaotic clutter is overwhelming. The experience of shopping at Honest Ed's feels much like the experience of watching LOST, and much like trying to find our way through the jungle that is the postmodern age.

After liberating ourselves from the horrors of modernity, with its "manipulative reason and fetish of the totality," we are left to our own devices, wandering aimlessly through the pluralistic 'shopping mall of ideas' of post-modernity.(1026) A typical postmodern woman may practice yoga, wear clothing from Indonesia, cook Mexican food, and attend a Catholic Mass on Sundays.(1027) She is able to adorn herself in whatever bits and pieces of various cultures she wishes, creating her own 'personal worldview style.'(1028) For with the rejection of the 'One True Culture' that characterized modernity, Western society has embraced the unlimited options of religions and worldviews that have been made available for our consumption. Walsh and Middleton give us the image of the modernist project being like the tower of Babel, and the postmodern situation like confusion of tongues, the overwhelming nature of the "cacophony of private languages and tribal agendas, all clamoring for our attention." They go on to say that "the cultural unity of the tower of Babel is replace by the culture wars of the post-Babel situation."(1029) With each idea and worldview given 'equal-footing,' they are available to us in the West to pick and choose whatever parts suit our fancy at any given time.

Peter Berger perceptively refers to this as the 'commodification of belief.' The pluralist situation, he explains, is essentially a market situation. For with the range of options available, each religion and worldview is forced into competition with one another, like Nike vs. Adidas, or like the plastic Elvis statues vs. jumping dolphin clocks at Honest Ed's. While the motto of modernity was the Cartesian "I think therefore I am," the motto of post-modernity is "I consume therefore I am."(1030) Essentially then, post-modernity aids and abets the Empire – the Western, market-run economy of globalized consumerist capitalism. It may disguise itself as being tolerant, willing to listen to the perspective of the 'other,' and open to diversity, but if the Western market system is dominant, isn't this still a modernist conquest – only this time of the global economy?(1031)

Thus, as Walsh suggests, there is no such thing as post-modernity; it is really just hyper-modernity.(1032) It is hegemony (a conquest-driven 'One True Culture') in disguise as heterogeneity ('diversity! freedom! tolerance!'). As Bruce Cockburn puts it, post-modernists are simply 'slavers in drag as champions of freedom.'(1033) While the postmodern critique and distrust of modernity is accurate, its response is nowhere near radical enough. The liberation from modernity has left us not only wandering through the disorienting postmodern jungle, but getting snared in its vines. Who will come and untangle us lost sheep from the thorny thicket? LOST shows the way to freedom through the transformative journey of the good Shephard we have come to know as Jack.

From Faith in Himself to Faith in The Island

Jack is constantly trying to overcome his father's harsh words to him as a child, "You don't have what it takes [to save everyone]." He has been trying for most of his life to prove his father wrong, and he does it by 'fixing' as many people as he can. He has a bona fide Messiah-complex, and believes he can, through his own rationality and medical abilities, help the lame to walk and the dead to rise. Before the crash, he 'fixed' the beautiful Sarah, enabling her to walk again and then marrying her. She left him a short time later, and as she was walking out of his life she said to him, "Look at it this way, at least now you have something to fix." On the Island, Jack resuscitates a nearly dead Charlie and becomes furious with himself when he is not able to 'fix' the young Boone, who dies after falling off a cliff. He even tries to fix himself, as when he needs his appendix taken out, he tries to do it himself! When Juliet, another doctor, tells him she can do it, he still demands to be kept awake in order to 'guide her through it' (although she eventually has him put out when it's apparent he is not handling the pain well). His mission to get everyone off the Island is just another broken situation to 'fix'. This controlling impulse does not come out of a selfless desire to help others, but out of a need to control, to master the natural world thereby putting himself in the center of it.

"Do No Harm" by Gideon Slife
Used with permission.

The modernist quest to master the unknown stems from people like Jack. For as Walsh and Middleton assert, "the whole view of the modernist project depends on this view of selfhood. Without an independently rational self there would be no reason to trust the results and achievements of modern science."(1035) It is Jack's view of himself as a rationalistic, independent being that allows him to see the world – and other people – as a set of mechanistic systems that can be studied, known, and conquered. Thus if something is wrong – whether it be paralysis or being stranded on an Island, his natural response is that he must fix what is broken, thereby achieving a mastery over it.(1036) Jack only believes in what rationality and science can help him see, feel, or touch. If it is not logical, it must not be true. This naturally puts him into conflict with the Island's ironically-named "Man of Faith," John Locke. It was the Island that healed Locke's paralysis, not Jack. As a result, Locke has tremendous faith in the miraculous nature of the Island, telling Jack that he believes it is "different...special... because I looked into the eye of the Island, and what I saw was beautiful." Locke believes that each one of them crashed there 'for a reason.' He says they have a 'purpose' on the Island, that 'the Island chose you too, Jack,' and it is his 'destiny' to be there. Jack thinks this is ridiculous, and consistently dismisses Locke as a delusional old man, telling him 'I don't believe in destiny.' When the two discover a hatch that leads down into the DHARMA Swan Station with the computer button that needs to be pressed every 108 minutes to 'save the world,' Jack refuses to believe that anything will happen if it is not pushed. Locke, on the other had, believes this is part of their 'destiny' and tries to convince Jack to push the button first. When Jack refuses, they have one of the most memorable shouting matches of the entire series.

> Locke: WHY DO YOU FIND IT SO HARD TO BELIEVE??
> Jack: WHY DO YOU FIND IT SO EASY??
> Locke: IT'S NEVER BEEN EASY!!

Locke spends his time on the Island struggling to find what exactly it is that the Island wants him to do, while Jack spends his time trying to rescue 'his people' from 'the Others' who kidnap some of them, and get everyone off the Island. Eventually, Jack makes contact with Widmore's freighter, believing it is there to save them, while Locke tries desperately to stop him from leaving the Island.

> **LOCKE:** But you're not supposed to go home.
> **JACK:** And what am I *supposed* to do? Oh, I think I remember. What was it that you said on the way out to the hatch—that crashing here was our destiny?
> **LOCKE:** You know, Jack. You know that you're here for a reason. You know it. And if you leave this place, that knowledge is gonna eat you alive from the inside out...until you decide to come back.
> **JACK:** Good-bye, John.
> **LOCKE:** You're gonna have to lie.

JACK: Excuse me?
LOCKE: If you have to go, then you have to lie about everything... everything that happened since we got to the island it's the only way to protect it.
JACK: (Sighs) It's an island, John. No one needs to protect it.
LOCKE: It's not an island. It's a place where miracles happen. And— and—if you—if you don't believe that, Jack, if you can't believe that, just wait till you see what I'm about to do.
JACK: There's no such thing as miracles.
LOCKE: Well...we'll just have to see which one of us is right.

…

Lie to them [when you get back home, about what has happened], Jack. If you do it half as well as you lie to yourself, they'll believe you.

Jack, as the typical modernist man, cannot believe in miracles, or a higher purpose, or destiny, because these things are rationally and scientifically inexplicable. He cannot produce miracles himself, therefore they must not exist.

Yet Jack is a 'Man of Faith' – faith in himself, and faith in science and reason as the highest possible ways of knowing. But his faith does not lead him to a very good place. Just as Walsh and Middleton suggest, when left to his own self-directed devices, the heroic, modernist individual inevitably does violence.(1037) Jack's controlling, self-reliant ways cause him to physically fight anyone (like Ben) who gets in his way of getting off the Island, and his 'rational' decisions gets many people killed. He guides the people from the freighter to the Island and they end up killing several people. The freighter eventually explodes, killing more and leaving them stranded on a helicopter, which crashes into the ocean. Only a handful of them, the 'Oceanic Six,' are rescued by another boat passing by. Remembering the last words of Locke, Jack convinces them all that they have to lie in order to protect those they left behind on the Island. The three years that they are off the Island become the most miserable of their lives. Jack succumbs to alcoholism and drug addiction. He ruins all of his relationships and loses his job. His modernist, controlling tendencies rebounded upon him. The last straw for Jack is discovering that Locke has committed suicide, after failing to convince the Oceanic Six that they all had to go back to the Island. Jack feels deeply responsible for Locke's death and, realizing his controlling, self-reliant faith in himself, reason, and science had led to nowhere good, begins to believe that maybe Locke was right after all. He becomes nothing but an emotionally bankrupt, deeply broken, shell of a man. I like to think Coldplay's sweeping ballad Fix You influenced Jack's decision to go back to the Island.

> Lights will guide you home
> And ignite your bones
> And I will try
> To fix you (1052)

Jack tries his best to get everyone rescued, but succeeds in 'saving' only six of them. He wants to get away from the Island, and he wants to 'win' Kate's heart, both of which he accomplished, but this was not what he needed. His life derails and he becomes a drunk, unable to sleep or move forward with his life. Thinking of all that he LOST – his father, his job, his friends, and his love with Kate – causes him to drown himself in tears. But there is hope for Jack. The Light of the Island will 'guide him home,' so he will no longer be LOST. Fulfilling his destiny on the Island will 'ignite his bones,' will help him come truly alive, and will bring him healing and redemption. And in the end, for Jack who becomes broken by trying so hard to fix things, the Island will be the One to fix him. Starting to believe that all these things would come to pass, Jack takes a leap of faith and goes back to the Island.

Once returned, now in 1977(1038), Jack slowly starts to show signs of change. He lets others lead and when a young Ben gets shot (1039), Kate tries to plead with him to save Ben and he replies, "You know, when we were here before I spent all of my time trying to fix things. But did you ever think that maybe the Island just wants to fix things itself? That maybe I was just getting it the way?" He believes now in the seemingly impossible – that the Island is a special, miraculous, relational entity, capable of choosing him to complete some important task. He believes now that he is 'supposed' to be there, yet at first he doesn't know why. When Daniel Faraday, the physicist who specializes in time travel, explains to them that if they were to drop a nuclear bomb into the pocket of electromagnetism (that would eventually be the site of the Swan hatch), then it would break the chain of events that would lead to their plane crashing on the Island, Jack, believing still in the weight of scientific knowledge, considers that this must be why he is there, to prevent all the misery that they had experienced since crashing on the Island. He drops the bomb into the pocket of energy, which only succeeds in killing Juliet (1040) and catapulting them back into the present day. Jack, confused that his plan didn't work and still struggling to know why he is on the Island, eventually sees his name on Jacob's mysterious dial in the lighthouse,(1041) and the images of his childhood home in Jacob's mirror. After some time, Jack is finally able to let go of his need for rationalistic answers and embrace faith in the mysterious ways of the Island. When the four final Candidates (to replace Jacob as Island Protector) are finally able to talk to Jacob and he explains that one of them must protect The Light, Jack speaks up in his first moment of complete clarity.

"What They Died For" by Gideon Slife
Used with permission.

Jack: I'll do it. This is why I'm here. I'm supposed to do this.
Jacob: [whispering gently, knowing Jack's previous confusion] Is that a question, Jack?
Jack: [shakes his head, without hesitation] No.
Jacob: [smiles softly] Good.

Jacob performs the New Island Protector Ceremony, and gives Jack a cup to drink while reciting a Latin incantation over it. The parallels to the Christian ritual of Communion are obvious and striking. Jack's destiny, of which he is now certain, is to protect the Light, thereby saving all of humanity from the the Man in Black (aka the Smoke Monster) who's soul now resides in John Locke's body (who I'll call Fake Locke, or 'Flocke' for short). Flocke's goal is to destroy and leave the Island, thereby killing all of humanity. Jack however, is now ready to do what is

155

necessary to protect the Light and destroy 'Flocke' (who up until this time, could not be killed by regular means).

Now with a deeper, mystical connection to the Island, Jack goes with Desmond (who has a unique resistance to electromagnetism) and 'Flocke' to The Light so that Desmond can turn it off. Jack believes this will enable him to kill 'Flocke', but 'Flocke' believes it will destroy the Island. They are both right. With the Light turned off, the Island begins to shake and sink into the ocean. Meanwhile, 'Flocke' (the Smoke Monster) becomes fully human again, allowing him to be killed by regular means. During an epic battle with the Smoke Monster on the side of a cliff in the pouring rain, Jack is stabbed in the side, providing yet another reference to Christian imagery. But with the help of Kate, Jack is victorious in killing him. Yet the Island is still shaking and sinking, and Jack knows he must turn The Light back on in order to save the Island – and all of humanity. He declares his love for Kate and they share a passionate embrace before he pleads with his friends to run for the Ajira plane that brought them back to the Island. He returns to the cave and turns on The Light again (by placing a giant stone back into the core of The Light). He weeps with joy as he realizes that his destiny has been realized. He saved the Island and protected The Light thereby saving the world.

The final moments of LOST are pure poetry. Jack, bleeding profusely from his side, slowly stumbles back through the bamboo forest – the same one he first woke up in at the beginning of his journey. All his strength gone, he collapses to the ground and gazes through the trees. (Here the camera flashes to the 'sideways world,' which we now know is a sort of purgatory—outside of time and after they are all dead—so that all the plane crash survivors can find one another so they 'move on' together. Jack and all his beloved friends that he saved—and some that he couldn't save, like the real Locke and Boone—are being reunited in a church sanctuary.) Flash back to the Island: Jack is lying on the ground and the same golden retriever, Vincent, runs to him from out of the forest, this time not to lick him awake but to lick his wounds and lay beside him as he dies. Jack musters a weak laugh at the sight of Vincent, knowing that his epic, destiny-ridden journey has come full circle. (Flash sideways to the church: Jack embraces Locke, Hurley, and finally, his love, Kate, who guides him to sit down beside her in a pew.) Flash back to the Island: Jack's final sight is the plane flying overhead, and he smiles knowing that his friends are safe. (Flash sideways to the church: Jack's father, Christian Shephard, with whom he had made peace, proudly squeezes Jack's shoulder. Christian walks slowly to the back of the church and opens the doors, allowing The Light—The Light of the Island that Jack had died to protect—to fill the church, and all the survivors—including Jack - are in awe of its pure warmth and radiance.) Flash back to the Island: the final image of LOST is Jack's eye closing shut.

Only by letting go of his modernist ways and embracing, in faith and against all logic, his place in the Story of the Island, was Jack truly able to do the one thing he never been able to do before: save everyone. In the end, Jack didn't need all of the ultimate, rationalistic answers. He didn't need to know why he needed to protect The Light, or what it was, or how it got to the Island. He recognized that his modernist drive to rely on himself, master the unknown, and 'fix' people and situations only ended in tragedy, both for those around him and for himself. For reasons far outside the realm of logic and science, Jack relied on faith in something outside of himself, faith in something beyond the limitations of rationality, to guide his path home. Only by indwelling the Story of the Island, embracing his place among the many Island Protectors that had come before him, and sacrificing himself (adopting a healthier Messiah-likeness) for the good of others was he able to find ultimate healing and redemption, and spend eternity in peace with his beloved fellow pilgrims.

From System to Story

Like Jack, the Church's hope for guiding this generation through the jungle of post-modernity is found in letting go of our modernist ways of knowing, and embracing, in faith, our place in a socially-embodied Story. We must abandon our misplaced and destructive faith in rationality as the highest form of knowing and interpreting the Scriptures. We must recognize that 'finding the objective principles' is not possible because we can never have access to a 'neutral' position outside of our socially, historically, and culturally rooted perspective.(1043) There is no such thing as an absolute, timeless, contextless system of Truth that simply 'floats in space' somewhere 'out there' for us all to grasp with the tools of reason. Our belief that truth must equal objectivity simply implies that we have been culturally captivated by the modernist quest to master the unknown which as we have seen inevitably leads to violence against the 'other.' Rather, truth in a faith text is always socially embodied in a tradition; rooted and intertwined in a culturally-infused overarching Story. Instead of pretending that we are able to stand outside a faith text, from a neutral position, and then able to apply it to our own lives in a completely different cultural context, theologian and cultural analyst Lesslie Newbigin says that we must "indwell" the story in such a way that it becomes our story.(1044) We can come to a more authentic interpretation of a faith story the same way that we can come to a more genuine understanding of the LOST story: by abandoning our modernist quest for absolute answers, understanding that the narrative itself contains a critique of this way of thinking, and seeking to see ourselves as 'lost' as the characters in the story.

This concept is nothing new; it has motivated many heroes in literature and film. Recall the scene in Peter Jackson's *Lord of the Rings* where Sam and Frodo are halfway through their journey, and they are distraught, and feeling like they want to give up? They are, in fact, feeling rather lost. In that dark moment, they remembered that they were part of a larger story. Sam desperately reminds Frodo of this, saying, "Why, it's still going on, don't the great tales ever end?" It's the state of mind that motivated them to continue on their journey. Also, the curious boy named Sebastian in the Never Ending Story becomes enthralled when he discovers he, too, is part of a larger story, one that depends on him for redemption. We all long to be part of a Story, a Great Story larger than ourselves. Though we abhor the kind of oppressive Story, told and defended through a modernist lens, that has led to the postmodern "incredulity towards Metanarratives." We long for stories that, like the story of both LOST and the Hebrew Scriptures, contains within its narrative a critique of the totalizing and inherently violent ideology that results from modernist, "objective" thinking.

If the Creator of the Universe wanted us to know truth as a contextless system of 'objective facts', why didn't the Creator instruct the writers of a particular faith story to create systematic theology charts, graphs, and lists? Instead, the Author of Creation revealed truth through a socially- and culturally-embodied Story. Spanning all of time from pre-existence to eternity, the Christian Sacred Story contains the epic tale of creation, fall and redemption. It is the story of a suffering people whose cry was heard by a compassionate God who responded by taking the suffering upon Godself. It is the story of God's purposes for the world – shalom (peace, wholeness), compassion, and justice - being worked out through the Hebrew people, Christ, and the Church.(1045) Because this story of redemption is for all of creation, any "violent, ideological, self-justifying ownership of the story— either by nationalistic Jews or by sectarian and self-righteous Christians—brings the story to a dramatic dead end that has missed the creationally redemptive point."(1046) The faith narrative itself—with its concern for every creature from every tribe, tongue, and nation, especially those who are weak and suffering—is a critique of the totalizing exclusionary violence that occurs when one person or group embarks on the modernist quest to master the unknown. Like those who seek absolute answers in LOST, those who interpret the Christian Sacred Story through modernist eyes are missing the very point that the narrative is trying to drive home.

Instead, we must seek to become part of the story. We can more authentically interpret LOST once we see that we are the stranded survivors - flawed, alone, and 'lost' in the chaotic, disorienting postmodern jungle; we are like those who arrogantly seek mastery over the unknown and thus cause harm to others; we are like Jack—struggling to let go of our need for control, to 'fix' people, to rely on ourselves and to seek absolute answers; we would be better off if we placed our faith in something beyond ourselves, something that cannot be known rationally, something as mysterious and beautiful as The Light; we could find healing and redemption by choosing to love, serve, and lay down our lives for the good of our fellow pilgrims. In a similar tone, we can find a purer interpretation of the Christian Sacred Story, as Walsh and Middleton write, by noting that "We are the people whom God liberated from Egypt and led through the Red Sea; we are the people languishing in exile and crying out for release; we are the disciples whom Jesus rebuked for misunderstanding his mission and to whom he appeared after his resurrection; we are the newly formed church who received the outpouring of the Spirit after Pentecost."(1047) By placing ourselves in the faith narrative, we are able to gain a much clearer, intuitive insight into the 'dramatic movement' of the story and learn how we are to carry it forward, in our own context, in a manner that is faithful to the Author's intentions.(1048)

How exactly are we to do this? Walsh and Keesmaat borrow from New Testament scholar N.T. Wright as they explain that the task of indwelling the story requires 'faithful improvisation.'(1049) They say it is helpful to think of the faith narrative as an unfinished six-act drama, with Act I being creation, where the Author's plot intentions are initially revealed, Act II being the fall or the initial conflict, Act III the story of Israel, Act IV the story of Jesus and the climax, 'the pivotal act which begins to unravel the conflict at its deepest roots,' Act V the story of the Church, and Act VI being the eschaton in which the Author's narrative purposes are finally realized. We are all like actors living in Act V, the story of the Church, but the problem is, we have been given no script and the Author wishes us to finish Act V ourselves. In order to do this well, with the help of the wise and comforting Creator we must, as actors, become so immersed in the script we have been already been given that we acquire an 'intuitive imagination' for how we are to improvise in a manner that is faithful to the Author's narrative purposes.(1050) To do this well, Walsh and Keesmaat say it "requires taking the risk of improvisation that is creative, innovative, and flexible." We must not simply cut and paste from the culturally imbedded stories of Israel into our cultural context, because "these earlier passages are not a script intended for our performance in a postmodern world but are the record or transcript of past performances of God's people."(1051) To merely copy what the prophets did without taking into consideration that their actions were part of a particular culturally embodied story would as absurd as trying to find the Island in order to kill the Smoke Monster. Instead, we must learn of the Author's purposes for the story and humbly seek to embody the spirit of the story – justice for the oppressed, compassion for the poor and marginalized, and sacrificial, selfless love for all of creation—in our own cultural context.

The Conclusion of the Matter

LOST was never about forming a systematic grid of answers, it was about engaging in the human story. It was a prophetic critique of the modernist quest for ultimate answers and an allegory for the manner in which life should be lived in the carnivalesque aftermath of modernity's demise. Those who cynically complain that we never found out why Walt was so special, how The Light got in the cave, and why the Smoke Monster makes mechanical noises, have sadly missed the entire point of the narrative. The lack of answers was an intentional, brilliant literary device so that we would struggle along with the characters that were just as disoriented and 'lost' as we were. Jack never got all the answers spoon-fed to him— he had to reject his need for rational answers and rely on his intuitive connection to the Story of Island in order to fulfill his destiny. Likewise, to come to a more authentic interpretation of LOST - and more importantly, the Christian Sacred Story - we must abandon our need for absolute, objective answers – a mindset that caused only violence and destruction on the Island – and so immerse ourselves in the narrative that we gain an intuitive sense of its overarching dramatic movement that is faithful to the intention of the creators. For LOST fans, to be faithful to the intentions of Damon and Carlton means that we must interpret it as a character study, and learn from the horrible mistakes of those who sought to control the

Island, as well as the redemptive sacrifice of Jack Shephard who died to protect it. For those who trust and believe, to be faithful to the intentions of the Creator means that we must seek to live out shalom, compassion, and justice within a community of fellow pilgrims. It is only by rooting ourselves in this Story of the Light that we may illuminate the Way for those who are lost at sea, battered by the crushing waves of the postmodern storm.

Jennifer M. Galicinski is a graduate student at Regent College in Vancouver where she studies theology of culture, philosophy, biblical literature, and creative non-fiction writing. She participates in the community of Grandview Calvary Baptist Church, which has taught her much about indwelling the Sacred Story. She enjoys back-country snowboarding, vegetarian cooking, and all things creative.

Parental Predicaments in LOST

Gozde Kilic
Erin Carlyle

"All The Best Cowboys Have Daddy Issues": The Centrality Of Father Issues in *Lost*

By Gozde Kilic

"All the Best Cowboys Have Daddy Issues"
by Gideon Slife
Used with permission

Lost has been praised as one of the most creative programs in the history of broadcast television, mostly because of its extremely intricate plot, innovative storytelling devices, and comprehensive and puzzling mythology. Writers, journalists, and scholars from various disciplines have viewed the show as a turning point in American television, since few shows would exemplify the storytelling possibilities unique to the television medium more dramatically and innovatively than *Lost.*

However, while the show has become best known for its narrative experimentation and confusion, it has mostly been passed over in terms of its thematic concerns. Father issues are a salient and recurring theme of the show, and as I argue, lie at the center of character formation and development, yet the theme has hardly been recognized as a scholarly subject. In my presentation today, I offer a critical discussion of this not-much-discussed aspect of the show: problematic father-son relationships and their significance in *Lost*'s overall narrative. By adopting a psychoanalytic perspective, I view the father more as a psychological construct, a mythic presence that comes to symbolize culture, society, and patriarchal order rather than an individual, and look at the ways *Lost* revisits and refashions this psychoanalytic construct in its portrayal of characters.

Lost's popularity lies in its unconventional narrative content and structure. As Jason Mittell suggests, "*Lost* critically comments on the condition of the individual in modern society, by challenging the conventions of narrative, genre and the medium of television itself" (1103). The novel structure of the series is apparent in the show's formal practices such as multiple story arcs, fragmentation of episodes, use of suspense and surprise, and shifting perspectives (to name a few) as well as its inclusion of the Internet as a narrative component. By destabilizing the established norms of representation, *Lost* assumes an 'unconventional' attitude towards the codes and conventions of television narrative, making the viewer suspicious of their forged sense of reality.

Lost demonstrates the same 'unconventional' attitude in its portrayal of family dysfunction and fatherhood crisis. It challenges the ideology of the stable and nuclear family unit by picturing family in various fractured forms such as blended, divorced, and single-parent groupings; dealing with a variety of family issues such as custody rights, alcoholism, and molestation; and presenting diversified portrayals of the father such as vanished, absent, unloving, oppressive, and molester. It constructs an image of family and fatherhood that departs from their traditional role and function.

However, although *Lost* abandons dominant myths related to family as a stable and nuclear unit with fixed gender roles, it still conforms to the psychoanalytic myth about the centrality of the father. I argue that, in spite of its unconventional stances in terms of narrative, description of gender, race, and physical appearance, *Lost* remains ideologically committed to the father's mythic importance in the lives of sons and daughters. The paramount significance of fathers is apparent in the show where most characters' motivations, actions, and objectives are greatly influenced and largely shaped by their past paternal conflicts. *Lost* survivors who are wounded and torn by their past relationships with their fathers repeatedly project aspects of their paternal drama onto their adult world. In this way, the show adopts Freud's conception of a patriarchal subjectivity while constructing its character profiles according to his theory of the Oedipus complex, thus the centrality of the father in the development of character.

Before I continue talking about the ways *Lost* perpetuates the mythic presence of the father, I would like to talk a bit more about the Oedipus complex for the sake of clarification. In its most facile sense, the Oedipus complex expresses an infant child's love for his mother and hatred for his father. These feelings are, of course, embedded deep in the unconscious and barely make themselves known to the conscious. According to Freud, the hostile feelings felt for the father have to be resolved in the unconscious in an early age in order for the boy to develop a mature sexual role and identity. So, hatred for the father should turn into identification with him and rivalry should turn into submission to his power. According to Freud, this stage in maturation, 'the resolution of the Oedipus complex,' is a crucial phase of the normal developmental process and is vital to becoming healthy, 'normal' and functioning individuals in a given society. So, in the Oedipus complex Freud equates paternity with individuation and selfhood. Fathers become the only means for our entrance into society, our formation of subjectivity; consequently fathers are responsible for who we are. If we are healthy, normal, and autonomous individuals reading these words, making sense of an essay, it is due to our fathers who liberated us from dependency to the mother and led us into reality and independence. Our identities as well as our destinies are intimately tied to our fathers.

Lost maintains and recasts these patriarchal assumptions pertaining to the Oedipus complex by placing 'daddy issues' at the center of the narrative. When you look at the backstories of the characters, you see that they are filled with problematic father-child relationships. Almost every character on the show has had negative experience involving either his own father, or himself in the father role. Jack had a father who was emotionally and psychologically absent from his life; Locke had a missing father, whose rather short existence in his life inflicted a deep wound that would take a very long time to heal; Sawyer's father killed both himself and his wife, leaving young Sawyer in his own struggle for life; Hurley's father abandoned him; Kate's father molested her; Michael continually struggled to father his estranged son. Not to mention Charlie, Sun, and Jin who suffered overly oppressive and almost tyrannical fathers.

When this group boarded Oceanic Flight 815, they were flawed and fractured, facing their struggles alone. They did not know that they were actually sharing a collective problem, united by the same feelings of injury, pain, and loss. They were all 'lost', not only geographically but also emotionally and spiritually, and this 'lost-ness' experienced by everyone on the island was largely a manifestation of the inner loss resulting from both physical and symbolic absence of the father.

On the island, their quests consisted partly of learning to come to terms with their paternal deprivation, resolving the painful circumstances of their previous lives. They were physically distant from their fathers, but that did not mean they were psychologically isolated from their influence. So, life on the island was at once a return to a traumatic beginning, a chance for change and redemption rather than the start of a brand new life. It was a constant struggle for the survivors to repair their broken selves and construct a better self-image for themselves. This, of course, was also the struggle of reclaiming what has been lost: the father. For Julia Kristeva, writes Sylvie Gambaudo, with the absence of paternal authority the subject goes into a crisis, which is marked by a desire to find other paternal substitutes in order to fill the void left by the father (1101). The subject's relationship to the declining paternal function highly influences its psychic structure and identity. It creates more need and yearning in the subject for the father with the hope of repairing the fragmented self, and reaching a unified, stable, and autonomous position that only the father is capable of filling. In the case of *Lost*, many survivors' quests on the island ultimately take on a search for the lost father – the father function is sometimes taken over by external figures such as Jacob, the island's ageless protector, or the island itself, or performed in the characters' own psyches through their super-egos as representative of their own fathers. Once they find their new father, they will know who they really are. That is why this is a singular, personal quest.

Now, I would like to give some examples from the show's two most prominent characters, John Locke and Jack Shephard, in order to support my point that these characters' perceptions of the world/island and themselves are shaped by the mythic construct of the Oedipus complex. First, John Lock is the self-assured spiritual leader of the island. He is a great hunter and a figure of wisdom and knowledge among the survivors. He stands out with his exceptional faith in and bizarre communion with the island. However, contrary to his strong and confident image on the island, Locke was, as we know from the flashbacks, a man of sorrows in his past life, greatly warped and wounded by his father's absence. His father was essentially responsible for every tragedy in his life, including his kidney loss and wheelchair dependence, and the reason he was such a feeble, helpless, and pathetic figure before he came to the island.

So, what happened that miraculously turned a shy and unassertive lowly worker in a box company into an assertive and self-assured leader? The answer is the island, which offered Locke not only the fulfillment of his dream to engage in a walkabout but also the magical healing of his legs. Locke interpreted this transformative experience as explicable only through phenomena outside of the realm of science or logic. He believed that there was a divine power at work and embraced the island as the source of this power. Gradually, he developed a special bond with the island, as the island assumed the role of his missing father providing him his unmet paternal needs such as security, protection, guidance, and a greater purpose in life. Locke's past essentially provided the fuel for his willingness to embrace the island as his new father-surrogate. Dennis Balcom writes that men who experience father loss always feel as if something deeper is missing with a sense of imperfect and unfinished self. They feel "obliged to turn their attention to their absent fathers"(1101) or cling to an idealized father image in an attempt to repair their relationship with their real fathers. Locke projected his need for paternal function onto the island and this became the base of his strong, and somehow blind, faith.

As the episodes unfold, Locke's attachment to the island as a father-substitute assumes a religious dimension, as the island becomes a divine presence, a God-like figure for him. Locke believes that nothing occurs in vain, or there is no purposeless conduct. For him, every event is a part of the preordained plan determined by the God-like agency of the island. For example, in the first season, when Boone died, Locke rationalized his death as a sacrifice the island demanded so he could fulfill his destiny. His belief system, as Christian Piatt argues, "does not allow something as significant as Boone's death to be a senseless loss, or merely a consequence of careless curiosity" (1104). That is why Locke must arrive at some kind of justification for Boone's death.

Locke's unshakeable faith in the island and the ideas of fate and destiny grow out of his need for a supportive father. He believes himself to enjoy a special relationship with the island and conceives of every happening in terms of fate because he needs to repair his broken self by finding a secure ground (such as belief in a divine power or destiny) to anchor his existence. Anthony Giddens notes that "a sense of fate whether positively or negatively tinged relieves the individual of the burden of engagement with an existential situation which might otherwise be chronologically disturbing" (1102). Locke's fatalistic vision (evident in his frequent bawling, "This is my destiny. This is what I am supposed to do") becomes a way for him to cope with his father absence. When he treats matters as above and beyond his control (attributing them to fate), he relieves himself from the pain of asking existential questions. In this way, his fatalism provides him psychological security and compensation. Therefore, Locke's quest on the island, his motives and beliefs, are revealed to be a response to his father loss. What drives him is the need to reclaim his lost father-son relationship and to find meaning and purpose in life.

Just like John Locke, Jack Shepherd deals with a problematic father-son relationship and the desperation to prove his self-worth. While Locke tries to prove his self-worth through his fabricated belief that he is a special person who is supposed to do important things on the island, Jack feels a constant need for achievement and success. From the beginning, Jack's inclination to take charge, medical treatment to those who are in need, and his supreme sense of responsibility and determination marked him as the *de facto* leader of the survivors. He was everyone's hero. His later name 'shepherd' also reflects his position as the leader and the potential savior. However, Jack's leadership was not without errors. As much as he benefited the entire group, sometimes he was quite destructive, especially when he took impulsive decisions putting others' lives in danger. He was a man of strength and courage at first sight, but underneath he was anxiety-ridden and insecure. His fragmented identity constantly oscillated between the feelings and needs of success and failure, confidence and self-doubt, power and impotence and was often tormented by their continual internal battle.

I believe that Jack's dysfunctionality, his split personality, can be traced to his former father issues. His conflicted relationship with his father, Christian, can be viewed as the underlying reason behind his typical narcissistic behavior marked by his need to be admired, becoming angry and moody when criticized, and depressed by failures. In support of this conclusion, I believe that

"White Rabbit" (Episode 1.05) occupies a very special place in Jack's overall narrative. In this episode's flashback story, Jack as a boy gets involved in a school fight and as a result has to confront his father to account for his actions. In this very important scene, he stands in front of his father, very quiet and fearful to talk, getting ready to listen to whatever he is going to say. Talking over a glass of whiskey, his father, Christian, advises his son: "You don't want to be a hero, you don't want to try to save everyone, because when you fail, you just don't have what it takes." So, here Christian's remark does not seem like fatherly advice to Jack, or probably to anyone viewing the scene. As the new episodes unfold, we understand the crucial importance of this remark in Jack's psychological development. We understand that Jack's desire for constant success and achievement is a reaction to his father's early remark. He acts in opposition to his father's wish, probably driven with a desire to prove him wrong, to show him that he indeed has "what it takes." However, his motivation for achievement also implants in him a substantial fear of failure. When he fails, (as he does in saving some of the castaways on the island or saving some of his patients at the hospital) he is severely tortured by his internal world (which probably tells him "You did not try hard enough!"). Jack's first and only childhood memory that we get to see in his back story in "White Rabbit" presents the underlying motivation behind his heroic actions, and also the root cause of his unstable personality, his quick temper, obsessions, stubbornness, which is his unresolved Oedipal drama with his father.

Lost is maybe the best example of postmodern television fiction with its aesthetic style and narrative complexity: complex and cryptic storyline, shifting perspective, unresolved questions, and time-space confusion, and also with its unstable, multiple, disoriented and fragmented character portrayals. The Lost characters are subject to dramatic transformations, constantly moving around on the scale of good and evil. But, despite all its postmodernist and deconstructivist attitude, Lost is ideologically committed to the mythic/psychoanalytic importance of the father in the lives of sons and daughters. It reduces the plurality of voices and multi-dimensionality of identities to a single originator: the father.

As Luigi Zoja contends, the search for the father is more than a material one; it is "a universal psychological need" (1105). All of us want to know whose child we are because family, and in particular the father, still survives in myths (psychoanalysis being such a mythic discourse). Zoja states that "the quest for the father is an ancient and archetypal theme, which symbolically tells both society and the individual that a father is an always continuing effort that never reaches a definitive end" (1105). If the father is an expression of the patriarchal society from which he derives, then he will be a powerful force in the lives of the children as long as the society remains largely patriarchal. After acknowledging this fact, when we analyze popular media texts such as Lost and discover the mythic construct of the father embedded in character construction, it won't be a surprise at all.

Gozde Kilic graduated from Brock University with an Master of Arts in Popular Culture, and has recently finished her master thesis on the father issues in *Lost* with the title: "[Post] Oedipal Father and Subjectivity in ABC's *Lost*." She is currently in the Cultural Studies PhD program at Trent University, Canada.

The Mother Image in *Lost*

By Erin Carlyle

Island Mother
5" x 7", Mixed Media on Wood Panel

Island Mother represents the island as a mother. She has the light of the world in her bag. In her womb?

<u>Interviewer's Note:</u>

I was privileged to speak recently with Erin Carlyle about her creative work around the mother-image in LOST. Ms. Carlyle provides fascinating and unique insight into the Island as feminine progenitor. For Carlyle, the Mother in LOST is not only the source of caring love, but also creator, instigator, and logos. Her thought and the stunning imagery of her artistic vision have given me an entirely new, vividly imaginative way of considering the progression of events through the six years of the series.

—Pearson Moore
December, 2011

PM: What do you see as the most important elements of the mother theme in LOST?

EC: First off, I wanted to mention that it is interesting to do scholarly work using art instead of writing. You are able to "talk" about things in a way that you couldn't because there is no need for words. Visual art is a language that speaks directly to the heart, so using it to talk about LOST is tricky. LOST is visual, but it is also written word. My work is similar to paintings of characters in mythology. They are my interpretations of LOST. I hope you keep all of this in mind when I attempt to discuss my thoughts in an intelligible way.

There is no question that many of the characters have parent issues—mother issues. Some have been hurt by their mothers, and some were mothers who hurt. In the past a statue of the Egyptian goddess Taweret used to stand. Taweret represents fertility and childbirth. Being a mother is something that, before the survivors of 815 get to the island, is impossible. It seems that the island has taken away that gift. We do know that women could have children at one time, but after Ben kills the Dharma Initiative, this is impossible. I think this is key when thinking about the mothers on the island.

Map of the Body
12" x 12, Mixed Media on Wood Panel

Map of the Body represents the island as a mother

Claire is the first mother to be on the island in years. Later, the "others" bring in Juliet Burke to help with this, but she is unable to do anything about it. So, right from the beginning, when we see the silhouette of a pregnant Claire after the crash, motherhood is established as a key theme.

Later in Season Six the viewer comes to understand that a "mother" was the keeper of the island before Jacob. Her lies set the story in motion (or lies her mother told her). Her need for children set the story in motion. It is possible that she is a mirror of the island. Maybe the island has a need for children. The island needs someone to care for. John Locke knows this, but loses his focus. Other characters want the island's power. Her power is a loving force, but people are often confused and side tracked by greed.

PM: Several of the figures in your LOST paintings contain round spots with yellow or purple color. What is the significance of these spots?

EC: The colors are purely for aesthetics (sorry, I wish I had a profound answer), but the circles represent the circular nature of the story. One mother's life influences another, and so on. Characters repeat the past. Characters become other characters. They also represent the holes we have in our lives—the need for a mother's love. They represent the cycle of life and death.

PM: How is the mother theme related to other important themes in LOST, and how does this theme help us understand the deeper meaning of LOST?

EC: Maybe I started to answer this already. I think that the deeper meaning of LOST is that of love and understanding. The world is a messed up place. The characters of LOST all have their issues.

Mother and Her Light
9" x 11", Mixed media on Wood Panel

Mother and Her Light represents "mother" or Jacob's mother. She holds the
secrets of the island, and she will never tell. Is she a bad mother?

I think this show is very similar to Stephen King's *The Stand*. A character in this novel, Larry Underwood, needs the love of God (the father?) and the purpose of ending Randall Flagg (evil force) to find peace within himself. In LOST I think the characters need the love of a mother. That is why the writers establish the absence of motherhood in the beginning. They need the love of the mother, the island, to find peace. Sounds hokey, right?

PM: Not at all! You've indicated that the Island itself acted as a mother. In what ways do you see the Island taking actions we would associate with motherhood?

EC: I think the island is a mother. I think she holds the light of the world in her belly—her womb. She cares for the characters, and provides for them love and understanding. It is hard for some of the characters to accept this love because of the paths their lives have taken. Some of them take advantage of that love. Another indication that the island is a mother is that each of the characters went through (or could have gone through if they worked on it) a rebirth.

PM: Was the Island a mother toward everyone or only toward select individuals?

EC: To me the island is a mother to everyone. The culture I live in is centered around the idea of the father. Many cultures are. The Father is the central focus of the family. God is seen as a father. Where is the Mother? I believe in the story of LOST the Island is a mother. She holds power in her center. She holds love, and if she was allowed to, she would give freely of that love. It isn't the island who holds the secrets, the resources, the love hostage; it is the characters.

PM: Do you consider that any of the characters were aware of the Island as mother? Did any of the characters behave unconsciously toward the Island as if it were their mother?

EC: I do think that John Locke felt the power of the island's love. He was healed by it, but he couldn't keep it. He kept forgetting his purpose, and kept forgetting to feel that love. The pain of the world kept him from the love of the island. Other characters clouded his judgment, but he knew.

Wash in the Water
12" x 12, Mixed Media on Wood Panel

Wash in the Water represents the hope of motherhood on the island. The island as a mother, and the rebirth the characters experienced.

The Man in Black said Locke died confused, but I hope he found some understanding. I think the finale suggests this. Locke was looking for love, yes a father's love, but maybe even the love of a mother.

PM: Which of the characteristics of motherhood were represented among the human inhabitants of the Island?

EC: You have many types of mothers in LOST. I think some of the female characters represent archetypes in a way. Archetypes but also developed with their own flaws and personality traits. The works that I have made are illustrations of those characteristics. I didn't want to make work that was just drawings of the characters/actors. I felt that was something like fan art, and this project is about scholarly research (not that there is anything wrong with fan art.).

Claire represents youth, she is the hopeful mother. She represents the hope of the return of motherhood on the island. On the other hand, Claire, along with Danielle Rousseau, also represent the wild woman, or the wild mother. They are women who would do anything for their children. They are driven mad because they have lost their children. Kate is the surrogate mother. She loves Aaron the way that, she perceived, her mother didn't love her. Eloise Hawking represents the sacrifice. She is similar to Mother Mary, of course I mean that with all respect to the Christian Religion. She gives her son, so that the story can proceed. In a way you could say that Carmon Reyes sacrificed her son, but he did not have to die. Sun represents the relationship aspect of motherhood. Her child is the result of her love with Jin.

I think it is important to keep in mind that many of these mothers, much like every theme in LOST, are complicated. They do not just represent one idea. What I have said is a portion of what they represent. That is the beauty of LOST.

The Little Birds
8" x 9", Mixed Media on Wood Panel

The Little Birds represents the two mothers who became "wild" mothers.

PM: Danielle Rousseau and Claire Littleton were arguably the most prominent mothers in LOST. How does their extreme behavior square with a balanced presentation of motherhood?

EC: Rousseau and Claire are prime examples of the importance of motherhood in LOST. They are driven mad because their children were taken from them. Claire was told that she had to be the one to raise Aaron. I think this is not because Aaron was particularly important to the island, but because he was important to Claire's life purpose. She was destined to be his mother. The same could be said for Rousseau. When Ben took Alex from her, her life's path was altered. They could represent the power of love and the absence of love, what the absence of a mother's love can do to a woman. Not just the love of a mother to a child is important, but the giving of that love is a quit a force as well. These women are examples of what happens when love is "lost (*LOST?*)."

PM: Jacob's adoptive mother, Eloise Hawking, Sun Kwon, Diane Janssen, and Carmen Reyes were among the most important mothers in LOST. How do you evaluate their work as mothers?

EC: In answering this question, I want to focus on mother or Jacob's mother. Her role as a mother pushed the events of this story. Maybe it was her mother that set events in motion, but "mother" is an important beginning point in the story of LOST. She cares for her sons, but she chooses a favorite. Her need for the Man in Black to love her and to take her position leads Jacob to act the way he does. He becomes jealous, and that jealousy influences how he acts in the position of keeper of the island.

"Mother" is a liar. She is ruthless in her protection of the island. She doesn't seem to want to share the love of the island with the new inhabitants. *She* tells Jacob that the people who crashed on the island, the people his biological mother was with, are bad, not the island.

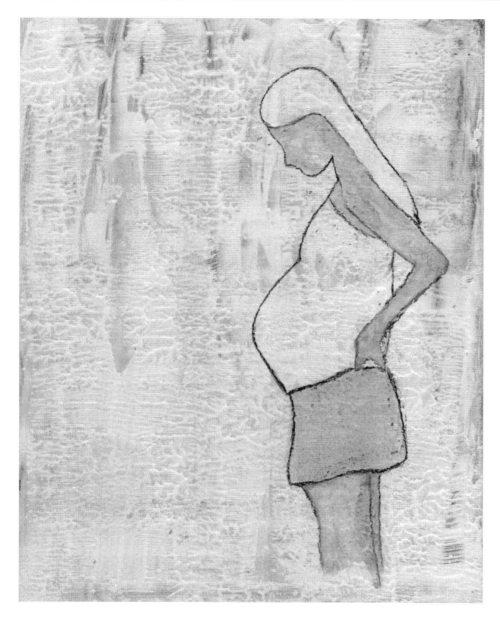

In Hope
8" x 10", Mixed Media on Wood Panel

In Hope represents the hope of Claire as the first mother on the island.

Reach
10" x 12", Mixed Media on Wood Panel

Reach represents the love aspect of motherhood. She is possibly Sun reaching into the water. She is reaching for love.

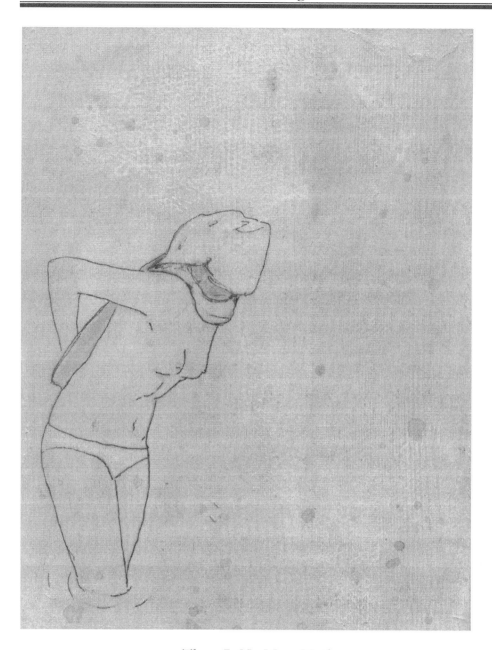

There Is No More Mother
8"x 10", Mixed Media on Wood Panel

There Is No More Mother represents the absence of motherhood on the island. The mother has been captured. The island as a mother has been captured by greed.

She is a hoarder of love. Maybe this is why Jacob runs the island the way he does. Maybe this is why he keeps people in the dark. Would Ben be different if "mother" was different? What about Charles Widmore? It is amazing that the mothers of LOST, much like in reality, change the course of their children's lives. It's amazing the complexity of this story—it's a human story.

PM: Do you include Kate Austen among the mothers of LOST?

EC: Yes, I do include Kate as a mother. She found great meaning in her life when she became Aaron's mother. She shows how motherhood is not limited to those who give birth. Jacob's Mother did not give birth to her sons, but she was a very important mother in Lost. Still, it wasn't Kate's place. It wasn't Jacob's Mother's place, and life paths were altered. People were changed. More confusion muddied the love of the island.

PM: You've mentioned the importance of Tori Amos and Margaret Atwood to your greater work around women's issues. Do you see the motherhood themes in LOST relating in any way to the work of these artists?

EC: Sure, I do think that motherhood is very important to both women. They are both influenced by being mothers. Tori Amos has been profoundly influenced by motherhood. The entire path of her career has changed since becoming a mother. Her 1998 novel *From the Choirgirl Hotel* was about her miscarriages, and her desire to become a mother. This year she released an album in which her daughter plays a central role. I feel this is an amazing full circle moment for her. Just like in LOST, she knew her purpose, and found great peace from the fulfillment of that purpose.

PM: Thank you so much for sharing your ideas with us!

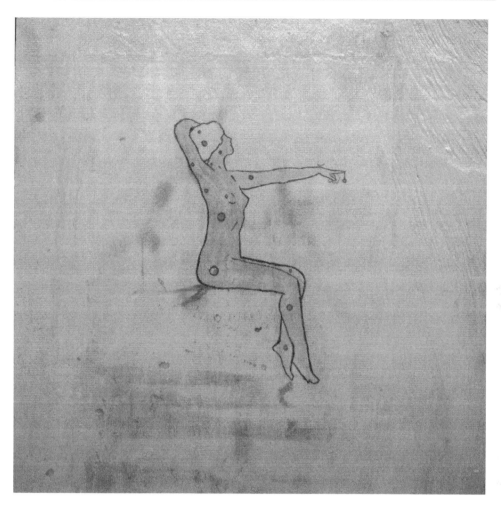

In the Distance
12" x 12", Mixed Media on Wood Panel

In the Distance represents the future in the distance. The mother characters do not know their future. They are stuck in their pasts.

Erin Carlyle is a graduate student in Gender and Women's studies at Western Kentucky University. She studied English literature and Visual Art as an undergraduate, and has shown art work regionally and nationally.

Free Will in LOST

Kevin McGinnis
Amy Bauer

"It's Never Been Easy!" A Stoic Perspective on the Personal Struggle with Free Will and Determinism in *Lost*

By Kevin McGinnis

"Jughead" by Gideon Slife
Used with permission

In one of the defining moments of the first season of *Lost*, Jack and Locke stop on their way to blow open the hatch and discuss their conflicting interpretations of what has happened to them on the island:

189

Locke: "I think that's why you and I don't see eye to eye sometimes, Jack, because you're a man of science."

Jack: "Yeah, and what does that make you?"

Locke: "Me? Well, I'm a man of faith. Do you really think all this is an accident? That we, a group of strangers, survived–many of us with just superficial injuries. Do you think we crashed on this place by coincidence? Especially this place? We were brought here for a purpose. For a reason. All of us. Each one of us was brought here for a reason."

The scene ends with Jack claiming he does not believe in destiny. "Yes you do," Lock responds. "You just don't know it yet." This exchange was the first to address head on the question of fate in *Lost*.

Others who have written about the topic of fate in *Lost* have focused on the question of whether or not fate exists within the context of the show. What is great about *Lost*, however, is not just that it raises such philosophical questions, but that it grounds them in a very human story about very compelling characters. Now that we can consider the show in its entirety, the question about fate is not whether it exists within the world of *Lost*, but how do these characters differ in their responses to the fact of fate. After all, as we now know, they really *were* brought to the island for a reason, Jack *would* come to believe in fate, and that journey to acceptance would be the driving narrative for his character. In this paper I hope to show how one's disposition towards the *fact* of fate significantly shapes the emotional state of our heroes, John Locke and Jack Shepherd, two characters whose stories exemplify the Stoic ideas about the necessity of aligning one's will with his or her destined path.

Stoicism was a school of philosophy based primarily on the writings of Zeno of Citium and Chrysippus of Soli, two philosophers who taught in Athens in the third century B.C.E. Though little known now, the Stoics were one of the most important philosophical schools of the ancient world. Their ethics especially would greatly shape Christian ideas of morality and sin as would aspects of their theology, political philosophy, and hermeneutical methods. Ethics was an especially important topic to the Stoics, but since they also taught that all things were governed by Fate, many of their contemporaries questioned the Stoics' reconciliation of moral rectitude with a belief that actions were predetermined. After all, you can either have free will and moral responsibility or you can have determinism, but you cannot have both.

The Stoics, however, disagreed. For the Stoics, the goal of life was to live in accordance with nature, which might also be understood as god's will, which established a predetermined plan for the manner in which events would pan out in the world. This plan was achieved through a nexus of external causes that led to certain necessary effects. What that left for the individual was not the ability to change what would happen, but to bring one's will into accordance with that plan—in a sense, to submit to the will of god through choosing to follow what was already ordained, or to align one's internal dispositions and judgments with the external influences that led one through life. In doing so, one gained a freedom from feelings of loss, or frustration, or anger; a freedom from pain was the goal of a life in accordance with nature.

One metaphor Stoics used to illustrate this was that of a dog tied to a cart. As the cart moves, the dog must move with it. The dog that chooses to keep pace with the cart willingly is going to be happier than the dog that resists the inevitable. Resistance only leads to frustration, pain, and confusion. Aligning one's own will with God's will, on the other hand, was the achievement of the wise and the only way to happiness.

This relationship between happiness, the will of the individual, and the path of destiny is precisely what is at issue in so many of the most emotionally charged scenes of *Lost*. This idea that happiness, will, and destiny are related helps us to better understand the struggles of some of our favorite characters. In what follows, I will apply this perspective to Locke and Jack, our man of faith and our man of science. The same insights apply to other characters as well, Charlie and Hurley especially, but not with as much significance and poignancy as with these two lead characters.

Locke, of course, is a man of faith. From the first Locke-centric episode, *Walkabout*, we learn that he believes there is something he is destined to do. In the final flashback scene of this episode we see the wheelchair-bound Locke arguing with the Australian tour guide about his ability to go on the walkabout. It is here that Locke first delivers the line perhaps most intimately connected with his character: "Don't ever tell me what I can't do, ever!" he shouts. "This is destiny. This is destiny. This is my destiny. I'm supposed to do this." This is the first time we have seen Lock lose his cool and he does so because someone is standing between him and what he thinks is his destiny. Locke may be a man of faith, but he does not know with certainty what it is he has faith in. Destiny, yes, but a destiny that will take him down what path? For Locke, that search for his true path is what defines his struggles and his frustrations. He wants to give himself up to his fate, he just does not know what his fate is, and in this instance he gets angry because he thinks someone is inhibiting him from attaining his destiny.

But Locke evinces a fundamental misunderstanding of destiny; that misunderstanding leads to his loss of emotional control, which was precisely what Stoic philosophy was meant to guard against. Since Locke did not go on the walkabout, then it clearly was *not* his destiny, and Locke, had he been trained in Stoic philosophy, would simply have accepted that turn of events stoically. In that same episode, Locke has his first encounter with the smoke monster, an encounter which seems to renew his faith in destiny and, more specifically, a destiny that has something to do with the island. Locke is unsure what he is supposed to do for the island, but his confidence in his mission is what drives him right up until his aborted suicide attempt in *The Life and Death of Jeremy Bentham* (Episode 5.07).

The most important episode for understanding both Locke and Jack in terms of their disposition towards fate is *Orientation* (Episode 2.03). As the episode begins, Locke is being held at gunpoint by Desmond and Jack mockingly asks, "Is this what you were talking about, Locke? Is this your destiny? 'All roads lead here.'"

Shortly thereafter, however, Jack and Locke are sitting down watching an orientation film and Locke seems to have a renewed sense of purpose, which leads him to believe that Desmond's work with the computer *must* continue. The computer has been damaged, though, and Desmond himself flees the Swan Station with Jack right behind him. "This isn't what was supposed to happen," Locke tells Jack. He believes he has been brought to the hatch for a reason and now the only obvious reason—to push the button—seems to have been taken away already. Locke, of course, loses it again, knocking over the tool box and screaming, perhaps to the island itself, "What am I supposed to do?"

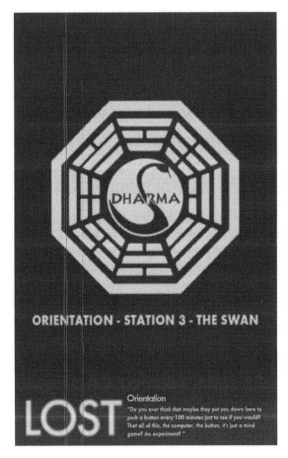

"Orientation" by Gideon Slife
Used with permission

As in his frustrating encounter with the tour guide, Locke again feels he has lost sight of his imagined destiny and has been left alone to wonder and to fear. This is paralleled in his flashback, as Locke clings to the gates of his father's estate and is only slowly coaxed to take "a leap of faith" by Helen, who assures him, "You don't have to be alone." As the episode comes to its climax with Locke asking Jack to push "Execute" on the computer, Locke confesses, "I can't do this alone, Jack. I don't want to. It's a leap of faith, Jack." His words echo Helen's as he shows himself at his most vulnerable. He needs Jack because, as he has just admitted, believing has never been easy. It is a constant struggle, but one that gives meaning to Locke's life and is something he cannot help but contend with. He is, after all, a man of faith, and to him falls the first shift, both at the computer, and at the role of leadership amongst those on the island.

Locke's newfound sense of purpose will become unraveled later in Season Two when Locke and Eko watch a different orientation video at the Pearl Station, a movie that Locke reads too much into, since he interprets the video as stating that the work of pushing the button is completely insignificant—*just* a part of a psychological experiment. Eko disagrees.

Eko: "It *is* work, John. We are being tested."
Locke: "Tested?"
Eko: "The reason to do it—push the button—is not because we are told to do so in a film."
Locke: "Well then what is the reason, Mr. Eko?"
Eko: "We do it because we believe we are meant to. Isn't that the reason you pushed it, John?"
John: "I was never meant to do anything! Every single second of my pathetic little life is as useless as that button! Do you think it's important? Do you think it's necessary? It's nothing. It's meaningless… and who are you to tell me that it's not?"

Locke is determined in his newfound nihilism to prove to Eko that the button on the computer accomplishes nothing, that pushing it only makes him a slave. In the finale of Season Two, Locke and Desmond take control of the Swan Station to prevent Eko from pushing the button. While they are there, Desmond realizes Locke is mistaken.

Desmond: "You say there isn't any purpose—there's no such thing as fate, but you saved my life, brother, so that I could save yours."
Locke: "No, no, no. None of this is real,"
Desmond: "I'm sorry for whatever happened that made you stop believing, but it's all real."

There *is* a purpose and Locke's frustration in trying to deny the existence of fate was just as strong as when he could not see where fate was taking him. In the end, however, he accepts that he was in fact wrong, that things are destined, that there is a purpose, and the rest of his time alive would be spent trying to find just what that purpose is.

Locke's confusion lasts right through to his final moments in *The Life and Death of Jeremy Bentham*. Having left the island to bring the Oceanic 6 back to the island, Locke still struggles with whom to trust and how to achieve whatever the island supposedly needs him to achieve. In his last talk with Jack in the hospital room, Locke continues to press the question of fate, but this time Jack does not go along and press the button. Instead he tells Locke, "Maybe you're just a lonely old man that crashed on an island." Locke has failed and he has been abandoned by the one person whose support and company he always felt he needed in order to achieve his destiny. He does not get angry this time, he simply gives up and tries to kill himself. With no direction and with a partial faith that could get him only so far, Locke is our failed, tragic hero.

Jack's story similarly takes him down a path in which his attitude towards fate vacillates, though in a very different way and for very different reasons. For Jack, our man of science, his frustration comes not from a lack of direction but from confirmations that fate may in fact have a role to play in his life. He wants to control everything, to be the leader, however reluctant, because he cannot help but try to shape things. We first see his frustration erupt in the caves when he is trying to save Boone from impending death in *Do No Harm* (Episode 1.20).

There is no hope for Boone. Even Sun can see that, but Jack insists that he has to amputate Boone's leg. When Sun tells him he cannot save Boone, Jack responds with Locke's line, "Don't tell me what I can't do." Boone's death is inevitable, but Jack does not want to believe that he cannot will something different to happen. The delirium Jack is exhibiting from his loss of blood is symbolic of the delirium that keeps him from seeing the truth about destiny.

As it is with Locke, so too is *Orientation* an important episode for seeing the way Jack's disposition towards fate plays such an important role in his emotional state. Throughout the episode, Jack is upset and resistant to the idea that the Swan Station and its computer could have any significance. Before they start the orientation films, Locke asks him, "Is the reason you're so upset, because he said he recognized you? Because *that* would be impossible." In that moment, Locke establishes Desmond's recognition of Jack as a possible proof for the existence of fate. To his logical mind, Jack seems to think that that really would be too much of a coincidence, although he seems to have already recognized Desmond. He does not want to admit that he recognizes him, though, because it will have to mean *something*, a notion to which Jack is adamantly resistant.

Jack interrogates Desmond while he is attempting to fix the computer. Jack is not interested in the details of Desmond's existence, though. What gets Jack worked up is when he starts asking Desmond if he really believes that it is all true, that it is all *real*. Jack does not want the computer to be significant because then there might be something even more powerful at play. Jack does not want to believe in the possibility and he abandons Locke to pursue Desmond, who had failed to fix the computer. In Jack's confrontation with Desmond in the jungle he has one of his most emotional breakdowns of the entire series. First, he seems upset because Desmond insists the computer is significant, but then, as Desmond starts to recognize him, Jack gets even more upset, to the point that it seems quite likely that he is going to kill Desmond. In the last moment, Jack gives in; he admits that he has indeed met Desmond before, and for a brief moment he allows for the possibility that there is something more going on. He returns to the Swan Station and corrects Locke on the final number that needs to be entered. Despite this, Jack still insists it is not real and he tells Sayid not to push "Execute." It is only Locke's pleading that persuades the reluctant Jack to push the button.

Jumping ahead to the end of Season Four, Jack's continued resistance and belief purely in himself is what gets him off the island. In Jack's farewell conversation with Locke at the Orchid Station, Locke asks him to stay.

Locke: "You're not supposed to go home."
Jack: "Then what am I supposed to do?! Oh I think I remember. What was it that you said on the way out to the hatch? That crashing here was our destiny."
Locke: "You know, Jack. You know that you're here for a reason. You know it. And if you leave this place, that knowledge is going to eat you alive from the inside out until you decide to come back."

Jack is worked up into another mini-frenzy here, but, as Locke predicts, it is nothing compared to the whirlwind of despair that claims Jack back in Los Angeles. Off island, Jack does exactly what Locke tells him to do—lie—lie to them like he lies to himself. But under the weight of those lies Jack turns to alcohol and drugs to smother his unhappiness, because he has in fact come to believe that he must return to the island—he can no longer live with the lies he has been telling himself. The only way out of his destructive path is to return to the island, to accept to his destiny, and to pursue it faithfully.

Jack's process of conversion starts with his belief that he is supposed to return to the island, but it is not a smooth ride. He *will* be convinced. After all, as Ben points out in telling him the story of Thomas the Apostle in *316* (Episode 5.06), "We're all convinced sooner or later." For Jack, the "later" does not come until the penultimate episode of the show, however. At this point, Jack still does not know how to accept fate, or how to align his own will with that of the island. In *Whatever Happened Happened* (Episode 5.11), Jack refuses to perform surgery on the young Ben. He tells Kate "When we were here before I spent all of my time trying to fix things. Did you ever think that maybe the island just wants to fix things itself? That maybe I was just getting in the way?" Jack thinks that he can passively put himself in the flow of destiny and things will just work themselves out. He does not know how to reconcile his old way of trying to control everything with his acceptance that things may be somehow predetermined. He is no longer angry, but he is no longer driven, no longer our hero. He seems weak, in some ways even weaker than when he was off island.

When Jack does perk up again, it is because Faraday, the *ultimate* man of science on the island, is convinced that he has found a way to cheat fate. In *The Variable* (Episode 5.14), Faraday tells Jack, "I've studied relativistic physics my entire life. One thing emerged over and over – you can't change the past. You can't do it. Whatever happened happened, right? But then I finally realized I had been spending so much time focused on the constants that I forgot about the variables!" Jack looks up at him, sitting at his feet like a good disciple, and when Faraday says, "We can change our destiny!" Jack looks hopeful, just moments after looking befuddled. Here is someone who knows more about science than Jack does, and he is explaining that fate can be beaten. Despite everything that Jack had gone through to return to the island, he still finds greater comfort trying to deny his destiny, and when Faraday dies he is determined to follow through with his plans even though, as Kate tells Eloise, he does not know what he is talking about, he only thinks he does.

"Daniel Faraday" by ArtGUS
Used with permission

Jack's final conversion experience begins at the temple when Hurley tells him that Jacob said that Jack "has what it takes." Jack, of course, knows what this means, much more so than Hurley does, and he asks to be taken to see Jacob at the

Lighthouse. Once there, Jack starts to believe things really *have* been set in motion by forces beyond his control. The realization does not come easily. Jack wants answers—he wants to know *why* Jacob had been watching him and in his frustration he destroys the mirrors of the Lighthouse. But then afterwards, he sits alone and quietly looks out to the sea piecing things together in his head—another process that Jacob sets into place because he knows what Jack needs to do in order to align his will with that of his destiny. Much like the Apollo bar that got stuck in the machine and just needed a push from Jacob, Jack too is moving through the machinelike motions of destiny, but still requires a little push. For Jack to take the last step in his conversion process, he still needs proof. That proof comes two episodes later in *Dr. Linus* (Episode 6.07) as Jack sits in the Black Rock with a lit dynamite stick between him and Richard Alpert. If he is right in his newfound beliefs, the dynamite cannot kill him. And if he is wrong, well, at least his journey will be over. In those final seconds Jack closes his eyes. He believes he will be okay, but he has found peace either way and, when the fuse blows out on its own, Jack exhales the breath he has been holding and gives one of his most jovial smiles of the entire series. Jack's a believer now. Jack is finally the hero the island needed.

This fact is given Jacob's seal of approval in *What They Died For* (Episode 6.16). Jacob explains to the remaining candidates that he brought them to the island to find a replacement for himself. Jacob tells them that he is going to give them what he was never given—a choice—but that if none of them choose it, it will all end very badly.

Jack: "I'll do it. This is why I'm here. This is what I'm supposed to do."
Jacob: "Is that a question, Jack?"
Jack: "No."
Jacob: "Good."

Jack might not know what exactly lies before him, but he sees that he is on a path, that he has a purpose, and it is one he has chosen freely. For the first time in the show, Jack seems to be at peace, and it is a peace that sustains him in his final battle with the Smoke Monster, it sustains him as he transfers the care of the island to Hurley, and it sustains him as he lies down among the bamboo and dies with Vincent at his side.

The philosophical question of how we are to reconcile free will with determinism is an interesting one, but it is one that is without meaning when disconnected from the experiences of real people. Among the many things that *Lost* has left us with is a beautiful story of fascinating, well-crafted characters who give life to what would otherwise be rather empty philosophical musings. The Stoics knew that the question of fate was not just an academic one, but one that had implications for the individual in terms of morality, happiness, and a sense of purpose. As I hope I have shown in this paper, the question of the relationship between one's happiness and the extent to which one has conformed to their destined path is a central theme in *Lost*, one that our lead characters struggle with throughout the show, and that gives shape and meaning to some of *Lost's* most moving scenes. In the mystery of the early seasons it was easy to be captured by the story as a whole, to argue about whether or not our heroes really did have free will, but perhaps the questions we should have been asking are the far more personal ones of why these characters are so unhappy and what might we learn from their examples.

Kevin McGinnis is a doctoral candidate in Religious Studies at Claremont Graduate University, where he has focused on the social history of early Christianity. He is currently a visiting instructor at the University of the Pacific in Stockton, CA, where he teaches on method and theory in the study of religion, early Christian history, and religious violence.

"So much for fate": Free Will and Narrative Closure in *Lost*

By Amy Bauer, Ph.D.

"Live Together, Die Alone" by Gideon Slife
Used with permission.

<u>Editor's Note</u>: *This essay was written in 2007, at the end of Season Three. However, time has affected the piercing relevance of neither Dr. Bauer's insightful discussion, nor her astute conclusions.*

From its inaugural episode, when Charlie wrote the word "fate" on his fingers, the spiraling narrative of *Lost* has turned on the issue of free will versus fate. During the course of Season One, Locke and Michael profess a belief in destiny, while other characters debate whether fate or happenstance led them to the island. Desmond, Anna-Lucia, Eko and Ben Linus join this discussion in Season Two. In Season Three Juliet and Ben address the question of free will, while the mysterious Mrs. Hawking appears as if an agent of fate personified, sent to ensure that Desmond remain on his pre-determined path.

This ongoing debate is signified by a symbol or action that—although woven into the larger narrative—holds particular significance for each of the first three seasons. These iconic signs or events appear time and again, their constant repetition at odds with the forward movement of plot and character development. In Season One tragedy and doom attach to "the numbers." In the second season several characters confront "pushing the button," the abstract, law-like requirement that they input the number sequence into the Swan hatch computer every 108 minutes to avoid certain catastrophe. These events are clearly distinguished from other narrative conflicts. For instance, discrete flashbacks relate actions taken in the past to those occurring in the island's present. Didactic morality tales of community life follow individual narrative arcs that move the larger plot forward. But each time the characters encounter the numbers or push the button, they reach an impasse, and are returned—figuratively and often literally—to the place from which they began.

In Season Three the ethical dimension of free will versus fate becomes explicit when Desmond reveals a precognitive insight to upcoming events: flashes of a future that include Charlie's death. Desmond's flashes complete a trifecta that began in Season One with the numbers and continued in Season Two with the button. As part of an escalating series of events that pit individual characters against fate, (the ultimate big Other), repeated glimpses of Charlie's demise assert the traumatic collision between fate and free will in its literal fullness. No matter how many times Desmond saves Charlie in *Lost*'s reality, Charlie's death will return like clockwork in the form of visions that predict the character's every move and moral choice. I will first analyze the numbers, the button, and Desmond's visions as they embody the conflict of predestination vs. free will through *Lost*'s first three seasons. I close with a discussion of Charlie's death as a summation of this theme, with implications for the new format of *Lost* in Seasons Four through Six.

Season One: The Numbers

The sequence 4-8-15-16-23-42 was officially introduced to us as a series in Episode 18 of Season One, *Numbers*, but each separate number – as well as 108, the series' sum - appeared as so-called "Easter eggs" throughout the season, as catalogued exhaustively, and assigned portents from the mundane to the cosmic, on fan sites such as "The *Lost* Numbers" and "Sledgeweb's *Lost* stuff."(1401)

Numbers in themselves, of course, resist semantic reinterpretation. But the ubiquity of individual numbers confounds our understanding of them as simple icons that order or quantify. The appearance of the entire series in diegetic locations that range from a radio broadcast to the shirts of a girls' soccer team further resists interpretation on the conventional level, and encourages us to invest them with an extra-nominal significance.

The *Lost* numbers refer to a long-standing narrative tradition in sci-fi and fantasy literature cited earlier by executive producer J.J. Abrams, when he incorporated the number 47 as a recurring symbol in the fantasy spy series *Alias*.(1402) Here specific numbers serve a dual function, as icons of conspiracy that link disparate events by association. But *Lost*'s numbers serve a different rhetorical function; more than mere signs, their connection to pivotal events suggests a veiled agency. In series they seem to advance or thwart not only the plans of individual characters, but – as revealed in the 2006 online game The *Lost* Experience – to control the fate of the world as we know it.(1403)

Like a virus passed on from one plot thread to another, the numbers move from background to foreground, from Hurley's flashback in "The Numbers" to other characters and situations, traversing decades and continents.(1404) They penetrate the realm of the public and private without distinction, as abstract entities located nowhere in particular, yet embodied everywhere in hatch inscriptions, connect four games, and lottery tickets. Until the producers assign a definitive interpretation within the textual frame of the show, the numbers remain opaque, with each viewer free to assign them provisional and contradictory meanings.

As portents of indeterminate value that may bode good or ill, their mimetic reproduction throughout the series pulsates with a sense of the uncanny. As symptoms of a repressed trauma more shocking than the plane crash itself, the numbers function as proxies for the mysterious workings of fate. Their irruption into the narrative is a subtle reminder that *Lost*'s central trauma is not the plane crash that began the series; of more importance is each character's confrontation with that fate, as well as Fate with a capital F. The juxtaposition of flashbacks with island narratives in Seasons One through Three underlines this theme, in a complex dance between characters as they once were and as they exist in the show's present.

Despite their mystery, the diegetic introduction of the numbers follows a progressive pattern: first broadcast over the air, the numbers drew Danielle Rousseau's crew to a disastrous fate, and "infected" Sam Toomey and his friend Lenny with their suggestive power. Lenny was institutionalized and spends his days vocalizing the numbers, which "spread" to Hurley, who serendipitously plays them to win the lottery.

The utter contingency of the numbers indirectly expresses the trauma of blind fate. Yet as a symptom they are addressed to the "other supposed to know." Hence Hurley's vigorous pursuit of Sam Toomey and Danielle, when he discovers that the very numbers that brought him both immense wealth and untold disaster led them to similar fates. But no one in *Lost* can interpret the numbers for Hurley, leaving the viewer to assume the position of analyst. We might note that, left alone, the number are but inert symbols, whose semblance of order tempts the unwary. The numbers have agency only when performed, broadcast over the air, used to win contests, or typed into a computer every 108 minutes. Thrown into the world like dice at a craps table, they return the user's message in an inverted form: to call lady luck invites good as well as bad. Sam, Hurley and Danielle don't yet know who programmed the numbers into the radio beacon, or who inscribed them on the hatch. But each made a choice to heed the numbers, and each became obsessed with their link to unforeseen catastrophe.

Season Two: "Pushing the Button"

In the premier episode of Season Two we meet Desmond, who is all too acquainted with the numbers.(1405) Desmond does not hear them, say them, or write them, but types 4-8-15-16-23-42 thirteen or fourteen times a day, every day, for nigh on four years. Like the sweepstakes winners, Desmond performs the numbers, towards an explicit if mysterious, end. And just as the numbers brought both good fortune and calumny to Sam and Hurley, so their import is paradoxical: the Swan Station numbers both count down to disaster and simultaneously prevent it. Desmond's success at pushing the button is signified only by the ghostly replication of the numbers in yet another form, as a countdown timer that resets with their sum, 108.

But unlike Hurley and Sam, Desmond does not encounter the numbers by chance; his performance represents Kant's classic ethical dilemma of the forced choice. Desmond appears to have little free will in the matter; not performing the numbers would result not only in suicide but mass murder. During the course of Season Two many fans wondered, why not build a completely mechanical fail-safe? Why must any character make the decision day in and day out whether or not to push the button?

When *Lost* began, the debate between free will and determinism grew naturally out of the characters' reactions to the plane crash; later we find that the characters felt connected to fate before they arrived. Season Two brought this theme to a sharp focus in the Swan station when the "hatch monkeys," a chosen few who represent the community as a whole, pushed the button every 108 minutes. In the classic paradox of the forced choice, one of the alternatives is always choice itself, for life and the world create the very condition of freedom. The button paradox leaves no room for free will, a choice through which Desmond, Locke, Eko or Jack could assert his subjectivity. John's fateful choice at the end of Season Two to not push the button, and to prevent anyone else from doing so was less an act of freedom than an hysterical outburst directed towards the force he feared was really in control, pulling the strings behind the castaway's fate. In contrast to Desmond, Locke's fantasy projects the island as big Other, a master constantly testing his servants with inscrutable demands which it is their burden to decipher.

The Scottish sailor faces a forced choice of a different kind when, following Locke's rash action, he employs the mysterious fail-safe key left for extreme emergencies. With only the barest hint of what might result, Desmond – to paraphrase his late partner Kelvin – takes his finger out of the dam and blows the whole thing up.(1406) To save the island – perhaps the world - from destruction he must, theoretically at least, destroy the island, with no idea if the cure is worse than the disease. Desmond faces terror at its most pure: the only way to prevent unthinkable destruction is to cause unthinkable destruction, to show fealty to his cause and sacrifice the island to the island.

The violent implosion of the hatch was the outward sign of a narrative turn away from the Dharma station toward a greater mystery. But it also indicated a character shift for Desmond, the perennial outsider. In the terms of Lacanian psychoanalysis, Desmond's choice to turn the key was an act, a truly free choice devoid of Kant's pathological necessity. Lacan called suicide the only successful act, but here suicide represents the death of the subject as a symbolic entity: that is, the death of the subject represents everything that defined his or her place in the symbolic order. Although saved from literal death, Desmond's internal change – and his new role in the *Lost* community – is externalized as he both travels back in time and experiences flashes of the future. The course of Season Three played out the full implications of that choice by forcing Desmond to continually repeat it, in a more intimate and ambiguous form.

Season Three: Charlie's Choice

Desmond and Charlie's parallel trajectories in Season Three played out the two logics of suicide, the two paths to the act as the Kantian definition of free will. In the third and fourth episodes of Season Three we suspect that Desmond might have precognitive abilities. These abilities and more are revealed in Episode 3.08, *Flashes Before Your Eyes*, where Desmond's ethical quandary is laid out in full. Fate – the big Other if ever there was one – has apparently set him on a preordained path, yet cruelly reversed that path for the sole purpose of offering the classic forced choice.

Desmond's quandary is straight out of the *Critique of Practical Reason*, where Kant suggested that no reasonable man would forfeit his life for a night with the woman of his dreams.(1407) The stakes are even higher in "Flashes," where Desmond is asked to give up a life with his beloved Penny in 1996 order to save the world eight years hence; the story's nods to the Odyssey along with the presence of the eerily omniscient Mrs. Hawking put Desmond in the role of a tragic Greek hero.(1408) As a truly ethical subject Desmond would not cede his desire: he would marry Penny, and to hell with fate. But to choose his fiancée over the world would be monstrous, a betrayal of his humanity, and so Desmond sacrifices the girl for the world.

Desmond's sacrifice follows the first logic of suicide, the sacrifice of one's life, or something of great value, (here Penny's love), so that another may live or thrive. But Mrs. Hawking's proposal is only the first (in one temporal stream) of a series of choices forced on Desmond by his horrific foreknowledge. As always with the logic of sacrifice, fate is a sadistic master, and will always come out the victor. Desmond's flashes compel him to choose between the girl or his comrade's life more than once: repeated visions imply that he may either save Charlie or reunite with Penny. Thus Desmond sacrifices love for honor over and over again, each time losing Penny to give Charlie a few more days of life. The only way to escape the sadism of fate is to choose the second logic of suicide: to deny fate its formal victory by commiting an act with no purpose in the eyes of the big Other. This brings us to Charlie's choice, the defining act that closed Season Three and set *Lost* on an entirely new narrative course.(1409)

Charlie's act followed yet another of Desmond's visions of his demise, but one with a rider attached: that his newfound family Aaron and Claire will be rescued by helicopter. With this development the logic of sacrifice shifts agents from Desmond to Charlie, who immediately rises to the challenge, even as Desmond attempts once again to intervene. In *Through the Looking Glass* (Episode 3.22), Charlie follows Desmond's vision to the letter. He finds that – as a musician who knows the melody of an old Beach Boys song – fate seems to have chosen him alone to break the code that will alert the outside world to their predicament, theoretically rescuing not only Claire and Aaron, but saving the castaways from death or incarceration at the hand of the others. Everything that happens, in fact, is as Desmond predicted until he flicks the switch that would allow contact with the outside world.

Two events happen at this point that reveal cracks in the big Other, that show fate to be nothing but a bit player on the *Lost* stage. The first is the flipping of the switch, whereupon Charlie is supposed to drown. He is delighted instead to receive an incoming video transmission from none other than Penelope herself. The second event occurs when Charlie asks Penelope about Naomi, the parachutist who claimed to represent Penny's rescue operation. Here Charlie surmises that the castaways have been duped: Naomi's party has no affiliation with Penny, and may prove more dangerous than either the island or the Ben Linus-led others. Desmond's vision of Charlie's death, and Claire's rescue seems to have no more predictive power: both Charlie and Desmond have been absolved of their duty to fate. Yet when Charlie finally dies it is not because he has succumbed to fate, but because he has embraced it. He consciously decides to warn Desmond about Naomi and to peacefully accept death by drowning, an end that – as many fans pointed out – he could have escaped. At the moment of death Charlie realizes the Other – his predetermined fate – doesn't exist. His choice is thus an ethical act of pure freedom, done not **for** but despite the Other. Charlie's role in the prewritten drama complete, he improvises a final act, choosing death not because he must but as a gift to his colleagues and friends; in accepting physical death he achieves "spiritual" rebirth, one of the few characters in *Lost* to achieve full subjectivity.

Charlie's act reveals the purpose behind the mantra "free will vs. fate" that ran throughout the first three seasons of *Lost*: only at the moment when a character accedes to the demands of fate does he realize his true freedom. Charlie's sacrifice was the culmination of three seasons in which characters were forced to confront a series of forced choices or tempt fate. It thus marks the tipping point when *Lost*'s narrative turned upside down, and began flashing forward to an ominous, uncertain future, instead of a static, preordained past. Charlie's "fate" strongly suggests that only when the remaining characters accept the contingency of the plane crash as destiny, will *Lost* resolve its founding trauma and achieve emotional, ethical and narrative closure.

Dr. Amy Bauer is Assistant Professor of Music at the Claire Trevor School of the Arts, University of California, Irvine.

Multi-Dimensionality in LOST

Jeffrey Frame
Sarah Clarke Stuart
Amy Bauer
C. David Milles

"Flashes Before Your Eyes": Augustine, Four-Dimensionalism, and the "Time-Grace" Continuum

by Jeffrey D. Frame

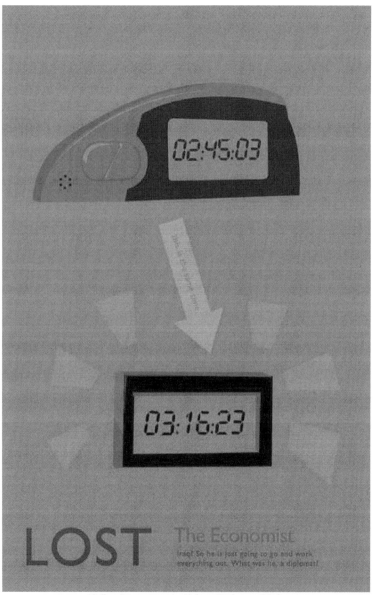

"The Economist" by Gideon Slife
Used with permission.

When the final episode of the hit television phenomenon *LOST* aired on March 23, 2010, the mood in the living rooms of 13.5 million viewers was expectant and pin-drop tense. ABC had experienced its best non-Oscar Sunday night ratings in more than two years, with an upsurge of two million more viewers than the sixth-season average (1502). Although the series premiere in 2004 boasted 18.5 million viewers, *LOST*'s menagerie of characters, mythologies, themes, and inventive threads had found staying power over the span of the series and, with them, so did the core of the show's fandom.

Even so, like the rollercoaster of narrative frustration and fulfillment experienced by the show's spoilerholics, spoilerphobes, fringe fans, and "the faithful" during the five years leading up to *LOST*'s final season, the overall fan base response to the series finale—"The End"—was predictably mixed. Some fans complained that the conflation of mythologies in the series badly dampened the narrative and its themes to the very end, while others readily and good-naturedly invested their faith in the imperfect, debatable riddles of Abrams' "magic box," one of his early metaphors for the island (1512). Throughout the discussion of *LOST*'s most highly trafficked unofficial and "official" websites—most notably "The Fuselage"—viewer responses landed along what was already a familiar continuum of heightened emotional and intellectual reactions to the series. At one extreme, viewers seemed to experience the vexation, anger, and perceived waste of time due to unanswered mysteries about the island accumulating every season (despite other mysteries being unraveled in carefully metered amounts by the "*LOST* Labs").

At the other extreme, viewers responded with exuberance at the seemingly sublime and fitting homecoming shared by the show's most beloved characters in what was revealed in the series finale by Jack Shephard's father, Christian, to be a kind of afterlife (or "bardo," as Nikki Stafford has rightly urged) where nearly each one in that strongly connected community of survivors could find one another again on his or her way to the next part of the journey. Here, the nomenclature for Season Six— particularly the misnomer of the "flash sideways"—only seemed to exacerbate the confusion among viewers who had already been led by the writers and by ABC to believe that the term "flash sideways" meant an "alternate universe" (as if these flashes might represent a parallel universe like the ones in Fringe).

On the other hand, referring to the narrative leaps of the sixth season more accurately as "flashupwards" might have been too easy. In the end, none of us seems to have been able to find that "easy button" from Staples® for the text of *LOST*. Viewers have sought closure to the protracted, puzzling, and emotional odyssey of *LOST*, closure that would satisfy in many directions; but, depending upon his or her particular "reading" formations—or lenses—with which a viewer watched and interpreted the *LOST* narrative, one's belief in the story and in the high concept of the show was either broadly authenticated or ultimately (even fiercely) blighted. Many of those in the academy who have followed *LOST* closely continue to find themselves talking about viewers of the season finale mostly in terms of a division between two primary opposing forces: a dissatisfied audience who felt the show to be character-driven, and dissatisfied viewers who considered the show to be mythology-driven. In their textual approach to reader-response theory, Russell A. Hunt and Douglas Vipond use the terms "story-driven readings" and "information-driven readings" to describe such dichotomies. They use a third term, however, to describe yet another category of textual transaction: readings that are "point-driven" (1506), meaning a story driven by its theme, gist, thesis, or overarching objective. It is this third category I'd like to focus on briefly in order to consider how *LOST* (particularly through its nonlinear narrative) might be less confusing to us if we were to understand it, in the end, as a television show that invites a point-driven reading.

Undoubtedly, one of the most widely debated ways in which the narrative of *LOST* has created (or confounded) meaning for its viewers is the nonlinear aspect of its discourse. As early as the first season, largely dissatisfied fans began grappling with the increasingly intricate flashback structure that governed each episode. One online poster by the name "Coca Lite," for example, created a thread board on *LOST*'s section of the *Television Without Pity* website entitled, "Lost Is Its Own Monster: The Bitterness Fiesta"—designed as "a refuge for my fellow disappointed viewers"—and initially commented that the show's apparent "decline in quality" early in the first season could be attributed, in part, to an "over-reliance on flashback as a way to drag out the A-story to daytime-TV-level slooowwwness [sic]."

Employing a more optimistic, "doubter-be-damned" approach, popular *LOST* writers like *Entertainment Weekly* columnist Jeff "Doc" Jensen devoted considerable attention to puzzling through popular discourse issues in the show on behalf of viewers throughout the run. In "Time Passages," his column spotlighted the widely-discussed, Desmond-centric, time-traveling episode, "Flashes Before Your Eyes"; in his article, "A Map of Lost," Jensen grilled Darlton about the end of Season Three, the "rattlesnake in the mailbox," and the discourse structure of remaining episodes; and, in another article, he closely reads the "Ji Yeon" episode in Season Four, which crosscuts between a flashback and a flashforward, each focusing on Sun and Jin. Over the course of the series, in addition to bloggers, posters, and the media, even the scholarly response to the unique challenges of *LOST*'s narrative and its renegade discourse has been strong, weighing in more and more regularly about how *LOST*'s experiment with story time and discourse time has emerged as one of the defining hermeneutics for the show. As early as Lavery and Porter's *Unlocking the Meaning of LOST*, the prominence of the show's narrative time and of its effect on character development, plot points, and thematic revelations has found its way into the discussion. Since then, the conversation has mushroomed with key contributions coming from voices such as Jason Mittell, Mark Dolan, and others, all demonstrating in some way how *LOST*'s unprecedented explorations in serial narrativity and discourse time have changed the strategies with which viewers unpack a televised text.

As Erika Johnson-Lewis describes *LOST* (in formalist terms) "The sjuzet [the order of events as delivered or presented to the viewer] deliberately impedes the ability of the audience to follow the fabula [the unfolding of events as experienced by characters in the world of the story]" in *LOST* (1510). Johnson-Lewis also points to Roberta Pearson's helpful essay "Chain of Events" in which she suggests that the wrestling between Darlton's apparent desire to achieve a character-centered show (or, what Hunt and Vipond would call a story-driven reading of the show) and many of the viewers' apparent desire to disentangle what they experience as a mythology-based text (or, an information- driven reading—again, Hunt and Vipond's terms) help to create the very tension that was largely responsible for the show's sustained success as well as the extraordinary conflict equally responsible for the tempestuous disparity in viewer responses after the series finale (1514).

Yet, arguably, the most useful means of understanding *LOST*'s narrative voyage is located in neither the story-driven [character-centric] vision of the show runners nor in the information-driven [mythology-centric] assumptions of the audience, but rather in the point-driven [theme-centric] aftereffect of the *LOST* text as a whole. Using a textual (rather than industrial) approach to better understand the thematic implications of the narrative discourse of *LOST*, I propose that we look to the confessions of the Christian philosopher Augustine of Hippo regarding time and eternity for a strong point-driven lens through which to interpret the uses of time in *LOST*. It's a context that moves us in the direction of four-dimensionalism and McTaggart's relational, B-theory of time as well—a context which, in the various iterations of time in the *LOST*verse, I regard as a sort of "time-grace" continuum for many of *LOST*'s characters.

In the Augustinian tradition, God, as such, exists in eternity, which is perpetually in the present, and outside of the dimension we know as chronological temporality, which Faulkner's Quentin Compson describes as the kind of time "clicked off by [the] little wheels" of clocks (1503). In Chapter 10 of his *Confessions*, Augustine argues that God's "vision of occurrences in time is not temporally conditioned [not affected by time]" (1501) and asks, "What times existed which were not brought into being by you? [. . .] you are the cause of all times [. . .]. You have made time itself. Time could not elapse before you made time. [. . .] Your 'years' neither go nor come. Ours come and go so that all may come in succession. All your 'years' subsist in simultaneity, because they do not change" (1501). Most importantly, Augustine asserts that "In the eternal, nothing is transient, but the whole is present. But no time is fully present. It will see that all past time is driven backwards by the future, and all future time is the consequent of the past, and all past and future are created and set on their course by that which is always present." In her book *The Fire in the Equations*, Kitty Ferguson highlights these Augustinian musings as a list of questions:

> What would it be like if events were not ordered in chronological time? If God knows everything in the universe that ever has happened and ever will happen [. . .], in what way would that affect God's power to affect the universe? What meaning could cause and effect have in such a setting? What would happen to 'predictability'? Where events are not filed chronologically, is there some other sort of filing system? (1504)

By considering an Augustinian perspective, we receive important clues into the behavior of the narrative discourse in *LOST*. From an ontological perspective, this conversation looks a lot like "four-dimensionalism" which is, as Theodore Sider explains it, a doctrine of temporal parts and a picture of persistence over time (1516). In four-dimensionalism, a person is comprised not only of spatial parts (head, feet, kidney, heart, and so forth), but also of temporal parts (infancy, adolescence, middle age, old age). And just as spatial parts can be larger or smaller (head, mouth, lips, skin cells), so temporal parts can be larger or smaller (adolescence, a year in the life of, a day, or one life-changing minute).

No other television text seems quite to have captured this concept of four-dimensionalism or Augustine's perspective on eternal time as ambitiously as *LOST* has done. The recent Terence Malick film *The Tree of Life* nobly attempts to do some of these same things with a four-dimensionalist ontology, or with a God-like view outside of time, in order to look at the temporal parts of one man's life and, from that, suggest the whole, or the persistence of time throughout that life, thus giving the life meaning. Likewise, *LOST* has become serendipitously and uniquely positioned to suggest the meaning of a life by looking at the sum of a life, or—in the case of our multiple island survivors—the individual meanings of their lives via the sums of the temporal parts of their lives as they are delivered to us nonlinearly. *LOST* accomplishes this feat in at least three ways which can be roughly matched with seasonal groupings.

Seasons One through–Three are etiological (related to cause and effect) in that they concentrate–primarily on the non-diegetic (occurring outside the story-world) causes and effects between backstory and the "island present." Part of the reason for this was industrial, to the extent that Darlton are said to have waited until they knew that the show would be able to continue after Season Three before beginning to play with time the way that they do in the second half of the series.

Needless to say, the first three seasons firmly establish–a cause-and-effect modus operandi, which allowed the show runners to set the audience up for an interruption in that routine. Seasons Four and Five, then, become prominently teleological (rooted in motivation and rationale) in that the attention of the text shifts to flashforwards and time travel, both of which demonstrate ways in which the core characters question their respective purposes in life. In the final season, narrative priority shifts again, this time to an eschatological (last or final matters) dimension in which many of the same core characters question their respective purposes in death. And in the series-long process of these transformations from an etiological text to a teleological text and finally to an eschatological text, we discover how time becomes an Augustinian means of grace for these characters, taking on a newfound point-driven importance as viewers compare and piece together the smaller temporal parts of character s' lives—the "flashes before their eyes"—in order to arrive at the sum of those changes—a fuller understanding of personhood in the persistence of time.

As an example of the etiological movement of the first three seasons, we could look to almost any episode. Each of them is predicated on the narrative strategy of backstory entangled with "present" island time. Some would argue that this approach isn't nonlinear at all, but rather a traditional use of narrative flashbacks. I'd assert that nonlinearity must include, by definition, what Gerard Genette refers to as "syllepsis" or "the fact of taking together [. . .] anachronic groupings governed by one or another kinship" (1504); in other words, "[a] group of situations and events governed by a nonchronological principle rather than by a chronological one" (1515).

Since *LOST*'s episodes in its first three seasons are governed by the kinship or nonchronological principle of backstory, intercut with scenes from the present, then syllepsis occurs, and the resulting nonlinearity can be said to serve as the critical formula for *LOST*'s narrative discourse in those episodes. This nonlinear formula allows viewers to measure character motivation (the past, or the "why?") against character intention (the future, or the "what for?). In the process of glimpsing the temporal parts of the lives of Jack, Kate, Sawyer, Locke, Hurley, Sayid and the rest of them through various nonlinear flashbacks set against the temporal parts of the present, we can draw conclusions about what personhood gradually means to each of these characters and how Augustinian time allows them to discover the meaning of grace through growth, change, and, eventually, substitutionary sacrifice.

In the teleological phase of the series (Seasons Four and Five), a beautiful example of the narrative "time-grace" continuum can be seen in the heart-wrenching episode called "Ji Yeon," which focuses on the incongruity of Jin's life working for Sun's father in the past and the absence of Jin during the future birth of his daughter. The conceit of the episode, of course, is that the audience has been set up to believe that Jin's purchase of the stuffed panda and his rush to the hospital is in the future, just as the flashforwards of Sun going into labor are in the future.

Upon the audience's discovery at the end of the episode about what they've just been witnessing, "there's not a dry eye in the house." More importantly, this brilliant, narrative playfulness with what has come before, what is simultaneously happening on the island and on the freighter Kahana, and what will come after, provides another glimpse of the "telos" or original seed—purpose for Jin's life, which is, essentially, "to be a good father." The temporal parts of Jin here include his subservient days to Sun's failed father, his desire to consider baby names with Sun in their togetherness on the island, and the result of Jin's imminent sacrifice on the Kahana for Sun and his daughter, as intimated by his eventual absence.

Craig Keen, professor of systematic theology at Azusa Pacific University, suggests that if a "purpose" is a telos, an end that is already present in seed form, then "martyrdom" is an eschatos, signifying a certain end—an end that has been prepared for, but is not initially an aim or goal, per se. Whereas the root of "teleology" signifies "to complete the circle," the root of "eschatology" actually signifies "outside." Applied to *LOST*, we learn that Season Six is primarily eschatological as it deals with the "certain ends" of lives "outside" of the seed-based or circle-completion plan—an end that may even result in martyrdom. The first clear hint of this new collection of temporal parts in Season Six comes as early as the sacrifice of Charlie at the end of Season Three. One of the many episodes from the final season that fully articulated this final phase of the time-grace continuum is

"Dr. Linus" in which we see Ben in the present finally expressing remorse for choosing the island over his daughter Alex, while we also see scenes of high school teacher Ben in his afterlife state, choosing to make personal sacrifices for his star pupil Alex. As Ilana forgives Ben on the island for killing Jacob, and as Ben voluntarily sacrificed his own goals for the well-being of Alex in his afterlife, we are shown how his life's temporal parts and his "certain end outside" of the church, reveal a newfound, overarching grace in his growth into full personhood over time and even into non-time.

In the director's commentary of his little-known nonlinear movie, *Eye of God*, Tim Blake Nelson tries to explain his choice for using nonlinearity to shape the discourse of the film:

> Now the reason for the film using time as it does in terms of showing scenes, [. . .] out of sequence with one another is not simply to create mystery around the story of Ainsley's death, or even why it happened, but to look at time in a way which is more divine than human. And the premise would be that if God is eternal, then God would not see time as we humans do—in chronological order—because we have finite lives. God might see events as they relate thematically or spiritually instead of seeing events as they relate chronologically. And so events and scenes in this movie are connected to one another editorially in ways that I hope are deeper than we experience events as human beings, one after another. And that's the reason for the way the film uses time—to find a deeper way that the events described in the movie relate to one another.

Whether by the writers' design or no, the text of *LOST* wants to do with readers precisely what Nelson describes about his film. It seeks "to find a deeper way that the events [and characters] relate to one another" by using a nonlinear approach to the discourse. In her scholarly discussion of *LOST*, Erika Johnson-Lewis really seems to be onto something when she analogizes the way *LOST*'s nonlinear narrative works as a Dr. Who quote: "people assume that time is a strict progression of cause to effect, but actually from a non-linear, non-subjective viewpoint, it's more like a big ball of wibbly wobbly, timey wimey stuff" (1510). In the case of *LOST*, the big wibbly wobbly ball is the Augustinian, four-dimensionalist, time-grace continuum of the text.

The unprecedented increase in the nonlinear playfulness of television narrative discourse in *LOST* and in other recent series such as *How I Met Your Mother*, *Daybreak*, or *Flashforward*, is symptomatic of a wider ongoing narrative trend that owes largely to film, which in turn owes much more to the fictional novel. Of course, the telling of stories out of chronological sequence is nothing new. From Shakespeare and his early modern English contemporaries to the novels of Faulkner, Vonnegut, and Morrison in the twentieth century, authors of literary fiction have tampered with time. Over the last century, in fact, one could come easily to believe that nonlinear discourse has nearly become the rule in contemporary literature, rather than the exception. Television is now finally not only tasting that narrative freedom with point-driven readings through nonlinear delivery, but has become emblematic of that trend, and so far, *LOST* remains clearly the leader of the pack.

Jeffrey D. Frame is associate professor of theatre and film at Trevecca Nazarene University and is a veteran of stage and voiceover work. Mr. Frame has spoken on various topics in film, theatre, and literature at professional conferences and has been a member of the Film and History Conference, the Popular Culture Association of the South (PCAS), and the American Alliance for Theatre and Education (AATE). In film, his research has focused on nonlinear narratives and, in television studies, his special interests range from narrative and seriality (*LOST, 24, Fringe*) to short-run phenomena (*Firefly, Daybreak, Flashforward*) to character edge and evolution (*The Sopranos, Breaking Bad*).

Jack Klugman and Tony Randall, "The Odd Couple" 1972 Publicity Photo, WMC PD

A conversation between Sarah Clarke Stuart and Pearson Moore

Sarah Clarke Stuart and Pearson Moore were both featured speakers at the 2011 Lost Mini-Conference in New Orleans, Louisiana. Although starting from divergent assumptions and backgrounds, they proposed similar theses for the take-home message of Lost.

Clarke-Stuart asserted that Redemption, salvation and the construction of memories (which is inextricably tied to salvation in Lost*) rely on social communion and group collaboration. There is no "one who will save us all" because the individual is never the saviour; in* Lost *the most heroic acts are accomplished through cooperative group effort. In the end Jack plays the role of the martyr, but it is Kate who shoots the Man in Black, making it possible for Jack to kick him off the cliff, and Desmond who removes the cork, which makes the Man in Black mortal. Meanwhile Sawyer and Hurley play vital strategic roles in saving the island, while Lapidus fixes the plane and Kate saves Claire from herself.*

Moore, on the other hand, proposed that the necessity of deeply meaningful one-on-one interactions constituted the core message of Lost. *In his conference address, Moore reiterated his idea of the Strange Attractor, claiming that* Lost*'s central lesson was the requirement for spiritually profound connections not only between two lovers ("Constant couples"), but even more importantly, between adversaries. Moore's presentation is offered in Chapter Five of this volume.*

Moore and Clarke-Stuart spoke in December, 2011, two months after the Lost *conference.*

PM: I was amused to find that we offered theses of such close similarity in our featured talks in New Orleans.

SCS: You weren't the only one.

PM: At first I thought your idea and mine were mutually exclusive. How can "It takes a village" possibly work in the context of "The Odd Couple"?

SCS: Felix Unger and Oscar Madison probably wouldn't get along very well with Hillary Clinton.

PM: Exactly. Secretary Clinton would attempt diplomacy, but then Oscar's stinky, unwashed socks would end up on top of the round table, and Felix would have an allergy attack.

SCS: Not a productive scenario.

PM: No. But it struck me, the more I thought about it, that maybe the Village Thesis and the Strange Attractor Thesis might be reconciled in some way.

SCS: We obviously end up with similar notions regarding the importance of certain outcomes, such as the way the Sideways World is intimately and necessarily tied to the Island. We both agree that the social outcome is unique to LOST.

PM: Absolutely.

SCS: I like this idea. And I think we agree on the necessity of Jacob's Progress, too.

PM: Yeah, and that's something I don't think a lot of people have agreement on, so there's an interesting and rare convergence of our ideas there, too. But I've asserted that one-on-one interactions form the basis of Jacob's Progress—that the society of crash survivors cannot make social or political progress until key players in the camp realize personal growth. I see personal growth as requiring the kind of Constant relationships and Strange-Attractor, odd-couple sort of investments I discussed in *LOST Humanity* and in my New Orleans presentation. It's not social, but personal—it's always one-on-one. Without the rough stimulus provided by Locke, Jack couldn't have been transformed from Man of Science into the Island's most important Man of Faith. Jack didn't acknowledge the importance of the group when he gave his dressing-down to the Smoke Monster—remember, when he and the Man in Black were lowering Desmond down into the Source? Jack said *Locke* was right, "about everything." Hurley, too, couldn't have moved from a position of extreme discomfort with even the smallest white lie to a facility with creating well-planned and executed fabrications if he hadn't been in his odd-couple relationship with Ben Linus. I'd say maybe the most visible Odd Couple example occurred in the Sawyer/Anthony Cooper coupling; in order to move beyond his past and his unhealthy mirroring of the confidence man who destroyed his parents' lives, Sawyer had to confront his Strange-Attractor nemesis, Anthony Cooper. I take the Jacob/Man in Black pairing as evidence that the Strange Attractor relationship was intentionally built into the very fabric of the Island. The need to propagate this strained counterpoint is seen in the fact that Hurley's Number Two is his opposing Strange-Attractor twin, Ben Linus.

SCS: Interesting point. I have always considered Hurley to be a kind of community bonding agent. The only pairing I considered was his partnership with Charlie, and then his adversarial pairing with Sawyer. Otherwise, he seems to play a significant role as the one who identifies the group's commonalities. He is a peacemaker. Especially in retrospect, with Hurley chosen as the protector of the island, we can see how he always put the group first.

PM: Yeah. He's absolutely the most social guy on the Island.

SCS: Yes! And that's essential. As I point out in my book, *Literary Lost*, the reason Hurley was chosen as the next Jacob is that Hurley alone recognized that it was never the island that was special; it was the people and their connections to one another. But I see how Hurley would not have been elevated to this final level if not for the push and pull of his relationship with Ben.

PM: That seems to fit quite well with Darlton's contention that in the end, LOST is about the characters, not about the mythology or the physics of it all. I recognize the insistence on the primacy of the one-on-one relationship could be misguided, or at least incomplete. But I think either one of our theses could satisfy the creators' professed emphasis. I see the final objective of Jacob's Progress not as Jack's heroic act on the lava cliffs or his heroic bravery in replacing the Cork Stone, but as the creation of a society based on the carved-in-stone precepts of the Cork Stone itself. Constant and Strange Attractor relationships involve intimate, one-on-one relationships, but in the end, they're intended as the foundations for a dynamic society—

SCS: We might even say 'postmodern'—

PM: Yeah, a dynamic, always-changing, postmodern society—that in its processes of change—that is, Jacob's Progress—ends up asserting the paramount, unchanging—or objective, realistic, and definitely *not* postmodern—importance of faith in a higher power. And that really just mirrors Rule #1 from the Cork Stone: Make A Way For The Osiris is just a way of saying that human beings don't get the final say. The Island—this thing that makes all the rules and sets individual destinies and all that—is the primary law. When that law is violated, the Island literally and figuratively falls apart, as we saw when Desmond pulled out the Cork Stone. The other rules are subordinate: balance—that is, Rule #2, where Horus and Set are guarantors of life, justice (Rule #3), and peace, which is the final rule. We see themes of faith, balance, justice, and peace throughout LOST, with the title itself alluding to the survivors' condition as people lacking faith, balance, justice, and peace.

SCS: Yes, I like this idea: the title suggests not only that they are lost but that they have lost important parts of the human experience: they are looking for a lost faith, lost balance, lost justice, lost peace, lost loved ones. These are all restored when they are all together in the final "moving on" place. There IS a higher power (faith is restored), in death everyone is equal (justice and balance are restored), violence is no longer necessary (peace is restored). I don't know if restored is the best term though. It seems that what they "find" together is as much created as it is discovered.

PM: Fascinating. I have to admit I hadn't thought of the Sideways reality as asserting the efficacy of volition or intention, and I find the idea exciting. "This is a place you all made together" takes on new meaning if we extrapolate from the Sideways World to the Island World, as you seem to be doing.

SCS: I suppose a lot of us thought the two worlds—the Island World and the Sideways World—would have to merge somehow. Long before the finale, I was thinking along the lines of how the two worlds would collide or interact, and it led me to wonder about how they might be connected on a conceptual basis—you know, the things they shared in common. Early in Season Six, it seemed like the Island was a sort of free-for-all experiment, but the Sideways World was more focused. So, yeah, if freedom or free will or choice or whatever you want to call it was important on the Island, I think it was important in the Sideways world, too, and I think the events we saw in the Sideways support that view.

PM: I love this idea. It means that volition/intention—free will—is a much greater component of Jacob's Progress than I acknowledged in my analysis, and was a primary or major influence through the six years. The idea is attractive in a text that certainly incorporates strong elements of postmodern thought, but appears to supersede postmodernism in its insistence on objective truths, and—

SCS: I don't think LOST ever makes us choose between objectivity and free will. I find it so significant that in *Literary Lost* I spend an entire chapter exploring this notion.

PM: Yes. And that's one of the really beautiful things about LOST. The idea that we don't have to choose between destiny and free will I believe is important. The fact that a choice doesn't have to be made seems to strengthen the notion that LOST is asserting a reality that goes beyond postmodern sensibilities, which I believe could be seen as bolstering either of our two theses. I see Hurley's van ride in "Tricia Tanaka is Dead" as supporting your idea that 'what they find together is as much created as it is discovered.' Hurley didn't discover that the van could be made to run, he ***made*** it run. And in support of the It-Takes-a-Village thesis, Hurley didn't do it alone, but with help from Charlie, Sawyer, Jin, and (the Island's ever-vigilant, all-seeing agent) Vincent.

SCS: Yes. I think "The End" is a tool that we can use to decipher all prior episodes. It instructs us, showing us that their lives aren't just about coincidence and accidental crash-landings, but about what they create when the crash landing happens to them. They are led to a seemingly enchanted place by "fate," but they must engage in the work of collaboration in order to really discover it. They have to make it significant to their own lives, and usually this involves the development of community. The inner turmoil of each individual serves as a catalyst to create growth and outreach, to construct the intricate bonds that will make up the special place: the village. A village is not just a geographical location; it is a living, breathing organism. It exists as much in a physical place as it does in the spirits of its inhabitants. This is why it's so significant that the island moves around in space and time. It is less important where and when it is, than *who* it is.

PM: A possible deficiency in the It-Only-Takes-Two thesis is that it can be seen as superfluous or not properly centered on the true foundation of LOST. Our two theses seem to concur in their assertion that a new social order is the message of LOST. If so, which elements of LOST demand the primacy of one-on-one interaction?

SCS: I don't necessarily think we are talking "a new social order" as much as a natural shift of power that will eventually shift again…and again. I think that LOST urges its viewers, more so than any other TV show that preceded it, to embrace change. The dynamic of the show was constantly changing with so much death and loss. The flashbacks also kept us on our toes, by changing our perspectives, and the time travel made it necessary for us to be flexible about what did and did not transpire. The most exciting thing about life is also the most heartbreaking: rapid change is the nature of all life. LOST does a compelling job of reflecting this truth.

As for the "It Only Takes Two" thesis, I think the Locke/Jack pairing is an essential centerpiece of the show, and it can be applied to so many other features of LOST. One of the more significant themes of the narrative—faith vs. science—is inextricable from this pairing. The faith/science dichotomy originates with these two.

PM: In the series finale we saw two pairs of odd couples lowering a man into the Source: Jack and Locke/MIB lowered Desmond into the light and a few minutes later we saw Hurley and Ben repeat the action when they lowered Jack into the darkened cave. These paired actions could certainly be interpreted as subsets of a larger society with an intention of fulfilling the parameters of Jacob's Progress. Jacob did not meet only with Jack at the final candidates' fireside chat. He met with all the remaining Candidates and one who was not officially a Candidate—Kate— but she really was a Candidate, at least according to the scheme I discussed in *LOST Humanity*. He made known some of the elements of Island life that only Locke had previously intuited. He spoke with them as individuals, but also as members of a society. These types of gatherings occurred throughout the six years.

SCS: The fire is an important image/metaphor for the convening of characters that we see throughout the six seasons. The fire and the light at the center of the island embody the concentration of energy that occurs when the group is together. Unlike my very positive characterization that this energy always has a good outcome, I would revise my thesis here by acknowledging the dichotomous nature of the human group dynamic. It can be likened to the destructive and creative forces of the Greek god of fire, Prometheus. Fire/light both destroys and creates life. Similarly, the human collaboration can be an unstoppable force of destruction or a light to guide humanity to a greater degree of clarity and progress.

PM: Fascinating again. We had fires in the Pilot, Walkabout, and White Rabbit. We had Jack leading the way with torches. We had Christian's lantern and "follow me" (Biblical references that also incorporate fire as a motif). The fire motif was certainly front and center in Jack's speech at the end of White Rabbit. The implication's gotta be that Jack is drawing from his earlier tête-à-tête with Locke; in the It-Takes-a-Village thesis, I imagine we would understand the one-on-one (Locke's "This place is different" speech to Jack) as supporting the later and more important group interaction and Jack's speech ("Live together, die alone"). The It-Takes-Only-Two hypothesis, on the other hand, would probably have to assert that Locke's "This place is different" speech is the thesis of White Rabbit, or at least the core of the episode's chiastic structure [see *LOST Humanity*, Ch. 11, "Literary Analysis"], which would elevate the importance of Locke's one-on-one with Jack to become the predominant interaction of the episode. If we look at this from the point of view that both types of interaction (couple and group) are essential and formative, I suppose we could argue that Jack is symbolically in the dark during Locke's speech, that Locke's words kick-start Jack's growth process, but that the group (who lit the fires) symbolically becomes Jack's lantern, allowing him to formulate a prototype of the series' thesis ("live together, die alone"). From this point of view, even if the one-on-one interactions and group interactions are equally important, the final objective, which is the building of a new kind of society, is the final determinant of relevance, and seems to point to group interactions as being the final, defining characteristic of LOST, with fire not only as motif but inextricably entwined in the thesis itself, as you said a bit ago, becoming metaphor for the level of enlightenment required to make the jump (to "move on") from the Lost state to the state of having realized (completed) Jacob's Progress.

SCS: The recurring image of the survivors gathering around the fire is not coincidental. Each fire-lit assembly illustrates "the one and the many." We usually see a long shot of the whole group, and then the audience becomes privy to the smaller groupings and the intimate conversations of pairings, even when we don't hear the dialogue. In the pilot episode at the end, for instance, we see relationships already forming by the way characters turn toward one another. In "Everybody Hates Hugo" [Episode 2.04], everyone sits around the fire as Hurley bolsters the group's unity by distributing items from the newly discovered food pantry. He is at once providing physical energy for the individual bodies and stoking the fires of camaraderie among them. One bread, one body. This feast illustrates how the one-on-one conflict between Charlie resulted in Hurley's decision to rise to the occasion of caretaker. As a result of this "rough stimuli" directed at Hurley, the group is elevated and united. More than once, Hurley moves through the group from one pair to the next, exhibiting his power to unite the survivors. The primal symbol of the fire is used throughout the series as a signifier of human engagement, both confrontational and peaceful. It illustrates the bonds of conflict, passion and cooperation. Much is accomplished around the fire: romance, strategic planning, mourning, friendship, feasting, and debate.

PM: I have to admit, when I think about the survivors' society—their Hillary-esque village—I see so many ways this might have been taken. We don't end up with Golding's bifurcation into civilized and uncivilized camps, we—

SCS: But we have everyone choosing sides at the end of Season Three, Locke and—

PM: —Jack. Yeah, but they're not choosing between Science and Faith or the *Lord of the Flies* choice between civilization and power—they're making choices based on their concept of the Island and its nature. Charlotte's 'This Place is Hell' versus Locke's 'This Place is Paradise.'

SCS: It's both.

PM: Yeah, and that's why I'm saying this breaking into two camps at the midpoint of the series was not a primary driver—it didn't have significance at the end of the story.

SCS: I see that, too. What you're saying makes sense.

PM: But we don't end up with a Great Hero, either. Naomi calls Jack "Moses," but even back then, we know he's not. He's much more like the knee-jerk kind of leader Sawyer described in Season Five, when he's giving Jack his dressing-down at the barracks—the Churchill speech [Episode 5.09].

SCS: 'Winston Churchill read a book every night, even during the Battle of Britain.'

PM: Exactly. Sawyer thinks things out, Jack just reacts on the basis of his logical appreciation of things. Unfortunately, logic is never enough—especially on the Island!

SCS: Science is never enough.

PM: Absolutely. So, there's no downward spiral à la *Lord of the Flies*, but there's no grand, glorious leader, either. And there's no Forrest Gump. It's not a village full of idiots, stupidly going out into a storm and becoming millionaires in the shrimping business. There's no hopeless spiral into barbarism and anarchy, there's no village leader, there's no village idiot.

SCS: Ha! But who's to say that the Hanso foundation didn't have a hand in Gump's success?

PM: Hanso Shrimping Enterprises, eh? I keep coming back to the idea that Jack needed Locke, Jacob needed the Man in Black, Hurley needed Ben. I think Jacob's Progress was captured perfectly in the two striking images of duality we saw in the finale, inside the cave.

SCS: When they were lowering Desmond—

PM: Yeah. It had to be Jack and the Man in Black lowering Desmond into the light, because by lowering him into that cave they were making progress—Jacob's Progress—and the only way to achieve that progress is through struggle. So you gotta have two guys with completely opposite views pitted against each other, yet working together, to make Jacob's Progress. You gotta have two guys who are 100% opposed to each other to spark the conflict that leads to one Strange Attractor couple making Jacob's Progress. Same thing later on, with Hurley and Ben lowering Jack into the cave. The ones making Jacob's Progress have to be complete 180-degree adversaries, and Hurley and Ben certainly are, not just around the contrast between honesty and deception, but around the dilemma between Ben's careful planning and Hurley's throw-it-to-the-wind spontaneity. It can only be Hurley and Ben lowering Jack into the cave, because only polar opposites can make Jacob's Progress toward human perfection, which was represented in the precepts literally carved into the Cork Stone. It's a village of Odd Couples. It has to be, 'cause that's the final meaning of LOST.

"New Otherton"
Photograph by KOS Tours, Oahu
Used with permission

SCS: Or, in other words, a village of struggle and progress, right? This is an interesting way to look at community: as a complex system of smaller conflicts. Or a series of little chemical reactions that keep life moving forward. If this is the case, if LOST is a village of Odd Couples, does every single character have a Strange Attractor?

PM: I think they do, yes. I've made a case that there are at least nine such pairings, but we could probably find more if we looked hard enough.

SCS: Okay, but if so, how do the pairings bond among one another? Is it important to explain how the two become four and then eight, and so on?

PM: If we're going to reconcile the two theses we probably have to do that. I'm just not sure at this point how we bridge the gap. Natural selection? I think no matter how we look at it, LOST would argue against anything like this. It's all about interactions—even "fate," really, seems to come down to interactions, if not between the humans, certainly between the humans and the Island.

SCS: It seems a little too easy—and not entirely supported—to ascribe all this directly to the Island's interference in the survivors' lives.

PM: I think your assessment is spot-on. I understand, though, that the mythic one-on-one interactions could be interpreted as drawing their real strength from the complicated ***structure of relationships*** on the Island. Jack's relationship with Locke was certainly informed by his strained relations with Sawyer and Kate especially, but to lesser degrees with Rose, Boone, the Others, and of course, his dead father. I think one could assert that the primary rationale for the depth of flashback, flashforward, and flashsideways was demonstration of the primacy of multi-tiered, interconnected relationship. One of the bonus materials on the Season Two DVD set, for instance, was a discussion of the theory of Six Degrees of Separation. The relationship web, even at the close of Season Two, was almost certainly the most complicated scheme ever seen on television, and certainly one of the most detailed in all of fiction.

SCS: I think it makes more sense to say that the complicated structure of relationships draw their strength from the one-one-one connections rather than the other way around. They are like the simple chemical bonds that make up something more complex.

PM: Hah! Using a chemistry metaphor with a chemist! Kudos! I think this is a useful way of looking at the issue, and again this way of looking at things—that one-on-one interactions are merely the building blocks for more complicated social structures—could certainly be seen as having broad support in the text of LOST. But it also calls into question my assertion that LOST must be seen through the lens of higher-order synthesis, not through analysis, reduction, or deconstruction [see *LOST Humanity*, the "nonlinear" chapters, 10-13 and 17-18]. Isn't the insistence that one-on-one interactions are primarily merely another way of reducing more complicated social interactions into something more easily understood, and therefore actually over-simplifying the narrative? If the final objective is the complicated molecule, with its many one-on-one chemical bonds, and not the chemical bonds themselves, why would we assert the primacy of anything other than group social interactions? If we reduce a molecule to single chemical bonds, what is to stop us from proceeding in our analysis to individual atoms (individual characters), or subatomic particles (single motivating factors or elements of characters' histories) as being the paramount structures informing LOST's thesis?

SCS: But atoms and bonds are no less important—and essential to the final structure of the molecule.

PM: Hmm… you're stealing all my thunder here! Do you watch *Breaking Bad*, too?

SCS: That's another discussion in itself! But I do think Walter White would agree with me about the structure of molecules.

PM: Who am I to argue with a chemistry teacher! You bring up valid points. The metaphor seems to fit LOST very nicely. It's obvious that Locke is Jack's nemesis, Kate is Claire's nemesis, Sawyer is Anthony Cooper's nemesis, and so on; each of the major players has a single nemesis. When Locke dies, the Smoke Monster has to take on Locke's form, because Jack could have only one nemesis. This was vital to the story, as we see in the way these one-on-one relationships are structured, even to the point of using a single actor for two roles. If the Strange Attractor relationship had not been critical to the story, Darlton could have employed Terry O'Quinn as Jack's visitor from the sideways world, giving him advice or goading him on or whatever—something akin to the way Obi-Wan appeared to Luke, for instance. That this was not done I think not only diminishes the importance of the hero motif, but also strengthens the Strange Attractor thesis.

SCS: But you're not just asserting a manifestation of duality in the Odd Couples.

PM: No. That manifestation is not coincidental, but inevitable, and essential. When the odd-couple pairings are attached to the notion of faith, and especially with the Jacobian faith in humanity's future potential, the Strange Attractor thesis seems inevitable. If Locke hadn't been the single necessary agent in Jack's growth, he would not have grown, he would not have become the Island's Man of Faith.

SCS: This seems to reduce the importance of Locke to the level of pure agency. He's a meaningless, thoughtless automaton—a weeping, sniveling, pathetic invalid—a gullible fool. I don't know that I agree with that assessment.

PM: No, I don't either. Locke held the key.

SCS: I think we've been talking too long. Or you're drinking Irish coffee.

PM: Ha ha! No, Locke was vital—agency was not his primary raison d'être. Locke was a fully developed and essential character in his own right, as Jack confirmed during his conversation with the Man in Black while they were lowering Desmond into the Light. As Nikki said [at the New Orleans LOST conference, October, 2011] when she commented on my statement about Locke's resurrection, one could easily conclude that Jack, upon his acceptance of faith, became the reincarnation (Canton-Rainier) of Locke.

SCS: Yes, I like this… I concurred [at the conference], invoking the early image of Jack and Locke superimposed over Locke and Jack: Jack becomes Locke, Locke becomes Jack.

PM: Yes. It's not that Locke is subordinate to Jack. They're both subordinate to Jacob's Progress. I see both members of the Odd Couple as equally affecting the path taken by the Strange Attractor pair. Jack's destiny—his trajectory on Jacob's Progress—is affected by Locke. Intellectually, spiritually, emotionally, and psychologically the two of them are "joined at the hip," as I tried to illustrate in one of my presentation slides in New Orleans. If Locke is uncoupled from Jack, he cannot reach his destiny. Therefore, this intimate, Odd-Couple relationship is necessary, and both characters are required in the final evolution of the Odd Couple pair.

SCS: But how does their struggle over faith fit in?

PM: Well, I think faith in LOST is not communal, but individual. Locke doesn't tell groups they need faith, he relays this assertion to individuals. Faith for Locke is concrete: He has faith in the Island. The Cork Stone is the key to Locke. This stone key contains the precepts of LOST, literally carved in stone. LOST dismisses the Great Man theory, and replaces it with the Strange Attractor. Locke is reincarnated as Jack, but Jack retains every positive aspect of even his negative character attributes. Thus, Jack the compulsive, self-oriented fixer becomes the thoughtful, planning, other-oriented fixer who makes the Island whole again. Jack is not the hero. If there is a hero, it is Jack-Locke-Kate-Christian (Locke is Jack's Strange Attractor, Kate is Jack's Constant, and Christian is Jack's Reconciler).

SCS: Right—faith is not communal in LOST but I think that developing faith in community is a central tenet of the show. It is clear that the "end game" was coming together and not necessarily rising to a higher power. Faith in each other, faith in human strength was the true religion. All of the symbols and statues and sacred texts that pointed to belief in a supernatural higher power seemed to be drained of their significance when we discovered that Jacob and the Man in Black were only men.

PM: I agree completely. But faith remains, even after most of the supernatural elements are withdrawn. The basic idea I'm trying to express is that LOST is not a pastiche grab-bag from which you can pull out any conclusion you wish to draw based on caprice. In the end, I believe LOST sets forth certain ideas—like the essentiality of the Constant Couple—that are unique to LOST and are also unambiguous. I reject the notion that LOST is pure postmodern expression left entirely to the whim of the observer or observer/participant to assemble into any coherence or incoherence she fancies at the moment. LOST is not a closed text, it does require active participation/redaction in order to resolve the nonlinearities into something the human mind can comprehend, but it sets forth universals—truths upon which everyone can find agreement.

SCS: When you say that you reject ambiguity, are you referring to the question of righteousness at the end? Was Jack's sacrifice based on a "worthy truth"? Certainly the Smoke Monster was working in opposition to the values of human dignity and "social health." I think that a study of moral ambiguity lies not in the final efforts of the heroes, but in the actions of Jacob. It is clear that the Smoke Monster was violating human dignity, but Jacob did not necessarily act as a clear nemesis to or antithesis of him.

PM: Fascinating idea! I hope you will expand on this notion that Jacob's actions were ambiguous. This is something I touched on in my chapter on Jacob [*LOST Identity*, Ch. 10] and also in the "Inversion" essays on *Ab Aeterno* [see http://pearsonmoore-gets-lost.com/Lost609PartI.aspx and http://pearsonmoore-gets-lost.com/Lost609PartII.aspx]. As for ambiguity, I don't think LOST is open to random interpretation—otherwise the most ridiculous "theories" abounding on the Internet would have relevance equal to anything we've discussed or anything anyone has ever posited, and I don't think that's correct. But I think it's reasonable—and necessary—to say that LOST is an open text, that we are the final redactors.

SCS: The text may support more than one thesis, then.

PM: Exactly.

SCS: That would seem consistent with LOST as postmodern expression—

PM: Or post-postmodern, as I think LOST is.

SCS: Now there's a word!

PM: Ha! I think it's pretty simple, though, in the end. Do you remember the Saturday Night Live commercials from the 70s?

SCS: That's a bit before my time.

PM: Now you're making me feel old! Say, could you pass me that bottle of Grecian Formula?

SCS: You mean the one labeled "Dharma Initiative Age Cream?"

PM: Ha ha! You spiked *both* coffee mugs with Irish whiskey, didn't you?

SCS: Seems only fair, if we're an equally balanced Odd Couple.

PM: Ha ha! I'd love to take one of your courses. No, here's what I was thinking about: Chevy Chase and Gilda Radner did this commercial parody—I think it was during the very first season of SNL, back in 1974 or 75. The commercial was called "Shimmer Floor Wax." Gilda picks up a yellow bottle and tries to spray the contents on her mop, saying "Shimmer is a floor wax." Dan Aykroyd takes the bottle from her hand, sprays it on the bowl of pudding in front of him, saying "Shimmer is a dessert topping." They get into a heated argument, but Chevy Chase comes in to save the day: "Hey, hey! Calm down, you two! New Shimmer is a floor wax **and** a dessert topping."

SCS: I'll have to see that. It sounds hilarious.

PM: It is—one of the best SNL commercials ever. It's so effective because it's ludicrous—but even more deadly effective because it's **true**.

SCS: How so?

PM: You ever buy orange-scented "natural" cleaners?

SCS: You mean like Orange Glo?

PM: Yeah—Orange Glo Floor Cleaner.

SCS: It smells good.

PM: And tastes good, too. It has real orange essence in it.

SCS: But you can't—

PM: No, the built floor cleaner is poisonous, but only because of the other stuff they put in it and not because of the orange essence. You **could** just smear the orange essence on your floor and it would do a pretty darn good job as a cleaner all by itself. The chemical name for the stuff is D-limonene, but it's one of the main components of orange rinds. And that's how they get D-limonene for the floor cleaner: they squeeze it out of orange rinds. Same orange rinds you use to make desserts—and D-limonene is the major component in orange oil that is used in dessert toppings. So, Shimmer is real: it is a floor polish, and it is dessert topping, too. It's both!

SCS: You're saying the Village of Odd Couples is our Shimmer, then?

PM: Exactly. We have two theses that are similar, yet diametrically opposed. Particle and wave, just like light. Light can be understood as a wave, but it can equally be understood as a particle—and in fact, both interpretations are necessary to a good physical understanding of light behavior. Shimmer can be understood as floor wax or as dessert topping, but it's really both. We can understand LOST's main idea as the necessity of creating a never-before-seen type of society, but we are equally justified in believing that LOST says one-on-one pairings are central to Jacob's Progress.

SCS: This is an excellent conclusion then. The message of LOST is both that redemption is achieved through community and that the development of individuals is dependent upon their Strange Attractor relationships. Both the village and the pairing slowly nudge them toward enlightenment. I like your comparison to understanding the nature of light behavior: LOST can be defined in particle form or wave form, and, I'm sure in countless other ways. But the idea that its thesis can encompass these seemingly divergent ideas illustrates the compelling nature of LOST. Interpreting through different lenses, and seeing the central tenets clearly through each lens allows the viewer to continue seeing it anew. After all, this is what makes good literature, right? Ambiguity and the potential for multiple interpretations? But it's always nice to be able to weave together two or more understandings of a text and perceive them at once. It's like the rabbit/duck optical illusion. The challenge is to view it as both rabbit and duck at the same time, to try and hold in your mind both images at once. So, I'm glad we were able to talk through this optical illusion of ours and share our differing perspectives to construct a richer, more complex image. Together! As a community composed of one odd couple!

Sarah Clarke Stuart teaches composition, literature and popular culture at Florida State College at Jacksonville and the University of North Florida. She is the author of *Literary Lost: Viewing Television Through the Lens of Literature* (Continuum Books, January 2011) and *Into the Looking Glass: Exploring the Worlds of Fringe*. She writes about television and other popular narratives on her blog, "Teleliterate: Reading Television and Other Flickering Media."

Pearson Moore, while best known for his work on LOST, also writes novels. His first novel, *Cartier's Ring*, an action-adventure historical novel, is available at bookstores worldwide. His second novel, *Intolerable Loyalty*, considers the early years of the American Revolutionary War from a Canadian perspective; *Intolerable Loyalty* will be published in late 2012.

17. Amy Bauer: Time *Is* the Essence

"Time *is* the essence": the split subject of *Lost*

By Amy Bauer, Ph.D.

"Desmond" by ArtGUS
Used with permission.

The second season of the ABC television series *Lost* draws to pulse-pounding close as Locke's rash actions threaten the existence of the world. With but seconds to spare, Desmond Hume the hapless Scottish sailor employed a mysterious fail-safe key left to implode the Swan hatch, sending himself and the show down the proverbial rabbit hole. For Desmond had acquired that power the Greek Agathon had forbidden even to God: to change the past. And with the simply turn of a key in a lock, *Lost* became a show not only about an improbable plane crash, a mysterious island, and a host of scientific anomalies, but about traveling in and unraveling time.

Desmond's encounter with the hatch may point to the traumatic kernel at the series' core, one long theorized about by fans, especially when the already circuitous plot began a three-way toggle among the present, flashbacks and flash-forwards and the end of Season Three. The mysterious disappearance of the *Lost* island at the close of season four paved the way for a video released by *Lost* producers at July's Comic Con convention in San Diego with a startling message to fans. In an ostensibly 30-years old recording meant only for the ears of the initiated, the enigmatic, long-dead Dr. Pierre Chang (aka Edgar Halliwax, Marvin Candle and Mark Wickmund) reveals a knowledge of 21st century life, and insists that "Time is not just *of* the essence, it *is* the essence." Rhetorical flourishes aside, if we take the pedant at his word, time itself may be viewed as the split subject of *Lost*. Desmond's two forays into his own past are but one part of *Lost's* overarching narrative, which is riven by discontinuous moments. The subtle shifts in Penny's photo between seasons, Miles Straume's changing Los Angeles stairwell or Daniel's prescient lab notes imply the mutability and instability of past events, of history as we know it.

In this paper I will analyze narratives in *Lost* that center on the questions of fate and causality involving Desmond, Charlie Pace, Daniel Faraday, John Locke and Benjamin Linus. Through the structural devices of doubling, the minimal difference, and the call of the other, I will demonstrate time travel in *Lost* as the circular logic of a subjective—as opposed to linear—time that literally enact the process Lacan called *après-coup*: the way the past is always already read by the future. Lacan's term *après coup* is the term used by French analysts to translate Freud's *Nachträglichkeit* (deferred action). Both terms refer to the way that, in the psyche, the past exists in the psyche only as a set of memories. Present events cannot help but affect past events *a posteriori*, since our recollections are constantly reworked and reinterpreted in the light of present experience. In fact all of our discourse is structured by retroaction; the first words of a sentence take on their full meaning with the approach of the final punctuation mark, as the meaning of an essay is sealed by its final paragraph.(1701)

As an accepted tenet of poststructural discourse, we tend to forget the novelty of Lacan's 1954 statement that "History is not the past."(1702) Yet the full implications of its followup, "History is the past insofar as it is historicised in the present," have rarely been played out on the broad canvas of a long-running series, 82 episodes and counting. This is played out in *Lost's* narrative gradually, as we come to revisit a past shown in earlier episodes, and come to see past objects and events in a new and unequivocally changed light. This is not the inconsistent past of an unreliable narrator; if the viewer could not accept *Lost*'s flashbacks, much less its "present," as valid, the tissue of the extended story would unravel into isolated and unrelated threads. *Lost*'s story line asks us to accept everything we see as fact, information with some place in the overall story, even if what we see now seems to contradict what we saw last year or, occasionally, before the last commercial break.

FLASHES BEFORE YOUR EYES

The Desmond centric season three episode *Flashes Before Your Eyes* can be read as an inverted retelling of another famous time travel story with a genteel moral, Frank Capra's "It's a Wonderful Life." Rather than witness a past world that existed without him, as did George Bailey, Desmond observes the world he left as if he were still part of it, as if he'd never left England for the high seas and shipwreck on a remote island. Desmond's very own Clarence Oddbody, in the guise of an eerily prescient jeweler Mrs. Hawking, convinces him that he must forsake his love and a chance at happiness to save the world. George Bailey decided not to join the War effort, but remained in Bedford Falls to battle evil Mr. Potter. He sacrificed life as a "great man" for the woman he loved, as he later sacrifices death to return to her. At the end of "It's a Wonderful Life," the entire town of Bedford Falls turns out to belatedly thank George, supporting him in his hour of need. By contrast, Desmond forsakes battle with the sinister Charles Widmore, leaving his beloved Penelope a second time to join the Army and see the world. The millions that Desmond has saved will never know of his sacrifice, if that sacrifice were indeed his to make. For what marks "Flashes Before Your Eyes" as satire is that, unlike George, whose will is celebrated as something that in and of itself makes the world a better place, Desmond is urged to passively give in, to let destiny soldier on with him in its wake.

In *Flashes Before Your Eyes* Desmond travels back in time for two related but opposed reasons, their duality echoing the light and dark polarity that runs through *Lost*. The fact that his future was always already prefigured in the past has one positive outcome. Mirror imagery pervades *Flashes Before Your Eyes* to tie the island of 2004 to 1996 London: similar paintings in Widmore's office and the hatch, clock faces frozen to ominous times, beeping alarms, and sudden rain showers. Yet from the vantage point of 2004, what Desmond knew as the past has altered in myriad, subtle ways: a photo of he and Penny has changed, her engagement ring is in the Thames rather than in a shop, he recognizes Charlie on the street, and he becomes the unwitting victim of a pub brawl. Yet–like the proverbial "house that Jack built"–the future remains what it was despite all that it housed. The only meaningful change in the past is Desmond's feelings about it. Traumatized by the decision to leave Penny in 1996, he has spent eight years in turmoil and regret. If he didn't leave Penny because of his personal weakness, then neither did he join the Army, leave England, join a round-the-world yacht race, or even visit a local pub for ignoble reasons. As a warrior of fate Hume's actions merit tribute, not rebuke.

Yet like all adult morality tales, Desmond's journey has a dark side. Season Three revealed as well Desmond's precognitive insight to near future events, all of which centered on fellow castaway Charlie's death. No matter how many times Desmond saved Charlie in *Lost's* reality, Charlie's death returned like clockwork in the form of visions that predicted the character's every move. Back in the past, the jeweler's cautionary example involves a man in red shoes. His death under a building– red shoes thrust out à la the Wicked Witch of the West–illustrates the inevitability of fate. But Desmond's own future resembles another character with red shoes, Hans Christian Andersen's unlucky girl, who must cut off her legs at the knees to stop from "dancing" through life. As in the fable, the red shoes haunt Desmond. Nothing he does will remove the curse they represent: his ability to forecast a grim future yet an inability to prevent it.

The 1946 film *The Red Shoes* was a recursively-nested retelling of the same tale. A prima ballerina leaves her true love for life in the theater, yet leaps to her death in the very shoes she wore in her performance of the Red Shoe ballet: a fable within a dance within a film. Within the film the Andersen story was retold as a cyclical horror plot, in which the cursed shoes were ominously bequeathed to another. Similarly, Desmond's lifetime battle with fate seems to enfold countless smaller tales. His abilities to connect past and present are another "gift that keeps on giving," as they draw in more characters and plotlines in ensuing episodes.

THE CONSTANT

Desmond starred in another of *Lost's* finest hours in the fourth season, "The Constant." As the episode opens, we see a helicopter piloted by Frank– containing Sayid, Desmond and Naomi's corpse–leave the Lost island for a freighter anchored offshore. As Prologue, the teaser kicks off the plot with the weekly MacGuffin: a freak electrical storm that sends Desmond careening back into the past, as the thunderstorm at the beginning of the H.G. Wells's short story "The Remarkable Case of Davidson's Eyes" caused Davidson to visit a far off island while in London. At that point Desmond's consciousness takes over from the omniscient narrator, with every other character's actions acting as thematic counterpoint to Desmond's journey.

This tightly-written tale is driven by the desperate solution for a resolution to Desmond's trauma before it kills him, and structured by the use of parallel narratives and alter egos in past and present. Desmond's mind appears to switch places with his consciousness in 1996, some time after his journey back in "Flashes" while he is a soldier in the Royal Scots Regiment. The drill sergeant and fellow soldiers in Desmond's past with the Royal Scots corrrespond to those of the doctor, Keamy and Omar on the freighter in 2004. These stock players confirm through physical duress and the imposition of their will the reality of both 1996 and 2004 (each reality contains an authority figure and underlings, who calm Desmond and encourage him to accept the authority's rule).

A Mirror character in each reality confirms the possibility of internal time travel, and serves as Desmond's alter ego, a counter to the mundane–and therefore possibly false–appearance of stock players. The Mirror in 2004 is George Minkowski. the freighter's second apparent time-traveler and communications officer, while the 1996 Mirror is Eloise, a time-traveling white rat subject to Daniel Faraday's covert experiments. The Witness character serves as an external observer to the time travel itself, and links the Mirror and Desmond in each timeline. As Frank the Pilot and the Stock Players see Desmond and George's condition as simple amnesia, physicist Daniel Faraday plays the Witness in both 1996 and 2004. Desmond encounters the Unexpected Friend as an unknown or possible foe, yet in each timeline the Unexpected Friend gives him the key to resolve his trauma and the plot. The Friend in 2004 is Sayid (who fixes the phone), while the Friend in 1996 is Charles Widmore, who in a surprising move gives Desmond the address of his daughter Penelope, Desmond's ex-fiancée.

Penny as eponymous Constant links both realities, but her role cannot be "activated" until all the other players have completed their tasks. In 1996 Desmond made an aborted phone call to Penny; he needed to make contact with the Witness and the Unexpected Friend in both realities before he could activate The Constant by phoning Penny in 2004. As in "Flashes Before Your Eyes," the time travel itself is never explained; what matters is the resolution of Desmond's trauma–the recovery of his sanity and rescue from the fate suffered by George and Eloise–by grounding himself through an emotional connection with someone in both realities. Desmond moves through each timeline in parallel, from beleaguered soldier/prisoner-patient to empowered, autonomous suitor who has accepted his plight and taken action to resolve it as best he can. The narrative inverts at the end, when Witness and Protagonist switch roles, and Desmond becomes Faraday's Constant and thus, implicitly, his Witness in some parallel future.

Just as "Flashes" paired sounds and signs from 1996 and 2004, so "The Constant" binds past and present together with portentous codes. The episode's title becomes an alias for one person, Penny, whose connection to Desmond remains the emotional heart of *Lost*'s expanded journey into the Real World. The Lost number eight denotes years and events: eight years pass between Desmond old and Desmond present, and eight flashbacks chart the missing time and missed attempts at communication before the Protagonist makes contact with his Constant. Water is everywhere as bad weather and cleansing ritual, there are two journals, and there are two people who "aren't supposed to be here." Finally there are two means– phones and notes–by which communication is breached, broken and occasionally made, miscues that build enormous tension directed towards the successful completion of the final call to Penny.

THE SHAPE OF THINGS TO COME

Up to this point I've discussed incidents of time travel that center on Desmond, and which involve a kind of internal travel confined –Billy Pilgrim-like– to a character's perceptions, and inflicted on him against his will. *Lost* has included only one diegetically-confirmed instance of physical time-travel on the island, in Dharma videos, one shown at the 2007 comic con convention and in the context of the 13th and final episode of season 4, "There's No Place Like Home"; both rely on the Casimir effect to displace a rabbit 100 milliseconds into the future. Yet the end of Season Four strongly implied that both the duplicitous leader of the Others and the island had been transported in time and space, a narrative structured more by anticipation of the future than retroactive historicization of the past.

The time travel storyline that culminated in *There's No Place Like Home* began in the ninth episode of Season Four, *The Shape of Things to Come*, in which Ben Linus comes to woozy consciousness in the middle of the Sahara Desert, wearing the same parka and sporting the same injuries we would later see in Episode 13. In the strict chronology of *Lost*, Ben put on the parka to descend into an icy cave beneath the abandoned Orchid station. The mysterious figure known as Jacob had demanded that Locke move the island; Ben has taken the onus upon himself, telling Locke that "Whoever moves the island can never come back." Injuring himself during the climb down, he nevertheless manages to turn a great wheel, creating a blinding light, a screeching wail, and the familiar purple sky effect last seen when Desmond turned the hatch key. As the camera point of view shifts to reflect those fleeing by helicopter, we see the island disappear completely beneath the waves. The Analepsis from the earlier episode drops Linus not only into the middle of the Tunisian desert, but into October 2005, where he immediately gets his bearings and heads to Iraq to recruit the services of Sayid—one of the Oceanic Six fleeing the island in 2004.

Despite his unplanned visit to the future, Ben seems to have anticipated his every need: he has money, lodging, weapons, false identification and a clear mission, in contrast to Desmond, who was quite unprepared for the past. Lacan's notion of *après coup* had a correlate in such anticipation, the way the future which has yet to occur affects the present. Every sentence begins in anticipation, every ego is constructed on the model of an anticipated, future whole, that which—in the future perfect tense—will have happened already in order for the present to exist. Anticipation is crucial to the tripartite structure of logical time, the moment when a decision is made based not on objective fact, but subjectively, in anticipation of future certainty. When that future certainty arrives, it is retroactively "desubjectified"; the future is now a shared, intersubjective truth, as if it always had already been so.(1703)

From the moment he was introduced under the alias Henry Gale, Linus has been portrayed as a master manipulator, one whose hunches and feints always succeed. Yet Ben remained in thrall to the island, to Jacob, to the agenda of the Other, at least in his own mind. His trip to the desert relates directly to the one instance of "anticipatory failure" he experienced on the island in 2004. At the moment in which the mercenary Keamy held a gun to the head of his adopted daughter Alex, Ben anticipated, with certitude, that Keamy would not pull the trigger. *The Shape of Things to Come* ends with him facing Charles Widmore in 2005, demanding revenge for her cold-blooded murder. He argues that her death broke the "rules," rules that seem to prevent the two nemeses from harming one another and their families. Yet this tear in the logical fabric of fate subjectifies Ben, sends him out into the world with Locke in charge of the island, as catalyst of Season Five and the future of the Oceanic Six. Ben's traumatic encounter with fate—the minimal difference between the future that should have been and the future he couldn't predict–is a tiny window through which free will enters, and allows him to complete the ethical act of forsaking all he holds dear and moving the island.

But what of Locke, left behind in the Orchid in 2004 with express instructions to lead the Others, and guard the island? The final shot of the series to date reveals the corpse of one Jeremy Bentham, alias John Locke, in 2007 Los Angeles, as a despondent Jack and Ben look on. As shadowy doubles, Linus and Locke share several traits: mothers named Emily, complicity in their fathers' deaths, special audiences with the spectral Jacob, and an unshakeable faith in the island's boons. In *No Place Like Home* they finally switched roles, as Locke assumed Ben's mantel as leader and Ben adopted John's former role of loner and vagabond. John's death counters Ben's rebirth as subject; Locke's story, however, has yet to end, as Ben insists that John Locke return to the island with the Oceanic Six.

No fewer than four different time travel scenarios inform the episodes under review. Yet they feature similar devices: character doubles, the minimal difference that indicates a gap in the smooth fabric of time, and the call of the other, whose summons seems to come from outside of time proper. Mrs. Hawking serves as a kind of temporal policeman, offering Desmond Kant's classic forced choice. The Critique of Practical Reason suggested that no reasonable man would forfeit his life for a night with the woman of his dreams. The stakes are considerably higher in "Flashes," where Desmond is asked to give up a life with his beloved in order to save the world eight years hence. As a truly ethical subject Desmond would not cede his desire: he would marry Penny, and to hell with fate. But to choose his fiancée over the world would be monstrous, and so Desmond sacrifices the girl for the world and regains his humanity. The message passed from Widmore to Desmond is the call of the other in *The Constant*. A version of Lacan's letter that always reaches its destination, Widmore's message allows Desmond to literally call his constant and regain his place in time, while demonstrating his faith in the humanity of others, including those he did not recognize when his past self visited the present. Jacob issues the inexplicable call to move the island in Season Four to Locke. Yet Ben's traumatic loss of not only his daughter but his ability to predict the future leads him to take Locke's place, and save the island while forsaking it.

As a structural category, time travel itself is but a subset of temporality, as *Lost* relies not only on Analepsis and Prolepsis as structural devices but enfolds entire cultural histories into its ongoing narrative through an expanding net of intertextual reference. These temporal devices, like the time travel scenarios themselves, are often mutually incompatible; yet more evidence that time *is* the essence of *Lost*, a radically split subject, whose fundamental inconsistency cannot be resolved at the same time that it propels the series into a fifth season and beyond.

Dr. Amy Bauer is Assistant Professor of Music at the Claire Trevor School of the Arts, University of California, Irvine.

LOST and the Power of Story

By C. David Milles

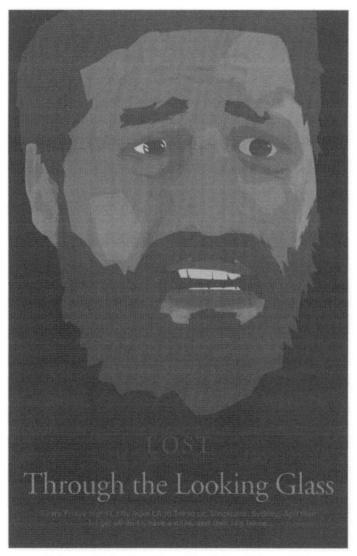

"Through the Looking Glass" by Gideon Slife
Used with permission.

LOST ended its on-air run on May 23, 2010. As the final scene played on our television screens, paralleling the opening of the series, we were left with a sense of wonder and sadness. Not because Jack died and was reunited with those he

239

loved in the afterlife. I believe it goes deeper than that. I think the finale left us with an emptiness that mirrored the same sense of loss we feel when someone we know leaves this world. We had grown attached to these characters, and we did not want to say goodbye.

LOST was simply a television series, and these characters were not real people, but actors playing a part. Yet a piece of us felt a connection to them, and we believed, at least for an hour each week, that they were real. There was something happening in the story of LOST, something powerful.

LOST was more than just a television show to be watched; it was a narrative to experience. The show reached across all demographics and provided a story that reached everyone who watched it. But why did LOST appeal to such a broad audience? Why did fans immerse themselves in the mythology created by the writers? Even though the show has ended, why does the story stay with us to this day? More broadly, what can LOST teach us about the power of story in the lives of an audience?

Something Different

I'll admit it. I did not watch LOST when it first came out. I remembered seeing small scenes of the Season One finale the night it aired, confused why some smoke-thing dragged a bald guy through the jungle. I remembered watching two men and a woman open a small door, staring down into the opening, and then the episode ended. Apparently, this show was not for me.

For several years afterward, a friend of mine continually prodded me to watch the show, and even offered to let me borrow it on DVD. I declined, saying that I didn't have the time or interest to watch it. My real reason for resistance was the fact that so many people liked the show. I reasoned that if the rest of America liked it, then it must have had a very basic, dumbed-down story to maintain their interest.

But my friend didn't give up, and at my daughter's first birthday party, he showed up with the DVDs for Season One, forcing me to borrow them. I told him I would watch them, but let them sit for at least another month and a half. I simply didn't see how a show about being stranded on an island could be so interesting to so many people.

But as Ben Linus says to Jack Shephard in *316* (Episode 5.06) "We're all convinced sooner or later."

I gave the show a chance, and by the time I had watched *Walkabout* (Episode 1.04) I, too, was convinced. There was something going on here.

Something different. I became hooked, sensing that this was one of the best stories on television. I watched four seasons in just a month and a half, and finally caught up with the rest of the world in time to watch Season 5. Today, as a Communication Arts instructor, I frequently cite LOST as an example of how to craft stories and how to use different writing techniques.

I've often reflected on why LOST was so successful during its run. How was it able to reach so many in just a few short years? I believe it was partly because LOST gave us something different in our menu of television offerings. While other shows were crime-of-the-week dramas, shallow reality shows, or comedies infused with laugh tracks to tell us what was supposed to be funny, LOST gave us a story. It gave us something *real*. And because it was real, it resonated with us.

It still does. And there is much we can learn about the power of story from LOST, from the way the story was crafted, to the way it created viewer engagement, and especially from the way it used its characters.

Raising the Bar

LOST was unlike anything aired on television before it. The story was different, from the locales, to the characters it featured, and even down to the way it told the story. If viewers didn't know any better, they would look at it as an experiment on television. Filled with twists and turns, the story grabbed us from the very first eye-opening frame and didn't let go.

Some didn't like the directions the story took. The unconventional techniques made them uncomfortable, and they stopped watching. Others wanted different explanations to the questions and situations. After "The End" aired, some fans were disappointed by the way it concluded, even becoming angry at the writers because it didn't mesh with how they themselves envisioned the ending.

Accusations were hurled at Darlton and the other writers for "making it up as they went along." But with all stories, there is a blueprint, a basic idea and skeleton of what will happen with the characters and situation. The same was true in LOST. But the writers also realized a crucial component of all good stories: they're living entities, and they need to be given room to grow and to evolve if they are meant to be real and resonate with us. LOST was alive, and that is why it continues to live with us to this day.

Long ago, writers viewed a story by its genre, categorizing it using simple terms such as *romance, science fiction, adventure, action,* or *fantasy,* to name just a few. The writers of LOST realized that as our culture evolves, so does the way we view and tell stories. If we were asked to label LOST as representative of any specific genre, what would we choose? Romance? Certainly the show featured love triangles and quadrangles, as well as true love relationships as evidenced by Desmond and Penny.

Would we label it as adventure, an island survival story? What about science fiction? Season Five threw us all for a loop with time travel and paradoxes. Fantasy? An island that contains seemingly magical properties would definitely qualify for this. But LOST was none of these.

And it was all of them. LOST defied genre, its writers realizing that to tell the best story, they would need to think outside conventional categories.

Blake Snyder, in his book on screenwriting called *Save the Cat!*, discussed the need for looking at stories through a new lens. Instead of having the traditional genres, we need to look at *story types*. For example, there is the "Monster in the House" story type. LOST is partly this, as we wonder what the Smoke Monster is, where it came from, and what it is capable of. There is the "Golden Fleece" story type, in which the characters are on a quest to find or discover something. LOST embodies this in many ways, especially with the inner struggles the characters go through, each on a quest for something they're missing. Some of their experiences fit the "Rite of Passage" model, as each character is trying to find their own way in a different aspect of their life. The story also reflects elements of the "Whydunit" and "Buddy Love" story types, reflected through the mysteries of the Island's past and the relationships between the characters.

Because the writers of the show did not limit themselves to one specific genre or story type, the story they created was itself not limited in its capacity to reach a wide audience. The story was multi-layered, deeper than anything that had been on television before, and this allowed viewers to experience the story in different ways.

In the same way LOST defied genre, it also defied the conventions of story structure. Each episode took us on a journey, although the journey was not always crystal clear at the moment.

I often use LOST as an example in my class of how anything can be possible if you know how to tell a story well. Sometimes, students will bemoan the fact that they need to write a story, saying they just want to "get to the action" and skip all of the exposition. I tell them that they can; it's their story. I then show them the opening scene of the pilot episode: Jack's eye opening, confusion and chaos everywhere as he emerges from the bamboo grove. The story opens in the middle, but we still get the exposition through the flashbacks as each episode explores one of the character's lives in the past.

This was particularly effective because by letting us see the characters in peril, we already care about them and their plight. Would we have felt the same if we had watched half a season of backstory, waiting for the characters to board Flight 815? I do not think so. I believe that by immersing us in the characters at that moment, we had a desire to get to know them, just as the other survivors wanted to learn more about those they were stranded with. Because we did not know who they were or whether or not they could be trusted, we experienced similar feelings to the other castaways.

Beyond the flashbacks, LOST also made us care about the characters through the flash-forwards. We knew that they had gotten off the island, and we were happy for them, but we felt a sense of longing for those left behind, and like Jack we wanted to go back. The story kept us intrigued as we watched to see how and why the Oceanic 6 left the island, and why they would leave the rest behind.

The writers did not stop there, and in Season Six they employed the flash-sideways. Because of the science fiction element to Season Five, we wondered if this was an alternate timeline. Was it a "do-over" for the characters? In these flashes, they did not know each other, and we were both happy for them receiving a chance to start over, yet saddened that they no longer had the same shared experiences, and we felt a loss. By weaving these different techniques into the storytelling, the writers *made* us care about the story and the characters.

The writers of LOST used these techniques effectively because they knew how to tell a story with substance and complexity. Looking back over the series, we realize that the sheer number of characters was huge, yet we can remember intricate details about each one and where they fit on the timeline of the show. Normally, the number of main characters in a show is limited so that the audience can keep them straight in their minds.

But the writers and producers of LOST trusted that their audience was smarter than this. They provided us with a story that opened up several new mysteries every time it answered one. We watched, we interacted, and we discussed theories online about the characters, the events, and the Island. Fans also created intricate timelines of the story, so drawn in by its complexity that they wanted to create a structure to make sense of it. How many other shows tell such a large story that their viewers go to great lengths to see it as a whole?

Since LOST debuted, many shows on television have attempted to mimic its format and its style. It's not uncommon to see stories that attempt to introduce the audience to a multitude of characters, that try to involve us in their backstory through flashbacks or some other plot device. Yet for some reason, many of them do not seem to work as well. I believe this is because at its core, LOST was not just about the storytelling techniques. While these likely played a part in helping us care about the characters, there was more to the story of LOST than just complexity.

LOST had complexity plus heart, and the overall narrative it told was about ourselves. Just as our lives are uncertain, the story in LOST was always uncertain as well.

With so many island survivors, we expected the writers to eventually eliminate some of the "red shirts" to thin out the cast. Imagine our shock when characters we truly cared about faced the same fate. Indeed, the storyteller giveth, and the storyteller taketh away.

Boone's death, the "sacrifice" that Locke spoke of, shocked us, but it made us realize the reality of the Island. Any one of these characters, as important to the story as they are, can die at any time. As a result, our connection to the story grew deeper, and we had a greater sense of urgency as we hoped they would all find a way off the island. We cheered with Michael, Jin and Sawyer as they set sail to find hope and a way home, and were disappointed when their plans ended in failure. We had become invested in their lives, and so when one of them faced the prospect of death, we felt it.

The writers knew this. Only by putting our beloved characters in harrowing situations could they create a more powerful story. There were stakes in this tale. As Damon Lindelof put it during an interview for the New York Times Talks Live program, in order to let the audience see the true reality of evil in the story, there had to be stakes for confronting that evil. There had to be sacrifice. And there could not be a perfectly happy ending for all.

Boone was not the only sacrifice, but he was one of many, each drawing us into the narrative and amplifying the power of the story that was unfolding. Self-sacrifice was also a prominent part of the series. As Charlie realized his destiny, he gave his life so that his friends could leave the Island, only to realize at the end that all was not as it seemed. He scrawled a final message on his palm, placed it on the glass, and succumbed to fate.

Locke's death was a complete shock for many viewers. He gave his life as a sacrifice for the Island, although his death was even sadder given the circumstances that surrounded his last days, and sadder still when considering his life as a whole. His search for meaning and purpose drew us into the story, and his death made us more determined to realize ours so that we might not feel the same hopelessness of his final moments.

The show's writers demonstrated the power of self-sacrifice even further when they paired it with redemption. As the submarine sank, Sayid atoned for his sins and died a hero instead of a murderer, but his sacrifice was not without further loss. We watched as Sun and Jin, reunited after their long separation, spent their last seconds together. They had come to the Island with a broken relationship, but left with an inseparable one.

Even though the writers demolished our expectations for storytelling on television by putting the characters in real peril, they made sure to use our minds along with our emotions to hook us into the story. By throwing mystery after mystery at us, the unending sequence of multi-dimensional events and interactions ensured that discussions surrounding the show would not be relegated to simply repeating the funniest joke on last night's sitcom or summarizing the plot of an episode. As an audience, we were thinking. We were engaged.

Active Involvement

"Argument Over a Card Game" by Jan Steen ca. 1670 WMC PD

LOST was successful as a story because it was active rather than passive. That is, audience members needed to involve themselves if they wanted to understand the story. They had to discuss, create theories, piece together clues, and organize bits of information and hold onto them until the end. Not many shows can say the same.

The mysteries of the show were an important part in creating a powerful story. There was, of course, the mystery of the Island. What was it? Why were the characters there? How could it be invisible to those who sought it, yet a plane could crash onto it? Was it magical? Holy?

I will admit that it was the mystery of the Island that first caught my attention. While watching the episode *Walkabout*, my jaw dropped open to see the camera pull back, revealing John Locke in a wheelchair. This same man who walked confidently on the sands of the Island had once been a paraplegic. How could something as violent as the crash of Oceanic 815 possibly heal him?

Then, in Season Two, the mystery of the Dharma Initiative opened a whole new door for theories. Well, really it was the opening of the Hatch door that opened the mysteries of the Dharma Initiative, in which the same numbers that cursed Hurley were not only imprinted onto the Hatch itself, but were entered into a computer—a computer that was supposedly preventing the end of the world. And this computer, mind you, was being monitored by the same Scotsman that had spoken to Jack Shephard years earlier.

How is it that so many coincidences could come together in one small place of the world? Did the writers expect us to believe that all of this was possible? They didn't have to convince us. We believed it because in this story, it was possible.

It was possible for Smoke Monsters to kill people, for polar bears to roam the jungle. It was possible for paralyzed men to walk. It was possible for cancer to go into remission, for drug addicts to break free from addiction like a moth from a cocoon. Relationships were healed and restored, murderers were free of their past, and good and evil battled for the soul of the world.

The mysteries, such as the Numbers, gave us something to think about beyond the weekly plots. We knew it had meaning, that it had relevance. And we sought to find that meaning, in every scene, every piece of dialogue, every repeated phrase. There were clues everywhere, and repeated viewings helped us find more substance than we ever thought possible.

The audience was drawn to the power that the story of LOST provided, and created theory after theory trying to explain them. Sometimes the theories were correct. Many times, they were not. One trick, Lindelof explained, was taking the "what" of a mystery and turning it into a "who." The coffin? It contained the body of John Locke, one of the greatest characters on the show. The Hatch? It wasn't just a thing. It was Desmond David Hume, isolated and afraid to leave the room, carrying out his duty of saving the world by pushing the button. The same button that, once neglected, set in motion the events of the story we witnessed.

But the story began long before Desmond neglected to push the button. The Smoke Monster, another "what" mystery, was also revealed to be a "who" in Season Six. No longer was it a thing that was chasing the characters, killing some and judging others. It was a person, and this person had a past with suffering and struggles. He had a brother.

By turning the mysteries into individuals, we could connect with them. If something is in the jungle, threatening to kill us, we fear it. But when that same thing is revealed to be a person with a past and with emotions, we no longer fear it, but we embrace it as part of ourselves. At the most basic level, we know what it's like to be lied to. We know what it's like to be alone, feeling like we're just pushing a button without purpose.

Some of the mysteries were never answered, at least not directly. And while that frustrated some fans, it is important that Damon Lindelof, Carlton Cuse, and the rest of the writers did *not* provide the viewers with easy answers. Lindelof called it the "midi-chlorian effect." A reference to the *Star Wars* films, it's the idea that in the original films, The Force was something mystical, something for us to be in awe of. It captured our imaginations. In later films, The Force was explained away as resulting from the activity of biological entities (midi-chlorians) in the bloodstream. By trying to provide answers, some of the wonder of the mystery was lost. The Force lost some power, and the power of the story was diminished as well.

If we were told exact, point-blank answers to questions such as "What is the Island?" or "What is the significance of the Numbers?" or "What is the Source?" it would erode the power of the story of LOST. Answer by answer, the story would be stripped down until there was nothing left. The fact that not everything received an answer to everyone's satisfaction means that people will still discuss it, will still find new insights, and will still learn from it. All good stories endure and stand the test of time. And while the story of LOST is still in its infancy, I believe it will stand that test.

The Power in Characters

I believe that at the core of a good story are characters that reflect us and resonate with us. Some stories are good, funny, or are filled with excitement and computer effects. But they are quickly forgotten until the next bit of technology is used to surpass its predecessor. As with all good books we read or movies we see, the characters are the key. And in this area, LOST truly is a model of the way stories that endure use exceptional characters that cannot easily be forgotten.

The world is a sea of characters from books, movies, television shows, video games, comics, and more. So what makes the characters of LOST stick out in our minds so much? Why are they, out of this vast ocean, so memorable?

"Tom Sawyer" unknown artist, attr. to True Williams
Frontispiece to "The Adventures of Tom Sawyer" 1876 by Mark Twain
WMC PD

The characters of LOST are memorable because they are unique. A doctor grieving the death of his father. A fugitive on the run for murdering her father. A washed-up, drug-addicted rock star. A manipulative father. An unknown, deity-like leader. A con man with heart. A knife-wielding former paraplegic.

They are all unique. They're all surprising. And they are all real.

They're real because at their core, they embody all that we hold dear, all that we hold at our core. While they may be one thing to the world on the outside, on the inside they are often something completely different.

Powerful stories like LOST build on the difference between *characterization* and *character*. This notion, explained in the book *Story* by Robert McKee, teaches that characterization is the aspect of story the writer uses to create the character that we see on the outside: the way they talk, act, dress, their past and mannerisms.

Their *character*, however, is something ultimately different. Character is what the individual is like deep down inside, or the way they would react in a difficult situation. The most powerful characters are ones in which these two elements, *characterization* and *character*, are opposites of each other. LOST does this very well.

Sawyer is the perfect example. At the start of the series, he is one of the most reviled characters, even more so than Iraqi torturer, Sayid. Sawyer is rude, he's judgmental, he's hateful, and we know from his past that he's a con man. He even murdered someone in cold blood. Mistakenly, of course, but that doesn't change the fact that he is a murderer. Sawyer hordes the supplies the castaways find, and he quickly earns our scorn. We want nothing to do with him. If only he would leave the Island, it would be a better place. We're happy to see him go at the end of Season One.

But as the show progresses, we slowly see the *character* of Sawyer. And it's the opposite of what we would expect, given his characterization. His past has shaped him into the con man we see, but deep down, we find that it's not who he really is. Locke is one of the first to realize this and calls him by his true name, James. In a difficult situation, we see Sawyer's true character, and he quickly earns our love because of it.

Sawyer is the first to put his life on the line for his friends. He jumps out of a helicopter so the Oceanic 6 can get home. He rushes into the gunfire of battle to protect Claire and Aaron. He's soon regarded as the true leader he has always known he could become once he faced his past, and leads a life of contentment with Juliet in Dharmaville.

Jin also reveals this difference. When we first meet him, he's overly-protective, harsh, and we soon learn he committed violent acts in the name of his father-in-law. We can completely understand why Sun wanted to leave him, and we bemoan the fact that she didn't until we see his true character. Jin's actions reveal that he's loving and learns from his mistakes. He forgives Sun's romantic indiscretions and commits himself to her well-being, scorning his father-in-law's respect in favor of her true love. He would give anything, even his life, for Sun. And he does, just hours after being reunited with her.

Ben Linus is one of the most despised characters in the entire series. Next to Charles Widmore and the Man in Black, Ben is considered one of the most evil characters to enter the lives of the castaways. And yet, he's also a character we love. Why?

His characterization is one of a young boy seeking the love and approval of his father, or seeking a way out of the Dharma Initiative. Ben, powerless as a child, will manipulate and lie to get and maintain power over others as an adult. He refuses to let go of it, even using his daughter in a standoff with Martin Keamy until Keamy unexpectedly calls his bluff.

Yet we see that deep down, Ben is a caring, misguided individual. We understand that he is not as evil as we once expected. He's misunderstood. He's sad, and he regrets many of his decisions. While his character may not be as golden as Sawyer's turns out to be, we see that it is a bit different from his characterization.

Deep down, Ben really *did* believe that the Others were the "good guys," as he told Michael. Only later did he realize that maybe things weren't as they seemed. As he stands in front of Ilana, a broken man, he surrenders to the thought that the only place he belongs is with the Man in Black because his decisions have damned him. But Ilana sees through the mask to the real Ben, the desperate and hurting Ben.

I believe that we get occasional glimpses into true character through the sideways world. In this world, some of the characters reveal a bit of who they truly see themselves as. Ben seeks power, but he is willing to put Alex's well-being and future ahead of his desires. This is something he wishes he would have done in his own life. In the same way, Sawyer is still the same, broken man who witnessed his parents die, but instead of turning to crime, he turns to justice.

Charlie Pace starts out as a positive character. He seems likeable, and he strives to be recognized by the others from Oceanic 815. The Island is a new start for him, because before the crash, in his attempt to find meaning and purpose, he turns to the hard-rock lifestyle. When he finds a stash of drugs, he returns to the temptation once again, hating himself for giving in. He is now a pathetic character, and we see how weak he is.

At the same time, he is protective of Claire and her baby, so we want to care for him. His characterization is one of someone we want to trust, but are not sure we can. He seems selfish, yet we know there's more there. His *character* has yet to reveal itself.

We see the full extent of Charlie's character at the end of Season Three, an act of self-sacrifice. In fact, his characterization and character are so well-written that my wife originally did not like him. She had little pity for the man Charlie had become, and did not like the drug-addict rocker that he embodied. He was her least favorite character, yet she cried when he gave his life. By seeing the full extent of his character, she realized that there was more to Charlie than the way he was portrayed on the outside. Deep down, he was good. He had changed. And in a story, change is powerful.

I tell my students that in all stories, characters must undergo some kind of change. If they don't, then the story is not worth telling. The Hero must have a Resurrection as someone new; otherwise, was his Journey worthwhile?

LOST provides examples of this throughout the entire series. One only needs to watch the transformation of Jack Shephard from the first episode to the last. A Man of Science at the start, he is transformed into a new Jack Shephard, the Man of Faith once embodied by his rival, John Locke. But there are other changes that transpire throughout the series, often several in an episode.

In the Season Three episode *Tricia Tanaka is Dead* (Episode 3.10), we see a powerful example of change in the lives of the characters. In that episode, three characters undergo significant changes during the course of events. Hurley moves from one who believes he is cursed to a new Hurley, one who believes he makes his own luck and is free from superstition. Jin learns he must work for his marriage, and commits himself to Sun even further. And Sawyer, back from New Otherton, arrives angry but is transformed by the love of Hurley and Jin as they work together on the Dharma van.

But powerful stories go beyond simply showing change in characters. There is a quality of a story well-told that makes the characters stand out to us, that stay with us and make us recall their experiences. LOST uses sympathetic and empathetic characters to accomplish this.

There's actually a slight difference between sympathy and empathy, and though small, it is significant. When we feel sympathy for a character, we feel *for* them. We have an understanding of what they're going through, and we feel for their hurt or happiness. But empathy is deeper. When we empathize with a character, we feel *with* them. We experience their emotions alongside them, having experienced their suffering or celebration ourselves.

According to Robert McKee in *Story*, whether characters are bad or good, we seek to find the Center of Good in them. We want to find a way to identify with them, and often we do this by finding a way to sympathize with them. The writers of LOST made this easy, as all of the characters have a Center of Good in them, and we seek to align ourselves with them.

It is difficult to think of many television shows in which the audience feels so connected with the characters. Sure, there are always characters we like or are our favorites, but to go so far as to identify with them is rare. Yet in LOST, the characters are crafted so well that we find ourselves transformed by their experiences.

The range of experiences endured by the characters is so universal that they are transcendent. That is, everyone from all walks of life can identify with at least *some* aspect of the characters or their problems. For almost every character in the show, the father/child relationship is an issue at the center of their troubles. No matter the degree of happiness in our own relationship with our parents, we can all sympathize with the characters and the struggles they face. Some of us have experienced more, and can empathize with them, creating a richer story experience.

Sawyer is one character we can all feel for. At first glance, we despise him, but as his story evolves, we feel sympathy for him as if he were a real person. We watch him hold the letter he wrote for the real Sawyer, the one responsible for his parents' death, and we know that deep down, below that tough exterior, there is a hurting little boy inside. Our hearts break for him, and we want to speak to him, to tell him we're there for him. Yet he's only a character, a figment of the writers' imagination. But he is more. He's the hurting child who has lost his parent, and we care for him. We are glad he's a fictional character, yet because his experience is so real, we have trouble remembering that he is only a character.

Good stories are powerful this way. They shape us as they force us to confront our deepest emotions, to see them in the characters onscreen, and to realize that they're everywhere. We are heartbroken to watch John Locke seek his father's love and approval, desperately wanting to believe he has worth as an individual. Our hearts break for him as he yells at the gate of his father, despondent and let down. We watch him alone in the jungle at night, crying at the Hatch, and we want his pain to end. John Locke's story is perhaps one of the most soul-wrenching stories in the show, and we desperately hope for him to find what he seeks by the end. And once again, our hearts sink as he dies in a dirty motel room.

We feel sympathy and empathy for Charlie, former drug-addict and protector of Claire and Aaron. We watch him leave behind his family's ring in Aaron's crib, and the image sticks with us because emotional meaning attaches to his action. It's not just a show; these people are real to us. We care about them. And so when Charlie dies, we mourn.

We feel for Ben Linus, master manipulator, deceiver of all. Ben, who allows his daughter to die at the hands of a mercenary and who is tricked into killing the Protector of the Island. Yet we feel for him. Why? Is it just because the writers gave us a good character? Or did they give us something more, something deeper? Did they understand that we have all felt alone, misled, uncared for and deceived, and decided to reflect those fears in Ben? I believe they did.

I also think they knew this when they let us get a glimpse of the Man in Black's true identity. A murderer at first sight, we come to known him as a sad individual, someone who only wants to be told the truth. The Man in Black is more than a "bad guy." He's Everyman. He's the person we can become if we choose to give into the darkness of our heart. We feel sympathy for him, because we wonder if we can see in him a spark of good, and we have hope for him that he is not completely lost.

As we watched the six seasons of LOST, we lived with these characters as if they were real. We cared because they *were* real. They were *us*. They *are* us. Much as the characters in the sideways world look into a mirror and see their true selves, we look at them, and they reflect who we are at the center of our being.

We Have to Go Back

LOST is over. But the story is not. No story that powerful ever can be. When the creators, writers and producers of the show set out to make it, they probably were not considering the profound impact the show would have on people.

But LOST is not just any story. LOST is *the* story of our lives, the story at the heart of mankind. As the creators have said, the title does not simply refer to a physical location, but to a spiritual or emotional reality. LOST changed the way stories are told, and in doing so, it taught us about the transformative power of story.

Once "The End" was over, I felt like people I knew were gone. Like Jack in the flash-forwards, I wanted to go back. I still do. I didn't want to say goodbye to these characters, to this story that moved so many. I wanted them to live on.

But they do live on. The story lives on in the discussions we still have about the elements of the show. It lives in the books that we write about it, eager to share what it has taught us. Not many television shows could claim as much.

LOST does make such claims, and rightfully so. The writers have created something that stands as an example of how an idea can become something much more than intended. They embraced the power of story.

C. David Milles has been teaching writing for nearly a decade. In his spare time, he writes Young Adult novels that seek to capture the power of story to transform his readers. When he's not writing, teaching, or listening to his collection of movie scores, he can usually be found reading more on the craft of writing or watching his favorite television shows, *Lost* and *Fringe*. He is currently writing his fourth young adult novel, tentatively titled *Paradox*. He recently began a blog on writing to connect with his young adult audience called "Attacking Ideas 101."

Read the blog here: http://cdavidmilles.blogspot.com

253

The Structure of LOST

Michelle Lang
Delano Freeberg
Antonio Savorelli

Lost: Poststructural Metanarrative or Postmodern *Bildungsroman*?

By Michelle A. Lang, Ph.D.

Editor's Note: *Dr. Lang wrote this paper in late 2007, at the end of Season Three. However, time has not affected the deep relevance of her thought or the power of her observations.*

The primary goal of this introductory paper is to define the terms "poststructural metanarrative" and "postmodern *Bildungsroman*," and to examine how they are relevant to *Lost*. I will also pose several questions that arise from the show when it is considered from this perspective. There are more questions in this paper than answers, but that was part of my goal: to generate a sustained dialogue with the *Lost* community on this and other conceptual issues relevant to *Lost*; and to encourage the development of the intellectual community concerned with the study of this innovative and important program.

In short, 'post-modern' and '*bildungsroman*,' two admittedly problematic terms, refer here to the largely self-contained narrative of the show: the story of the castaways that takes place in the present, past, and since the final episode of Season Three, the future. 'Post-structural metanarrative' could refer to larger self-reflexive, metafictional framing elements - such as the *Lost* game, the *Bad Twin* book, and the extensive Internet commentary - but here I am concentrating on those elements embedded within the primary narrative that have the potential to undermine its core realism, elements that question the nature of memory and identity, fiction and reality.

I will begin then, with the primary narrative - the story of the castaways after the crash of Oceanic Flight 815 on the island - which of course includes a backstory for each of the main characters that has only gradually been revealed through flashbacks. Together these narratives do not combine to form a *Bildungsroman* in the sense of the German novel of education and formation - a story of growing up *per se*. But *Lost* seems to be about growth into emotional maturity for many of the characters, regardless of their age - a theme that is consistent with our contemporary emphasis on adult self-improvement and self-knowledge. Thus Charlie overcomes his addiction, Jack takes charge of the group, Claire assumes responsibility for her child, Hurley finds a new courage, and Sawyer allows himself to fall in love.

In his study of the *Bildungsroman*, John R. Maynard comments that a major element of the form is the theme of identity: the nature of human nature. The *Bildungsroman* is not necessarily committed to the idea of an essential human nature, but it often examines the relative effects of environment and individual predisposition, or moral choice, for the creation of character.(1901) In *Lost* we do have the context of a dramatically-shifted geographic and social setting—the result of a traumatic event that, for most of the castaways, seems to have occurred when they were already in the midst of a personal crisis. Suddenly torn from their usual lives, they have plenty of time, and stimuli, on the island to provoke a meditation on who they really are and how they got to this point, on core beliefs that no longer seem valid, and on maps of the world inherited from family systems that now need to be redrawn. We see this largely through the flashbacks: Charlie's initial use of heroin, Jack being bullied by his father, Locke's exploitation by his parents, Sawyer's early lessons about the dire consequences of passion and jealousy, and most disturbingly, Ben's rejection of his abusive father. For Executive Producer Carlton Cuse, "these are heroes born out of moments" who "always act most nobly when they act in the spirit of community."(1902) This is human nature strongly affected by circumstance but also rooted in established traits that become increasingly evident over time.

While in the larger sense *Lost* is a story about character development, at every age, midway through the series it is not clear if this will emerge as a primary theme. After all, it is difficult to change who you are, and the characters are of sufficient complexity that the inevitable darker, more destructive sides of their personalities have emerged, and continue to do so. Despite behavior to the contrary, Desmond may still be a coward, Sawyer a con man, and Locke a self-destructive victim. Jack has a grace and maturity on the island that is much less evident in his flashbacks, or flashforwards. They are all both the people of the past and the present, and now, future, and it is hard to tell which, if any, of these time frames, will dominate, or if these pieces will come together to form a coherent gestalt of self-actualized personality.

Much of what we know about these characters is from flashbacks of an uncertain etiology. They could be moments of soul-searching clarity or self-affirming, self-protecting denial. If their function is to illuminate the larger theme of that episode, it is unclear how much of this information is for the benefit of the viewer alone. Are these lessons already learned, now re-remembered? Or are they events that have been reframed, a process stimulated by the circumstances of the present? There is a tantalizing ambiguity about these memories, given the motives they reveal about their narrators. We are encouraged to trust the characters by the sincerity with which they seem to remember, and the depth of feeling displayed in the past and present. But the degree to which a flashback is an accurate re-creation of an actual event is rarely clear, as the isolated setting provides so little corroborating evidence. And all of the characters are provided with motives that might compromise the construction of memory, which is at best a subjective process. Does Sayid really want to confront his past as a torturer? Is John really as naïve as he seems? To what extent is Kate capable of loyalty? Do we trust the characters to remember their lives with clarity, and anything approaching objectivity? As a narrative device, memory often has a precision that we know does not exist in real life. Nevertheless, the authorial intent might still be to provide additional access to a character's essential self, seen through their own perspective of increasing self-reflexive maturity. But I think what we are getting, at least in part at least, is a postmodern search for a fragmented 'truth'—one that does not exist in any objective sense. Characters are seen making decisions and performing actions, and suffering the consequences in both the present and past, but it is the latter that foregrounds the role of memory, suggesting that these recalled 'truths' might indeed be a condition of subjectivity.

This post-structural aspect of *Lost* is one of its most interesting elements, existing as it does in tension with a very un-postmodern sincerity. On the one hand *Lost* plays with the idea of absolute truth through the destabilization of identity, history and perception. Within its own fictional universe, the self is presented, in part, as a fictional construct. Certainly the characters are complex and realistic, but at the same time *Lost* has a certain new Historicism about it—identity is a social construction, mediated through the language of memory, and all truth is relative.

The island too has an uncertain status. It seems like a real place, but it has so many unreal aspects—the crashing black cloud of a 'monster,' the mysterious healing effect, the bizarre coincidences with Hurley's numbers, the relationships between some of the castaways in both the past and present—that we are again prompted to consider the structure of the narrative. There is also a prevalence of references to other texts beyond the immediate narrative. Philosophical names like Hume, Rousseau and Locke, books with related themes, such as *Watership Down*, *The Lord of the Flies*, and numerous other examples draw attention to the constructed, fictional nature of *Lost*.

At the same time there is an unmistakable authenticity to the characters—or at least to the castaways—that is at the center of each episode, in both timeframes. Some of the most intense moments of the show are starkly realistic in their emotional content: Jack's anger and grief over his father's death, his face when he sees Kate with Sawyer, and the loss he experiences in the flashforward; Sawyer's killing of Anthony Cooper; Rose's reunion with Bernard; Juliette watching her sister and her child, to name just a few examples. This is reinforced by the contrasting lack of affect usually displayed by the Others. These intense, very believable moments mitigate the ambiguity of the characters, suggesting that although memory may be unreliable, its associated feelings are real. I suspect that just as the gradual unfolding of logical reasons for what earlier seemed odd reasserts the realism of the plot—the polar bears having been brought to the island by the Dharma Initiative, for example—this may too be a device designed to enhance one of the core elements of the show, its mystery. But whether or not the characters end up having solidly integrated humanist selves or not, sincerity and believability are strong elements that dominate the show's more post-structural aspects.

And while *Lost* is to some degree about narration itself, it also contains a less reflexive totalizing meta-narrative. For even though it follows the postmodern dictum that all narratives are local, it has several overarching themes, including the complexity of the human heart and the possibility of redemption, that are more in the mode of universal truths embedded in a particular mythology than fictions to be deconstructed. There is also a strong suggestion within the narrative of a larger order lurking behind it—of answers that once revealed that will ultimately explain the lingering mysteries, rationalize the improbable coincidences and tie all of the loose ends together. *Lost*'s creators describe it as a 'mosaic' with elements from the past, present and future that will fit together in the end.(1903)

Lost also does not have a particularly postmodern hyperconsciousness— what Jim Collins calls "a hyperawareness on the part of the text itself of its cultural status, function, and history, as well as of the conditions of its circulation and reception."(1904) Individual characters provide plenty of sarcasm and irony, but this is never self-referential with respect to the show as a whole—it doesn't degenerate into parody. When the larger narrative alludes to its status as fiction it does so without compromising the emotional integrity of the individual castaways and their memories. They are not aware of being characters, or vehicles for larger themes. Locke does not comment on his distinctive name, or its possible associations with the situation in which he finds himself; Sawyer says that Watership Down is 'about bunnies,' without examining the irony that this particular book survived the crash. Again, the sincerity of the narrative is primary, and the hints that all may not be as it seems remains in the background. There is, then, a tension between the foregrounding of the structural aspects of *Lost* and the maintenance of the 'fourth wall' within the story itself - with the island as a self-contained thematic narrative within the larger contemporary sea of intellectual context, as it were.

Dr. Michelle Lang, for many years a professor of art at the University of Nebraska, is Managing Director at Critical Management Services in Edinburgh, Scotland. She is the author of *Saturn's Apprentice*.

Quantum Mechanical Pastiche Pie: Postmodernism on Jacob's Island

By Delano R. Freeberg

Abstract: *Lost* is most consistent with dispersive, participatory models of literary thought. The story is postmodern not only in structure and methodology but also in its insistence on local narrative and its outright rejection of culture-independent objective metanarrative. The popular disillusionment with the finale is properly interpreted as unfamiliarity with the postmodernist agenda, which centers around the emergence of community-centered circular (logically ungrounded) subjective texts. *Lost* does not claim objective truth. This paper uses some of the formatting and thought conventions associated with physical science, in part as parodic homage to the playful nature of *Lost* in general, and to the Dharma Initiative construct in particular.

Introduction

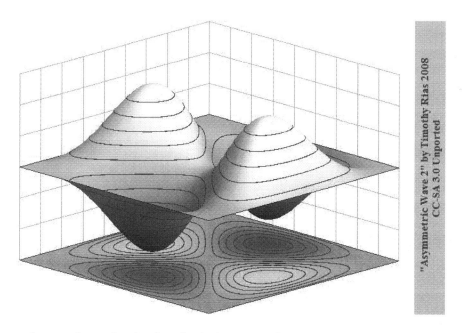

Asymmetric wavefunction for a fermionic two-particle state in an infinite square well potential. The asymmetry represents the deconstructionist binary opposition of dominant and marginalized narratives according to the Derrida school of post-structuralism.

We should not be surprised that speculative fiction is in the avant-guard of literary development; any such assertion would probably seem axiomatic to those with even a modest interest in literature, film, and theater. That the most speculative of genres, science fiction, has often been at the fore of advances in literary structure is likewise well accepted. However, the postmodern affinities of *Lost*, arriving a quarter century after the formal establishment of postmodernist theory and fully 55 years after the publication of George Orwell's *1984*, seem to have caught us off guard.

After all this time *Lost* could be considered cutting-edge only in the sense of having imported well-established literary principles to an artistic medium heretofore untouched by writing conventions more recent than those developed by Hemingway. Cookie-cutter, relentlessly linear stories based on dessicated logical syllogisms have been the norm in televised drama for over sixty years. *Lost* finally updated small-screen literary forms from the 1930s to the 1960s. Its greatest accomplishment is generally understood to be the dramatic ratcheting up of viewer expectation regarding story complexity, cultural relevance, and intellectual engagement. Most observers of pop culture seem to concur that no television successor to *Lost*'s storytelling magic has yet been identified; some have stated they do not expect to experience again such a compelling story in their lifetimes.

In this chapter I am not interested in *Lost* as story or as cultural phenomenon, but *Lost* as literary structure. I will bring to bear the simulated (hyperreal) concepts of Jean Baudrillard, the classification scheme of Ihab Hassan, the binary confrontation of opposites in Jacques Derrida's deconstructionist analytics, as well as supporting postmodern ideas first articulated by Jean-François Lyotard and other thinkers.

Postmodernism as applied to literature certainly extends at least as far back as *1984*, published in 1949. Orwell depicts an inner-party ruling elite in Oceania as continually destroying and rewriting history, replacing standard English with Newspeak, and in general denying proles and outer party members any objective reality other than the fluid truths promulgated by the party. Thus, the party destroys any independent means of establishing truth. Without an enduring hierarchical structure of historical and moral values, the masses in Oceania must accept the central party's manufactured reality. This rejection of objective reality is one of the core tenets of postmodernism, and the idea finds possibly its most complete development in Orwell's masterpiece.

Of immediate interest to any literary analysis of *Lost* is William Golding's *Lord of the Flies*. Golding asserts the complete lack of a moral center in the human psyche. When a group of pre-adolescent boys crash land on a deserted island, their society, unguided and unpoliced by British social expectations, quickly devolves into an uncivilized, self-destructive anarchy, ruled only by animal lusts. The absence of a moral compass—or any other discernible focal point—is yet another defining feature of postmodern thought. Lostpedia has mapped dozens of allusions to *Lord of the Flies* in *Lost* (http://lostpedia.wikia.com/wiki/Lord_of_the_Flies), including character names, situations, symbols, events, and themes.

While *Lost* is similar in form and structure to early postmodern science fiction, its methodologies, especially its broad use of philosophical pastiche, are closer in nature to those of later works, such as Philip K. Dick's *Do Androids Dream of Electric Sheep?* I believe the conclusions of both works are similar, also.

To many postmodern thinkers, especially to adherents of the Baudrillard school of criticism, television has long been a purveyor—perhaps even the premier source—of the enormous volume of disconnected and disorienting consumer-driven, value-encoded imagery at the core of postmodernist expression. Self-referential televised metadrama did not begin with *Lost*, and many popular programs, such as *The Simpsons* and *Seinfeld*, are considered to have moved from ordinary irony and double-entendre into the realm of double-encoded humor devoid of overriding metanarrative. In *Seinfeld* nothing makes sense, anarchy rules, and any attempt to apply logic or hierarchies of any kind only leads to further entanglements in nonsense.

Lost may not be the first example of small-screen postmodern drama (*Twin Peaks* and *Alias*, for example, are frequently mentioned as ground-breaking postmodern creations), but it is certainly the most celebrated and heavily analyzed.

Materials and Methods

The conceptual frameworks listed here provide the major criteria I used to establish *Lost*'s literary adherence to the cluster of parameters associated with a particular classification. These frameworks are not necessarily those of the thinker cited, nor should they be considered a full or even balanced representation, but ought to be viewed as merely my interpretation of the thinker's system for the limited purposes of this investigation. I understand nonlinearity to be a practical and essentially *de facto*, though not formally necessary or unique, outcome of the imposition of postmodernist forms, and I add this quality to the following list of postmodernist criteria.

The Hassan Criteria: Ihab Hassan understands postmoderism to reject universals: Truth, knowledge of any kind, values, history, science have no objective existence. Reality is a social construct and therefore subjective, pluralistic, temporary, valid only to the group creating it, and self-referential and circular to the point that no syllogistic proof is required or even possible. Process is deemed to have greater value than outcome. Postmodern qualities are best understood in their opposition to modernist parameters:

Modernism	Postmodernism
Objective	Social
Universal	Communal
General	Local
Result	Process
Design	Chance
Hierarchy	Anarchy
Distant	Participative
Synthesis	Deconstruction
Presence	Absence
Centered	Dispersed
Genre	Text
Semantics	Rhetoric
Paradigm	Syntagm
Transcendence	Immanence

Jencks Criteria: According to Charles Jencks, postmodern constructions convey eclectic double-coded icons that provide a sense of contradiction, paradox, irony, or parody.

Derrida Criteria: Jacques Derrida teaches that rationalist centers (universal, objective truths) exclude, creating in-groups and marginalized groups. This leads to the creation of binary opposites with a central term and a marginalized term. Poststructural deconstruction inverts the terms, so that the formerly marginalized becomes central.

Baudrillard Criteria: According to Jean Baudrillard, postmodernism projects simulacra (artificial copies of real things or events) that confirm the death of the real. Postmodern texts rely heavily on bombardment of the viewer-participant with a plethora of disconnected, deeply-encoded images of the type most frequently experienced in mass media (radio, television, Internet, newspaper, podcasts), and advertising of all kinds. Simulacra present digitized, binary, superficial or horizontal on/off or yes/no conditions that result in the minimization of differences and choice.

Jameson Criteria: Fredric Jameson asserts that postmodernist works include multiple instances of pastiche, defined here as a hodge-podge of literary styles, techniques, or motifs borrowed from multiple sources. Satire and parody are properly the province of earlier literary styles, such as modernism. Thus, a heavily satirical work may be considered to violate postmodernist principles, and may be aligned more closely with other classification schemes.

Lyotard Criteria: Jean-Francois Lyotard says postmodernism rejects grand narrative or metanarrative—text that asserts objective truth. Art cannot faithfully represent the Other. Even if it tries to do so, there is always another Other that the artist neglects. Text can only apply to the group that creates it.

Deleuze Criteria: Gilles Deleuze believes postmodern knowledge structures are horizontal, not hierarchical or vertical. Postmodernism does not concern itself with origins or destinations, roots or conclusions. Instead, this type of art makes a dizzying array of radically horizontal, rhizome-like connections from one artistic statement to another.

Results

I watched *Lost* on television and online over the six years of its broadcast life. I also purchased and viewed both the DVD and Blu-Ray versions of *Lost* and generated a full manuscript for the entire six years (including mobisodes) as a general reference for the confirmation of quotations. My assessments are recorded in the Discussion section.

Discussion

It is here, at the point of initiating a discussion regarding a work thought to exemplify postmodern patterns, that any resemblance to traditional analytical science breaks down. We cannot "prove" that a text is properly assigned to the province of postmodernism, but more importantly, we cannot dissociate ourselves from the discussion, or from the work itself. Passion-free movement from hypothesis to experimental design to description of observations to discussion of results (evaluation of alignment with the original hypothesis and prevailing theory) and final statement of conclusions is not possible. I am a participant in creation, and therefore entitled to comment on the work's impact in my life, or I am not. I am entitled to display unbridled passion, or I am not.

Lost, and any other postmodern work, requires that we subscribe to the Heisenberg Uncertainty Principle. We cannot have simultaneous knowledge of two intersecting properties of a subatomic particle. This idea may seem meaningless gibberish, but it really is a defining reality of postmodernism. In simple terms, we can know something only by measuring it, but in measuring the object of our interest, we change the object. We have touched it, or deflected it from its path, or made it aware of us as an entity requiring some degree of interaction. The notion of an independent, inert observer who does not affect the system being observed is a fallacy, especially in science. The observer *always* affects the system, and this truth becomes essential to quantum mechanics. This is also true in narratives, because the viewer or reader or "observer" is actually a full participant in the event. There are no outside observers in story, or art, or any facet of life, and postmodern interpretation makes us sensitive to this fact. Life and depictions of life in art are a quantum mechanical pastiche pie. We may resist the idea that we are participants, we may believe ourselves the independent and vicarious benefactors of others' creative work, but like it or not, we are the paint on the canvas, the actors on the stage, the characters in the novel.

I listed seven criteria to serve as the horizontal, rhizome-rich, comparative basis for this discussion. Each of the seven postmodernist authorities I cite offers emphasis or ideas different from or even at odds with those of his colleagues. I plan to compare my redactive understanding of our common creation, *Lost*, with the thought of these seven foundational thinkers.

The Meaning of *Lost*

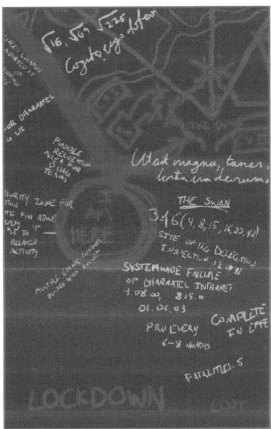

"Lockdown" by Gideon Slife
Used with permission

The characters of *Lost* were confused and lost in their lives until they fully participated in and bought into a narrative that had meaning to them personally at every level of their beings. Each of the characters ended up buying into a different narrative reality. For instance, Kate decided to devote her life to the narrative reality that included herself, Aaron, and Claire. She did this even though it meant leaving the men she loved, Jack Shephard and James Ford.

Each of the narratives enjoyed some degree of overlap. This was demonstrated in the horizontal or "sideways" world-narrative, where the characters "found" each other. While the church provided the backdrop for an ***artificial*** understanding of metanarrative, we know such an "objective" reality was not possible, since the island they believe they remembered inhabiting was actually located somewhere at the bottom of the Pacific Ocean. This did not mean that in the equally valid horizontal reality they knew as "the island world" they were imagining things. In fact, everything they experienced on the island was real, as Christian Shephard explained to Jack in the sideways church's outer room. The island narrative was different from the sideways narrative, but both were in the same sense real.

In the end, *Lost* was about building community in spite of multiple overlapping and sometimes conflicting narratives. The world we inhabit cannot subscribe to a single grand metanarrative, for to do so would be to continually erect barriers to the full participation of everyone. Metanarrative engenders a distancing of subjects and an exclusion of the Other. On the other hand, the depiction of multiple, overlapping narratives—understood by participants as the reality of their own lives—is a practical way of indicating the horizontal truths associated with people who experience their reality in different ways. People can live together in harmony only if they are not marginalized, treated as an inferior Other, and told that their way of life or their dreams and aspirations do not conform to the expectations and constraints of a metanarrative created by the politically powerful or religious elite.

Lost was postmodern from the very instant Jack first opened his eye after the crash to the moment he closed his eye in the same spot three years later. Lindelof and Cuse used the language of postmodernism, from their decision to call Ben's group "the Others" (Lyotardian terminology!) to the sideways (horizontal—Deleuzian terminology) world, to their nonsensical importation of hundreds of cultural quotations spanning thousands of years of history and representing virtually every religious, literary, and artistic tradition known to humankind, *Lost* was about the destruction of metanarrative and the assertion of local, socially-based text that allowed the participation of everyone.

Lost was not about the triumph of faith over science. Faith in what, exactly? The point of the Jack/Locke science versus faith debate was that there is no metanarrative into which everyone on Earth can be squeezed. Jack realized the shortcomings of science in trying to unravel the mysteries of Jacob's island. Locke came to understand the pointlessness of faith. Faith only temporarily gave him an inner sense of peace, but it all came crashing down when he realized his faith was baseless.

I do not believe *Lost* claimed that science and faith cannot serve as the basis for texts that are complete in themselves, or that they cannot serve as excellent starting points for systems of thought or spiritual guides. I think the island was a discontinuity to any text its participants believed to define reality for everyone. Jacob's island was the very sharp pin that burst the balloons the survivors considered the full definition of reality. The island forced everyone to erase their slates and start over. Jack told Kate in Episode 1.04, *Tabula Rasa*, that they were entitled to begin again, their slates wiped clean. I don't believe tabula rasa was a choice. I believe the survivors were being forced to confront an experience so foreign that not a single one of their pre-conceived notions of "reality" allowed them to deal with the scenarios and choices the island presented.

"It only ends once. Everything else is just progress," Jacob said. Yes, of course. The end did not matter. *Lost* was about the characters because the characters had to choose a narrative they were comfortable with, and that text changed from one person to another. That was the whole point of the sideways (horizontal) world, in which people realized their connections in different ways. They had to "find" themselves in different ways because their experience of reality—their narrative text—was different, virtually unique to the individual. The sideways world consisted of mini-clusters of narratives and their participants agreeing to co-exist amiably with each other. There was no grand narrative. The six religious symbols depicted on the church window did not represent coalescence into a single vision but rather a pastiche in which every narrative had relevance, and every narrative retained its fully unique flavor.

Sayid, for instance, did not spontaneously rise from his prayer on the *Elizabeth* and begin singing Christmas carols (it was, after all, close to Christmas when he set off on his quest to find the Others). No, Sayid never surrendered even one iota of his identity as full participant in the Islamic way of life. The star and the crescent on the church wall, for him and for all Muslims, did not mean merging with the other religions, or "equality" with the other religions. It meant simply that his religious views were entirely valid and true within his narrative. He was not an Other in the postmodern sense. His views were complete in themselves, inferior to no other view, even opposing views.

Live Together, Die Alone

Some commentators believe *Lost* presented an objective reality, and they claim it was based on the island. After all, Locke proclaimed the island was the focal point for everyone. "This place is different. It's special." (Episode 1.05) And, "The island brought us here." (Episode 1.24) The island did indeed bring the survivors to its flea-infested shores and its polar bear-infested jungle, but we saw with our own eyes the immediate effect of the island. There was no coalescence into a unified group. There were always multiple factions competing with each other, and others, like Rose and Bernard, that wanted no part of any of the factions. We rarely, if ever, saw any indication of unanimity of purpose.

The example of Ben Linus is instructive. He was never really connected to Jacob. He was concerned about his place on the island, though, and he worked with extraordinary diligence to maintain his vaunted place as leader of his people. When he saw his influence waning, he seemed to join forces with some of the survivors, but he was always looking toward what he perceived to be his best interests, and he returned to his own agenda and again opposed the survivors. When they shackled him and forced him to dig his own grave, he accepted the Man in Black's offer and ran into the jungle to get a rifle to kill Ilana. With great emotional fanfare, he held Ilana at gunpoint while she listened to his story, forgave him, and said "I'll have you." So, for an episode or two he was back in the survivors' camp. But that didn't last long. When the Man in Black threatened Ben, he gave his full support to the knife-wielding brother of the dead Protector. In the last few minutes of the story, he pulled a gun on Sawyer in his capacity as first lieutenant to the Man in Black. But a few minutes later, Ben again switched sides, this time pledging his all as lieutenant to Hurley.

The point of Ben's continual flip-flopping was not that he was a weak character, but that he was between narratives. His worldview did not include following, but leading. When Charles Widmore committed a sin against the Others' narrative by bedding a woman off-island, his violation gave Ben a ticket to island leadership. Ben was stable in his position as leader for over ten years, enjoying a narrative that seemed built for him. The appearance of the Flight 815 survivors on his island destabilized his narrative reality and led to three long years of insecurity, sometimes as prisoner, sometimes as valued source of information, but always truly as an Other existing outside the new majority's various text-realities. It was not until the installation of Hurley as Protector that Ben was again given the opportunity of occupying a leadership position, this time at the next level above Leader. He was offered the Advisor position, and he accepted immediately. His narrative-reality again made whole, he found himself in a stable worldview until the end of his life, when Hurley thanked him for being a "good Number Two."

The importance of Ben to the greater story is that people can "live together" only when they buy into a narrative-reality, fully immerse themselves, and participate unreservedly. Ben remained lost at the end of the series because he could not reconcile his life with the murder of his adopted daughter, which he believed he had caused.

The maintenance of socially-based narrative had such monumental significance to *Lost* that even the two main characters, Jack and Kate, were obliged to part company in the last few minutes of the series. Kate could have stayed with Jack, but her narrative—that helping Claire was more important than anything—meant she had to be willing to sacrifice even the man she loved. Jack died alone because Aaron needed a nanny.

The narratives were so different that the six passengers on the Ajira plane behaved virtually as strangers to each other. Only Kate and Claire bonded in a meaningful way, holding hands as the plane left the island. But the other passengers were off in their own worlds, perhaps contemplating their individual futures off the island. Meanwhile, Jack was dying all by himself, and Hurley and Ben were on another part of the island, apparently having forgotten about Jack entirely.

Redemption, and the full realization of "live together" as an event, did not occur in the island life, but in the horizontal (sideways) life, when the participants in multiple text-realities decided to "live and let live" without having to share each other's narratives.

But this ending was really inconsequential to *Lost*. The story was about the ***process*** of coming to identify valid text-worldviews. It was not about proving that faith was better than science, or that being trapped on a weird island had any significance in itself. The island was nothing more than a catalyst to force the characters to consider the awful, distasteful reality that their narratives were insufficient to interpret and encompass the different kinds of text-realities they saw (but never understood) inhabiting the space and time all around them. This is why Damon Lindelof and Carlton Cuse correctly insisted that the story was about the characters, not about the run-amok mythology or about any over-arching themes. All the mythology-based theories that inhabited the Internet for so many years now amount to amusing curiosities, but they contribute nothing to our deeper understanding of *Lost*. The *Lost* vision of community—live together—is achieved only when communities drop their infantile, modernist insistence on metanarrative and get on with the business of living out their own narratives and make a decision to accept others' views as having validity equal to their own.

The Heisenberg Pastiche Pie

I have spoken so far of *Lost*'s correspondence to several of the Hassan criteria (social, communal, local, process, participation), the Derrida view (marginalization as an outcome of modernism), the Lyotard assertion of local narrative, and Delueze's contention that postmodern knowledge structures are horizontal. In this section I will explore the story's deep commitment to Fredric Jameson's rhizome-like pastiche. This section will also serve to connect with Baudrillard's understanding of postmodernism.

Lost quoted hundreds of novels and plays, scores of authors, dozens of philosophical traditions (especially in character names, such as John Locke, Rousseau, Edmund Burke, and the like), mythology from several ancient traditions, pop culture (such as Star Wars), and the icons and rituals of every major religion. An in-depth comparison of these rhizomic signs and images and their connections to each other would require hundreds of pages, certainly beyond the scope of this short paper, but also unnecessary to the development of my thesis. Rather than an open-ended exploration of thousands of signs and images, I will restrict my commentary to a discussion of the syntagmatic signs connected to the Swan Station.

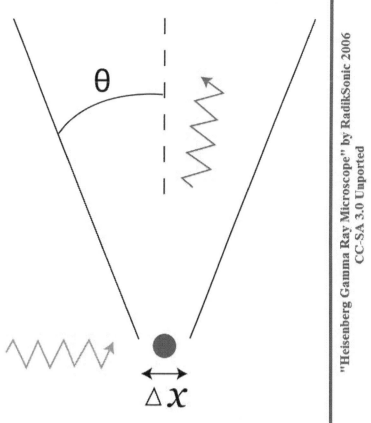

Picture of the gamma-ray microscope described in Heisenberg's 1927 paper on the uncertainty principle ("Über den anschaulichen Inhalt der quantentheoretischen Kinematik und Mechanik", Zeitschrift für Physik, 43, 172-198). The blue circle is the particle, the green wave is the incoming gamma-ray and the red wave is the gamma-ray scattered up into the aperture angle θ of the microscope (depicted as solid black lines). The uncertainty in the particle position is △x, as shown.

The Swan Station, one of the several Dharma Initiative stations found throughout Jacob's island, did not symbolize anything. Rather, it served as a drop zone for the placement of multiple cultural and literary references. For instance, the station itself was named after an important element of the ancient Greek myths associated with the sun god, Apollo (Swans were sacred to Apollo (http://www.theoi.com/Phylos/Hyperborea.html accessed January 4, 2012)), but the Swan Station logo, the Dharmachakra, was borrowed from Buddhism, and the Swan Station orientation video depicted Dr. Marvin Candle using a Hindu salutation, "Namaste." The countdown clock featured ancient Egyptian symbols, which Carlton Cuse said could be translated to mean "Underworld." (Carlton Cuse at Comic Con 2006) The underworld reference seemed to be tied to the Dharma Initiative's understanding of the Smoke Monster as the island's version of Cerberus, the three-headed dog who guarded the gates to Hades in ancient Greek mythology, but considered by the DI as a "security system." The six famous numbers, on the other hand, added up to 108, which is a sacred, perfect number in the Hindu religion. The numbers included a prime number (23), and 42, which may have been an homage to Douglas Adams' humorous view that 42 was the "Answer to the Ultimate Question of Life, the Universe, and Everything." (*The Hitchhiker's Guide to the Galaxy*)

The station featured an expressionist (modernist) painting attributed to Desmond Hume (actually created by artist/director Jack Bender) and a geodesic dome, a modernist design patented by R. Buckminster Fuller (U.S. Patent 2,682,235, granted in 1954, and U.S. Patent 3,197,927, granted in 1965). The dome was filled with the 1970s-era accoutrements of early computer science. If this lair of modernist thought "symbolized" anything, we would have to say it pointed to the great failure of modernism. The inability of the station to deal with simple electromagnetic phenomena, long known to science, was testament to the pathetic nature of modernist thought. The station's implosion at the end of Season Two could be interpreted as a visual sign tied to the conceptual implosion of the thought system represented by Gertrude Stein, James Joyce, and Ernest Hemingway.

Desmond David Hume was the second major personage in what became a long line of characters named after the representatives of various philosophical schools of thought. David Hume was an empiricist. This choice provided a subtle basis for eventual reconciliation of multiple narratives. If Lindelof and Cuse had chosen a theorist for the name of the Swan Station's single inhabitant we might have expected a higher level of tension between advocates of the science and faith metanarratives, since postmodernism rejects theory as a hierarchical imposition. But in choosing David Hume, the representative of a philosophical tradition that can coexist with postmodernist thought, the writers made broader allowance for the reconciliation we witnessed in the final minutes of the series.

The bookshelf was the most interesting feature of the station, and also the source of the Swan's richest trove of pastiche treasures. We saw dozens of titles, including

After All These Years
The Brothers Karamazov
Dirty Work
High Hand
An Occurrence at Owl Creek Bridge
Our Mutual Friend
Rainbow Six
The Third Policeman
The Turn of the Screw
Valis

The point was not that Desmond Hume was a Renaissance man, but that *Lost* was asserting the horizontal, crabgrass-like significance of dozens of literary points of view. I believe the bookshelf also served to deflect any thought that the writers were attempting to create a modern-day *Lord of the Flies, The Stand, The Dark Tower,* or the other works thought to have had influence on the show; *Lost* is not derivative, it is unique.

I cannot find any basis for the idea that Desmond's book, *The Turn of the Screw*, serves as a literary foundation for Desmond Hume's character, or the conceptual root of the Swan Station, the Dharma Initiative, or any of the other pastiche elements of *Lost*. Certainly the other books on the shelf have even less direct connection to Desmond or any of the Dharma stations. I would imagine that each one of these books, somewhere on the Internet, serves as the basis for a mythology-based theory about Desmond's origins or the true meaning of the Swan Station or the Dharma Initiative's connection to Jacob's mother's second cousin, but any such theory is going to be based on speculations having no real bearing on the story. These books are pastiche, and nothing more. They serve as intricate, horizontal knitting, weaving themes and conceptual threads into an immense patchwork tapestry that signifies the interconnected yet distinct nature of the disparate elements of human diversity. The books point to the rich, pluralistic, postmodern heritage that *Lost* embraced.

The Swan Station was one of many feeding stations for the passive acquisition of the thousands of images, signs, and double-coded icons that bombarded us into passive acceptance along the lines of Baudrillard's understanding of late capitalist mass media advertising and image propagation. The sheer weight of so many images competing for space in our jumbled and fragmented thoughts had to lead to the implosion of any hierarchical connections to history or precedent or symbolic significance. This was certainly the showrunners' intention, made manifest in the physical implosion of the Swan at the end of Season Two and demonstrated again (for emphasis!) at the beginning of Season Six.

Conclusion

The way Lindelof and Cuse chose to end *Lost* should have confirmed in every viewer-participant's mind the writers' postmodernist intent. Throughout the six seasons of *Lost*, we were treated to binary oppositions in the form of a majority-view character berating a marginalized character.

The purpose of these binary oppositions became clear in the final episode, when first the Man in Black and Jack, then Hurley and Ben were portrayed as meting out rope to a man descending into the light cave. In both cases, the tables were turned, with the individuals representing the initial marginal view (Jack and Hurley) being portrayed as carrying fire for the now-majority position. The binary positions were deconstructed, indicating movement from modernism to postmodernism, following the inevitable pathway described by Jacques Derrida. But Benjamin Linus delivered the socially-derived deconstructionist frosting on the postmodernist cake:

> HURLEY: It's my job now... What the hell am I supposed to do?
> BEN: I think you do what you do best. Take care of people. You can start by helping Desmond get home.
> HURLEY: But how? People can't leave the Island.

BEN: That's how Jacob ran things... Maybe there's another way. A better way.

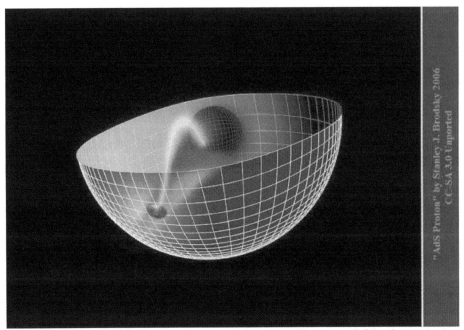

A small proton created at the AdS boundary falls into AdS space pulled by the gravitational field up to its larger size allowed by confinement. Due to the warped geometry the proton size shrinks near the AdS boundary as perceived by an observer in Minkowski space.

Hurley and Ben, two opposites working together toward development of a social construct, not achieving a goal, but just a **process**, "just progress," as Jacob said, would fashion their own way of doing things. That is, they would develop their own narrative to replace the outdated Jacobian narrative that no longer fit their styles. The island and everything on it would bend to their construct because, in the end, that's the way the world works. In fact, that's the **only** way the world can work. Communities and civilizations fashion their own way of dealing with the world as they understand it. Jacob's way of interacting with people and the sea and all of history could not become Hurley's way, unless he made the choice to accept Jacob's narrative as his own.

Hurley and Ben embraced the liberating, inclusive, horizontal nature of local postmodern narrative. They left us with the final, crucial thought: Life on the island continued. Even after the show ended, the **process** went on.

It was a wild six years. But if Ben's words to Hurley mean anything, they mean something to us, because we are the actors to whom Ben's words were really addressed. Ben's words mean *Lost* is not a closed text. *Lost* continues, the text lives, and therefore there is no reason for us to leave the island.

As for me, I think I will join the hunt Hurley is organizing. Roast boar, a nice snifter of Dharma Initiative boxed cognac (from the generic district of the Cognac region!), and a generous helping of Heisenberg pastiche pie will top off the perfect meal as we lean back on the warm sand, enjoy the setting sun, and listen to Glenn Miller's "Moonlight Serenade." "Perhaps," we think to ourselves, "we will not be caught off guard this time." We will know to ask when we are, not where we are. It could happen. But we will certainly be caught off guard by other bits of pastiche, other fascinating elements that eluded us the first time around. After all, this time around, we know we are fully entitled—to enjoy the boar, the cognac, the pie—to display unbridled passion in every moment we enjoy here, in this place, in this time.

Delano R. Freeberg is an analytical scientist. He holds more than a dozen patents and received an honorary doctoral degree for his work on adjustments to the Debye–Hückel limiting law. He enjoys murder mysteries, running, Tae Kwon Do, and theoretical physics.

By Antonio Savorelli, Ph. D.

"George Burns and Gracie Allen"
Publicity Photo, CBS Television, October 1952 PD

Editor's Note: *Semiotics is the study of the processes of production and communication of meaning, beyond the realm of linguistics—which in turn can be considered a branch of semiotics specialized in verbal signification systems. Structural semiotics, particularly, is centered on the complex processes that govern the existence of texts, intended as the self-contained products of a specific system or, in the case of syncretic texts such as those of television and other audiovisual media, of a combination of systems.*

This essay was born during the first month after the *Lost* finale. My initial idea of writing a simple, informal blog post got a little out of hand, in terms of both length and content. During that month, one of the most frequent questions I got from people—not only *Lost* watchers—was whether or not I liked the series finale. I wasn't sure what answer to give, which is why this essay came out on my website over a month late, after the whole world had already written about it, one way or another.

Fans had tweeted their satisfaction or disappointment, while non-fans had reiterated their lack of interest (and also openly mocked the disappointed fans). Academics had already had enough time to dissect, analyze, interpret the episode, the season, the series, and, possibly, the fans' reactions to all of them.

I was torn. I could be a fan and voice my feelings about the outcome of the series, or I could wear my structuralist's hat (which I admit I generally have a hard time taking off, not for academic snottiness but because I think I'm just wired that way). As it turned out, trying to separate the two perspectives wouldn't quite make sense, as they're always inextricably linked.

The Truth About Season Six

The title of this section is misleading, since I'm not going to reveal any previously unknown secrets. The truth in question concerns my attitude toward Season Six, which, up until the last few episodes, I claimed was illuminating and as engaging as the previous two. In reality, I was underwhelmed and slightly disappointed with what I perceived to be a lack of narrative involvement: information was being given, but I didn't feel that enough stuff was actually happening.

It seemed to me that *Lost* was violating one of narrativity's cardinal rules, that of "show, don't tell," which can only be taken literally in the case of an audiovisual medium. Surprisingly enough, even an audiovisual medium has very powerful ways to tell and not show.

One of the trademarks of the early seasons of the show was the sense of "a-ha!" the viewer got when things were revealed. The fifth episode of Season Four, "The Constant," can be considered the single most important of the series, not only because of the themes involved, but especially because it's the perfect model for the show's peculiar textual mechanics. This episode alone succeeds at doing what the entire sixth season mostly fails at (or simply refuses to do): providing revelations instead of explanations.

Most of the frustration I got from Season Six depended on the fact that all these explanations were spoon-fed to me very carefully, lest I miss anything. It was almost as if the whole season had been designed as a system of footnotes to the previous five—and the last three episodes confirmed this feeling.

Of course, I already knew that every season had its own special quality, which meant I had to accept Season Six as having this peculiar one. It still didn't mean I had to like it.

The Fan and the Semiotician

Accepting this new quality of the show meant that, as a semiotician, I was acknowledging a shift in its textual construction, exactly like I had previously acknowledged the time travel, the paranormal activity, and every other seemingly odd element of *Lost*'s discursive and narrative fabric—up to the very idea that a bunch of people had survived a plane crash of that magnitude.

But this is what fiction is about, isn't it? It's exactly what suspension of disbelief means. As long as the different shifts in textual construction hold together, there would and should be no grounds for complaint. If everything holds, the text can be assumed to be semiotically sound (until proven otherwise). This is nothing the inexpert (or the skeptical) reader should be scared of: humans are constantly involved in some kind of semiotic endeavor, when they try to construct meaning or to make out the meaning of things.

If, so far, the semiotician doesn't judge (and he never should, really), the fan is allowed some margin of discomfort. But since the fan and the semiotician are bound together, both perspectives have to be taken into account in my understanding of the *Lost* finale and, consequently, of the whole series.

The Myth of the Lack of Revelations

One of the most common complaints I've read online is that the series finale didn't provide enough explanations of things that had happened before. I want to be daring and unpopular here, and say that I think the finale (and the entire Season Six) provided way more information than it should have. Everyone who has watched *Lost* for at least a few episodes knows that it is by no means the usual kind of American drama, where everything gets a nice explanation at the end. It's no procedural drama, and it's definitely no Gilmore Girls. (Pardon the reference here, I was trying to go for the least *Lost*-like show I could think of.)

It's not only because the complexity of the storyline is so high that it would have been impossible to explain everything—who wants six more seasons raise a hand—but because the semiotic process at the foundation of *Lost* requires viewers to fill in the gaps. It's what we do in real life in every single moment, which is why I don't think it should be considered so outrageous for a work of art to require us to do the same. (Yes, a work of art: if we put it this way it's not so outrageous anymore, is it? Did Dante write his own footnotes to the Comedy? I don't think so. Did I just compare *Lost* to Dante? You betcha.) Ultimately, it would have been an insult to the viewers if every single detail of the story had been accurately explained. However, television has gotten us accustomed to receiving explanations, which I think is why many viewers expected them.

Why would I need to know who Mother is or how the light at the center of the island works? (As Jason Mittell brilliantly puts it, "Unless you want to build your own, why do you care?").(2101) Frankly, I'm not even sure I needed to know there was a Mother or a light. This, in my opinion, is why *Lost* works much better when some things are left unsaid or ambiguous.

One particular example is the moral polarization between Jacob and his brother. On the one hand everything points to a semisymbolic (2102) relationship between the two: one wears a white shirt and seems to be the good guy, the other one wears a black shirt and seems to be the bad one. (The white:black::good:evil semisymbolism is so conventional and culturally ingrained to be nothing short of a cliché.) This opposition also seems to be confirmed in Mother's discourse, when she tells Jacob's brother that he's special because he can lie (as opposed to Jacob, who apparently can't), and also when she tells Jacob that he was always meant to be the next guardian of the island (because he's the good guy, one would assume). While it could be argued that Mother is lying to Jacob, her discourse consolidates this moral opposition as the official axiology according to which Jacob will rule the island. Since lying is supposed to be wrong, the "moral math" should follow very simply. Nonetheless, Jacob is seen doing (or having people do on his behalf) very bad things, while his brother—even after becoming the smoke monster—shows to be capable of mercy and perhaps even of honoring his word. Yet no precise revelation about the true nature of this opposition is ever provided.

Partly as a consequence, the one big detail *Lost* leaves unsaid is the question of what would have happened had "Locke" been able to leave the island. All we know is Jacob's metaphor of the wine bottle (the island), according to which if the red wine (his brother) spills out it will be bad news for the whole world—which is why someone must guard the island (acting as a cork). Since Jacob cannot lie, we can only assume he is telling the truth to the best of his knowledge, but we cannot know whether that truth is, well, true. And it doesn't matter. The final fight between Jack and "Locke" is by no means less powerful or less meaningful because of this uncertainty or lack of relevance of the ultimate truth. Better yet, it's a perfect deployment of the theme of faith, which used to be Locke's prerogative and now, in the final season, gets transferred to Jack.

Moving Sideways

At the beginning of Season Six I felt that the time-travel dilemma had been brilliantly solved with the introduction of a parallel universe. I'm sure I wasn't the only one who had to wait until the last episode to understand that it was not at all like that. (In retrospect, I should have known better than to take what I was seeing at face value.) Even more strikingly, it wasn't until maybe a couple of episodes to the end that I realized the writers (and consequently the hard-core fans) used the term sideways to denominate this special universe.

I don't think this term is too descriptive, and it wouldn't have given anything away if I had known about it, except for the fact that I would have noticed the producers' implicit refusal to talk about a parallel universe. After all, meaning emerges in difference, doesn't it? And isn't absence a very notable kind of difference?

Here's where the semiotician—so far intent on explaining and motivating what the fan couldn't accept—becomes himself uncomfortable with the turn of events. The feeling is that the producers decided, sometime in Season Five, to make

Lost break out of the text, and to turn themselves into the masters of a game where some of the players had more knowledge than others. Specifically, the hard-core fans (that is those who discuss the show at length in web forums and blogs, and actually have some level of interaction with the producers) had access to information that was not directly derivable from the text of the TV show.

It's way more than what happened with the invention of the Valenzetti equation back in Season Two. Not knowing what that was didn't change the (lack of) understanding the viewers had of the numbers. On the other hand, this unforeseen interference between television and its web-based metatextual world had, in my opinion, far deeper effects on the sixth season.

"Interferenz" by Dr. Schorsch 2005 CC-SA 2.0 Generic

The degree to which this interference is actually unforeseen is open for discussion. Let me just say that a television system still largely based on traditional broadcasting, where little room is left for interaction, makes it harder for the majority of viewers to even be aware of such interference—let alone participate in it. But I'll keep this particular door shut.

Lost: an Exposé

Not that it hadn't happened before. The fourteenth episode of Season Three, *Exposé*, was exactly the product of such an interference. Nikki and Paulo were killed off the way they were (buried alive by mistake, in an episode that was completely out of context) simply because the fans didn't like them. (2103) Despite Damon Lindelof's claim that the characters were "universally despised," I must assume the decision was based on a relatively small number of fans—the ones who gave constant feedback. The others probably had no idea who these two characters were. As Sawyer would say, "Who the hell is Nikki?"

This unequal distribution of knowledge and awareness among the fans had a big impact on the reactions to the episode: those who knew and did dislike Nikki and Paulo could, of course, understand exactly what the episode was about (and cheered); those who didn't dislike them (having barely noticed them at all) simply remained clueless about the ultimate meaning and function of the episode, and just thought of it as a dud, a low point in the whole series—even lower than Mr. Eko and Ana Lucia (there, I said it).

Then there are people like me, who may have picked up on the episode's odd nature and realized it didn't happen by accident. Like I said (and it's not something I came up with, (2104) unfortunately), meaning lies in differences: the discursive structures of the episode—as well as its structure of enunciation—are significantly different from anything that comes before. Also, while "Exposé" may have influenced future choices, no other episode that follows behaves the same way. Due to its placement midway through the series it can afford to be odd, since the show's semiotic mechanisms have already been established.

I won't go into the details of how the episode plays with these mechanisms. (2105) Suffice it to say that it's the show's first attempt at overflowing its established textual boundaries—if it were an actor, it would be breaking the proverbial fourth wall.

Back to the End

The single most interesting feature of the series finale is the revelation of the fake parallel universe. This illusion, carried on for a whole season, fits perfectly into *Lost*'s general strategy of deception and withholding of information, even more so considering that the revelation comes in an absolutely unexpected way. (2106) My first reaction to it was to think that it made the whole season lose sense—which is in fact the exact opposite of what it's meant to do. Then I regained my semiotic awareness (not before watching the episode again, after a whole day during which I felt as if I had been drugged) and realized that not only was meaning not taken away, but that there was a whole new level of meaning to be considered.

Here's where the "sideways" denomination came into play, as the marker of the meaning to come—a marker that is completely extratextual, since up to a certain point no one within the text is aware of the parallel universe. A whole class of viewers must have been tipped off by this word. Those who were more actively involved with the off-the-air discussion about *Lost* had to be closer to an understanding of the season before I ever was.

What bothers me about this interference of an extratextual world with the final outcome of the text is that it challenges all the partial conclusions I had drawn about the meaning of the show. Whether or not I like the outcome as a fan, as a semiotician I cannot but take into account the finale's pragmatic implications. After watching the episode, I had the bitter feeling that I would eventually be able to reconcile my discomfort, and justify the structural shift in the name of a sort of postulated textual consistency.

The feeling I had about it was bitter because I realized that's exactly the sort of thing non-semioticians think semiotics does: find arbitrary justifications in the name of some abstract principle. I was also feeling bitter because the finale forced me to change my pragmatic approach to the whole text—better yet, to have one, after years of basically ignoring the pragmatic component and treating *Lost* as a self-contained and -sufficient text. If my initial approach was probably too conservative (but I will deny ever admitting to this), the pragmatic shift in Season Six was what broke the series' textual consistency.

The enunciative structure of the text, which for five seasons had been functional to its narrative tension—that is, to creating those mechanisms of suspense and anticipation that drove the whole story—in Season Six was bent, once again, but with the new goal of creating a device that would deceive the audience, and ultimately split it into two unequal parts: a participating audience with considerably more (albeit not necessarily accurate) knowledge and insight, and one, possibly much wider, that had no access to a certain amount of extratextual information on the show—information that, let's not forget, often came directly from the very people who ran the show.

Quenching the Fans' Thirst

Season Six was designed to answer the fans' questions—as anticipated by Carlton Cuse and Damon Lindelof in the Season-Five DVD extras—and that's exactly what it does: it takes single issues and gives explanations. Sometimes it does so by devoting entire episodes to relatively minor details with the sole purpose of gratifying the thirsty fan (by which I mean the kind of fan who's interested in the smallest detail without much consideration for its weight in the general structure of the story).

This is the case with the ninth episode, *Ab Aeterno*, where we finally get to know Richard Alpert's back story. We do learn more about the dynamics between Jacob and the Man in Black (although we still don't know they're brothers), but the episode-long flashback serves almost exclusively as a setup for the scene where Hurley acts as an intermediary between Richard and his long-dead wife (a scene that seems taken from an episode of Ghost Whisperer, with Jorge Garcia as an unlikely Jennifer Love Hewitt), in order to restore the immortal man's faith in the mission Jacob bestowed upon him one and a half centuries before.

The episode's real mission is revealed: shaking up the viewer's faith by displaying Richard's own crisis, only to restore it—along with Richard's—at the end of the episode. But was the viewer's faith all that solid to begin with? And does the episode ultimately restore it? Does it even want to? All plausible questions with a bunch of different plausible answers, but more than else these questions are a confirmation that the text has engaged in a duel with the viewers: via a not-too-subtle simulacrum (Richard) it challenges its own veridictive premises by tickling the audience with the seasons-old questions about the nature of the island and the existential status of its inhabitants. This is all the episode seems to care about, as it otherwise shows very few signs of narrative advancement.

Say Goodnight, Katie

Lost's final season, and particularly the last episode, is way more self-reflexive than the show ever was, or than it ever wanted to appear. By breaking out of its established pragmatic model—where the enunciative device played cat and mouse with the audience without ever letting itself get caught—*The End* engages the audience directly, and voices out a number of issues that had bothered the viewers for six seasons. It even goes as far as to make fun of its own creation, through some of the characters' smirky remarks (such as Kate mocking Christian Shephard's name). Once again, even if only briefly, by moving up a level and engaging with the audience, the text finds it easier to assume some distinctly comic traits.

What I see is that the sixth season was designed as a long setup to the finale, which couldn't not be a long goodbye. And despite the fact that I may not approve—as a fan, mostly—of the way it was deployed, I think everything about it was built almost to perfection. Once again, and for the last time, *Lost* was able to create expectations and give us something unexpected in the end: it was able to surprise us. As Jason Mittell also remarks, (2107) *The End* reminded me somewhat of the finale of *Six Feet Under*, from an emotional point of view. Contrary to Mittell, though, that's exactly what I didn't like about it—and I don't mean I didn't like it being emotional: I thought the *Six Feet Under* finale was unnecessarily and nauseatingly rhetorical, a way not to end a story but to part from the viewers.

This need for a rhetorical goodbye can be understood in the case of a series that, like *Lost*, had such an interactive history, and considering that the final season—and even more so the last episode—was a veritable worldwide event. I think this is what made the final episode generate strong emotional reactions even in people who didn't particularly care for the way things ended—or who stubbornly refuse to accept it (I know some of those).

Ultimately, though, what makes me uncomfortable about this kind of finale is not the rhetorical approach per se, but the fact that, in my opinion, it works only upon first viewing and possibly just for a limited subset of viewers. It works quite well for a text that is perceived as ephemeral and perishable not only by its audience but also—if not primarily—by its producers.

But, contrary to general opinion, *Lost* isn't over: it's only just begun.

Antonio Savorelli holds a Ph.D. in communication and new technologies, and runs a small web-design studio in Imola, Italy. As an independent scholar, he pursues his interest in the application and expansion of semiotic theories to the fields of televisual narratives and digital design. His research on the transformation of American sitcom was published in 2010 by McFarland & Co., with the title *Beyond Sitcom: New Directions in American Television Comedy*. On the web: antoniosavorelli.it.

Lost as the Neo-Baroque

By Michelle Lang, Ph.D.

"Madonna and Child in Glory" by Isaac Oliver ca. 1610
WMC PD

Editor's Note: *Although Dr. Lang composed this paper during the third season of LOST, her argument—and conclusions—are as vital now, two years after the conclusion of LOST, as they were five years ago. At issue is the question of whether LOST proposed universal or objective truth or instead obeyed the tenets of postmodern, subjective (social) relativity. Dr. Lang's conclusions are controversial and her analysis makes for fascinating reading.*

In *Neo-Baroque Aesthetics and Contemporary Entertainment*, Angela Ndalianis evaluates the transhistorical, metamorphic and enfolded spatial formation that is the postmodern Neo-Baroque. In doing so she describes the forms that are characteristic of this contemporary incarnation of what was once called a style, but is more precisely and comprehensively presented in her text as a mode, a poetic, and a logic. Ndalianis is primarily concerned with contemporary cinema and its associated media, but this Neo-Baroque aesthetic can also be located in the medium of television, for example, in the series *Lost*. *Lost* uses all of the major Neo-Baroque elements defined by Ndalianis: the persistent, if partial, violation of the frame that contains the artistic illusion; the emphasis on intertextuality, complexity and virtuosity; and "the active engagement of audience members, who are invited to participate in a self-reflexive game involving the work's artifice."(2201) But the Neo-Baroque in *Lost* is no mere referencing of a popular creative mode; rather, *Lost* engages with that foundational element of the Baroque - the fidelity to nature - with an ambivalent complexity seen in the most vivid examples of the original style.

Definitions and (Art) History

Madonna of the Long Neck, Parmigianino (1534-40)

The term Baroque derives from the Portuguese *barrocco* which refers to a deformed pearl;(2202) it also was used in late sixteenth-century French speech to denote something unusual or bizarre, and may relate to *baroco*, a type of syllogism described by scholastic philosophers.(2203) Although popular in its own time, by the later eighteenth century—an era dominated by the Neo-Classical style—Baroque was widely criticized on both aesthetic and moral grounds. Diderot (1758) described 'baroque' architecture as "the ridiculous taken to excess."(2204) Compared to the clean lines, local colors and idealized forms of the Renaissance and Neo-Classical art to which it was being compared, Baroque art was seen as too extravagant and intense. But there was also recognition that after the more extreme distortions of Mannerism—seen in such works as Parmigianino's *Madonna of the Long Neck* (1534-40)—the Baroque was at least a return to Renaissance principles of unity and the observation of nature. Writing in 1855, Jacob Burckhardt conceded that the principal methods of the new 'Baroque' style were "naturalism in form as well as the whole conception of what had happened (reality) and the display of emotion at any cost."(2205) Although overstated here, the core of Burkhardt's observation about the Baroque—the increased veracity in the representation of both the natural and human worlds—is now understood to be a typical component of the style.

Baptism of Christ, Andrea del Verrocchio (1470s)

It was Heinrich Wölfflin, however, who achieved the most important, early critical rehabilitation of the Baroque.(2206) Wölfflin contrasted the Renaissance and

Baroque styles using five opposing pairs of elements: linear versus painterly, plane versus recession, closed versus open form, unity versus multiplicity, and absolute versus relative clarity.(2207) The typical Renaissance form Wölfflin describes is illustrated by Andrea del Verrocchio's Renaissance *Baptism of Christ* (painted in the 1470s), a Renaissance painting, a reproduction of which was displayed on the wall of Charlie's childhood home and recreated in his dream in *Fire + Water*. This painting has the multiplicity of elements, absolute colors, even lighting and parallel planes, all contained within the frame, that are typical of this style. By contrast, Rembrandt's *Nightwatch* (painted in 1642), a Baroque example, is more unified, with more relative color, naturalistic and dramatic lighting, and recession into space.

Nightwatch, Rembrandt van Rijn (1642)

Wölfflin's system has since been criticized for being reductive and deterministic, but his description of the essential qualities of the Baroque style remains influential.(2208) Subsequent art historical scholarship has refined, rejected and now it seems, largely resigned itself to the continued use of the term 'Baroque' to characterize the constellation of formal and thematic elements that dominated seventeenth-century Western European art. For painting and architecture, these may include: a commitment to naturalism (which in the seventeenth century meant that nature was still idealized, but to a lesser degree than during the Renaissance); an increased interest in human character and emotion; a penchant for allegorical and symbolic meaning, especially with reference to transience and mortality; quasi-theatrical staging and lighting; the representation of intense often violent scenes designed to capture attention and, in the case of religious art, inspire devotion; the projection of the artistic and thematic space into the realm of the viewer; and the use of multiple media to engulf said viewer in a *Gesamtkunstwerk*—a total work of art.(2209)

The Baroque can also be conceived in more philosophical terms, useful for bridging the historical distance between the seventeenth and twenty-first centuries. As an aesthetic, it uses technologically sophisticated forms and complex themes to first attract viewers, and then suspend them in an uneasy, yet pleasurable, state of apprehension. This emphasis on the moment just before the event - a device essential to horror films - "actually has the effect of suturing [the viewer] into the image and its emotions."(2210) The philosophy of the Neo-Baroque is intertwined with postmodernism, where 'truth' and 'reality' have no absolute definition and rigid, static boundaries exist to be transgressed. In both the Baroque and Neo-Baroque, time and space can be elements of form and content, emotion and perception can be both process and theme. The contemporary film *Matrix reloaded*, for example, is Neo-Baroque in its use of intense visual spectacle intended to overwhelm the viewer and foreground the process of vision itself - a theme supported by the multiple levels of reality in the narrative and the explicit references to the spiritual and the sacred (including Christianity).(2211)

Gesamtkunstwerk and the Edge of the Frame

Ecstasy of St. Theresa, Bernini (1652)

The Baroque *Gesamtkunstwerk* was intended to surround the viewer with visual spectacle. Bernini's *Ecstasy of St. Theresa* - a statue group depicting an angel piercing the medieval saint with a golden arrow, igniting her with a burning love for God - captures the viewer's attention on its own, with its astonishing naturalism and presentation of rapture as both physical and spiritual. The work of art extends beyond this sculpture however, to include actual and sculpted rays of light from above, an image of a skeleton on the floor below, exquisitely patterned marble columns and an elaborate, quasi-architectural structure, and to the sides, sculpted portraits of the Cornaro family who commissioned this chapel. Here there has been no attempt to confine the artwork, either physically or thematically, to a narrow frame. Instead, the space of the image is thrust forward to include the spectator, just as in Rembrandt's *Nightwatch* Captain Banning Cocq's arm seems to gesture out from the picture plane, into the realm of the viewer.

One of the primary themes of Ndalianis' text is that the Neo-Baroque, like the Baroque, is defined by its seriality and polycentrism - its refusal to be contained by the traditional edges of the frame, particularly with respect to narrative and genre. Beginning and endings may be hidden, stories continued across many installments (and not necessarily in temporal order) and hybrid media employed as vehicles for expression.(2212) *Lost* is widely recognized for each of these Neo-Baroque elements. *Lost* has quickly expanded beyond the confines of a television series. On the Internet alone there has been an explosion of fan-based, related content: websites, forums, unofficial transcripts, fan fiction, detailed documentation of shooting locations, and more.(2213) On the corporate side, ABC has orchestrated the production of tie-ins through both traditional and new media: novelizations, including *Bad Twin*, podcasts, an online alternate reality game, and coming soon, action figures, mobisodes and the *Lost* video game.(2214) *Lost* television series also periodically embraces the concept of the spectacle. The pilot, the most expensive in history, was a visual and narrative tour de force that has been matched on a narrative level by a large cast, numerous reoccurring guest roles, and a storyline with both synchronic and diachronic complexity. The complementary content available on other media is designed to draw viewers further into this slowly unfolding storyline and increasingly Baroque mythology. So far at least, these efforts at blurring the line between marketplace of reception and the economics of production have not impinged on the core of the *Lost* experience - the television series itself. The Baroque illusion of naturalism remains intact within the experience economy, which follows the current best practice marketing model by including both revenue and non-revenue activities so as not to alienate viewers.(2215)

Mortality and Transience

Wölfflin's statement that "the Baroque never offers us perfection or fulfillment, or the static calm of 'being', only the unrest of change and the tension of transience" is an apt description of *Lost*.(2216) The dramatic shift to the survivors of the tail section of Oceanic Flight 815 in Season Two has been followed by yet another spatial and narrative re-location, to the perspective of the 'Others.' Indeed, time and space have never followed the rules on *Lost*. As J.M. Berger has noted, the Dharma Initiative's logo has its roots in Eastern tradition of time as a cyclical phenomenon, where repetitions are never exactly the same and there are "consistent relationships between cause and effect (and past, present and future) that are not strictly logical-linear outcomes"—with the seemingly miraculous appearance and reappearance of people and objects from the past into the present, and back.(2217) When, in Season Three, Ben plays a tape of the Red Sox winning the World Series for Jack, it is a jarring insertion of the outside world into a narrative that has hitherto existed apart from normal time and space. By this point the viewer has gradually become acclimatized to castaways' singular, often baffling, and gradually increasing,-inteconnections in the present and the past. Hurley's boss at Mr. Cluck's Chicken Shack is John's superior at the box company, which it seems Hurley now owns; Kate's father is seen in Sayid's flashback; Shannon's father injures Sarah, Jack's future wife—to name just a few examples. Actual time—the mundane act of taping a baseball game (however odd that it is available)—seems pedestrian by comparison. The island seems to be caught in a relativistic matrix, where cause and effect are gradually becoming non-linear, and where the theoretical conception of time as a function of space, still so far ahead of popular understanding that it typically appears only in science fiction (and then with copious amounts of physics for dummies-style exposition), has been allowed free reign. On the island, time doesn't work the way it is supposed to at the speed of everyday life; events and memories unfold in a realistic manner, but they are framed by a time and space that appears strange and irrational to the outside observer, giving the appearance that "the Island's 'present' [is] resonating into the past."(2218)

This foregrounding of time links directly back to the Baroque. The pendulum clock was invented in the seventeenth century and the discoveries of Kepler, and then Galileo, brought a new awareness of an infinite universe where humanity, once thought to be the center of biblical time and history, was relegated to an ever diminishing role. Erwin Panofsky, the pioneering art historian, went so far as to state: "No period has been so obsessed with the depth and width, the horror and sublimity of the concept of time as the Baroque, the period in which man found himself confronted with the infinite as a quality of the universe instead as a prerogative of God."(2219) While the Christian faith still offered salvation, there was, for the prosperous Netherlands in particular, a sense that one must not forget that human accomplishments were insignificant compared to one's eternal soul. Neo-Baroque works that present symbols of both mortality—human skulls, hourglasses, rotting fruit, dying flowers are most common—and the ultimately futile human accomplishments, are in the tradition of the Baroque *vanitas*, which has its source in Ecclesiastes (1:2): "Vanity of vanities, and all is vanity."

On the island, most of the castaways have lost that which gave them status in the outside world. As the only doctor on the island [until Juliet in Season Three], Jack's medical skills are essential to survival, and this places him above the other castaways. But we soon learn that Jack has mixed feelings about accepting this responsibility, and he continues to be involved in dangerous situations that would be prohibited to a leader in a more structured chain of command. In stark contrast to contemporary Western society, money, even the promise of future gain, has no value on the island. It does not matter that Sun is from a wealthy, powerful family, or Hurley won the lottery. Instead, before the crash both characters had already begun to realize the extent to which their wealth was ruining their lives. Goods are bartered, most ruthlessly by Sawyer, who seems to have had the greatest need to acquire wealth in his previous life. But under physical and moral pressure, Sawyer's loyalty to this system weakens, and it has been suggested that his hoarding may have its roots not in greed, but in his traumatic and insecure childhood. Of all the characters, Shannon was the most committed to maintaining the vanities of her previous life: dieting, tanning, willful ignorance and ineptitude. This did not survive in the face of increasing demands that she shed her frivolity for emotional authenticity, an inner journey which continued into the realm of mysticism, as she began to have visions of Walt. In the Baroque era, such soul work could expect reward in the next life; in a more secular, Neo-Baroque context, there is no such certainty. But there is still the message that inner quality—the person each castaway is gradually revealed to be, in both the past and present—is more important than status, passions, or fleeting pleasures once enjoyed.

Divine Light

The Blinding of Samson, Rembrandt (1636)

Unlike twenty-first century Western society, the culture of the Baroque was deeply entwined with Christianity. The Protestant reformers in the North of Europe who embraced the Word and rejected visual traditions they considered inappropriately non-biblical, but did not spurn all art outright, influenced the establishment of the first open art market in Europe. Here paintings and prints of subjects not previously considered 'art'—landscapes, still lifes, genre scenes—were available for purchase. Catholic Reformers pursued the opposite strategy at the Council of Trent (1545-63), where they reaffirmed the power and utility of the visual arts for proclaiming the new, purified Counter-Reformation faith. By the seventeenth century Catholic clergy began to patronage artists who used the vivid and naturalistic Baroque style to inspire devotion in the faithful. Baroque artists were particularly effective in conveying both the naturalistic and more traditional, symbolic, aspects of light. Depending on the narrative context, light could allude to Jesus ('I am the light of the world. He who follows me will not walk in the darkness, but will have the light of life' - John 8:12), refer to the Holy Spirit, or suggest the general presence of the divine. Actual light could also imply inner light, or enlightenment, as in Rembrandt's rendition of *The Blinding of Samson*. In this narrative the biblical hero, in a moment particularly devoid of insight, has revealed the source of his strength to the treacherous Delilah. Rembrandt represents the moment the Philistine soldiers literally blind Samson as a physical and spiritual fall from the spotlight area of the canvas into the darker area to the right.

In the contemporary, secular context of mainstream television, Christian content, if present at all, usually exists only in relation to other, primary themes. *Lost*'s multiple references to religion and spirituality follow this norm. As a self-proclaimed priest, Eko exists at the margins of established religion; his faith is strong but unpredictable, with an as yet ambiguous relationship to his violent past. Charlie's religious leanings are balanced, perhaps even negated, by his history as a dissolute rock star and heroin addict. This is conveyed visually by the kitsch statues of the Virgin Mary that have been turned from their original purpose as devotional objects, and whose generic blandness—a visual sign of the post-Baroque split between mainstream Christian theology and art—makes them ideal drug mules. Each character has been presented as seeking some sort of redemption, whether they know it yet or not. In the Baroque this would be understood in terms of the sin that ultimately resulted from Adam and Eve having eaten from the Tree of the Knowledge of Good and Evil and being thus expelled from the Garden of Eden. In *Lost*, Christian references are more implicit. In *The Moth* Charlie may state the words, 'Bless me Father, for I have sinned,' but he does not relive and overcome his failings—weakness, fear, insecurity—within an explicitly Judeo-Christian framework. There are numerous allusions to this rich tradition of visual imagery, however. When Charlie crawls into a cave to rescue the trapped Jack, he literally moves into darkness—without his flashlight it would be pitch black. The flashback accompanying this segment is, appropriately enough, to the beginning of his drug addiction. When Charlie reaches Jack he provides physical illumination, by way of his flashlight; he also soon broaches the subject of enlightenment.

Charlie: "This place reminds me of confession—those little claustrophobic booths."
Jack: "I wouldn't have taken you for a religious man."
Charlie: "I used to be."

Here it doesn't matter that Charlie isn't feeling religious—his experience will still be one of atonement and redemption. With their dirty, unidealized faces, illuminated by the unseen flashlight, Charlie and Jack form a tableau that in both form and content has direct roots in the Baroque, specifically in the innovative, theatrically lit (*tenebrist*) works of Caravaggio (1571-1610). Caravaggio used real people as models, and he often set them in shallow pictorial spaces with almost black backgrounds. Often we are not shown the source of the light which shines in this darkness - instead it seems to either emanate from divinity, either within or outside the figures (for example in Caravaggio's *The Inspiration of St. Matthew*, 1602). The similarity to Caravaggio in the placement and lighting of Charlie and Jack in this scene is striking. Although we know its actual source, the light seems to emanate from the two men themselves, mirroring a moment of emotional, if not spiritual, illumination. Later, Charlie literally sees the light from above that leads them to safety (a light denied to the viewer), and thus moves from the darkness of the cave, and the envy, bitterness and fear that is the shadow within, to personal enlightenment.

The Inspiration of St. Matthew, Caravaggio (1602)

John, the character most directly aligned with, or against, faith, also sees a light at a moment of a crisis in belief when he pounds on the hatch in frustration at the end of *Deus ex Machina*. That this is later revealed to be Desmond does not deter from the metaphysical significance of the event: grace (only by accident does John save Desmond) working through human means, a primary theme for Christianity, based as it is on a concept of God as incarnate in the world.

Naturalism and Artifice

While the Baroque was primarily concerned with naturalism, it also was deeply imbued with allegory and personification. *Lost* often presents complex ideas in simpler forms. John compares Charlie's journey to that of the moth, Sun breaks something inside herself when she lies about the shattered glass ballerina. Symbols abound. Without the seventeenth century's strictly defined and recognizable emblematic tradition, the island's physical and social structure, particularly the ominous but still largely unknown 'Others', implies an allegory that is not easily interpreted.

Lost may be overdetermined with signs but they have not yet been allowed to overtake the naturalistic core of the show. Situations are bizarre but reactions to them—what Descartes (1649) termed 'the passions of the soul'—are not. Jack, Kate and John all weep for their fathers—appropriate reactions under their circumstances. Or so it seems; without the full story of each of their lives we cannot be sure. *Lost* makes clear the ultimate futility of such a narrative, while nonetheless pursuing a strategy of increasing information over time. Multiple perspectives on a single event—such as Jack's check-in at the Oceanic counter—dramatically increase the emotional veracity of a scene, but at the same time this broadening of our view to include many perspectives does not mimic reality. We rarely know another person's experience of the world so directly. But while this narrative structure demonstrates that 'truth' can never be completely known, this abstract concept is marginal to *Lost*'s gradual unfolding of present and past events and the characters' resulting moments of personal revelation. This consideration of the constructed natures of time, meaning and art is embedded in a commitment to verisimilitude and emotional authenticity—a particularly Baroque quality. *Lost* does not spin its illusions without providing some truths to ground them. In this world at least, sometimes things are what they seem, and people say what they mean.

Indeed, unlike the postmodern aesthetic, *Lost* is rooted in sincerity, not irony. Other texts are referenced, but without the 'hyperawareness on the part of the text itself of its cultural status, function, and history, as well as of the conditions of its circulation and reception" that characterizes postmodern popular culture.(2220) Sawyer's nicknames for Hurley alone read as a catalogue of pop culture references but his cleverness is not self-conscious, and wit does not become parody.(2221) Locke and Rousseau and Hume do not comment on their namesakes or their corresponding philosophical doctrines. The four-toed statue may remind the viewer of the remains of the colossal statue of the Emperor Constantine, and to the fact that all empires collapse in time, but the cleverness of this allusion is not allowed to contaminate the text. *Lost* is its own world—the characters may joke about their surroundings but they are entirely real to them, and therefore to us. *Lost* may be Neo-Baroque in its violation of frames, active integration into media-dominated consumer society and complex, reflexive narrative strategies, but in a twist on the postmodern denial of the integrated subject, the core of the series remains the integrity of human agency. Outside forces may be revealed to be pivotal—Fate is certainly is playing a strong hand—but the modernist grand narratives of heroic human agency and the gradual unfolding of truth prevail.(2222) When these themes—heroism and the search for understanding in the face of constant change—are presented as constituents of the intelligible world rather than myths, *Lost* deviates from the tenets of postmodernism. Instead, *Lost* belongs to the Neo-Baroque.

Dr. Michelle Lang, for many years a professor of art at the University of Nebraska, is Managing Director at Critical Management Services in Edinburgh, Scotland. She is the author of *Saturn's Apprentice*.

Notes

All fine art reproductions courtesy Wikimedia commons from The Yorck Project.

23. Jamie Smith: Sayid Jarrah

Sayid Jarrah and American Orientalism

By Jamie R. Smith

"Sayid Jarrah" by ArtGUS
Used with permission

"My name is Sayid Jarrah, and I am a torturer." (*One of Them*, Episode 2.14)

What are we to do with a character like Sayid? With the exception of perhaps Ben Linus, he is the most unpredictable character on the show. Over the course of six years we see him torture people, romance a valley girl, fix electronic equipment, shoot strangers in cold blood, organize rescue missions, fix more electronic equipment, break a guy's neck with his feet, build schools for underdeveloped countries in Central America, work as a hitman, go to the opera, kill more people, shoot a kid in the stomach, disarm and then rearm a nuclear bomb, see kids safely onto a school bus … to make a long story short, confuse the hell out of anyone trying to pin him down as a "good guy" or a "bad guy." This makes sense considering J.J. Abrams' previous television success, *Alias*, the show that set the precedent for moral ambiguity in TV's new heroes: "The show was about good guys working with the bad guys, many of whom thought they were the good guys."(2301) He grinds this ax once again in *Lost*, but when the writers decided to include a particular "bad guy" type whose persecution has become a divisive force in our country's psyche in recent decades, they complicated the good guy/bad guy dichotomy considerably.

Not only are we struggling to sort the heroes from the villains, but we are also left questioning our own attitudes towards Islam and Arabic culture post-9/11. Overcoming the fear, bitterness and hatred that stems from such attacks and turning instead toward a desire to understand difference is a long and complicated process, and often fictional characters and situations are required to push us forward in the real world. Sayid's process of redemption and letting go mirrors the Western, specifically American, surrender of the perception of Islam as "other."

I doubt it is coincidence that this character's first name is phonetically identical to the last name of the theorist who made the concept of the East as "other" famous in his controversial work, *Orientalism* (2302). It seems to me an obvious connection to Edward Said, despite the fact that his entry is currently absent from the Philosophy References section of *Lostpedia* (although there is a brief note connecting the two in Sayid's character profile). Nevertheless, his stance on the Orient as "other" in the European psyche is analogous to the place of Islam in the traditionally Christian American psyche: "European culture gained in strength and identity by setting itself off against the Orient as a sort of surrogate and even underground self."(2303) Margaret Miles, author of *Seeing and Believing: Religion and Values in the Movies,* takes this notion and extends it to film audiences' reaction to the "other" on the silver screen: "Identifying and excluding people who differ in race, class, religion, and gender … is an ancient strategy for self-definition" (2304). Miles elaborates on this thesis to examine such odious films as *Not Without My Daughter,* a film which portrays Iranian culture as monstrous and barbaric. *Lost,* however, takes the opposite approach—this show demonstrates the *inclusion* rather than the *exclusion* of the Islamic "other," and even takes the trouble to address the psychological process of identifying the stereotype and its roots, grappling with the truths and falsities of it, and eventually overcoming it in favor of understanding.

The pilot episodes of *Lost* set to work in identifying those stereotypical elements that define someone as "other." Setting Sayid apart as "other" is the first, most primitive, instinct, because it reaffirms our own position in the "us and them" dichotomy. Sawyer acts as a surrogate for the audience's role in this right away. He picks a fight with the Iraqi, claiming Sayid is the reason the plane crashed, and that he was the one the U.S. Marshall had in handcuffs. Sayid immediately responds by calling Sawyer a redneck. By all rights this should make the audience cringe: here we are, Americans behaving badly. An interesting dynamic then develops between Sayid and Sawyer in the first season: although Sawyer continues to foster mistrust with regards to Sayid, he follows the group to higher ground anyway. In the ending montage of "Tabula Rasa" (Episode 1.03), Sayid is seen tossing a mango to a confused Sawyer, grinning as he walks away. Little by little, barriers are torn down.

When we first meet Sayid and Sawyer, the impulse is to side with Sayid simply because Sawyer, at least at first, represents our own internal "other," that "in the wild" caveman attitude that we are desperately trying to exorcise in these modern, civilized, politically correct times. Once the altercation is over, the audience gets a new, more acceptable surrogate in the form of Hurley, the show's moral compass, the "puppy dog whose presence makes *others* feel safe," according to Nikki Stafford (2305, my emphasis on *others*). He enters the scene to reassure us that it is okay to toss out fear in favor of acceptance: "I like you. You're okay." Of course this affirmation is deflated with Sayid's admission that he fought in the Gulf War as a communications officer for the Republican Guard *against* U.S. forces. Over the course of the show, the idea of "other" is further distorted and is eventually no longer useful. "The Others," the community that was on the island before the Oceanic 815 passengers, insist that they are "the good guys," being the original inhabitants, and that our heroes are the invaders. In short, the others are us. This becomes even more apparent when we take into consideration the acts of aggression that are perpetrated on both sides by various players; out of all of these acts, Sayid's are typically the most violent and extreme.

The remaining seasons, at least through Season Five, set out to grapple with the stereotype of the inherently violent Muslim. It could hardly be considered coincidence that Jarrah's family name can be translated into "cutter," "wounder," or "surgeon" from traditional and modern Arabic (2306). By writing Sayid as an Iraqi Republican Guard interrogator, the show pinpoints the contemporary root of the stereotype: the War on Terror. Although Western views of Islam as a violent theology are centuries old, the campaign against terrorism has breathed new life into this problematic assumption. Rollin Armour, Sr. reiterates that this view has become more readily accepted in recent years, particularly in the U.S. (2307):

> "[t]he September 11 attacks have caused the United States to announce a war on international terrorism, a war American leaders say they will prosecute with all of the resources in their possession. Westerners have been repulsed and embittered by these attacks, and a new spirit of patriotism has emerged among Americans. Many Muslim leaders have called these attacks a violation of true Islam. Unfortunately, because of these events, many are again claiming that Islam is a religion of violence. The ancient charge against Islam is in danger of returning."

This charge finds its way into popular culture, according to Jack Shaheen: "Television tends to perpetuate four basic myths about Arabs: they are all fabulously wealthy; they are barbaric and uncultured; they are sex maniacs with a penchant for white slavery; and they revel in acts of terrorism…. The image can best be described as "The Instant TV Arab Kit." (2308). This isn't exactly what we

301

find in Sayid; he is, even in the first impression, intelligent, sophisticated, and often quite helpful, in a McGyver-improvise-a-radio-out-of-a-laptop-battery kind of way. There is nothing overtly barbaric about him, although Sawyer is quick to point out that his propensity to torture first and apologize later isn't exactly "show[ing] everybody how civilized you are" (Episode 2.13). Regardless of whether he fits Shaheen's type, he begins as a type nonetheless.

Sayid's is a peculiar case in that from the beginning he is out of context, at least more so than any other Oceanic 815 passenger. We are not immediately told the reason for travel for any of the passengers; we learn this gradually as the show progresses. One of the first things we do learn, however, is that most of the passengers are either from Australia or the U.S., with a few exceptions: Charlie, Sayid, and the Kwons. Out of these four, only one is from a country that the U.S. was in a war with at the time. Even this would not be out of the ordinary; the U.S. received immigrants from Iraq on a regular basis even in 2004. What puts him out of context is that he was a soldier who fought *against* U.S. forces and should by all rights be an enemy of the state. Why, then, is he flying freely into the U.S. with no trouble? Why is he on the plane? The fact that we cannot readily explain these things leads us to even more questions about what we know and don't know about what we fear most, and that's the whole point.

All of this is at times forgotten as the first season progresses and Sayid, through his talents with communications electronics, quickly makes himself useful and becomes Jack's right hand man and an invaluable strategic resource for people like Locke and Kate. It quickly becomes apparent that whatever he was before the crash, on this island, under these circumstances, Sayid gets a chance to start fresh with a group of people who were once his enemies. In fact, everyone gets a clean slate, according to Jack in *Tabula Rasa*. Locke later reiterates this point; however, starting over isn't as easy as it sounds, even for the island's new spiritual guru. He reverts to his old self, at times doubting his own faith and purpose in the face of challenges such as an impenetrable hatch and six stubborn Losties who just won't cooperate and go back to the island. Some people just have a hard time letting go. As a wise con-man once said, "[A] tiger don't change their stripes." (Episode 2.13)

Sayid's process of self-forgiveness and affirmation as "one of the good guys" is more trying than anyone else's on the show, which is why his takes so long to accomplish the inner transformation. His duty to the Republican Guard required him to separate his emotions from his actions and to develop a psychological detachment from the knowledge of right and wrong, at least long enough to get the job done. "[S]ocial scientists have discovered that 'one of the most important antidotes' to torturing 'is to break through the chasm that separates the torturer from the humanity of his victims'" (Goleman, quoted in 2309). Sayid has an especially difficult time letting go of his past to the point that he commits all over again the atrocities he vowed never to repeat. He has internalized his role as communications officer (and part of that job is the unsavory task of getting people to communicate); as a result, he shows no hesitation when torturing Sawyer to get Shannon's asthma medicine.

He does, however, show guilt, and exiles himself from the other passengers in order to atone for what he did. It is implied that this at least was the right choice for him to make based on the music playing as he walks into the sunset: "I just reach for mother Mary, and I shall not walk alone." Although this is an overtly Christian reference, it is implied that he needs to seek some kind of redemption to rejoin the group. Ironically, his atonement comes in the form of an obsessed Rousseau torturing him in order to get something she wants. Later, he is asked by Shannon to "do something" about Locke after Boone dies as a result of his misguided leadership, but he refuses to solve this with violence. This does not stop him from later on torturing Henry Gale/Ben Linus out of anger over her death. He ends up, ironically enough, working as a hit man for this same torture victim, only to run away to Central America to help impoverished villages out of guilt. This pattern continues throughout the show; it only ceases when he dies and is resurrected, but pays for his new life by forfeiting the ability to feel anything like human emotions.

Sayid's struggle with his own identity echoes the process the human psyche undergoes when dispelling an internalized stereotype in favor of a more complete picture. Robert Jewett and John Shelton Lawrence offer methods for overcoming stereotypes fostered by life during wartime in their book *Captain America and the Crusade against Evil: The Dilemma of Zealous Nationalism,* an important one being the humanization of "the Bad Person. This … must be done skillfully, lest the critic fall under suspicion of disloyalty by picturing an enemy as a person of virtue. It must be a fully believable and natural story in which the audience is led on its own assumptions to break with past stereotypes of enemy behavior" (2310). The best way to do this in the context of *Lost,* of course, is the convenient flashback that shows how, exactly, a character came to be flawed in the first place.

In the episode *He's Our You* (Episode 5.10), in which Sayid is captured by the Dharma Initiative and assumed to be a Hostile, a flashback shows how a young Sayid steps in to kill a chicken for his frightened older brother, thus sacrificing his own innocence. This is a somewhat watered-down version of the sacrifice Eko is forced to make in *The 23rd Psalm* (Episode 2.10), in which he kills an old man in the village in order to save his younger brother from a life under the militia's control. Eko is labeled "a born killer," while in Sayid's case, his father simply exclaims, "at least one of you will be a man." This once again brings up the stereotype of a violent culture which expects men to know how to kill. Sayid's destiny is not complete, however, with the killing of mere chickens. As a member of the Republican Guard, his ability to interrogate suspects and maintain his cool leads to a promotion, which in turn puts him into enemy hands once the U.S. gains control of his division. In *One of Them* (Episode 2.14) he is forced to torture his own commanding officer, and then left to his own devices "with a new skill he can use." But the U.S. isn't done with him yet; the CIA later encourages him to aid in the process of turning his former college roommate into a terrorist in *The Greater Good* (Episode 1.21), using the whereabouts of Nadia as incentive. The fact that part of Sayid's cultivation into a hardened torturer and killer came from official U.S. influences is particularly intriguing. This addresses guilt on the part of the American audience for helping to cause the situations that lead to the creation of our own enemies. According to Armour, "In light of the history of the Western involvement with Islam, one must admit there is reason for Muslims to be angry with the West …. Western governments and businesses can be greedy and thoughtless, and the baser sides of Western society would be a threat to classical Islam" (2311). Like Eko, Sayid was not born violent; he was pushed by circumstances to make the best of what he had in order to survive and keep his family and friends safe.

A life-long struggle to shrug off circumstances that would insist on his innate violent nature even leads to an uncertain destination for his soul after death. Although Ben Linus labels him a killer, he professes that he "does not like killing" in *He's Our You*, and tries again and again give up his violent past. However, unlike Eko, he is unable to let go of these influences and accept a straight and narrow path. Once Eko chooses the life of a priest, he never waivers; perhaps this is why we do not see him again in the sixth season parallel universe, in which the rest of the main characters are coming to terms with their lots in life before moving on. We do see Sayid taking this journey in what might as well be called the Purgatory timeline, along with many of his fellow castaways, where he continues to work out ways to resist violence in favor of a more peaceful alternative, despite the situation.

Sayid is not the only hero of the show to face the dilemma of "letting go" of persistent character flaws. Most, if not all, of the main characters are deeply flawed and complex, even if we don't see it at first. Our first impression of Jack is of a hero who thinks of others before himself, and who is not afraid to run headfirst into burning wreckage to pull strangers to safety. Even so, we find out, at first through hints and intimations, and later more directly, that he is an alcoholic and a drug addict with daddy issues. Even the heroic and helpful Kate is a fugitive and a murderer. In fact, everyone starts out as an easily identifiable "type": the heroic doctor, who looks suspiciously like Clark Kent, the redneck, the hot fugitive on the lam, the drug-addicted musician, the domineering Asian husband and his submissive wife, the deadbeat dad and son, the creepy old guy, etc. If these types had been maintained as they were initially established, I most likely would have stopped watching. Categorizing people in this way is simply too easy, and although the plot of *Lost* is especially intriguing, it would not have been enough to carry a show with mind-numbingly predictable characters. Instead, the writers chose to show characters that are not at all what they appeared to be at first, and developed them into complex, real people with real problems – a significant one being the inability to let go of the past, which led to trust issues. An expected, and therefore trite, ploy to heighten this emphasis on trust and mistrust would have been to target the ready-made stereotypical enemy, Sayid; however, this would not please Abrams in the least, considering his wish to not "dumb it down or simplify it to the point of being lowest-common-denominator television" (2312). What happened instead was much more appealing to an audience that thrived on complexity and critical thought.

Sayid Jarrah's character arc is a mirror for changes in the contemporary American psyche concerning Islam. He is at once "other" and a part of us, and the process of acceptance of difference is at once atonement for our sins and exorcism of our demons. There is still work to be done, however, when it comes to representing the "other," a real Muslim, truthfully. Part of the problem with the way that Sayid is represented is the Western/Christian context into which he is assimilated. In order for him to change from the shameful racist/xenophobic stereotype lingering in the American psyche as a result of the War on Terror, he must conform to a model more readily acceptable to that context. He is no longer a militant Muslim; he is, however, Americanized, like any immigrant idea into our conceptual melting pot. He still retains some of the old attributes of the stereotype, but these are simply modified to become more palatable.

The best instance of this modification of stereotype occurs when he is blown up with the submarine in *What They Died For* (Episode 6.16); he in effect becomes a friendlier version of a suicide bomber, killing himself in order to save the lives of those around him. Miles expresses a similar concern: "[I]n my view, there is no adequate way, no matter how sensitive or insightful the outsider, to represent 'the other' truthfully. One can best listen and look, carefully and without comment, at the self-representations of those who have been marginalized from public discourse and from the institutions in which this discourse occurs" (2313). The creation of Sayid as first a flat stereotype and then a complex human being who wishes to cleanse himself of the identity that was forced upon him through sporadic acts of contrition, such as self-exile and devotion to charity work, is not a representation of a "real" Muslim, but a representation of our image of the Muslim as he is transformed from a violent barbarian "other" to something more akin to ourselves. As Edward Said puts it, "as much as the West itself, the Orient is an idea that has a history and a tradition of thought, imagery, and vocabulary that have given it reality and presence in and for the West. The two geographical entities thus support and to an extent reflect each other" (2314). By attempting to create a representation of a "true" Muslim in response to negative stereotypes and dangerous generalizations, *Lost* has, in fact, simply reflected back to us, the American audience, our own evolving assumptions about the "other."

I will end with a slightly modified quote from the Qur'an that exemplifies this endeavor:

"We [i.e., God] have made you peoples and tribes so that you can get to know each other [and yourselves]" (Qur'an 49:13, quoted in 2315).

Jamie R. Smith earned a Master of Arts in English from Middle Tennessee State University, where she teaches Freshman English and ESL courses. She plans to pursue a PhD in English with emphases in Film Studies and American Literature. She is currently working on research projects on the portrayal of the American Family in Independent Cinema, as well as the role of alternative sexualities in the work of Carson McCullers.

On *Paradise Lost* and *Lost*: The Island and Eden as I-land and Eye-land

By Julia Guernsey-Pitchford, Ph. D.

"Paradise Lost" by Gustave Dore 1866
WMC PD

In the ABC television series *Lost*, the island is above all else an I-land: a laboratory designed for the personal development of chosen individuals. The show focuses on past determinants of the characters' ways of experiencing self and the world and on the emergence of Island-transformed subjective understandings. (2407, 2408). At the same time, the "eye" is a symbol, first seen when Jack awakens in the jungle, his opening eye mirrored by the sun and later as part of the Oceanic logo, where the O looks like an eye (2404, 2408). Hence the I-land is also "eyeland," a place of Others, with "eyes that fix you in a formulated phrase" to quote Eliot (2403, line 56). The island is, from the very first scene, intricately concerned with I and Others, with subjectivity and intersubjectivity, topics also deeply relevant to Milton's *Paradise Lost*.

Two ways the self may apprehend itself in the eyes of another are defined by Jacques Lacan and D.W. Winnicott respectively. Lacan discusses Sartre's notion of "the gaze," elaborating on Sartre's sense of someone else's watching, a sense of the self's objectification in the eyes of another: "This window, if it gets a bit dark, and if I have reasons for thinking that there is someone behind it is straightaway a gaze. From the moment this gaze exists I am already something other in that I feel myself becoming an object for the gaze of others" (2405).

Self-alienation then is one internal, psychic response to the eyes of others (2401). Another is defined by object relations, such as those in psychoanalyst D.W. Winnicott's research when he discusses the holding and mirroring functions of a young child's primary caretaker. Before an infant is old enough to recognize a mother's separateness, Winnicott says, when the baby looks into a good-enough mother's eyes, the baby sees him or herself (2410). Later as a toddler begins to separate from the mother, the mother performs a mirroring function by reflecting through the look in her eye, the tone of her voice and other affirming gestures that she recognizes and approves of the baby's emerging sense of self (2410).

In brief, while Lacan argues that the self is irremediably decentered (by becoming an object of others' perception and cognition), Winnicott, theorizes that the self is inherently geared toward wholeness, which is realized over time through the baby's relation to the good-enough mother, who empathically knows and responds to her infant's needs and who mirrors the toddler's emerging sense of wholeness with affirmation, making the baby's self real and permanent. Self-alienation may occur when a not-good-enough caretaker creates a premature and too rigid false self in the child rather than mirroring and establishing the true self at the center. The false (or objectified, socially-constructed) self is necessary at the appropriate time in every child's development, but the socially-constructed self should be established on the foundation of a true self who has had time to emerge at the core of the personality. Otherwise the person will be overly compliant and will feel unreal, fragmented and inadequate (2409).

The idea of true and false selves may be applied to both *Paradise Lost* and *Lost,* though the sense of their relative desirability in response to an Other varies according to context. In the Renaissance, though historically autonomous individuals were emerging across a wider social spectrum than had been conducive to selfhood in the past, ambiguity toward the experience of individualism informed Reformation attitudes toward the self in relation to God (2402). As characters in *Paradise Lost* choose others who mirror the true self over a God who expects to be mirrored by his creation, the transformation of self is not typically positive. A transformation from joy to misery, good to evil, beauty to horror, occurs as Satan conceives and gives birth to Sin, and he and Sin beget Death. Falling in love with his own image, Satan becomes an Other to the Father and to himself. Human beings have two paths of transformation available. They may remain true to God, obeying his commandment not to eat the forbidden fruit. In this case, they will eventually transcend their current state of existence, becoming ethereal like the angels as they graduate to a higher spiritual plane. Or they may sin and catalyze the transformation from immortal to mortal beings, alienated from one another and from God, thus bringing "death into the world and all our woe / With loss of Eden" (2406).

This transformation is one encompassing their entire subjective and intersubjective existence as death turns out to mean not only physical mortality and with it aging, disease, and other deforming conditions, but a different sense of self, of each other, and of the Divine Other. Adam and Eve first express their different sense of self and each other by using each other sexually, and then they have a vehement argument, each blaming the other for their fall. They express their transformed sense of the Divine Other by trying to hide themselves from Him rather than greet Him when He comes to talk to them.

Paradoxically in their innocent state, Adam and Eve are the inadequate and compliant beings who lack the affirming Mother's mirroring of the "true self." However, in their perfect, pre-eviction state, they are not without personal traits inclining toward the possibility of their fall and eviction from the garden. On being created, Eve falls in love with her own reflection in a pool of water, and when she is introduced to Adam, she prefers her own image over him. The moment of her narcissism all but predetermines her later inclination toward overconfidence in her capacity to withstand Satan's temptation alone and her incapacity to discern flattery as Satan piles compliment upon compliment in the attempt to get her to eat the fruit. Adam, on the other hand, is lonely when he is first created. He is by himself in the garden except for God and the animals. Thus, he begs his creator to make him a mate, and when the creator does so, Adam falls so deeply in love with Eve that Archangel Raphael later upbraids him for esteeming her more than himself. When Adam discovers the fallen Eve and she offers him the fruit, he resolves to die with her rather than to live alone.

From Winnicott's standpoint both choose the true self—the one at the core who needs the mirroring other—over the false self, the one created free to comply with God's authority. The story makes sense when one considers Winnicott's claims on the name of God:

> Does not this name (I AM) given to God reflect the danger that the individual feels he or she is in on reaching the state of individual being? If I am, then I have gathered together this and that and have claimed it as me, and I have repudiated everything else; in repudiating the not-me I have, so to speak, insulted the world, and I must expect to be attacked. So when people first came to the concept of individuality, they quickly put it up in the sky and gave it a voice that only a Moses could hear (2409).

Especially as Milton tells the story, Adam and Eve choose to *be* rather than to mirror another. Adam and Eve insult God by choosing their own sense of being (the true self) over compliance. In other words, they take from God the "I AM" and their being coalesces around individual being.

Eve loves the self. Mother Nature mirrors back to her from the pool more than she loves Adam or God in Adam, for whom she was created. Adam loves Eve, who emerges from and mirrors him, more than the Other in whose image he was made. Both choose the self bound by "the link of nature" to a mirroring other rather than the self bound by the Law of the Father to God (2406).

This same pattern, this reclaiming and rebuilding of the adequate and whole self, is apparent in *Lost* as well. In *Lost* the characters live from the beginning in a fallen world, and many are guilty of terrible crimes before they crash on the island. Most have been used (objectified) and abused in the fallen world. As victims, they have been rendered "it" rather than "I" in their own eyes. But at the heart of the island, a cave offers a source of life, death and rebirth. The island and Others on it become Winnicott's good-enough mothers who hold, nurture and mirror some of the most wounded characters. The victims are then able to reorganize in Winnicottian terms, from pathological false selves to whole persons cohering around a true, core, self.

John Locke is the consummate victim, having been reunited with his biological parents only in adulthood after growing up in foster care. Then his disabled father manipulated him out of his kidney and again abandoned him once the surgery was over (Episode 1.19, *Deus Ex Machina*). Locke's birth father filled a psychic hole within him only to use him and desert him again, this time with a literal hole inside. Locke's paralysis also resulted from an injury his father caused (Episode 3.13, *The Man from Tallahassee*). Other victims include Sawyer, Eko and Hurley. Although Sawyer fights the role, he may be Locke's foil as victim, since when he was a child, a con man called Sawyer tricked and betrayed the little boy's parents so much that the father killed the mother, then committed suicide. The boy hid under the bed, overhearing the whole catastrophe. (Episode 1.16, *Outlaws*). Eko, once a warlord, is the child victim of warlords who turned him toward evil. He chose to kill his first victim only to protect his younger brother from being forced by a gang of war lords to do so. (Episode 2.10, *The 23rd Psalm*). And Hurley is a victim of abandonment by his father and more recently of circumstance (3.10, *Tricia Tanaka Is Dead*). Hurley won the lottery with a series of numbers he learned from an obsessed man in a psychiatric facility (Episode 2.19, *Dave*), and ever since, he has experienced one tragedy after another, for which he blames the numbers, believing them to be cursed (Episode 1.18, *Numbers*). These characters, who from Winnicott's point of view show symptoms of pathological false self organization—an experience of inadequacy, a sense of powerlessness, and lack of agency—all undergo corrective experiences on the island, emerging as the selves they had the potential to be from birth.

Before coming to the Island, Locke worked at a menial desk job in a company that produces boxes. Having little opportunity to express himself authentically, he made plans to go on a walkabout, but on arriving in Sydney he presented himself to those leading the tour, who told him that due to his disability he couldn't go. Locke arrives on the island as a man confined to a wheelchair, who has been repeatedly frustrated by what he could not do. On the island, though, Locke becomes the man he has always fancied himself to be. Not only does he walk again; he emerges as a capable hunter and becomes the primary provider of meat for the survivors (Episode 1.4, *Walkabout*).

It is as if the island itself provides the maternal holding and mirroring that facilitates John Locke's emergence as a whole and capable self. Locke then extends this parenting to others. He advises several of the young people on the island—Walt, Charlie, Boone, Claire—becoming a collective father figure. Even the deficit he retains, the missing kidney, becomes an asset. Locke survives after Ben shoots him only because where the bullet enters, there is no kidney to bleed out (Episode 4.02, *Confirmed Dead*). Thus for Locke, whose absurd, pitiful existence has been tortured by his search for reasons, the island becomes the good-enough mother, providing coherent reason for all that has ever happened to him and thus allowing him to bring his story together around a coherent center, the true self.

But Locke still has one false self-conflict to overcome. That conflict is his relationship with his biological father, Anthony Cooper. We see this point most clearly when Locke refuses to kill Cooper (Episode 3.19, *The Brig*). Because Cooper is also the original Sawyer who was behind the tragedy of James'/ Sawyer's parents, Locke manipulates James/Sawyer into doing the murder of Cooper. Locke is double bound psychologically even though the island allows him to act physically. His delusional love for the parent he never had vies with hatred based in real life experience of abandonment, violation and betrayal by a con man who shares his genes. Only by appealing to a split-off version of himself—Sawyer, the projected true self, whose parents were taken away by Cooper's cons—can Locke accomplish what he must, the death of the man who has tangled him. Locke's refusal to kill is not virtue. Neither is it cowardice. It is the very problem for which killing is the solution: it is paralysis. Like Kate's mother, he cannot kill the abusive other whom he hates and loves.

Originally named James, Sawyer has chosen to become the man who ruined his life—and also to kill him (1.16, *Outlaws*). Thus, at one level, he becomes the master of situations, while at another he replicates his father's suicide by deconstructing himself: killing the actual Sawyer while becoming Sawyer (a false self) in his own life, thus attempting to erase his true [vulnerable] self.

Sawyer's transformation evolves more slowly than Locke's over the course of the entire series. We first meet him as a tough guy who hoards the property of dead passengers and barters with other survivors over items that they need. Jack frequently squabbles with him, and Kate more successfully cajoles or manipulates him into relinquishing these items. Kate, who has sex with Sawyer on several occasions, is initially attracted physically while she continues to distrust him at a deep level. Gradually her feelings for him deepen as her knowledge of who he really is develops.

The real Sawyer—the true self—is not named Sawyer at all. It is the boy, James, who addresses the actual Mr. Sawyer in a letter that tells Mr. Sawyer about how his conning of James' parents has resulted in their murder/suicide and how James plans to take action against him. Kate gradually unravels the mystery of the letter and confronts Sawyer with it (Episode 1.08, *Confidence Man*). Momentarily vulnerable to her, James lies passive, speechless, marshaling his false self's response later as he tries to uncover her identity and her secrets.

Hurley also functions to facilitate Sawyer's transformation. In one episode, he tricks Sawyer into believing that the group has voted to banish him unless Sawyer makes an effort to be nice to them. Hurley coaches Sawyer on good deeds that Sawyer can perform for each survivor who remains after Jack has been captured by the Others, and Locke has defected to their camp. At the end of the episode, Sawyer discovers the prank, and Hurley explains that it's time he step up and be a leader, helping the group rather than insulting individuals in it. He is needed now that the group's leaders are gone (Episode 3.15, *Left Behind*).

Juliet is a third person who calls forth a more authentic and cooperative self from Sawyer. She and Sawyer get stuck back in time together, and as part of the Dharma initiative in the 1970s, they fall in love and spend years as husband and wife. James functions effectively within the Dharma group and also aids others survivors when they arrive in the same time frame. (Episode 5.08, *LaFleur*). He and Juliet, along with Kate and Miles, help Jack set off the explosion in the Swan Station that results in their return to their own time and also creates the sideways reality that develops in the show's last season (Episode 5.17, *The Incident, Part 2*). Sawyer turns combative toward Jack, his ongoing rival, when Juliet is buried in the drilling shaft where the Station is to be erected, but over time he calms down and continues to serve the group (Episode 6.01, *LA X, Part 1*). He becomes a double agent, going between the smoke monster / Locke's and Widmore's camps as island events draw toward the climax (Episode 6.08, *Recon*). Beginning as a character the other survivors hate and no one trusts, Sawyer evolves until, in the final season, even as he plays a double-faced role, others within his group trust him to lead them to safety (e.g. Episode 6.13, *The Last Recruit*). In Winnicottian terms James has progressed from living as a false self to living with the true self at the core of his being, capable of deploying a false self as needed to survive.

Eko is a harder case to analyze, since theological issues come into play in understanding his rebirth experience. Several times during his early stay on the island, Eko kills an Other in defense of his group of survivors. Regretting this necessity, he observes 40 days of ritual silence, and later confesses these murders to Ben and cuts off locks of his hair for each man he has killed (Episode 2.15, *Maternity Leave*). Eko thus does penance for acts committed starting when he arrived on the island. He never expresses guilt over the countless murders and other crimes he committed in his past as a drug trafficker and warlord, however. In fact, quite the opposite, Eko argues with the Man in Black, disguised as his brother's ghost, that he did what he had to do (Episode 3.05, *The Cost of Living*).

Eko seems to believe that his past self was absolutely determined by circumstances, but that the grace of God, as manifested through Eko's arrival on the island, affords a new self-freedom to choose. From an object relations psychoanalytic perspective, this new self may be understood as the recovered "true self," available to Eko in his childhood but renounced for the sake of his brother the day that Eko first chose to take an innocent man's life rather than let his brother do so. On that day, Eko relinquished to his brother the cross he wore around his neck.

On the island, this true self has re-emerged. As a sign, miraculously, Eko has found his brother's remains and taken back his cross (Episode 2.10, *The 23rd Psalm*). As if newly baptized, Eko has been symbolically buried to his past self, his record cleared. Yet, even the true self has found it necessary to kill again in order to protect Eko's own group against the Others. Because he has done penance for these murders, Eko seems to believe that he can look God himself in the eye, as mediated through his brother/priest, and face the judgment. Eko's imperfect transformation comes in the very area in which the smoke monster judges him to be deficient—his moral being—and thus it is possible to overlook the extent to which he has become a renewed man in spiritual terms.

The question is, does the smoke monster represent the Divine perspective? Is there a God in the world of *Lost*, or is Jacob one face and the smoke monster the other of a universe where equally matched opposing powers battle, each taking forever the spoils of a skirmish that goes his way? Would the skirmish end differently in Milton? We are given no easy answers since Eko does not appear in the survivor's sideways reality at the end of the series. Like Walt he vanishes; like Ben, he does not move forward. For Sayid, the torturer, there is light; for Echo only darkness.

Hurley's transformation is quiet but not to be overlooked, especially because Hurley becomes the guardian of the island after Jack is gone. Hurley arrives on the island as a former psychiatric patient, at times unsure of the difference between his perceptions and reality. (Episode 2.18, *Dave*). When he encounters the numbers that the survivors type into a computer in the hatch, he begins to relive the nightmare of feeling cursed; he believes that all bad things that happen around him are his fault, the consequence of a curse he incurred by using the numbers in the lottery (Episode 1.18, *Numbers*). He has little self-esteem and is convinced, though he gets along well with people, that he is unworthy of a relationship with a woman, and thus, he is shocked, though thrilled, when Libby proves the belief wrong (Episode 2.20, *Two for the Road*).

Hurley's conviction that he is bad luck is impervious to the arguments of others. Only when it occurs to him to take the reins of his destiny and make his own luck do things begin to change. Remembering how his father left him on a day when they were repairing an old car, Hurley decides to repair a van the survivors have found on top of a hill. Others who accompany him believe that he is doomed to fail when, after making the repairs, still unable to start the engine, Hurley gets behind the driver's wheel and starts the car downhill. But Hurley decides that luck is with him, that the van will start. And the van starts. (Episode 3.10, *Tricia Tanaka is Dead*).

Exactly where Hurley's change of heart came from is not entirely clear. It was an epiphany—perhaps inspiration from Jacob or from the island itself. In any case the epiphany was life changing. Hurley no longer feels cursed. He remains the humble character always in the middle of things but seemingly never out front. He is not the first to volunteer when Jacob asks that someone take over the island. In fact, Hurley seems a little taken aback when Jack appoints him Jack's successor. Hurley questions his ability and asks for help from Ben. And therein lies his magic.

313

For it is through Hurley's team spirit and lack of inflated ego that at last two characters from opposing groups end up not competing to the death but cooperating to keep the island going for the remainder of their lives. Hurley is the one whom Jacob has believed in all along—the one whose choice is not to exploit resources and kill others in competition for them but to cooperate with whomever remains—with the Other, with Ben!—for the sake of keeping the island safe and those on it happy (Episode 6.17, *The End*).

In one way or another, numerous characters experience a second birth during their stay on the island. Like the mother of a small child, the island becomes an I-land, helping the self to emerge and meet his full potential. At the same time it becomes an eye-land, teaching the self to perceive himself, as if though the eyes of others, as whole and capable. People learn to see themselves differently, as closer to their true potential, and thus to view others with empathy, seeing them as more like themselves.

Some character transformations in *Lost* are so dramatic as to appear at first glance like second births; others seem more subtle. But in all cases I have discussed, the island facilitates the emergence of subjective potential and intersubjective harmony. The island functions as paradisal motherland, allowing subjects to find new life. In contrast, in *Paradise Lost* Adam and Eve lose both themselves and Eden and are banished into a world where struggle and death are inevitable.

Dr. Julia Guernsey-Pitchford is Associate Professor of English at the University of Louisiana at Monroe. She was formerly the faculty coordinator of the Master of Arts program for the English Department, and has published several articles on assorted Renaissance writers. Her book, *The Pulse of Praise: Form as a Second Self in the Poetry of George Herbert*, is available at bookstores and online.

The Audacity of the Empty Tomb

By Pearson Moore

He is a drunkard, a philanderer, a man of secret shames and uncontrolled compulsions—the very antithesis of the dedicated father. Death does not deter him from tormenting his son and everyone who would help Jack. We hear the characteristic ticka-ticka-ticka as Jack stalks him through the jungle. Even so early in the story, in the fifth episode, we know what that sound means. In death he becomes death itself: Cerberus, the black smoke, the capricious judge, he who brings discord, fighting—he who destroys and corrupts. Jack's father is The Man in Black.

He is in every way evil, yet his words are honey-coated and irresistible. Jack must follow him because no one can resist the summons of his own father, even a dead father, even a man who in life provided only hardship and torture for his son. Jack is no different from us; he prefers agony and discord over emptiness and loss. Even if everyone in the world tells us we have what it takes, if we do not receive these sweet words of affirmation from our father, we forever long to hear his voice intone their sound, even from whisky-stained lips. Even though he be dead.

So it is that Jack follows the phantom into the jungle. He cannot but follow the image of the man who withheld the affirmation Jack needed more than food or even life itself. Man of science, master of logic, he abandons every shred of reason, safety, and sobriety, following the ghost of his dead father over a cliff. Only faith—though perhaps I should say the **personification** of faith, John Locke—saves him from a fall to certain death. Killed, murdered—we might even say **assassinated**—by the Island's own Prince of Darkness.

There is nothing this man—the hero's father—would not have done to thwart Jack's generous intentions, his good plans, his deepest hopes. Let us agree, in fact, that this dark ghoul is no man at all. He enjoys not a single thread common to the strong and good fabric of our humanity. He himself admits it: "He took my body. My humanity." (Episode 6.09) If we can imagine a being of pure evil, we should acknowledge that this demon exceeds every capacity of our understanding, that the darkness of his soul admits not the feeblest ray of light, and can produce only injury, decay, corruption, and death.

He is an apparition, a terror, a ghost. As Jack approaches the coffin we hear the familiar strains of Michael Giacchino's *Life and Death* theme, but it's tentative, rendered on what sounds like a pipe organ, imparting an unearthly feel to the darkness and the sputtering flame of the torch, and bringing unnatural depth to the anguished features of Jack's glowing face. He finds water—life-giving water. The same water he had been seeking for days. He sees the casket, anchors his torch, pauses—and lifts open the top.

The symbolism is breathtaking because it is unmistakable, and the unabashed statement of it negates everything that came before. Jack stands before the Empty Tomb. The tomb that once held Christian Shephard.

KATE: Who died?
DESMOND: A man named Christian Shephard.
KATE [chuckling]: *Christian* Shephard? Seriously?

Seriously.

Christian, meaning a follower of Christ. Shephard, meaning shepherd, or pastor—an unabashed reference to the Good Shepherd, Jesus of Nazareth, Jesus the Christ, whom Christians worship as God Incarnate.

The Empty Tomb, of course, is the most potent symbol in all of Christianity. It is invoked once a year, in the early hours of Easter Sunday. Parishioners gather outside the church, process around the building and return to the front, where the priest opens the main door. Finding the church (now symbolizing the Empty Tomb) without occupants, the priest proclaims, "The tomb is empty. He is risen! Alleluia! Alleluia!" Then begins the most joyous celebration on the Christian calendar: The Grand Solemnity of Easter, the Great Feast of the Resurrection.

"Satan's Pact With God" by Taddeo Gaddi ca. 1350 PD

He is Evil Incarnate: He led his son to a cliff to kill him and destroy him. He is God Incarnate: He led his son to water to sustain him and nurture him. He gave us his only begotten son who was pierced in his side and died so that we might live. He is the devil himself, focusing his prodigious energies on the destruction of humankind.

He is the source of our greatest confusion and untempered angst.

Who is Christian Shephard?

A Spirit Broken

Depressed Man WMC 2007 PD

Every element in Christian Shephard's life conspired against him. His training, abilities, and experience were beyond compare, but even the best physicians are no match for the forces of life and death. Not even a first-rate surgeon can cajole, coerce, or cheat the Grim Reaper out of his due. Fate forced him to occupy the antechamber to death, where he became the last hope of those too injured to avoid final reckoning with a surgeon's tenuous skills. Too often, he did not measure up. Can we fault him for having sought solace in the company of Jack Daniels and Jim Beam? They did not judge him, after all.

His family, on the other hand, not only judged him, but convicted and sentenced him. His wife was cold. The son in whom he had placed all his hopes and dreams found his single weakness, exploited it without mercy and without appeal to human dignity, leaving him a shell, withering and waiting to die. The surgery department he led with steady distinction disowned him, took away his privileges, and barred him from practicing medicine.

A decades-long career destroyed, connections to family and friends severed, his dignity hacked to bits by dependency and the condemnation of his peers, he sought out the only refuge he had ever known, in the Land Down Under. But even there his broken spirit could find no respite from shame and desolation. His Australian lover and his illegitimate daughter wished to live their lives without him. Even his "bodyguard," Ana Lucia, found him lacking in any quality worthy of her admiration or even her respect.

We should expect him to harbor bitterness and anger, especially for his son. As he began his last, fatal meeting with Jack Daniels, in the company of another wounded and broken soul, he gave voice to words that should have found no place in his heart. This is what Christian Shephard said to Sawyer in Sydney, Australia, on September 16, hours before he died:

> Don't let the air conditioning fool you, son. You are here, too. You are suffering. But, don't beat yourself up about it. It's fate. Some people are just supposed to suffer… I have a son who's about your age. He's not like me, he does what's in his heart. He's a good man, maybe a great one. And right now, he thinks that I hate him. He thinks I feel betrayed by him. But what I really feel is gratitude, and pride because of what he did to me. What he did for me. It took more courage than I have.

Everything he had savored in life—everything that affirmed his value as a human being—had been violently taken from him and broken into unsalvageable shards. Even in this hopeless state, though, in abject debasement, he continued to believe in values worthy of his respect. He felt pride, hope, gratitude. Most of all, he felt love for his son.

When the medical examiner allowed Jack a final glimpse of his father's corpse, he zipped up the body bag one final time, locking in not just a body, but a hope and a prayer: "My son is a good man, maybe a great one."

Listen to Christian's words. Read them again. Think on them. "It's fate. Some people are just supposed to suffer." I suffer, I'm supposed to suffer. But someone I love, someone who shares my blood, does not suffer, *cannot* suffer. "He's not like me." That is, he is not destined to suffer. Fate cannot be allowed to deal him anything less than the goodness he carries in his heart. "He does what's in his heart." He treats people with respect, fixes them, cares for them, loves them. "He's a good man," and good must be continued at all costs. "Maybe a great man." More than ordinary goodness, Jack Shephard, my son, carries within him something rare, profound, extraordinary—something that must not be allowed to succumb to strained fate.

If Christian Shephard, by some miracle, were permitted to reach his hand from the Sideways reality of spirits and dreams to interfere in the world of women and men, he would expend every available energy to guide his son away from bitter fate and instead toward blissful destiny.

An Island Broken

"Lanai Lookout 02" WMC 2008 PD
Modified by Pearson Moore 2011

Like Christian, the Island was broken. It was not always thus; at some point in the past, the Island had been whole. We do not know when the Island lost the fullness of its identity, but we have sufficient information to wager a valid guess.

> Damon Lindelof: If I were to have a theory that that apparatus we see in the finale with the stone sticking in the middle of the pool that's sort of blocking the light, maybe that apparatus wasn't created until after this event [the creation of the Smoke Monster].
> Carlton Cuse: I think that's an incredibly likely deduction, Damon.
> Damon Lindelof: It's possible people went down there and basically...
> Carlton Cuse: They built something.
> Damon Lindelof: Some people think the light went out in that shot [when the Smoke Monster rose out of the cave for the first time] but it was just the smoke monster obstructing the light. The light has not been diminished in any significant way but is probably largely responsible for what just happened.
> (Across the Sea Audio Commentary transcript from http://lostpedia.wikia.com/wiki/Across_the_Sea_audio_comment ary, accessed on January 26, 2012)

Sometime in the ancient past, Jacob's brother, unconscious, fell into the Source. We don't know exactly what occurred, but we know the results. Thanks to Darlton we also know something of the mechanism of transformation. Jacob's brother became the Smoke Monster due, in part at least, to the light, which was "… largely responsible for what just happened."

The fundamental relationship between light and water at the Source changed after the creation of the Smoke Monster. Soon after the Monster came roaring out of the cave of light, the Source was given an overhaul. The "apparatus we see in the finale with the stone sticking in the middle of the pool" was not present before the Man in Black's visit to the Source. "That apparatus wasn't created until after this event."

Changes to the Source were probably effected not by choice, but by necessity. Jacob explained the function of the Source to Richard Alpert in Ab Aeterno (Episode 6.09):

> [Jacob raises a corked bottle of wine] Think of this wine as what you keep calling hell. There's many other names for it too: malevolence, evil, darkness. And here it is, swirling around in the bottle, unable to get out because if it did, it would spread. The cork is this island and it's the only thing keeping the darkness where it belongs.

We should understand Jacob's words not as irrefutable canon, but simply as his understanding of the function of the Source. If we took his interpretation to be the complete truth of the Island's function, we would have to conclude the Island was naught more than the abode of darkest evil—hell, in other words. I should note, though, that a call sheet from The End (Episode 6.17) and the script for scenes 143, 145, 149, 156 and 157 refers to the Source as "hell" (http://screenrant.com/lost-series-finale-spoilers-aco-60480/all/1/, accessed on January 27, 2012).

LOST provides ways of understanding the Source entirely at odds with Jacob's view. The Guardian ("Mother") said the Source was the origin of life, death, and rebirth (Episode 6.15). The light emanating from the Source is "The warmest, brightest light you've ever seen or felt… It's beautiful… a little bit of this very same light is inside of every man."

But we should not believe that this portrait of a heavenly abode is the complete picture, either. This island "heaven" is subject to the ongoing survival of the very fragile Source, which depends on the actions of human beings:

JACOB: Can they [people] take it [the light away from here]?
GUARDIAN: No. But they would try. And if they tried they could put it out. And if the light goes out here… it goes out everywhere. And so I've protected this place.

The Guardian had a realistic, practical understanding of the Source. She knew of its power, its ongoing reality as the source of all constructive goodness in human life, but she also knew the Source was not something ordinary human beings could approach without being harmed, not just physically, but at every level of human identity:

JACOB: What's down there?
GUARDIAN: Life, death, rebirth. It's the source, the heart of the island. Just promise me: No matter what you do, you won't ever go down there.
JACOB: Would I die?
GUARDIAN: It'd be worse than dying, Jacob...much worse.

We could interpret the Guardian's words as an indication of her concern for Jacob's wellbeing. I do not think of her words in this way. It was evident, from every action she performed or attempted, that the supreme motivation at every point of her conscious existence was the safeguarding of the Source. I believe her injunction on entry to the Source was the result of her understanding that great harm would come to the unique place on Earth she had pledged her life to defend.

Some will argue that the Guardian could not possibly have felt so strongly about the Source. I would argue that she valued the Heart of the Island more than her own life. I think her insistence on Jacob's acceptance of the transfer of power proves the value she placed on the Source (Episode 6.15):

GUARDIAN: Here. Drink this.
JACOB: What happens if I do.
GUARDIAN: You'll accept the responsibility that you will protect this place for as long as you can; and, then you'll have to find your replacement.
JACOB: I don't want to protect this place.
GUARDIAN: Someone has to.
JACOB: I don't care.
GUARDIAN: My time is over.

The Guardian could not "let go" until her replacement was at his post and committed to protecting the Heart of the Island. We knew she wished to die, for the only words she said after being stabbed were "Thank you." But her readiness for death was contingent on the installation of the next Protector, meaning that the Source was more important to her than even her own life or death. If so, the Source would certainly have occupied a place of greater concern in her mind than the lives of any other human being, including those of Jacob and the Man in Black. Her manipulation of the Man in Black to carry out her execution can be understood well in this context. So too, her warning to Jacob about entering the Source.

We don't know who reconfigured the "apparatus" at the Source. Some will argue that the Man in Black, with his decades-long interest in the mixing of water and light, must have been the architect. I don't see this as at all likely. At *The End*, we know he required Desmond to enter the Source; for whatever reason, he could not approach the Heart of the Island on his own. Also, we know the Source in its most recent configuration (with the Cork Stone in place) prevented the Man in Black from leaving the Island. It seems improbable at best that he would have rebuilt the Source in this manner.

The party most likely to have been responsible for the reconfiguration of the Heart of the Island is Jacob. However, if he put the "apparatus" in place, it seems probable that he would have understood the mechanism and the fact that it controlled not only the interaction of water and light, the flow of water throughout the Island, and the very health of the Island itself, but also that it controlled both him and his brother. Based on his discussion with Richard, he certainly seems to have understood that removal of the Cork Stone would result in the Man in Black's ability to leave the Island. He either didn't understand or didn't fully appreciate the Source's other functions, though.

If we consider the reality of the Heart of the Island through Jacob's eyes, we may better appreciate something of the Source's history. He did not learn until well into adulthood that he could not enter the light. As a teen, a young adult, and well into his thirties and forties, he knew only that the light was "beautiful," and nothing less than "the warmest, brightest light you've ever seen or felt." The only danger he was aware of was the desire of self-absorbed women and men to take the light for themselves. The Guardian never so much as implied the Source itself was dangerous. Not until Jacob had experienced his first gray hairs was he obliged to reevaluate his understanding. He certainly never would have understood the Source or the Island as a "cork," not even after the Guardian's warning about entering the Heart of the Island.

For all of Jacob's formative years he understood the Source as an entirely positive force on the Island. He could not have conceived of the possibility that it contained within itself the ability to inflict harm. He could not have understood it as a container for evil.

Something occurred after the unleashing of the Smoke Monster that caused Jacob to completely change his understanding of the Source's function. The Heart of the Island was not "the warmest, brightest light you've ever seen or felt" and only coincidentally or peripherally the cork that imprisoned the Smoke Monster. Suddenly, upon the unleashing of the Smoke Monster, Jacob understood the highest function of the Source as a cork in a bottle imprisoning the worst evil in the world. For Jacob, that it was a source of human goodness was not even worth communicating to Richard. If this truly was the way in which Jacob understood the Source—an understanding that denied the reality he had known during the most impressionable years of his life—it seems to me something more than his impression of the Source must have changed.

The Source itself must have undergone actual change, and much more than cosmetic physical change. That is to say, the physical "apparatus" was not much more than a superficial reconfiguration. The true change at the Source was in the way it affected Jacob and the Island as a whole. The *quality* of the Source and the Island was not the same after the Smoke Monster. The Man in Black lost his humanity. The Island lost its grounding in human goodness. Both the Man in Black and the Island were broken.

The Smoke Monster

"Black Smoke" by Hunter O'Eeils 2008 PD

Somehow, in interacting with the light, a new entity was born. The former entity—Jacob's brother—was dead. More than his body was dead; an important part of the man who had form and substance before the event no longer existed. The Man in Black did not complain simply that Jacob had taken away his body. "He took... my humanity," also.

His body was lifeless, decaying in the caves next to the mortal remains of his "mother." He appropriated the form he had inhabited, but not the body itself. By the time he appeared to Richard in the mid-19th century his bodily remains had long since decomposed to nothing more than bone and sinew, but he continued to project the same persona he had always known. He needed to occupy an individual's persona to maintain human appearance, but the range of choices was limited only to individuals who were dead.

At least a few of the on-Island appearances of Christian Shephard were due to the Smoke Monster:

> Once [the Man in Black is] the Smoke Monster, he only can assume the form of dead people on the Island. The Man in Black appeared as Christian Shephard. He most notably takes the form of John Locke. (Carlton Cuse, "LOST: The Final Journey," May 23, 2010)

We need to remember, especially as we make the final connection between the Smoke Monster and Christian Shephard, that the Man in Black did not use dead bodies to project human images. He never used his own body to project the image of his former self, for instance, and he never would have used Christian Shephard's body, or anyone else's body, for that matter. Therefore, the Empty Tomb has no causal connection to any activity of the Man in Black.

More than this, though, I believe it is essential to point out that the Man in Black did not merely appropriate a bodily form, but a persona—a personality, a way of interacting with the world. When he projected the image of Richard's love, Isabella, for example, he did not maintain the sour disposition that belonged to Jacob's brother. Remember, the Smoke Monster lacked not only a body; more important to our discussion is the fact that he lacked *humanity*. He lacked personality. So it is that when he appropriated Isabella's persona to his use, he was obliged to project not only her physical beauty, but also her inner beauty. As a being with neither physical form nor spiritual existence, he had to occupy all aspects of an individual in order to project an image anyone would recognize as human. He appealed to Richard, then, not as Man in Black, but fully—in ways psychological, emotional, and spiritual—as the person whose entire personality and inner self he now projected. He appealed to him, and in fact he *was* in almost every way that matters, the person Richard knew as Isabella. The only way his being differed from hers was in those aspects of existence that were not stripped away at the Source: will, desire, resolve.

The will—the lusts and desires of our being—can motivate us to act on behalf of our humanity, but if we lack the essentials of human existence (an ability to care for anything other than our selfish desires)—that is, if we lack a heart—the will becomes an instrument oriented entirely toward the satisfaction of whatever whims strike our fancy, everyone else be damned. The human will, in other words, becomes an instrument of terror and pure evil.

We have historical precedent for the appropriation of human will toward the fulfillment of individual and collective evil. National Socialist propaganda of the 1930s was aimed at severing any affinities the German people had for anyone other than pure-blooded Aryans. People of African descent were called "monkeys," while Jews, gypsies, homosexuals, and anyone other than Protestant Christians of pure Germanic ancestry were deemed to be less than human.

"Triumph of the Will" National Socialist Party movie poster 1934 PD

The Smoke Monster, lacking a human heart, devoid of any aspect of humanity, was the purest expression of the inhuman beings, driven entirely to realize their individual or collective triumph of the will, that we know as intolerant, racist, or selfish people.

The Smoke Monster had no choice but to inhabit a dead person's entire being, subsuming their personalities only to his twisted and heartless will. But their personalities showed through, at times even directing his actions and his lesser desires. Often, and especially in tense situations, the Smoke Monster was unable to suppress the appropriated soul's innermost thoughts. So it is, for instance, that the most characteristic aspects of John Locke showed through when the Smoke Monster fell in the jungle when he occupied Locke's form while chasing the teenage vision of Jacob (Episode 6.04):

[Young Jacob begins to run]
MONSTER: Hey!
[Locke chases him but trips on a root and falls ... young Jacob stands over him]
JACOB: You know the rules. You can't kill him.
MONSTER: Don't tell me what I can't do...
[Jacob shakes his head and walks away]
MONSTER: Don't tell me what I can't do!

"Don't tell me what I can't do," of course, is John Locke's signature phrase. Though John Locke was in closest communion with the Island, at the spiritual plane of his existence he was wracked by insecurities around physical disability and intellectual lack of ability. These insecurities invariably showed through in the Smoke Monster's appropriated personality, when he inhabited Locke's personality.

Note that the Smoke Monster's thoughts, actions, verbal expressions, and interactions were often guided almost entirely by forces outside his volition. His will, strong as it was, was not the unique controlling force responsible for all of his activities; aspects of the appropriated persona often exercised almost complete control over him.

Note, too, that the Monster was often obliged to act not of his own accord, but on behalf of a higher power. We understand such instances of obedience to an outside force as "summoning the Smoke Monster," as Ben did in Season Four.(Episode 4.09)

"Anubis and Pan" by Pearson Moore 2011

Benjamin Linus, of course, was no "higher power." He was able to summon the Monster because he invoked a property of the Island—the peculiarities of water and the way it mixes with light in the high-magnetic-field, subterranean regions of the Island—that controlled various phenomena on the Island. One of those phenomena was the Monster's propensity to respond to Island needs.

When Ben pulled the plug in the earthen "bathtub" beyond the hieroglyph-carved door in his secret room, he was not activating some Stone-Age system of water and pulleys that would flash a light in the Smoke Monster's bat cave so the Dark Knight would come to Ben's rescue. The Monster was no Dark Knight, and he didn't care a hill of beans about Ben's problems. Water mixed with the light in certain ways, and this changed the behavior of space and time, the flow of water, the intensity of the light at the Source, and other phenomena.

The Smoke Monster was affected by Ben's summons not because he felt any compassion for Ben, but because he was obliged to act on the Island's behalf under certain conditions, as determined by the mixture of water and light. The Man in Black, when he entered the Source, lost his humanity, but acquired something of the Island's essence. In ways we can never fully understand, he became something like the Island. He became what the Dharma Initiative understood as Cerberus—the Island security system that seemed more like the guardian of the gates of hell. Ben was no higher power. But the Island certainly was. The Island directed Jacob's will and every aspect of his being. Under certain conditions, the Island could even overcome the Monster's will, bending him to the Island's own purpose. One of those purposes was self-preservation. The Monster answered Ben's call because it was the Island's call. Keamy's men posed a real threat to the Island's survival. The Island, then, summoned (better: ***roused***) itself—the part of itself that resided in the Smoke Monster—and neutralized the mercenary threat.

The Smoke Monster had a will of his own, but his will did not always determine his actions. The Island often decided the Monster's thought and activities. In a similar way, the Monster's thought, action, and will were sometimes suborned to the personality and innermost desires of the persona he had appropriated as image and likeness.

Follow Me

Christian Shephard's on-Island apparitions were qualitatively different than any appearances of the Smoke Monster that did not appropriate Christian's form. Even without deep analysis, we immediately grasp a connection between the Smoke Monster's outward appearance and his inner disposition during his interaction.

Smoke Monster Appearances				
Episode	Physical Form	Appeared To	Type	Issue
3.05	Yemi	Eko	Judgment	Eko's Sin
3.14	Spiders	Nikki	Judgment	Nikki's Sin
5.12	Smoke	Ben	Judgment	Ben's Sin
3.15	Smoke	Kate	Judgment(?)	
3.15	Smoke	Juliet	Judgment(?)	
5.12	Alex	Ben	Coercion	Obey Locke
5.17	Locke	Ben	Coercion	Kill Jacob
6.09	Isabella	Richard	Coercion	Kill Jacob
1.05	Christian	Jack	Guide	Find Water
4.14	Christian	Michael	Messenger	You can go
4.11	Christian	Locke	Guide	Move Island
5.05	Christian	Locke	Guide	Move Island
5.09	Christian	Sun	Guide	Find Jin

Notice that every apparition of Christian Shephard has the objective of helping the person he is interacting with. On the other hand, whenever the Smoke Monster appears in any other form he is either judging or he is attempting to coerce people to perform an act we know will benefit him directly. Notice also that, except in the case of Christian's appearances to Jack, the people seeing him do not know him personally. Michael, Locke, Sun, and Frank Lapidus never met Christian before their Island encounter with him. On the other hand, Eko was well acquainted with his brother, Yemi, Ben immediately recognized Alex, and Richard of course knew of Isabella's presence even before he could see her clearly.

In those cases in which the Monster wishes to coerce someone, he takes on the personality of the dead person spiritually or emotionally closest to the individual he wishes to influence. In his apparitions as Christian, he could never have any hope of coercing anyone, since neither Michael, nor Locke, nor Sun have any emotional ties to Christian Shephard. While he may yet be attempting coercion, the immediate benefit to him of reuniting Sun and Jin, leading Jack to water, or petitioning Locke to move the Island is not immediately clear. However, the Monster's benefit in convincing Ben to obey "Locke" (the Monster under Locke's form) or in talking Richard into killing Jacob is so obvious as to stand beyond any need for explanation or debate.

The theory that behaviors, expectations, and objectives are tied to the form under which the Monster appears seems incontrovertible. The matching of behaviors with appropriated personality is also in perfect accord with our previous discussion of the Monster's dependence on the nature of the person whose being he projects.

Locke is an emotionally and spiritually immature person. It follows that the Monster's appropriation of Locke's personality should allow him to suppress Locke's natural personality and exercise most fully his will. This indeed seems to be the case, since Locke's personality seems most evident only in certain unusual situations.

On the other hand, if the Monster were to project an individual of strong will, someone possessed of indefatigable drive and perseverance, we might expect that person's personality to manifest in a particularly strong and unique manner.

Recall that Christian had an objective. Nothing in this life or the next would deter him from helping the person he loved more than anything—more than even his own life. He loved his son Jack so much that not even the loss of everything he had worked decades to achieve could diminish that love. Has anyone ever loved as deeply as this man loved his son?

The most inspired, animated soul aboard Oceanic Flight 815 resided in the cargo hold, in a cheap wooden casket.

When the Monster appropriated the form and personality of this impassioned man he probably could not have known that outer appearance would so relentlessly drive inner purpose and will. In fact, Christian Shephard's love so informed his will and determined his objective that nothing—not even a being of pure volition—could steer him away from his goal.

LOST began with a man driven, a man who understood the Island's needs and the needs of his son to intersect perfectly. So it was that Christian Shephard became not the instrument of the Smoke Monster, but the living, breathing shepherd of souls who guided his only begotten son and everyone who would assist in the triumph of his son's humanity over the Smoke Monster's will.

CHRISTIAN: Come here… Come on. [Vincent runs towards him] Good boy… [He leans down and pets him.] I need you to go find my son. He's over there in that bamboo forest, unconscious. I need you to go wake him up. Okay? Go on.
[Vincent whines and runs off.]
CHRISTIAN: He has work to do.

By the time Christian says, "He has work to do," he is speaking to the empty grass in front of him, for Vincent has already disappeared to wake Jack and begin the survivors' six-year adventure. If he is under the complete control of the Man in Black, why does he not instead say, "I need to destroy him," or words to that effect? Why, in every on-Island apparition of Christian Shephard, do we meet a compassionate man bent on saving the Island or helping those in distress? Why do we see not Evil Incarnate but the Good Shepherd?

The End

"Everyone dies sometime, kiddo."
LOST

"The End" by Gideon Slife 2011
Used with permission

We know of the Smoke Monster's strong aversion to the concussive force of loud explosions. When he went out of his way to drag John Locke into a hole in the ground (one of the so-called "Cerberus Vents"; see Episode 1.24), he must have been unwilling to allow anyone to wrest his prize from him. Yet when Kate threw a stick of dynamite into the vent and it exploded, the Monster immediately released Locke. The explosion was more than unpleasant—it harmed him enough that he was forced to relinquish his hold on Locke.

Horace Goodspeed, who led the Dharma Initiative's security research effort, loved playing with dynamite, and was almost certainly the inventor of the sonic fence, which stopped the Smoke Monster in his tracks. In fact, the Smoke Monster's aversion to dynamite must have been known long before erection of the fence; Horace's familiarity with dynamite indicates he was using it as an early Monster avoidance device. The sonic fence was perfectly effective against the beast. Even when a mortal enemy like Charles Widmore stood on the other side of a sonic fence, the Smoke Monster could do nothing to physically harm his foe.

We know with certainty, then, that the Man in Black did not find loud sounds merely objectionable, he found them deadly to his person and something he was obliged to avoid at all costs. When we see Christian Shephard aboard the Kahana a split second before an enormous mound of C4 explodes directly in front of him, we know the Smoke Monster is nowhere near the freighter. The apparition Michael sees is not the Smoke Monster in physician drag, but the Island's true representative, thanking Michael for his selfless dedication and service to the Island.

Christian Shephard is LOST's shepherd of souls, leading them with his lantern from a state of Lost confusion into the fullness of the Island's light. "Follow me," he says, holding the lantern before him (Episodes 5.05, 5.09). We are more than familiar with the words and the imagery (Matthew 4:19, 8:22, 9:9, 16:24, Mark 1:17).

The Enemy With a Thousand Faces

"You don't have what it takes," Christian told his son (Episode 1.05). Were these the heartless words of a thoughtless and mean-spirited father? Perhaps. Perhaps they are something else, though. It could be they share more in common with the strategy of the man who named his son "Sue." As Sue's father said:

"Son, this world is rough
And if a man's gonna make it, he's gotta be tough
And I knew I wouldn't be there to help ya along.
So I give ya that name and I said goodbye
I knew you'd have to get tough or die
And it's that name that helped to make you strong."
(Listen to Johnny Cash's rendition of "A Boy Named Sue" at San Quentin Prison, February 24, 1969: http://www.youtube.com/watch?v=IcQKtl3MGCE)

The on-Island apparitions were not those of a milquetoast Peter Pan. Christian was there to lead his flock, but he would not hold their hands or ease the pain of their wretched lives (Episode 5.05):

CHRISTIAN: Hello, John.
LOCKE: [Amazed] You! What are you doing down here?
CHRISTIAN: I'm here to help you the rest of the way.
….
LOCKE: Richard said I was going to die.
CHRISTIAN: Well, I suppose that's why they call it sacrifice.
….
LOCKE: [Winces in pain as he attempts to stand] Could you help me up?
CHRISTIAN: [Bluntly] No. Sorry. I can't.

Somehow, in ways we will never understand, even as he worked to help Locke and Jack and Sun, he did so as if through clenched teeth, for underneath the determined skin of a devoted physician and father was the undeniable will of an even more determined being who had lost both his body and his humanity, whose only motivations were force of character and strength of desire.

"The Man in Black appeared as Christian Shephard," Darlton told us. That is, Evil Incarnate appeared as the Good Shepherd. The statement cannot be understood in logical terms. We cannot appeal to any tradition of literature, culture, or religion to make sense of these words. The system of thought most easily applied to statements of identity involving the Good Shepherd would be obliged to declare the words an unthinkable blasphemy and dismiss their validity.

Perhaps we can understand the tough but loving father. More difficult, but possibly still within the limited scope of our understanding, is the idea of the neglectful but loving father, or the abusive yet loving father.

If you see the Buddha, kill him. The perfect father does not exist, therefore, if someone tells you of any such father, you can be sure she is delusional, or wishes to assert the truth of a falsehood. If you see the Buddha, kill him. Not because he is illusion, but because the path toward enlightenment is followed by means of process, not by means of achievement, not by comparing your progress with others' positions on their paths. If you see the Buddha, it means you are not following your path. If you hear evil words from the mouths of your enemies, it means you are seeking evil, not good.

So, yes, the Man in Black appeared as the shepherd of Lost souls. It is not logic. It is kōan. Kōan "consists of a story, dialogue, question, or statement, the meaning of which cannot be understood by rational thinking but may be accessible through intuition or lateral thinking." (Wikipedia; http://en.wikipedia.org/wiki/K%C5%8Dan, accessed on January 27, 2012).

Island is mixed with Man in Black is mixed with Christian Shephard. Locke is mixed with Jack is mixed with Christian. Jack is mixed with Kate is mixed with Claire is mixed with Jack. Locke is mixed with Island is mixed with Jacob. Not logic. Kōan.

The Island kōan is relationship. The most enduring and necessary relationships, in LOST, are those that drive us along the path of Jacob's Progress. These are not lovey-dovey, kiss-and-make-babies kind of relationships, but tense, uncomfortable, strife-ridden battles of enmity and discord that place one determined individual in fierce, diametric opposition to an unrelenting mortal enemy. In the dynamic that governs LOST, to say a force of purest evil is coupled with a force of unsullied, divine goodness is not only a permissible statement, it is verbal prerequisite to any truth we should expect to declare. Satan's Pact With God is the starting point for human progress.

"Christian Shephard" by ArtGUS
used with permission

This is nothing less than the great audacity of LOST. We know, intuitively, that we will never see Christian in his coffin. He is the Good Shepherd, meaning he is Evil Incarnate. He stands in the full light of the Source wearing bright white running shoes, meaning he is not worthy to stand at the Burning Bush, even though he remove his shoes. He is the abusive alcoholic father, meaning he is the father who cares for his son more than any father has ever cared for a babe in arms. He is the irresponsible addict unsuited to the lowest leadership role, meaning he must be leader and shepherd to the most important flock the Island has ever known. He leads his son off a cliff, meaning he leads his son to running water. He is dead, meaning he will never die, and his coffin will forever remain empty.

Christian Shephard is inscrutable mystery because LOST is not result, but process toward a result. We never come to the end of the path we call Jacob's Progress. We will never understand our fathers, or love them as much as we should. We never see in our own lives the excitement, the wonder, the extraordinary nature of days that are filled with love and strife, lies and truths, faith and science, compassion and desire. This is our daily reality, obscure to us in our insistence on surmises as dogmas and prejudices as solutions. The beauty of the Source—and the beauty of Christian Shephard—requires that we live the journey into the Light, into living water, into the halls of Shambala, open to all, shared by all.

Every now and then, we see the beauty in the kōan. We find fanciful and wonder-filled symmetry in the posing of the question. We come to love the journey, and suddenly we find ourselves in the shadow of the statue. There, in the shadow of greatness, we become truly excited. For it is here, in the place to which destiny calls us, we throw off the shackles of complacency, conformity, and mediocrity, and we learn to ponder, to create, to dream, here in this place—here, on this Island.

3:16 PM
February 8, 2012

Pearson Moore is the author of *Cartier's Ring*, an action-adventure historical novel set in 17th century North America. The novel explores the culture shock of First Contact between Europeans and Native North Americans from an Aboriginal (Native American) point of view. The protagonist, Myeerah of Hawk Clan, starts as a slave, but over several decades she rises to become the most influential matriarch in her village and the leading voice for a new way of thinking that will come to represent the philosophy of a nation.

Afterword

Pearson Moore

"Light and Dark" © Pearson Moore 2011
Created for "LOST Humanity" © Pearson Moore 2011

"We deserve answers!"

Horace's exasperation spoke for many of us in the summer and autumn of 2010. Ben must have sensed his frustration; he addressed more than just "one question" in his brief meeting with the two Dharma Initiative warehouse workers. In fact, his responses and the Hydra Station orientation film answered more than a dozen of the more difficult questions dealing with LOST mythology: Why polar bears on a tropical island? Why did Dr. Chang adopt so many aliases? Why did the DI drop point coordinates always change?

It wasn't enough.

"What did they do to those bears? And what the hell's a 'Hostile'?" Perhaps you could find solace in knowing a bit more than Horace, but you had questions, too, and you found them neither in the severance envelope nor in Benjamin Linus' smug responses.

After days or weeks, though, you came to understand and appreciate the mythology of LOST. Virtually every one of the hundreds of mythological questions received full explanation in one way or another during the course of the six years. You returned the DVDs and Blu-Rays to their honored place on the shelf. "Remember," Christian said, "and let go." Perhaps, now that the mythology of

LOST made sense you could "move on." Something inside chafed, though. "A tiny itch," you thought. "It will go away."

Then you bought this book—and the itch became intolerable. Any thought of moving on evaporated in the fire of a thousand new questions.

Twenty-two experts in fields ranging from film theory to postmodernism to semiotics challenged us with ideas we never thought to invoke, creating questions we never thought to ask. We are confronted again with the inscrutability of characters we thought we knew, of an island we thought we understood.

But these 22 scholars have only quickened us, schooled us in matters outside our knowledge, but matters yet close, vital to our restless minds, immediately relevant to every faculty of perception, intellect, and desire. LOST is not a momentary diversion, a respite from the ordinary, a brief foray into the mythological. It is not without, but within. As theologians Kevin McGinnis, Paul Wright, or Jennifer Galicinski might say, LOST indwells. It is not only imminent to our conscious scrutiny, but *immanent* to our essential selves—to our thought, our humanity, our identity.

As the 22 scholars represented in this volume might say, the mythology of LOST is finite, but the subtext is inexhaustible. Not one of us deemed "experts" in LOST can ever claim to have made sense of every aspect of this most enigmatic of television creations.

"What made you think you could mess with my life? I was doin' just fine 'til you dragged my ass to this damn rock." We realize the excitement of this Island is not that it becomes a place of answers, of satisfactions to intellect and will, but a place of questions, of challenges to spirit and mind. We are never comfortable on this damn rock, and we never will be. There are too many questions, and nothing we discover will diminish the excitement of experiencing an eye pop open to a strange bamboo forest, to the desperation and disorientation of a wreckage-strewn beach. Yet more exciting when we realize we are not witnesses or observers—that we can never stand outside the events in which we are sometimes unwilling and overwhelmed but deliriously captivated participants.

LOST has immanence, vitality, immediacy to our hungry spirits because it juxtaposes a vision of Self, Other, and Society that transcends fiction. We know ourselves to be subjects, not objects, and we see in the Source the same light, the same fire that kindles our souls. We are not the mean stuff of atoms, molecules, of animal lusts, grand ambitions, but those for whom life, death, rebirth are signs of an alpha and omega that orients us to the never-fully-achieved possibilities of our full humanity. LOST addresses the fundamental questions of our existence as people of light, the bearers of unquenchable fire.

LOST is metafiction. We must subsume ourselves to the story, allow it to indwell, become the final redactor, the director, the hero who puts things right, the heroine who kills the monster. LOST rekindles the knowledge we once had, as toddlers, as children again, free of the stifling constraints of adult surmises and smug prejudices. Life is to be more than a surrender to the comfortable conformity of mediocrity. The Light that indwells, the fire that burns is not to be hidden under a bushel, but raised up for all to feel and see. This Light that is in every man cannot be stolen from the Source, but neither can it be become the property of any single human being. The Light, you see, is subject, too, not object. The Island is not servant of our will, but joy of our desiring.

"A little bit of this very same light is inside of every man." But that brilliant yellow light, "the warmest, brightest light you've ever seen or felt," finds its origin in fierce crimson fire—a fire so far outside our comprehension that "good" and "evil' become useless adjectives. The fire is outside, surpassing our understanding, yet indwelling, the source of every passion, every motivation of the heart. LOST, as metafiction, tells us we are not permitted to sit on the sidelines. But life, too, tells us we cannot sit out tragedy and comedy: Whether we like it or not, life not only entices and cajoles, but obliges and compels. LOST reminds us that, even in darkest times, unreserved engagement in life is exciting, thrilling. Just as we share in the Light, we share in life, in each other, in the fullness of our humanity.

Some of us will move on. But some of us stay. The Island never grows old, because the questions never cease. But whether we move on from the Island, in some way we will already have moved on from petty concerns to the greater end of fulfilling Jacob's Progress. No matter where we go from here, we will carry the Light, aware of ourselves as participants in the overwhelming incomprehensibility of life, knowing that amidst the awful wreckage of our lives there is something "different, special." We all know it. We all feel it.

No matter where we go from here, we will be grateful to our fellow passengers on Flight 815—Jack and Kate, Locke and Boone, Charlie and Claire. We will be grateful to the capable crew in the cockpit—Damon, Carlton, and Jack, Eddy, Adam, and Elizabeth. They gave us Light to see, hatches to discover, ideas to explore.

As for me, I've decided to stay. A thousand unanswered questions beckon. As Ben said, peering at me with severe and intense eyes, "You have work to do." Vincent is waiting, after all. Is he symbolic, or semisymbolic? Hyperreal sign or agent in a grand hierarchy? Postmodern simulacrum or realist metaphor? Truly I am Lost, but I know I belong here, in this place that beckons me, in this place that bids me abide—here in the shadow of greatness.

815 PM

February 16, 2012

Featured Artists

Gideon Slife
ArtGUS

LOST, One Poster at a Time

By Gideon Slife

I am delighted to be involved in the *LOST Thought* project!

I am a graphic design artist. The concept of one poster per *Lost* episode began as a personal project: one poster per day, starting with the premiere of season six and ending three days after the series finale. The posters were uploaded to Flickr and posted on the DarkUFO forums, where after a month or so they spread through the *Lost* community and eventually onto other sites like SlashFilm and NYMag.com's Vulture section.

Usually I try to make each poster something that people who have seen the episode will remember. However, it's important to me that those who haven't seen the series won't be spoiled by the images. Generally I finish each poster in an hour, although a few took more time, like Jack's face for *Through the Looking Glass*, which I wish I had been able to spend more time on. All of the posters are completed in Adobe Photoshop or Illustrator, but a few have other mediums, particularly The Candidate, which was screenprinted at a smaller size.

Deus Ex Machina: I think this is definitely one of the most memorable scenes of the entire show and one that really represents *Lost* as a whole. It takes something that was currently a mystery in the show (the hatch) and uses it to develop a character. Locke's desperation is obvious, and it really boils his character into a man with no hope left. But this character movie also reveals more about the mystery AND more about the character.

The Man Behind the Curtain: Another great scene. I can remember watching this for the first time. I'm really happy with the way this turned out; representing Jacob and not just the chair he's in.

346

The Variable: I'm also really happy with the concept of this poster: relating Faraday's life to the metronome he played as a kid. I'm also really interested in great time travel stories, like the tragic storyline of a man who dies at the hands of his mother months before he was born. If you liked Daniel's storyline, I'd definitely recommend the short French film Le jetée.

On the controversial subject of the finale, I liked it all right. The on-island stuff was awesome, but I didn't really like the revelation of the flash-sideways as an "afterlife waiting room." it just seemed they took a lot of time up with those story-lines that weren't really relevant to that reveal. I wouldn't have minded so much if they didn't take up as much time, or if the afterlife was something different.

Minimalism: Minimalist art is very tough to do right. I think that minimalism is more of a building up of elements. You build up what you need to represent a subject, an idea, or a form, then take away as much as you can until it hurts. Minimalism is hard.

I graduated from the University of Delaware in 2012 from the Visual Communication program. You can find some of my other work at gideonslife.com.

347

"Fuerte Kate" by ArtGUS, Created for *LOST Identity*

I am a Spanish artist and painter, specializing in realistic portraiture. I love to capture the personality and expression of the characters I draw; beyond technical issues, I consider it most important that the work embody the expression and the dynamic that convey LIFE.

John Locke by ArtGUS

As a fan of the immortal television program *Lost*, I decided to draw the fascinating personalities of this series. The obvious question was 'Which do I draw first?' The response was rapid and clear: Desmond Hume. I agree with many fans who believe the episodes in which Desmond appears are the best of the series.

Having finished the great Desmond, I continued with the main characters (Locke, Jack, Ben Linus, etc), and completed 25 character portraits for this marvelous series.

To create a drawing, I first seek a reference photograph or screencap from one of the episodes featuring the chosen subject. When I'm making my selection, I look for features such as light contrast and facial shadow that will help in transmitting the personality of the character.

Hurley by ArtGUS

Once I've chosen the subject, I sketch on paper (I always use heavyweight paper, 220 gsm, medium grain, dimensions 29.7 x42 cm), setting the basic features of the face (eyes, mouth, nose , etc). Once I'm happy with the result, I begin applying the face details. Usually I start with the eyes, first with hard pencils (6H, H, which are lighter) and then use soft pencils (4B, 7B, dark) to bring the depth and relief that a face needs to be realistic. I find a bit of cotton or rolled paper helpful for the shadows of the face. All of this is done with great care to get realistic skin tone and texture, and to avoid a blotchy look.

For the brightness of the eyes or clear parts of the face, I always leave that area untouched, unlike other artists, who use either the eraser or apply white paint (pastel or acrylic type) directly to the face. Each drawing requires somewhere between 15 and 20 hours.

For paintings, I use acrylic on canvas of varying sizes. I begin with a very soft pencil to draw the face on the canvas and then I apply a soft flesh color to the face. From there, I focus on dark areas and finally work up the bright areas of the face.

Clint Eastwood by ArtGUS

My works can be found in various countries throughout the world (USA, France, Italy, Spain), and you can see more of my work at my website. If you would like an original ArtGUS, please contact me: http://agusgusart.jimdo. com /

ArtGUS, February, 2012

Translated from Spanish by Pearson Moore

Citations

1. Abraham Heschel, *Moral Grandeur and Spiritual Audacity: Essays* (New York: Farrar, Straus and Giroux, 1997), 341.

2. The Reverend Frank Krebs, "In the Shadow of Greatness We Walk" (sermon, Saints Claire and Francis ECC, St. Louis, MO, January 21, 2012).

101. I'm not going to analyze the finale. If you want that, check out my book, *Finding Lost: Season 6*, where I devote 22,000 words and 50 pages to a full analysis of "The End." Instead, I want to talk about where we are a year later.

601. Mittell, Jason, "Narrative Complexity in Contemporary American Television." *The Velvet Light Trap* 58 (2006): 29-40.

602. Jen Chaney, "Talking 'Lost' with Damon Lindelof and Carlton Cuse." thewashingtonpost.com. *The Washington Post*, 20 May 2010. (Accessed September 10, 2011).

603. Interviewer identified by the initials "BJM," "Re: 'Lost' - 'The End': See you in the other life, brother." by Allen Sepinwall, Hitflix.com (May 24, 2010), (Accessed September 10, 2011).

604. "Judge me Tender," *The Simpsons*, Television broadcast (Fox, May 23, 2010).

701. Anthony Mercatante, *Who's Who in Egyptian Mythology*, 2nd ed. (New York: MetroBooks, 2002), 12, 133-135, 160, 217.

901. Umberto Eco, *Foucault's Pendulum*, trans. William Weaver (New York: Mariner Books, 2007).

902. Lifetime, Wow! Blog, "Lost Finale: Sad Trombone," http://lifetimewow.blogspot.com/2010/05/lost-finale-sad-trombone.html (accessed January 8, 2012).

903. Patrick George McCullough, Kata ta biblia, "Nauseating Religious Soup," http://patmccullough.com/2010/05/24/lost-finale-reflections-part-2-nauseating-religious-soup/ (accessed January 8, 2012).

904. William Faulkner, *Requiem for a Nun* (New York: Vintage, 2012).

905. For more on Christendom and European identity, see Denys Hay, *Europe: The Emergence of an Idea* (New York: Harper, 1966).

906. Theodor Adorno and Max Horkheimer, *Dialectic of Enlightenment*, trans. Edmund Jephcott (Stanford: Stanford University Press, 2007).

907. Jean-François Lyotard, *The Postmodern Condition: A Report on Knowledge*, trans. Geoff Bennington and Brian Massumi (Minneapolis: University of Minnesota Press, 1984).

908. See Friedrich Nietzsche, *On Genealogy of Morals: A Polemic*, trans. Douglas Smith (New York: Oxford University Press, 2009); Thomas Kuhn, *The Structure of Scientific Revolutions* (Chicago: University of Chicago Press, 1996); Michel Foucault, *The Order of Things: An Archaeology of the Human Sciences*, trans. anonymous (New York: Vintage, 1994).

909. This injunction is inspired by John 17: 6-19.

910. For the best introduction to Pico's life and thought, see Paul Oskar Kristeller, *Renaissance Thought and Its Sources* (New York: Columbia University

Press, 1979), 165-210. See also Kristeller, *Eight Philosophers of the Italian Renaissance* (Stanford: Stanford University Press, 1966).

911.   For a readily available and accessible translation of Pico, see Ernst Cassirer (ed.), *The Renaissance Philosophy of Man* (Chicago: University of Chicago Press, 1969). For the most scholarly translation with facing Latin original, see the Brown University website, "The Pico Project," http://www.brown.edu/Departments/Italian_Studies/pico/ (accessed January 8, 2012).

912.   Jürgen Habermas and Joseph Ratzinger, *The Dialectics of Secularization: On Reason and Religion* (San Franciso: Ignatius Press, 2007).

913.   For a rich exploration of the complexity and cultural power of "vast narratives" across all contemporary media, see Pat Harrigan and Noah Wardrip-Fruin (eds.), *Third Person: Authoring and Exploring Vast Narratives* (Boston: The MIT Press, 2009).

914.   Reuters.com, "*Lost* writer gives detailed account of show," http://www.reuters.com/article/2011/09/25/us-lost-idUSTRE78O2JM20110925 (accessed January 8, 2012).

1001.   This reference was removed.

1002.   J. Richard Middleton and Brian J. Walsh, *Truth is Stranger Than It Used to Be* (Downer's Grove: Intervarsity Press, 1995), 35.

1003.   Ibid., 62.

1004.   Heath White, *Postmodernism 101* (Grand Rapids: Brazos Press, 2006), 31.

1005.   Ibid., 33.

1006.   Middleton and Walsh, 34.

1007.   Ibid., 34.

1008.   Ibid., 35.

1009.   Lostpedia, http://lostpedia.wikia.com/wiki/Sri_Lanka_Video. (Accessed June 10, 2010).

1010.   Lostpedia. http://lostpedia.wikia.com/wiki/Valenzetti_Equation. (Accessed June 10, 2010).

1011.   Middleton and Walsh, 34.

1012.   Ibid., 35.

1013.   We never saw her do this, but it was alluded to by the way the entire village was killed. Bloggers theorize that many years prior she must have gone into the Light herself, which caused her to become the Smoke Monster. The Smoke Monster is able to take the physical form, and all the memories of any dead body on the Island.

1014.   Middleton and Walsh, 34.

1015.   Pearson Moore. Email to the author. May 15, 2010.

1016.   James K. A. Smith, *Who's Afraid of Postmodernism?* (Grand Rapids: Baker, 2006), 36.

1017.   Smith, Ibid.

1018.   Ibid.

1019.   Ibid.

1020. She is appropriately named after Stephen Hawking, a contemporary theoretical physicist who has written about the possibilities of time travel.
1021. Desmond is a Scottish man who crashed on the Island and spent 3 years entering the numbers into the computer in the hatch (the Swan Station). One day he failed to enter the numbers within 108 minutes, which caused the survivors' plane to crash. Some theorize the electromagnetic energy that was released when the button was not pushed melted the instruments of the plane and made the Island visible to the world for a brief minute.
1022. 'The Lamp Post' is a reference to C.S. Lewis' The Lion, The Witch, and the Wardrobe, where the lamp post marks the passage between Narnia and our world. The Lamp Post serves a similar function with regard to the Island.
1023. Daniel believed that if they dropped a nuclear bomb into the drilling site of the Swan Station, than the electro-magnetic energy would be destroyed, and the Swan Station would never be built, and Desmond would never not press the button that caused the plane to crash.
1024. Cari Vaughn, "Lost in Hypertext." Society for the Study of Lost. Issue 2.1. March 1, 2010. http://www.loststudies.com/2.1/hypertext.html. (Accessed February 4, 2012)
1025. J. Richard Middleton and Brian J. Walsh, *Truth is Stranger Than It Used to Be* (Downer's Grove: Intervarsity Press, 1995), 42.
1026. Ibid., 37.
1027. Heath White, *Post-Modernism 101* (Grand Rapids: Brazos, 2006), 128.
1028. Ibid.
1029. Ibid., 44.
1030. Brian Walsh and Sylvia Keesmaat, *Colossians Remixed* (Downer's Grove: Intervarsity Press, 2004), 32.
1031. J. Richard Middleton and Brian J. Walsh, *Truth is Stranger Than It Used to Be* (Downer's Grove: Intervarsity Press, 1995), 43-44.
1032. Brian Walsh, "Post-modernity lecture." Wycliffe College. Februrary 9, 2010.
1033. Brian Walsh, "Cockburn, 'Justice' and the Postmodern Turn," 7.
1034. Middleton and Walsh, 47.
1035. Ibid., 48.
1036. Walsh and Keesmaat, 123.
1037. Walsh and Keesmaat, 49.
1038. When Ben moved the Island, it skipped through time until it 'rested' in 1977 until Jack and the others returned.
1039. This was during 'DHARMA times' and Ben, whose father joined the DHARMA Iniative in 1973, is just a small boy.
1040. Juliet, another doctor, was a member of the Others who joined up with Jack's people when she tried to get off the Island. She became close with many of them, including Jack. She died by getting sucked into the pocket of electromagnetic energy.
1041. The large and lovable Hurley is told by Jacob to lead Jack to the Lighthouse, where hundreds of names are written beside numbers on a large dial. Jack's number is 23 (like the 23rd Psalm, the 'Lord is my

shepherd') and when they turn the dial to point at 23, Jack sees his childhood house in the mirror. This is how Jacob was able to watch them, and mysteriously draw them to the Island.

1042. J. Richard Middleton and Brian J. Walsh, *Truth is Stranger Than It Used to Be* (Downer's Grove: Intervarsity Press, 1995), 66.

1043. Ibid., 174.

1044. Ibid.

1045. Ibid., 68-69.

1046. Brian Walsh and Sylvia Keesmaat, *Colossians Remixed* (Downer's Grove: Intervarsity Press, 2004), 109.

1047. Walsh and Middleton, 174-175.

1048. Ibid., 183.

1049. Walsh and Keesmaat, 133.

1050. Walsh and Middleton, 183.

1051. Ibid.

1052. Coldplay performing "Fix You" (London: EMI Records Ltd., 2005).

1101. Dennis A. Balcom, "Absent Fathers: Effects on Abandoned Sons," *The Journal of Men's Studies* 6 (1998): 283-97.

1102. Anthony Giddens, *Modernity and Self-Identity: Self and Society in the Late Modern Age* (Stanford, CA: Stanford University Press, 1991), 133.

1103. Jason Mittell, "Film and Television Narrative," *The Cambridge Companion to Narrative*, Ed. David Herman (Cambridge: Cambridge University Press, 2007), 178.

1104. Christian Piatt, Lost*: A Search for Meaning* (St. Louis, MO: Chalice Press, 2006), 82.

1101. Luigi Zoja, *The Father: Historical, Psychological, and Cultural Perspectives*, Trans. Henry Martin (Sussex: Brunner-Routledge, 2001), 281-285.

1401. Sledgeweb's Lost...Stuff: The Numbers (lost.cubit.net), The Lost numbers (thelostnumbers.blogspot.com). (Accessed prior to February, 2012).

1402. Alias inspired a cottage industry of fan speculation regarding its underlying conspiracies and mysterious backstory, although network interference and the decreasing involvement of creator Abrams muted fan interest in the mythological aspects of the show; see http://alias-tv.com for more information.

1403. The Lost Experience was charted in detail by Truffula in Lost 1.2 and 1.3; a summary is available at lostpedia.com.

1404. "Numbers," *Lost*, Written by Brent Fletcher and David Fury. Directed by Daniel Attias. ABC, March 2, 2005.

1405. "Man of Science, Man of Faith," *Lost,* Written by Damon Lindelof. Directed by Jack Bender. ABC, September 21, 2005.

1406. "Live Together, Die Alone," *Lost,* Written by Damon Lindelof and Carlton Cuse. Directed by Jack Bender. ABC, May 24, 2006.

1407. Immanuel Kant, *Critique of Practical Reason*, Ed. and translated by Mary Gregor (Cambridge: Cambridge University Press, 1997), 27 (5:30).

1408. "Flashes Before Your Eyes," *Lost,* Written by Damon Lindelof and Drew Goddard. Directed by Jack Bender. ABC, February 14, 2007.

1409. "Through the Looking Glass," *Lost,* Written by Damon Lindelof and Carlton Cuse. Directed by Jack Bender. ABC, May 23, 2007.

1501. Augustine of Hippo. *Confessions.* Trans. Henry Chadwick 1991 (New York: Oxford University Press, 2008). 221, 229-230.

1502. Carter, Bill. "Viewers of '*LOST*' Finale Stay Tuned." *New York Times* on the Web. 24 May 2010. 2 June 2011. <http://artsbeat.blogs.nytimes.com/2010/05/24/ratings-for-lost-finale-are- sweet-dude/>. (Accessed prior to February, 2012).

1503. William Faulkner, *The Sound and the Fury.* Ed. David Minter. 1929 (New York: W. W. Norton and Co., 1994), 14.

1504. Ferguson, Kitty. *The Fire in the Equations: Science, Religion, and the Search for God* (Philadelphia: Templeton Foundation Press, 1994), 226.

1505. Gérard Genette, *Narrative Discourse: An Essay in Method* (Ithica: Cornell University Press, 1980), 85.

1506. Russell A. Hunt and Douglas Vipond. "Crash-Testing a Transactional Model of Literary Reading." *Reader.* Vol. 14. 1 September 1985. 23-40.

1507. Jensen, Jeff, "Totally '*LOST*': Time Passages." *Entertainment Weekly* Online. 21 Februar y 2007. 2 June 2011. <http://www.ew.com/ew/article/0,,20313460_20012336,00.html>.

1508. Jensen, Jeff, "A Map for 'Lost'." *Entertainment W eekly* Online. 9 May 2007. 2 June 2011. <http://www.ew.com/ew/article/0,,20038202,00.html>.

1509. Jensen, Jeff, " '*LOST*' : Cheating Time." *Entertainment Weekly* Online. March 14 2008. 2 June 2011. <http://www.ew.com/ew/article/0,,20184253,00.html>.

1510. Erika Johnson-Lewis, "'We Have to Go Back': Temporal and Spatial Narrative Strategies." *Looking for LOST: Critical Essays on the Enigmatic Series.* Ed. Randy Laist (Jefferson: MacFarland and Co., 2011), 15.

1511. Keen, Craig. Facebook message post. Facebook.com. 12 April 2011. (Accessed June 6, 2011).

1512. Jon Lachonis (aka "DocArzt") and Amy Johnston (aka "hijinx"), *Lost Ate My Life: The Inside Story of a Fandom Like No Other* (Toronto: ECW Press, 2008), 40.

1513. Coca Lite, "Lost Is Its Own Monster: The Bitterness Fiesta." *Television Without Pity* (December 2, 2004). (Accessed February 2, 2012) <forums.televisionwithoutpity.com/index.php?showtopic=3120925>.

1514. Roberta Pearson, "Chain of Events: Regimes of Evaluation and *LOST*'s Construction of the Televisual Character." *Reading LOST.* Ed. Roberta Pearson (New York: I.B. Tauris, 2009), 143-144.

1515. Prince, Gerald. *A Dictionary of Narratology.* Rev. ed. (Lincoln: University of Nebraska Press, 2003), 97.

1516. Sider, Theodore. *Four-Dimensionalism: An Ontology of Persistence and Time* (New York: Oxford University Press, 2001), 3.

1517. Nikki Stafford, Keynote address, *LOST* Mini-Conference. (New Orleans, October 7, 2011).

1701. Jacques Lacan in *The Subversion of the subject and the dialectic of desire in the Freudian unconscious, Écrits*. Ed. and trans. Bruce Fink in collaboration with Héloïse Fink and Russell Grigg. (New York: W.W. Norton & Company, 2006), 671–702.

1702. Jacques Lacan, *The Seminar of Jacques Lacan, Book I: Freud's Papers on Technique 1953–54*. Ed. Jacques-Alain Miller, Trans. John Forrester. (Cambridge: Cambridge University Press, 1988), 12.

1703. See Lacan, Reference 1601.

1901. John R. Maynard, *The* Bildungsroman: *A Companion to the Victorian Novel*, Patrick Brantlinger and William B. Thesing eds., (Oxford: Blackwell, 2002), 286-287. See also: Marian Hirsch Gottfried and David H. Miles, "Defining Bildungrsroman as a Genre," *Proceedings of the Modern Language Association* 91 (Jan. 1976), 122-23.

1902. "Lost: the Answers" (ABC Television Network, May 17, 2005).

1903. Nellie Andreeva, "End in Sight for Lost: 48 Episodes, 3 Seasons," *The Hollywood Reporter* (May 7, 2007).

1904. Jim Collins, "Television and Postmodernism," *Film and Theory: An Anthology*, Robert Stam and Toby Miller eds. (Oxford: Blackwell, 2000), 763.

2101. Jason Mittell. "Lost's Lingering Questions." Just TV (May 26, 2010). (Accessed February 10, 2012) <http://justtv.wordpress.com/2010/05/26/losts-lingering-questions/>.

2102. The concept of semisymbolism sounds weird only the first time one hears it. If a symbol is defined as an association between a signifier and a signified that's both arbitrary and conventional, semisymbolism is the arbitrary association between two oppositions: one on the plane of expression (that is, two signifiers that are presented in opposition to one another within a certain text), one on the plane of content (two opposite meanings). The association between the two planes may be arbitrary, but the oppositions between elements of each plane are not, hence making the semiotic relationship only half symbolic.

2103. Jeff Jensen and Dan Snierson, "'Lost' and Found." EW.com (February 11, 2007). (Accessed February 10, 2012) <http://www.ew.com/ew/article/0,,20011203_3,00.html>.

2104. It may be frowned upon, academically, but Wikipedia comes in handy in explaining the concept of value in Saussurean linguistics: "Value (semiotics)." Wikipedia, The Free Encyclopedia (December 12, 2011). (Accessed February 10, 2012) <http://en.wikipedia.org/w/index.php?title=Value_(semiotics)&oldid=465487765>.

2105. Some of it can be found in the seventh chapter of my own *Beyond Sitcom*, where it will also become clearer why there's a section about *Lost* in the book. (Antonio Savorelli. *Beyond Sitcom: New Directions in American Television Comedy* (Jefferson, N.C.: McFarland & Company, 2010).

2106.   Or at least it came as unexpected to me. It's one of the reasons why I generally don't read online fan forums: not just because I'm a textual purist, and claim that kind of stuff doesn't fit my approach; I actually mostly do it because I don't want other people's understanding to randomly influence my own. Also, I'm afraid the possible extra knowledge some of the viewers and forum posters inevitably have may spoil my discovery of the text. Once again, it's not my semiotic snottiness (and stubbornness) but rather my being a fan that makes me stay away from that sort of discussion.

2107.   Jason Mittell, "Lost Monday: The End." Antenna: Responses to Media & Culture (May 24, 2010). (Accessed February 10, 2012) <http://blog.commarts.wisc.edu/2010/05/24/lost-monday-the-end/>.

2201.   Angela Ndalianis, *Neo-Baroque Aesthetics and Contemporary Entertainment* (Cambridge, MA and London: The MIT Press, 2004), 25.

2202.   On the term 'baroque' and its history see Greg Lambert, *The Return of the Baroque in Modern Culture* (London and New York: Continuum, 2004), 1-14.

2203.   Germain Bazin, *The Baroque: Principles, Styles, Modes, Themes* (New York: W.W. Norton and Company, 1968), 15.

2204.   Cited in Kerry Downes, "Baroque", *The Dictionary of Art*, ed. Jane Turner, Vol. 3 (New York: Grove Press, 1996), 262.

2205.   Jacob Burckhardt, *The Cicerone: An Art Guide to Painting in Italy for Travellers and Students*, trans. Mrs. A.H. Clough (London: T. Werner Laurie, 1908), 220.

2206.   Heinrich Wölfflin, *Renaissance and Baroque*, trans. Kathrin Simon (Ithaca: Cornell University Press, 1966).

2207.   Heinrich Wölfflin, *Principles of Art History: The Problem of the Development of Style in Later Art*, trans. M.D. Hottinger (New York: Dover, 1950/1932).

2208.   On Wölfflin's continued importance for art history, see Vernon Hyde Minor, *Art History's History* (Englewood Cliffs, NJ: Prentice Hall, 1994), 113-115.

2209.   For a comprehensive discussion of the Baroque style within the context of the seventeenth century see John Rupert Martin, *Baroque*, Boulder, CO: Westview, 1977.

2210.   Patrick Fuery and Kelli Fuery, *Visual Cultures and Critical Theory*, (London: Edward Arnold Publishers Ltd., 2003), 24-25.

2211.   Angela Ndalianis, "Caravaggio reloaded: neo-baroque poetics," *Caravaggio and his World: Darkness and Light* (Sydney: Art Gallery of New South Wales; Melbourne: National Gallery of Victoria, 2003), 72-76.

2212.   Ndalianis, 23-25, 97.

2213.   www.lostvirtualtour.com.

2214.   For a list of *Lost*-related multimedia see http://en.wikipedia.org/wiki/Lost_(TV_series).

2215.   knowledge.wharton.upenn.edu/article.cfm?articleid=1514 - 39k - Oct 13, 2006. (Accessed prior to February 12, 2012).

2216.   Wölfflin, *Renaissance and Baroque*, iv.

2217.   J. M. Berger, "Flashbacks, Memory and Non-Linear Time," *Lost Online Studies* 1.2. (Accessed prior to February 12, 2012).

2218.   Berger, 2.

2219.   *Studies in Iconology*, New York: Harper and Row, 1962, 92.

2220.   Jim Collins, "Television and Postmodernism," *Film and Theory: An Anthology*, Robert Stam and Toby Miller eds. (Malden, MA: Blackwell, 2000), 763.

2221.   For example, Pillsbury, Jabba, Babar, from the episodes 'The Hunting Party', 'Fire + Water', and 'One of Them', respectively.

2222.   Perry Anderson, *The Origins of Postmodernity* (London: Verso, 1998), 25.

2301.   Nikki Stafford, *Finding Lost: The Unofficial Guide* (Toronto: ECW Press, 2006), 3.

2302.   Said, Edward W. *Orientalism* (New York: Vintage Books, 1978).

2304.   Said, *Orientalism*, 3.

2305.   Miles, Margaret R. *Seeing and Believing: Religion and Values in the Movies* (Boston: Beacon Press, 1996), 68.

2306.   Stafford, *Finding Lost: The Unofficial Guide*, 11.

2307.   *Lostpedia: The Lost Encyclopedia Online.* (Accessed November 27, 2011).

2308.   Rollin Armour, Sr., *Islam, Christianity, and the West: A Troubled History* (New York: Orbis Books, 2002), 178.

2309.   Robert Jewett & John Shelton Lawrence. *Captain America and the Crusade Against Evil: The Dilemma of Zealous Nationalism* (Grand Rapids, MI: William B. Eerdmans Publishing Co., 2003), 235.

2310.   Jewett and Lawrence, 241-242.

2311.   Jewett and Lawrence, 240.

2312.   Armour, 177-178.

2313.   Stafford, *Finding Lost: The Unofficial Guide*, 4.

2314.   Margaret R. Miles, *Seeing and Believing: Religion and Values in the Movies*, (Boston: Beacon Press, 1996), 70.

2315.   Said, *Orientalism*, 5.

2316.   Armour, 167.

2401.   Sandra Bonetto, "No Exit . . . from the Island: A Sartrean Analysis of *Lost*." *Lost and Philosophy: The Island Has Its Reasons.* Ed. Sharon M. Kaye (Malden MA: Blackwell, 2008), 125-135.

2402.   Jean Delumeau, *Sin and Fear: The Emergence of a Western Guilt Culture, 13th-18th Centuries,* Trans. Erick Nicholoson (New York: St. Martin's Press, 1990).

2403.   T. S. Eliot, "The Love Song of J. Alfred Prufrock," *The Complete Poems and Plays, 1909-1950* (San Diego: Harcourt Brace, 1971), 3-7.

2404.   Charles Girard and David Meulemans, "The Island as a Test of Free Will: Freedom of Reinvention and Internal Determinism in *Lost*." *Lost and Philosophy: The Island Has Its Reasons.* Ed. Sharon M. Kaye (Malden MA: Blackwell, 2008), 89-101.

2405.   Jacques Lacan, *The Seminar of Jacques Lacan: Book I: Freud's Papers on Technique, 1953-54,* Ed. Jacques Allain Miller, Trans. John Forrester (New York: Norton, 1988).

2406.   John Milton, *Paradise Lost. Complete Poems and Major Prose,* Ed. Merrit Y. Hughes. 1957 (Indianapolis: Hackett Publishing, 2003), 211-469.

2407.   Brett Chandler Patterson, "Of Moths and Men: Paths of Redemption on the Island of Second Chances," *Lost and Philosophy: The Island Has Its Reasons.* Ed. Sharon M. Kaye (Malden MA: Blackwell, 2008), 204-220.

2408.   Nikki Stafford, *Finding Lost: The Unofficial Guide* (Toronto: ECW Press, 2006), 45.

2409.   Donald W. Winnicott, *Home Is Where We Start From: Essays by a Psychoanalyst.* Ed. Clare Winnicott, Ray Sheperd, Madeleine Davis (New York: Norton, 1986).

2409.   ---. *The Maturational Processes and the Facilitating Environment: Studies in the Theory of Emotional Development* (New York: International Universities Press, 1965).

2410.   ---. *Playing and Reality* (London: Tavistock Publications, 1971; 1982

Glossary of Terms

Editor's Note: *All definitions in the glossary are drawn directly from my limited understanding, and are provided in my own words. These definitions should not be considered as authoritative, but merely as a starting point, for better or for worse, toward a more informed understanding which I encourage all readers to acquire through independent research. I am solely responsible for any incorrect or misleading statements.* —PM *January 23, 2012*

Agonistic behavior – Behavior, often ritualized, related to fighting. The term is considered stronger than "aggressive behavior" since the phrase encompasses not only aggression, but also threats and violence. The term originated with Scott and Fredericson in 1951. Agonistic behavior is seen in many animal populations due to scarcity of food, other necessary resources, or potential mates. The behavior often involves proofs of physical strength, technical or ritual prowess, or physical or sexual health or attractiveness. Scientists recognize three general types of behaviors in this category: threat, aggression, and submission. The range of behaviors includes simple ritualistic display all the way to a fight to the death.

Analepsis – Flashback.

Après coup – A concept in psychoanalysis conceived by Sigmund Freud (using the German term *Nachtraglichkeit*) and developed by French psychoanalyst Jacques Lacan as a tool for understanding temporal and causal elements in the human psyche. In *après coup* the patient interprets current events in terms of past, usually traumatic and often sexual, experiences due to their sudden re-emergence in response to a trigger event. The *après coup*, literally translated "after punch," constitutes the remains or after-effect of past events, reinterpreted and made suddenly relevant by recent events. *L'après coup* is sometimes called "deferred action."

Auteurism – A concept in film theory in which the director of the film is understood to have brought to bear such creative influence on the work that she is considered the primary author (French "auteur") of the original piece. That a single person could exercise such a degree of influence, in spite of the present-day complications inherent in large studios and the competing influences of producers, writers, production staff, and actors, is often considered remarkable. Auteurism has influenced legal understanding, especially in Europe, where the director, as auteur, is the copyright holder in the film. Auteurism had strong beginnings in the mid-1950s, when renowned director François Truffaut created an enduring connection between the concept and the movement he initiated, the French New Wave. Film critics at two influential publications, les *Cahiers du Cinéma* in France and *The Village Voice* in the United States, helped to perpetuate and eventually firmly establish the idea in mainline film theory.

Bardo – A Tibetan word meaning "in-between state of existence," or "liminal state." The term was first used to describe the Sideways World of LOST by Ms. Nikki Stafford, a leading LOST scholar. The concept is used in conjunction with the Buddhist and Tibetan traditional beliefs in reincarnation. During the Bardo, a consciousness is between physical death of the previous incarnation and physical birth of the next incarnation.

Bildungsroman – A literary genre concerning coming of age, but with great attention given to the spiritual, moral, or psychological growth of the protagonist. The idea was first publicized by Karl Morgenstern, a German philologist, but the genre itself is generally considered to have begun with the publication of Johann Goethe's *The Apprenticeship of Wilhelm Meister* late in the 18th century.

Billy Pilgrim – A fictional character created by Kurt Vonnegut in his 1969 novel *Slaughterhouse-Five*. Billy Pilgrim is the protagonist in the novel. The character is often invoked in discussions about LOST due to Billy Pilgrim's similarity to Desmond Hume in being "unstuck in time." That is, like Desmond, Billy Pilgrim's consciousness is able to move about in both the past and in the future.

B-Series Theory of Time – The McTaggart theory of time stipulates that there are two routes through which all temporal events can be understood to move. In the A-Series, temporal activity is ordered by means of non-relational terminology, employing strings such as "is past", "is present", and "is future." In the A-Series scheme, positions along the temporal continuum are envisioned as being in continual flux, so that any particular event is first of all seen as occupying a position in the future, then in the present, and finally in the past. Any statements about events in the temporal chain are understood as being relative to the person making the statements, with cognizance of that person's inability to speak objectively, since she herself is positioned on the temporal continuum. In McTaggart's B-Series theory of time, on the other hand, temporal events are described as having relational asymmetry and transitivity, so they "occur before" or precede, or "occur after" or follow. An interesting linguistic distinction between the two modes of considering temporal events is the idea of tense. A-Series events carry a tense, but B-Series events carry no tense. "Today Jane has a headache" carries present tense, and the statement is understood as being relative to the temporal position of the person making the statement. But "Jane has a headache on March 9, 2012" has no tense, and is independent of the position on the temporal continuum of the person making the statement. From a strictly logical point of view, assuming the two statements both refer to the same event, there is no difference in truth value between the two statements. However, the understanding of the two events in temporal relation to an observer, and the way in which they proceed through the continuum, is quite different.

Cabal – A group of individiuals cooperating in a close association, often aimed at increasing the influence of interests or agendas common to the group. The interests of the cabal often center on social structures, such as political organizations, organized churches, government, or local community organizations. Cabals frequently work in secret since members of the group often hold controversial or minority views, and their agendas are often self-serving.

Colossus of Constantine – An enormous stone and brick statue statue of the Roman emperor Constantine the Great (ca. 280–337). The statue originally stood in the west apse of the Basilica of Maxentius, not far from the Forum Romanum in Rome. Most of the remaining fragments of the Colossus, including the head, hands, and feet, may be found in the Courtyard of the Palazzo dei Conservatori of the Musei Capitolini, on the Capitoline Hill in Rome, just off the west side of the Forum.

"Campitelli campidoglio cortile dei conservatori" Lalupa 2006 WMC PD

Constantine's Statue – See the Colossus of Constantine.

Darlton – Damon Lindelof and Carleton Cuse, the executive producers and showrunners of LOST.

Derrida, Jacques – An Algerian-born French philosopher, Jacques Derrida developed the theory and methods of Deconstructionism, and is considered by many to be the father of Post-structuralism, a movement conceptually similar to Postmodernism. A prodigious writer, having authored more than 40 books, Derrida made significant, often seminal contributions to literary theory, semiotics, anthropology, cultural studies, sociology. His thought directly influenced disciplines as diverse as art theory and jurisprudence. He is frequently cited by leading theorists and investigators in areas such as ethics, language theory, epistemology, and esthetics. Jacques Derrida died in 2004.

Diachronic – Occurring over a (usually) long period of time.

Didactic – Concerning the art or practice of teaching. A didactic text, play, or film has the intention of teaching. The term may also be used to describe an instructor or a text that is too intent on teaching, or a teacher or text with an overly moralistic tone.

Diegesis – Concerning the fictional world in which the events of a story take place *as related and interpreted by a narrator*. The term is to be understood as being in contrast to Mimesis, in which the events of the fictional world are to be observed and interpreted by the audience member or reader, not by a narrator established in the fictional story. Diegesis is often characterized as "telling," while Mimesis is described as "showing." Plato understood Diegesis as descriptive reporting by a narrator, while Mimesis was representative or imitative demonstration. Diegesis might also be understood as expository, while Mimesis could be understood as demonstrative. Most authorities on the art of storytelling believe fiction must be demonstrative (mimetic) to best engage readers in the story and immerse them in the fictional world.

Emperor Constantine's Statue – See the Colossus of Constantine.

Epistemology – the discipline in philosophy dealing with the nature, limitations, and range of learning and knowledge. It addresses the questions: What is knowledge? How is knowledge acquired? To what extent is it possible for a given subject or entity to be known? How do we know what we know? Heated discussion often centers around the precise definition of the concept, since it necessarily has intimate connection to other highly contentious ideas, such as belief and truth.

Eschatology – Concerning "the end times," or the end of human history, often in an apocalyptic context. Eschatology typically deals with subjects related to death, judgment, and reward or punishment after death, often described using the terms "heaven" and "hell" or "the inferno."

Etiology – Having to do with cause and effect. Also, the formal study of causation.

Ficino, Marsilio – Also known by his Latin name, Marsilius Ficinus. Born in 1433, Ficino was perhaps the most widely-quoted humanist philosophers of the 15th century Italian Renaissance. An advocate of Neoplatonism, Ficino corresponded with every major scholar and writer of the time, translating the known works of Plato from Greek into Latin for the first time. In establishing the Florentine Academy, a contemporary revival of Plato's Academy, his Neoplatonic emphasis virtually determined the flavor of the Italian Renaissance and subsequent

Renaissance and Enlightenment eras in European thought. Marsilio Ficino died in 1499.

Flocke – Fake Locke. This name refers to the Smoke Monster in Seasons Five and Six when he is in the guise of John Locke.

Foucault, Michel – a leading French philosopher, social theorist, and historian of thought whose contributions were felt in broadly diverse fields. In the present volume, his ideas are most strongly brought to bear in areas touching on postmodernist problems. Lecturing widely in Europe and the United States, Foucault's ideas on social institutions and professional conventions, and especially in the study of prison systems and psychoanalysis, carried great influence. He wrote extensively on human sexuality, knowledge systems, and power hierarchies, gaining a worldwide following. Though often invoked by adherents of poststructuralism and postmodernism, Foucault rejected the classification of his work in this way and made clear his disdain for postmodernist approaches. He preferred to think of his work as flowing naturally from the thought of Immanuel Kant and Friedrich Nietzsche.

Fourth Wall – In theater productions, the imaginary wall separating the actors on stage from the members of the audience. The Fourth Wall is sometimes broken for humorous or shock effect, as in the closing, post-credit minutes of *Ferris Bueller's Day Off*, when the protagonist stared into the camera (the audience) and asked, "You're still here?" The film virtually abandoned the Fourth Wall throughout the film, but in a distant way, with the protagonist taking the role of an off-stage narrator. The complete removal of the wall did not occur until the speech after the credits.

Gestalt – A German word for form or shape.

Habermas, Jürgen – a German philosopher concentrating on issues in sociology. Habermas focuses on epistemological systems and social theory, the sociological context for legal systems, German politics, and the study of late capitalism and capitalist societies. He is perhaps best known for his work on concepts centered on modernity, especially ideas connected to Max Weber's concept of rationalization. Much of his work is considered to have been influenced by Marxist thought. He is an ardent critic of postmodernism on several fronts, but his most vocal denunciations contend that postmodernists do not address the practicalities of life. Habermas was born in 1929.

Hegemony – an indirect type of political control in which the imperial state rules subordinate political entities though political imposition rather than through conquest or military enforcement. While 19th century critics applied the term to political situations, the idea came to be used more frequently in the 20th century to describe the imposition of the cultural will of a dominating country over less culturally less intrusive countries.

Hermeneutics – The interpretation of a text; also, the theory of interpretation, usually as applied to texts in social philosophy, religious studies, and literary criticism. Hermeneutics is somewhat more flexible and more widely applied than the similar idea of Exegesis, which is usually applied only to written texts.

Heschel, Abraham – One of the leading Jewish theologians and writers of the 20th century, Abraham Heschel's influence extended into the Christian world as well, and into the thought of leading representatives of almost every major religion. Heschel contended that spirituality is a fundamental human reality, and therefore authentic religious experience is open to adherents of all faith traditions. According to Heschel, no single religious denomination can claim unique ownership of spiritual or religious truth. Abraham Heschel was a presence in the Civil Rights movement, as well as at the Second Vatican Council, where he was instrumental in convincing Pope John 23rd and the hierarchy of the Catholic Church to remove or modify liturgical texts that vilified or demeaned Jews or the Jewish faith tradition.

Historicization – A bias in favor of historical law over human agency. Historicism often understands historical development as immutable or inevitable; individual human attempts to subvert the natural historical flow of events, according to this scheme, are doomed to fail. Karl Marx's belief in inevitable social progression through historic periods of well-defined economic and political structures is an important example. In the context of LOST, Eloise Hawking's contention that the universe "course corrects" and that individual actions opposed to historically determined outcomes are futile can be interpreted as historicism. Less frequently, historicization may be understood as simply placing an event within a broader historical context.

Hypertextuality – A postmodern concept in which all literary materials within a culture are linked, and therefore any particular text must be viewed in the context of the greater literary culture. Hypertext is often invoked to discuss particular texts that explicitly or implicitly cite other literary works.

Induction – The logical process through which the validity of observations or conclusions about a large class of objects is determined as part of an effort to construct a general statement or conclusion applying to the entire class of objects. Also known as inductive logic, the concept is often simplified to a process of generating general propositions based on a large number of single objects or occurrences. Induction can be seen as contrasting with deduction, in which a proposition or conclusion obtains from a general theory or principle. In simplest terms, induction moves from single instances to general statements about an entire class, while deduction moves from broad theoretical statements to the analysis of specific cases. However, any such contrasts are overly simplistic in that they ignore aspects of induction and deduction having enormous bearing on practical problems. For instance, deductive arguments are valid if a proposition follows necessarily from premises, while in inductive reasoning a general conclusion does not necessarily follow from premises. For example, most contraptions fueled by an internal combustion engine and bearing four wheels are automobiles; the Ore Crusher has four wheels and an internal combustion engine; therefore, the Ore Crusher is likely to be an automobile. Since this is an inductive argument, it cannot be said that the Ore Crusher is an automobile. For instance, later investigation may determine that in fact the Ore Crusher is fixed in place and the wheels are merely used to move metal ore along a conveyor belt. The soundness of a philosophical argument based on induction is predicated on solid apprehension of the many nuanced facets of the method.

Intertextuality – the use of texts outside the main text to bring meaning to the main text. Intertextuality is typically achieved through the transformation, borrowing, or contextualization of an outside text by the author or participants within the main text. The distinction between intertextuality and simple allusion is not always clear, and may depend on the definitions employed by the person asserting the use of intertextuality in a narrative.

Kuhn, Thomas Samuel – Author of *The Structure of Scientific Revolutions*, published in 1962. Kuhn contended that the study and understanding of science and scientific knowledge periodically undergoes what he called a sudden "paradigm shift," rather than progressing through steady, linear development. The "paradigm shift" brings sudden change to the way in which sciences or knowledge are understood, allowing scientists not only to dramatically and quickly expand the knowledge base, but to do so by means of tools or ways of thinking that had not been available even months or short years before. The upshot of this way of thinking about scientific progress, according to Kuhn, is that objective consensus regarding the nature and methods of science cannot be attained. The subjective analysis of science is not only valid, but due to paradigm shifts, must be considered in some ways actually necessary to the more complete understanding of science. Kuhn died in 1996.

Lacan, Jacques – A French psychoanalyst in the tradition of Sigmund Freud. Jacques Lacan died in 1981.

Lagomorph – A member of the taxonomic order Lagomorpha, including rabbits, hares, and pikas.

MacGuffin – An object, event, or situation in a fictional work that draws the reader's or viewer's attention or serves to accelerate the plot. The MacGuffin usually has an immediate effect on the main characters in the drama, causing them to feel urgency around the fictional element, usually with the goal of possessing the MacGuffin itself or some benefit believed to be associated with it. The central players are often willing to say or do anything, even to make great sacrifices, to obtain the MacGuffin or a situation or benefit that would naturally derive from the item or situation. MacGuffins are most often employed in films.

McTaggart, John – A 19th century British philosopher, McTaggart considered himself Hegelian in his understanding of metaphysics. He is probably best known for the A-Series and B-Series theories of time. McTaggart taught at Trinity College, Cambridge, until just before his death in 1925.

Metanarrative – A metanarrative is a transcendent, master story that determines the course of lesser narratives and knits them together into a cohesive, consistent whole. It is often considered a culturally- or socially-derived grand story intended not only to explain all of knowledge and human behavior, but also to entrench and solidify cultural, political, or economic power hierarchies. Metanarratives typically are not recorded, even unofficially. Particular cultural truths drawn from the metanarrative are typically illustrated through one or more of the lesser stories sewn into the metanarrative quilt. For instance, the concept of Manifest Destiny could be considered a lesser narrative derived from a religiously-based metanarrative proclaiming the United States as the divinely-favored New Jerusalem destined not only to tame the North American continent, but to become the divinely-inspired and -approved hegemon to the entire world. Metanarratives are generally considered to exist independent of historical events. In simplest terms, metanarratives can be thought of as being culturally-based "theories of everything." Examples from LOST include Science, Faith, the Numbers, and the Island.

Modernism – A philosophical reaction to realism, modernism also rejected the broader precepts of the Enlightenment. The modernist movement began in the late 19th century but reached its most far-reaching expression in the 1920s as a result of the horrors of World War I. Not only war, but also industrialization and the failure of traditional philosophies to explain the socio-economic and political predicaments of modern society caused leaders of the modernist movement to reject religion and virtually every traditional way of evaluating the human condition. Modernist expression was often self-conscious, with feelings of angst often invoked to denote the pessimism and despair over identifying universal truths. Existentialism took modernist subjectivity to an extreme, claiming that truth was an entirely individual matter. Thus, modernism, existentialism, and postmodernism can be considered three quite different reactions to realism or the Enlightenment. While modernism continued to seek truths outside the subjective purview of the individual psyche, postmodernism found shared truth only in subjective, culturally-based images, and existentialism rejected all non-subjective truths. The modernist movement is generally considered to have lost most of its influence by the beginning of World War II.

Narrative – A story containing descriptions of a sequence of events. Narrative may relate either nonfiction or fiction stories, and may be part of related narratives or metanarratives. From a purely literary point of view, narrative can be considered one of the four rhetorical methods of communication, with the other three being argumentation, description, and exposition, though some scholars collapse narrative and description into a single category. More useful to the analysis of literature may be the concepts of Diegesis and Mimesis (see Diegesis above), which considers narrative from the point of view of exposition and demonstration.

Nietzsche, Friedrich – Friedrich Wilhelm Nietzsche was an influential 19th-century German philosopher. His work is frequently considered to be the forerunner of several modern schools of thought, including existentialism, postmodernism, and nihilism. Expanding far beyond traditional philosophy, Nietzsche contributed novel ideas in the areas of culture, science, poetry, religion, and philology. Nietzsche originated the idea of the Übermensch and the Will to Power. Long before modernism and postmodernism, Nietzsche proclaimed the death of God. He convincingly demonstrated the limitations and pitfalls of a reliance on objective truth. Nietzsche's ideas continue to have wide circulation far beyond the constraints of formal philosophy. Friedrich Nietzsche was born in 1844 and died in 1900.

Novikov Self-Consistency Principle – A principle developed around 1985 by Russian physicist Igor Dmitriyevich Novikov to address some of the problems of paradox associated with time travel. Novikov approached time travel as a possibility inherent in some of the more widely held technical understandings general relativity, with particular emphasis on solutions relying on closed time-like curves. A simple way of understanding the Novikov self-consistency principle is to consider the possibility of the occurrence of a paradox. According to Novikov, if an event would necessarily cause the occurrence of a paradox, the probability of the occurrence of that event is zero. It is likely, according to Novikov's scheme, that a change of any kind in any past event would require the satisfaction of at least one paradox condition, meaning that any such change would have a zero probability of occurrence. Temporally-induced paradox, according to Novikov, is not possible.

Orthodoxy – The adherence to a traditionally approved version of a cultural practice, religious belief, political persuasion, or philosophical system. The word may also be used to describe conformance to a generally or widely-held position or belief system, or a conventional attitude or disposition in general.

Osiris – The ancient Egyptian god of the underworld responsible for the dead and the afterlife. Osiris is most often depicted as a man holding a crook and flail. Though he was god of the dead, he was also known as god of the living, since the afterlife could entail reincarnation or rebirth into the ordinary world of the living. As the theology of Osiris developed in ancient Egypt, Osiris came to be understood as judge of the dead and the source of all human, animal, and plant life, even to the point of being credited with the growth of vegetation along the Nile. Osiris was considered the arbiter of eternal life. A detailed analysis of Osiris mythology and its possible relation to LOST is provided in Chapter 14 of *LOST Humanity*.

Pico della Mirandola – Possibly the most visible representative of Renaissance humanism, Count Giovanni Pico della Mirandola was an Italian philosopher and famed author of the *Oration on the Dignity of Man*, sometimes referred to as the "Manifesto of the Renaissance." The Oration provided a spirited unorthodox and humanistic defense of some 900 ideas in religion and philosophy. Pico della Mirandola lived 34 years, from 1463 to 1497.

Pilgrim, Billy – See Billy Pilgrim.

Postmodernism – A philosophical system which denies objective truth. An amorphous set of philosophical positions generally organized around the principle of socially- or communally-held truths understood to have relative or subjective but not objective value or absolute truth. Postmodernism can be thought of as a broad reaction to modernism, but it shares with modernism a disdain for the rigid objectivity of the Enlightenment. Postmodernism, however, denies the possibility of any objective truth, while modernism tended to seek a center, even if it could not always be identified. Postmodernism sees science and any other assertion of truth as socially constructed and having value only for the members of the group from which the system of knowledge or belief is derived. Postmodernism is generally considered to have its origin in post-World War II Europe and the United States, though the leading architects of the movement, mostly French philosophers, did not lay out recognizably postmodernist positions until the mid-1960s to the mid-1970s.

Prolepsis – Flashforward.

Realism – The philosophical position that truth or reality exists independent of observers.

Rhizome – A literary construct that permits horizontal (non-hierarchical) interpretation or representation. Rhizomes are found in large numbers in the literary works that employ them, and they usually serve to unite disparate elements of a composition into a "multiplicity" that demonstrates a kind of conceptual uniformity or unification across elements. The concept of the rhizome was developed by the postmodern theorists Gilles Deleuze and Félix Guattari, using the language of biology from which the term is borrowed.

Romanticism – An artistic movement beginning in Europe around 1850. Romanticism was a reaction to the social and political hierarchies of the Enlightenment, the changes brought about by the industrial revolution, and the Enlightenment-era attempts to reduce nature to a set of scientific principles. The best known advocates were found in the visual arts, literature, and music, but came to have vocal adherents within the realms of education and natural history as well. Romanticism stressed the value to be found in emotion, intuition, and nature, especially as an expression of philosophical opposition to logic, science, and industrialization.

Sartre, Jean-Paul – A French existentialist philosopher and leader of the 20th century existentialist movement. Jean-Paul Sartre died in 1980.

Saussure, Ferdinand de – Ferdinand de Saussure was arguably the most influential linguist of the late 19th and early 20th centuries. Saussure taught that the understanding of the world is necessarily achieved through language; without language, there can be no science and indeed no understanding of any natural phenomena. He is considered the founder of semiotics. Saussure died in 1913.

Self-Consistency Principle – See Novikov Self-Consistency Principle.

Semiotics – We use the definition of semiotics as provided by Dr. Antonio Savorelli (Chapter 21): *Semiotics is the study of the processes of production and communication of meaning, beyond the realm of linguistics—which in turn can be considered a branch of semiotics specialized in verbal signification systems. Structural semiotics, particularly, is centered on the complex processes that govern the existence of texts, intended as the self-contained products of a specific system or, in the case of syncretic texts such as those of television and other audiovisual media, of a combination of systems.*

Semisymbolism – An arbitrary connection, juxtaposition, or concomitance between linguistic or signifier oppositions. According to Dr. Antonio Savorelli, *"If a symbol is defined as an association between a signifier and a signified that's both arbitrary and conventional, semisymbolism is the arbitrary association between two oppositions: one on the plane of expression (that is, two signifiers that are presented in opposition to one another within a certain text), one on the plane of content (two opposite meanings). The association between the two planes may be arbitrary, but the oppositions between elements of each plane are not, hence making the semiotic relationship only half symbolic."*

Simulacrum – A simulacrum is a reproduction, copy, or an artificial creation bearing likeness or similarity to a real object. In some philosophical systems, such as postmodernism, the simulacrum in a sense reflects reality more completely than any object, and becomes "hyperreal". This is because postmodernism denies the existence of anything that can be universally understood as real; only the image, as seen by a particular viewer, can be real for that person.

Smith, James K. A. – A professor of philosophy at Calvin College, Smith is a leading voice in the postmodern Radical Orthodoxy movement within Evangelical Christianity. Applying the tools of critical thought to modern ecclesial practice and the church's relation to the greater world, Smith concentrates on proselytizing those within the evangelical community to the insights of Radical Orthodoxy. Smith and others in the movement feel their approach constitutes perhaps the most promising way of countering what are perceived as the deleterious effects of modernism within the Church. James K. A. Smith was born in 1970.

Syllepsis – A clause couplet in which the two parts disagree grammatically or in their meaning. An example: "You are free to execute your laws, and your citizens, as you see fit." (*Star Trek: The Next Generation*) Syllepsis is often found in a Zeugma, which is a two-part sentence containing a figure of speech in which a single verb or noun is common to both clauses. In the example, the verb execute unites the two clauses, but this single verb usually carries two different definitions when applied to laws and citizens; however, in the example, grammatical considerations force a single meaning. The result is a particular type of humorous declarative absurdity called a Solecism. Syllepsis and Solecism are often intentionally created for rhetorical or stylistic value.

Synchronic – Two or more events coincident in time.

Syncretism – The fusion of different belief systems, often achieved through combining the thought and practice of diverse philosophical or theological traditions. Syncretism can result in the unification and equation of originally distinct schools of thought, especially in religious theory and practice, leading to inclusive tendencies toward other faith traditions. While the concept is most frequently applied to the interface between philosophy and theological inquiry, the idea has been used to express movements in politics, culture, society, and the arts.

Teleology – See Telos.

Telos – A Greek term similar or identical in meaning to Aristotle's Final Cause. Telos is the end purpose or final intention of an entity or thing. It is the etymological root of the more commonly used word "teleology", which is the formal study of the objectives of an entity or thing. The idea is typically applied without difficulty in superficial human discourse, but can become a center of dispute and controversy when applied to non-human biological systems or inanimate, non-biological materials. That a plant may have "goals" without direct causal relation is considered by some to be problematic. Teleological assertions often undermine the usual etiological (cause and effect) relationships, and can become problematic to discussions of logic or scientific method. Another problem relates to design. If non-human biological organisms and even non-biological entities have a Final Cause, design by an entity outside the biological system is often asserted and may be a direct logical necessity in some teleological arguments. Teleology is often used to support the tenets of Creationism or Intelligent Design, for example. However, even biologists who do not generally support teleological creationism are often forced to concede teleological arguments for the goals and purposes of discrete organ systems or biological processes, for example. Teleological arguments are often made and accepted in the case of such topics as secondary metabolites (natural products), which can become difficult to rationalize without appeal to teleological thought. Teleology is often considered a logical, a posteriori argument for a universal Creator or God, but an assertion of divine activity is not necessarily the root of every teleological argument. Even those who may concede the consistency and validity of teleological assertions may question the validity of attempts to couple the premise of intelligent design to the tenets of theism.

Text – A coherent string of written, aural, or visual communication, or mixtures of these, that may serve as the basis for exegesis (interpretation), redaction, collation, or critical analysis or response.

UF – Unexpected Friend.

Veridictive - True, genuine, corresponding to facts.

Verisimilitude – The appearance of truth or resemblance to reality, facts, or truth.

Winnicott, Donald – An English physician specializing in pediatrics and psychoanalysis, Winnicott made major contributions to the field of psychology. His ideas on True Self and False Self, as well as his work on the Transitional Object, are widely cited.

Participant Notes

Participant Notes

Participant Notes

Participant Notes